UNDERSTANDING
CONTEMPORARY
CHINA

SECOND EDITION

UNDERSTANDING CONTEMPORARY CHINA

edited by
Robert E. Gamer

LYNNE
RIENNER
PUBLISHERS

BOULDER
LONDON

Published in the United States of America in 2003 by
Lynne Rienner Publishers, Inc.
1800 30th Street, Boulder, Colorado 80301
www.rienner.com

and in the United Kingdom by
Lynne Rienner Publishers, Inc.
3 Henrietta Street, Covent Garden, London WC2E 8LU

Library of Congress Cataloging-in-Publication Data
Understanding contemporary China / Robert E. Gamer, editor.— 2nd ed.
   p.   cm. — (Understanding : introductions to the states and regions of the contemporary
world)
   Includes bibliographical references and index.
   ISBN 1-58826-045-3 (alk. paper)
   1. China. I. Gamer, Robert E., 1938– II. Series.

DS706.U47 2003
951—dc21
                                                                          2003046721

British Cataloguing in Publication Data
A Cataloguing in Publication record for this book
is available from the British Library.

Printed and bound in the United States of America

5   4   3   2

Contents

Illustrations

■ **Figures**

■ **Photographs**

Preface

A s China's importance in the world's economy and political structure grows, so too does the number of books discussing it. For the teacher of introductory courses, that is a mixed blessing. Keeping current with the research requires increasing amounts of time, and bibliographical searches reveal that most of these works pertain to topics too particular and advanced for students with little prior knowledge of China. Few are designed especially for such students.

Understanding Contemporary China was conceived to address this problem. It brings together a group of scholars who have published extensively on China within their varied disciplines and also teach introductory courses on China. We all began this enterprise with a strong sense that such a book was missing and needed. As we have worked on two editions over the past eight years, we have become even more aware of the important niche we are filling. We have created a single text with readable chapters that introduce China from the perspectives of a number of disciplines. These chapters not only give overviews but also emphasize issues currently being researched—complete with bibliographical citations, so students can look into those sources themselves and also find other introductory texts offering additional information on different topics—and are highlighted with facts, narratives, experiences, and observations derived from the authors' close personal contact with China. Because the chapters are designed to be complete in themselves, they can be assigned individually. Yet, they cover a number of complementary themes, introduced in Chapter 1, to which each succeeding chapter adds form, focus, and nuance. This makes the book useful for courses offering broad multidisciplinary coverage of China, as well as courses that approach it from the perspective of a particular discipline. Some of the topics covered—geography, history, politics, economy, family and kinship, religion, literature, and international relations—are essential components of any introduction to China. Others—such as the environment, the roles and problems of women, popular culture, sexuality, demographics, and urbanization—are important topics that are often ignored in introductory works. All chapters give historical overviews along with a discussion of the most current events and the problems and prospects facing China in the future.

Chapter 1 introduces the book's themes and how they relate to our lives and concerns in the West and to Chinese living outside of China. The next two chapters introduce China's geography and long history. Readers will find some useful reference points here to which they can return when reading later chapters of the book: the maps in Chapters 2 and 3 and the dynastic chart in Chapter 3.

The rest of the book covers topics of major interest regarding China today. Chapters 4 and 5 discuss the evolution of China's political institutions and entrepreneurial traditions and how they interface with the current reforms. Chapter 6 covers four topics of special concern to China: Hong Kong, Taiwan, Tibet, and the large number of overseas Chinese. Chapter 7 gives an overview of China's foreign policy. The rapid political and economic changes in today's China have contributed to and been affected by population growth, urbanization, and environmental problems—the topics of Chapters 8 and 9.

Then we turn to an examination of China's society. Chapter 10 looks at China's family structure and the rapid changes currently taking place in sexual behavior and family relations, especially in urban China. Far more than in most countries, the family plays a central role in economic relations and political ideology, which makes these changes especially consequential. Chapter 11 focuses especially on how women are involved and affected, both positively and negatively, as the economy grows. Chapter 12 provides a historic overview of how China's indigenous religions and those of nearby neighbors shaped Chinese society and how these traditions are being challenged by Christianity, communism, and consumerism. Chapter 13 discusses how China's literature and performance art have always had their roots in popular culture and what people are reading, watching on television and at the movies, and exploring on the Internet today. This chapter, too, elucidates the rapid changes taking place in contemporary China's social and family life.

The closing chapter on trends and prospects returns to the themes introduced in Chapter 1 and points briefly to how they may play out in the near future. It gives alternative scenarios of where China's reforms may lead and also indicates some outcomes that are unlikely to occur.

—*Robert E. Gamer*

Acknowledgments

I have been the sole author of my prior books. Collaborating with others in writing this book has been a new and pleasant experience. I enjoyed passing chapters around among the authors so they could make comments to one another. With their diversity of backgrounds and wealth of experience in both teaching and research, this has been an enriching experience. E-mail makes it possible to instantly transmit chapters to one another and exchange data and comments when making revisions, even with fellow authors halfway around the world in China, Singapore, and Hong Kong, and across the Atlantic in Britain.

During the writing of the two editions of this book, People to People International, a visiting lectureship at Shanghai University, the University of Missouri–Kansas City, and the Edgar Snow Memorial Fund helped me make trips to keep abreast of current developments in China. As usual, I have many people there to thank for leading me to information and insights found in these pages. I can only mention some of them: Wang Junyi, Li Qiang, Zhang Xizhen, Chen Zhenya, and Chen Qiuji, at Beijing University; Chen Hui of the *People's Daily* and his wife, Chen Xiuxia, of the China Society for People's Friendship Studies; Huang Hua and Ling Qing; Fan Hengshan of the State Planning Commission; Shao Lei of the Ministry of Civil Affairs; Zhu Yukun of the Ministry of Labor; Jonathan Lange, H. Y. Cheung, and Lina Ting of Hong Kong Government Services; Stephen W. K. Chiu and Yvette Poon at the Chinese University of Hong Kong; Deans Liu Dezhong, Wang Ximei, and Jiang Yongkong in Shanghai; Guang Shi Long of the Zhuhai Nanfang International Trade and Economy College; and Li Jian of the Shenzhen Economic Trade Committee. All were generous with their time and rendered assistance beyond the call of duty.

In addition to our own exchanges of opinions on drafts of chapters, our authors benefited from several anonymous reviewers who read individual chapters and two who read the entire manuscript with great care. Along with skillfully directing that process—and creating the innovative model on which this book is based—Donald and April Gordon provided considerable help in improving the book. Editors Dan Eades and Leanne Anderson provided support and encouragement, not to mention frequent insightful input. Cheng De and Jane Cheng helped ensure consistent transliteration. Shou Huisheng kept me grounded and helped on many fronts. The Geographic Information Systems Lab at Miami University created the maps in the volume.

My friend and colleague Henry Mitchell devoted much of his life to reopening dialogue between the United States and China. I am frequently reinvigorated by his boundless energy.

My wife, May Lim Gamer, collaborated on this volume in many ways. She located many volumes and facts from libraries, shared observations from her reading and experience, maintained regular contact with a host of Chinese friends here and in China, helped me achieve cultural immersion in China (and rescued me when I did not), helped me create the index and review the manuscript, and patiently abided many long evenings when I was in the house but not of it.

—*R. E. G.*

UNDERSTANDING
CONTEMPORARY
CHINA

Introduction

Robert E. Gamer

Ayear ago two friends and I were climbing the Simatai section of the Great Wall of China, a less-frequented section high atop the craggy and sparsely populated mountain range northwest of Beijing. From its highest tower you can see Beijing. The young lady who followed us to sell a souvenir guidebook loves taking in that view. To her it is almost a mirage; she has never been to Beijing. And she has only visited the township capital, a modern town with tall buildings and a new park and shopping strip about ten miles away, twice in her life—on her wedding day and one afternoon to window shop with her son.

As any visitor to China will tell you, its cities teem with people amid new highways clogged with new cars, buses, and trucks, soaring modern buildings, and big new commercial complexes. Stores and shopping centers are filled with a vast array of goods. Preservationists fret as old structures give way to the wrecker's ball for more construction. On the outskirts, new suburbs rise from the landscape, and a system of freeways is rapidly linking all of the nation's cities. Villages around these hubs and along these ribbons operate factories and market farms to supply not only those cities, but also China's growing international market. Your home undoubtedly contains many goods manufactured there. Yet beyond those horizons lies well over half of China's population. Their benefits from the reforms have been far more modest. Hundreds of millions of them do not even have electricity. Many males from those villages have spent time as migrant workers helping with the massive urban construction projects. There they can witness a rapidly growing gap between their way of life and economic prospects, and those of city dwellers.

There is also a gap between the realities of life in China and the perception of many people outside China about the nature of life there. Today China

1

has the world's fastest-growing economy, a fifth of the world's population, and escalating trade and travel through its borders. It has a highly motivated populace spreading to all corners of the world, a modernized army, world-class movie makers, and competitive Olympic teams. It is a major market for Coke, Pepsi, Boeing, Avon, Butler, Sprint, Black and Veatch, Warner Brothers, and a host of other Western companies. Its goods line the racks in our stores.

Yet, while China has been moving in around us, our comprehension of it often remains mired in the past. We think of Mao, Red Guards waving little Red Books, water buffaloes in paddy fields, laborers wearing Dixie Cup hats, pagoda temples, crowds of people riding bicycles, communist officials with red stars on their caps ordering around workers in great factories, school-children singing socialist songs, and a lone student stopping a tank on Tiananmen Square. All these are true images of China, past or present, but contemporary China offers other images as well: lunchtime crowds lining up in front of Pizza Hut and McDonald's, businessmen talking on their cell phones over lunch, modern office buildings filled with rows of computers, construction workers wearing name-brand jackets and jeans produced in sweatshops up the road, shantytowns for temporary workers, unemployed youth chatting or begging on street corners or running in gangs, popular talk radio shows discussing sex and relationships, steamy novels selling at corner bookstalls, young people dancing to rock music late at night in discos, and engineering projects transforming entire valleys and islands from swamp into metropolis. All help China achieve the dubious distinction of being among the world's greatest purveyors of air and water pollution.

China is ubiquitous—its clothes, electronics, food, people, and even its air are ever-present in all places. Check the labels next time you go shopping. And this presence has another unique element: China still regards the 60 million Chinese living overseas as part of China. Although many of those overseas Chinese have become loyal citizens of other countries, they are often tied to China's 1.2 billion inhabitants by custom, family, and tradition. The richest of those families in Hong Kong (now part of China), Taiwan, Southeast Asia, Australia, and North America control very large amounts of investment capital; much of that money is invested directly or indirectly in China and in the Pacific Rim, including the coast of North America. This investment constitutes a major bond linking China to the Americas and Southeast Asia, one that the United States can ignore only at its own peril. It is important to note that 22 million of these overseas Chinese live in Taiwan. China still claims Taiwan as part of its own territory, while Taiwan's government still claims to be the true representative of China. China must be understood in the context of Chinese living outside its borders. China's prosperity has depended upon the investment of overseas Chinese; their prosperity, in turn, depends upon China's prosperity. Such interdependency explains a lot about how the communist nation of China can be as immersed in free markets as it is; those markets are embedded in the social structure of this widely dispersed Chinese community.

The dispersed community shares some attitudes and habits that have been passed from generation to generation for thousands of years. It is also quite diverse. As you read *Understanding Contemporary China,* you will see these attitudes and habits, along with social divisions, showing up in a variety of contexts. The rest of this chapter will give you an overview of those attitudes, habits, and divisions. But first I should say a bit about something that can be confusing without a brief introduction: Chinese words.

China has no alphabet. Its written language, which is thousands of years old, consists of single characters that represent entire words. Often these began as a simple stick drawing of a man, the sun, or another object that gradually became more complex and stylized over time. People had to memorize the individual characters for thousands of words. Only the educated scholar-officials and families of merchants in cities were in positions to devote the time it took to memorize these characters and learn to create them with careful brush strokes. After the communists came to power, they created about 2,200 simplified characters that could be taught to schoolchildren and used in newspapers, so as to spread literacy. But when Westerners arrived in China during the nineteenth century, they needed to transliterate the sounds of Chinese words into their Roman alphabet (romanize them). Two English sinologists, Sir Thomas Wade and Hubert A. Giles, devised a system (Wade-Giles) to do that. For geographical names, some other romanizations fell into common usage. During the 1930s a new system, *pinyin,* came closer to replicating the sounds of the words as they are pronounced in the Mandarin (literary) Chinese used around China's capital, Beijing. In 1958 this system was adopted by the People's Republic of China for its official publications, and in 1979 *Xinhua* (the China News Agency) began using *pinyin* for all dispatches. The *New York Times* and many other newspapers and scholarly publications now use *pinyin;* we use it throughout this book, except for a few words still commonly transliterated in other spellings (e.g., Yangtze, Sun Yat-sen, Kuomintang) and when referring to people and movements in Taiwan, where Wade-Giles (or often-careless variations on it) is still in vogue. Some fields like history still use a lot of Wade-Giles, and it is used often in transliterating literature. So you will encounter it in other books. Table 1.1 compares the *pinyin* names of some provinces and cities with transliteration common on older maps, and the names of dynasties and some other words in *pinyin* and Wade-Giles. It includes many of the Chinese words used in this book.

It is common for Chinese words to have only one or two syllables; when there are two, they are given equal emphasis in pronunciation. Words with similar sounds (and identical transliterations) may be differentiated by inflection of the voice—up, down, down-up, or flat—as each syllable is pro-

Table 1.1 Romanization of Chinese Terms

Pinyin	Older Geographical Transliteration	Pronunciation
Provinces		
Fujian	Fukian	foo jian
Gansu	Kansu	gahn soon
Guangdong	Kwangtung	gwong doong
Guizhou	Kweichow	gway joe
Hainan	Hainan	hi! nanh
Hebei	Hopeh	hü bay
Hubei	Hupeh	hoo bay
Jilin	Kirin	gee lin
Shaanxi	Shensi	shahn shee
Shanxi	Shansi	shehn shee
Sichuan	Szechwan	sü chwahn
Xinjiang	Sinkiang	sheen jyang
Zhejiang	Chekiang	juh jyang
Cities		
Beijing	Peking	bay jing
Chengdu	Chengtu	chung doo
Chongqing	Chungking	chawng ching
Hangzhou	Hangchow	hong joe
Nanjing	Nanking	nahn jing
Qingdao	Tsingtao	ching daow
Tianjin	Tientsin	tien jin
Xi'an	Sian	shee ahn

Pinyin	Wade-Giles	Pronunciation
Dynasties		
Han	Han	hahn
Qidan	Ch'i-tan	chee don
Qin	Ch'in	chin
Qing	Ch'ing	ching
Song	Sung	soohng
Tang	T'ang	tahng
Xia	Hsia	shah
Names		
Deng Xiaoping	Teng Hsiao-p'ing	dung sheeaow ping
Jiang Zemin	Chiang Tse-min	jyang dze min
Mao Zedong	Mao Tse-Tung	maow dze doong
Zheng He	Cheng Ho	jung huh
Zhang Xueliang	Chang Hsüeh-liang	jang shuey lyahng
Zhou Enlai	Chou En-lai	joe un lie
Zhuang-zi	Chuang-Tzu	jwong dz
Other terms		
baojia	pao-chia	bough dja
danwei	tanwei	don weigh
Dao	Tao	dow
guanxi	kuan-hsi	gwahn shee
Guomindang	Kuomintang	gwaw min dahng
Tiananmen	T'ienanmen	tien ahn mun
Xinhua	Hsin-hua	shccn hwa
Zhong guo	Chung-kuo	djohng gwaw

nounced; each would have a different character in written Chinese script. When looking at names, Chinese give their family name first and then their personal name; Mao Zedong's family name was Mao, and his personal name was Zedong.

And on another practical note, a reminder about Internet search engines, such as google.com. You will notice at the end of each chapter a bibliography, and within each chapter parentheses calling attention to books and articles where you can learn more about topics being discussed. In addition to this, typing words that interest you into google.com, teoma.com, or askjeeves.com will quickly alert you to a great deal of additional information.

■ Creative Tensions

A rubber band's ability to stretch helps it hold things together; its elasticity actually lets it wrap tightly around objects. China has many traditions that combine those traits, pulling apart while unifying. Chapters in *Understanding Contemporary China* highlight many tensions between

- Confucianism and both petty and modern capitalism,
- Confucianism, Christianity, and communism,
- popular culture and formal traditions,
- regions and the capital city,
- cities and the rural hinterland, and
- the heartland and its global outreach.

China is slightly larger than the United States but has four times the number of people. Its rivers cross high, dry plateaus to connect the world's highest mountains with enormous floodplains. Its eastern provinces are among the world's most populous, its western provinces among the world's least inhabited. It first became a unified nation 200 years before the birth of Christ, with the north conquering the south; that unity has waxed and waned ever since. At the time of Christ, China was abandoning feudal states and starting to adopt both petty capitalist trade among family-run enterprises (often associated with the south) and a Confucian ethic (coming from the north). Since that ethic emphasizes family loyalty and hard work on the one hand and interfering government bureaucracy and unquestioned loyalty to northern-based leaders on the other, it both benefits and interferes with capitalism. Daoism (deriving from folk culture) and Buddhism (from India) helped individuals cultivate their inner personal lives while conforming to the rigid social conventions associated with Confucianism and family enterprises. So did popular forms of entertainment, which at the same time provided inspiration for China's highly refined art and literature. China developed some of the world's earliest large cities, which sent Chinese to ports and oases in distant parts of Asia to establish a lively trade.

By the late eighteenth century, these cities were in contact with the emerging capitalism of western Europe, which increasingly competed with China's petty capitalist enterprises. These foreigners also brought with them Christianity and Western ideas about human freedom and progress, which competed for favor with China's established religious traditions. As large factories and cities began to widen the divide between city and countryside and among social classes, communist ideology began to compete with Christianity and capitalism for favor among workers, urban intellectuals, and peasants. Like many previous movements, those ideologies developed some Confucian traits as they adapted to China, especially those associated with strong rule emanating from the north. Today, as China strengthens its ties with international capitalism and capitalist nations, weakens its actual and ideological ties to international communism, and experiences rapid social change, traditions of both Confucianism and popular culture help fill its spiritual void. And overseas Chinese help fill its investment coffers.

Thus China blends many traits and traditions, which seem to pull people apart and at the same time bring them together. People are expected to give their highest loyalty to their families and friends with whom they have special *guanxi* (relationships); yet the same traditions simultaneously bid them to follow the directives of the nation's top leaders. For thousands of years, China has both encouraged and strictly controlled small manufacturers and traders. China's regions have held closely to their own traditions while sharing in a common Chinese culture. That culture viewed itself as civilized and the outside world as barbarian yet continuously absorbed civilization from the barbarians. Today China has dazzlingly modern cities short distances from peasants tilling fields with primitive plows and water buffaloes to supply those cities with food. China has vast numbers of laborers toiling with simple tools to support their families and the world's highest level of economic growth. Younger computer-literate leaders take the reins of power from old men who remember the era of Mao.

These diverse traits and traditions have come to support one another. Their distinctions and competition create tensions but do not hold back progress. That has not always been so. Between the 1839 arrival of the Christian West in the first Opium War and the introduction of communism after World War II, and during the cataclysms of the Great Leap Forward and the Great Proletarian Cultural Revolution, many millions lost their lives in conflict among contending social forces. But China has learned to use conflict as a means of adapting to change. It has a disciplined social core, weakened but still strong despite television, the Internet, cell phones, consumerism, crime, and other assaults of modern culture. Its families have shown an ability to control their size, save, work hard, engage in creative entrepreneurship, and divide labor between the sexes. China's civilization has focused on an attachment to the land that has survived amid many centuries of urbanization. People who have migrated to China's cities are welcome to return to their home regions, keeping alive rural social bonds and safety nets even as people move out to the ends of the earth. When the Central Pacific Railway found its European immigrant laborers fleeing the arduous task of building a transcontinental railway across the United States in the 1860s, it turned to Chinese laborers, who arrived already organized into disciplined work units under their own foremen. For millennia, China has used this labor and considerable scientific skills to channel its vast amounts of water, mine rich seams of coal, enclose its cities and borders with walls and towers, and manufacture a variety of goods prized for their excellence around the planet. Even when divided by ideology or temporary political division or separated by vast distances after migration, families and clans deriving from the same villages have habits of cooperation to further such enterprises by sharing capital, labor, markets, and special connections. They hold together tightly even while stretching to take on global challenges.

As a result, China can contribute to global capitalism without being absorbed by it. These traits that help make it a great producer also make it a great consumer; its enormous population produces ever-increasing amounts of goods not only for world markets but also for itself. Extensive use of low-skilled labor holds down the cost of manufacturing while providing millions of people with income to buy these new goods. Unlike many third world countries, China has developed huge budget surpluses stemming from a favorable balance of trade. Yet China's form of capitalism holds back many of the processes (e.g., impartial civil and criminal law, bureaucratic independence, investigative reporting) required for modern capitalism to thrive. If it wishes to sustain its current rates of growth, it must find new ways to adapt to global capitalism. Global capitalism, in turn, must adjust to the needs of China's dynamic sector of the world economy.

■ New Challenges

China still has great challenges ahead of it. Like many third world countries, China's traditions offer little support for democracy. With its focus on obeying family and community leaders, China has suppressed individual expression. It has never allowed independent interest groups to form. Although it has long had laws, it has no tradition of rule of law. Competing political parties clash with Chinese traditions of harmony and unquestioning obedience to authority. This lets all elements of Chinese society support movements rejecting foreign influences even as they adapt to world technology, trade, and popular culture, yet this balancing act is becoming increasingly harder to maintain.

China's development has resulted in major problems. Deforestation, removal of ground cover and wetlands, water and air pollution, and giant engineering projects pose serious threats to China's food and water supplies, health, and standard of living. Despite the "one-child" policy, a growing population increasingly moving to cities is a growing strain on resources. Women made many advances during the twentieth century; fast development enhances some of those advances but brings setbacks to others. The growing economy widens the gap between rich and poor individuals and regions and brings new opportunities for corruption; as a result, much capital that should go into development ends up in nonproductive pursuits. This inefficiency, fast economic growth, and reduction in central planning have caused both severe inflation and severe deflation, resource shortages, unemployment, and declines in social services. The inefficient state industries are hard to phase out because they employ large numbers of workers and still make essential goods, but they constitute a major drain on national treasuries as political and taxation powers devolve to the provinces. Their unrepaid loans strain the resources and integrity of the banking system.

These problems are amplified by an unpredictable legal system that leaves business contracts and individual liberties unprotected and makes both foreign investors and educated Chinese uneasy. In addition, China has put inadequate resources into educating a work force with skills to run all the new enterprises. Hong Kong and Taiwan, both critical to China's economic future, are especially sensitive to these concerns. The coastal provinces that have been experiencing the world's fastest economic growth resist directives from central government and party organizations. Meanwhile, ethnic minorities living in interior provinces are among those receiving the fewest benefits from economic growth; they are politically and culturally marginal. China has in the past split apart into regions controlled by warlords, and competition between China's center and regions for support from the military remains intense. Military threats to Taiwan or offshore islands and crackdowns on dissidents and ethnic minorities frighten away foreign investors. These problems challenge China as it strives to retain its fast-paced economic growth. Its leaders are sensitive to all these problems, and have devised an array of programs to address them. Will those programs work? Can they work without democratic reforms? What is the potential for such reforms to occur?

Young people who marched in the 1989 demonstrations and elders who once fought for a worker's revolution are preoccupied with making money and enjoying consumer goods. Many younger Chinese also revel in newfound freedoms to express themselves in music, dress, sexuality, and other nonpolitical ways. They are buying new flats and filling them with nice furniture and possessions—even cars. Meanwhile, the security of guaranteed jobs, housing, and social services provided by work units during the Maoist years fades away. Increasing numbers of people cannot find full-time work, and it is common for men and women to have two or three sources of income. Inland and rural regions lag behind in development. Both citizens and leaders are profoundly torn by whether to follow traditional Chinese ways or trends from the outside world. They want to solve the many problems accompanying the rapid change without destroying the fabric that has held China together as a great nation over the millennia. And they are increasingly desirous of becoming a part of the world. One of the greatest challenges in this regard is sorting out the relationship between China and Taiwan. A growing number of younger, and many older, people in Taiwan would like it to declare full independence from China and go its own way; few citizens of China share that sentiment. Will China find creative or destructive ways to deal with these tensions?

We explore all this in the pages ahead.

China: A Geographic Preface

Stanley W. Toops

C hina is moving onto our horizon. Though most of us know little about it, we are increasingly aware that somehow it is going to be a big factor in our lives. With over 1.2 billion people, China has more than a fifth of the world's population (Blunden and Elvin, 1998). Just slightly larger than the United States, covering 3.7 million square miles, it is territorially the world's third largest country (Hsieh and Hsieh, 1996). And its economy, already among the world's ten largest, is growing faster than that of any other country; soon its overall economic output could surpass that of the United States (Hsieh and Lu, 2003). Once isolated from the outside world, China's goods, people, and culture are rapidly penetrating all corners of the globe and heavily affecting the U.S. economy and society (Donald and Benewick, 2000). The next few pages will quickly introduce you to how China connects with its neighbors, its habitation, and the features of its natural environment. These facts will prepare you for an overview of its history in Chapter 3 and give you a convenient reference point when geographic places and features are mentioned in later chapters.

We will start by looking at where China is located on the map and its historical connections with neighboring states. Historically, China's culture and imperial power strongly influenced its closest neighbors, Korea, Japan, and the countries of Southeast Asia; in modern times, neighboring Russia, Japan, and Southeast Asia have had a powerful effect on China's political and economic development. Then we will look at China's internal divisions, north and south, and east and west. Those regions have starkly different histories, and the differences persist. Finally, we will examine China's natural landscape, which contains the world's highest mountains, huge deserts, and major rivers emptying into the world's most abundant floodplains. China encompasses a great diversity of cultures and physical features (Hsieh and Hsieh, 1996). It consists of much more than peasants tilling rice fields.

In simplest terms, we're talking about space (Linge and Forbes, 1993; Li and Tang, 2000), region (Goodman, 1989; Cannon, 2000), and landscape (Pannell and Ma, 1983; Tuan, 1969). What space do China and its neighbors occupy on the map? How do its regions vary? How does China's natural landscape affect the way its people live?

■ Space

Where is this place, and how is it linked to its neighbors? China is located on the eastern end of Eurasia, the planet's largest continent (see Map 2.1), but its land connections on that continent consist of poor roads over harsh terrain.

Geographic Information Systems Lab, Miami University, 1997 M.A.

Map 2.1 Regional Map of Asia

To the west are expanses of Central Asian dry lands and to the north is the cold steppe of Russia. To the south are the high mountains of the Himalaya, and to the east is the Pacific Ocean. China occupies an area not easily accessible to travelers and traders. The distances are far and the physical barriers formidable (Sivin 1988:78–79).

China's closest cultural and physical connections are with Japan and Korea. These three countries are not separated by high mountains, deserts, or long stretches of ocean. Together they constitute East Asia. Sometimes Westerners call this the Far East, but that term only refers to the distance from Europe. East Asia is a better term for this region, describing its location at the eastern end of Eurasia: it is only far from places that are far from there. Southeast Asia (from Vietnam down to Indonesia) is situated to the southeast (Kolb, 1971:21–24).

To situate China, look at the country in an East Asian context. China, Japan, and Korea have very distinct cultures, histories, and natural experi-

Wet-rice agriculture in Yunnan

Laurel Bossen

ences. Their religions are quite different. Unlike China, Korea is located on a peninsula, whereas Japan occupies a series of islands. But all three have been heavily influenced by Confucianism, a philosophy that began in China and has guided its ruling elite for centuries (about which you will read much more in subsequent chapters), and by Chinese art. Though their spoken languages are radically different, both Japan and Korea used Chinese characters (discussed below) to write words before they developed their own alphabets; the Japanese still use Chinese characters blended with words written in their alphabet, and many Koreans use Chinese characters for scholarly writing. This diffusion of philosophical ideas, artistic expression, and writing practices connects the people of East Asia (Kolb, 1971:531).

The connections to China's other neighbors are not as strong, but these linkages are not insignificant for China. The Buddhist religion began in India and came to China via the "Silk Roads" (see Map 2.1 and Chapter 12), which also brought China's silks and other luxury goods to other parts of the continent. Confucianism influenced bordering countries in Southeast Asia, which in turn developed the technology of wet-rice agriculture (planting seedlings in wet paddy fields) that spread throughout south China. Islam, born in the Middle East, has a stronghold in western China. From the north came historically powerful external threats, the Mongols and the Manchus (Sivin, 1988:80).

■ The Middle Kingdom

China's name has historical and geographical significance (Cannon and Jenkins, 1990:269). The Chinese call their country *Zhong guo*. In the simplified characters used in the People's Republic of China, it looks like this:

$$中 \quad 国$$

The first character *(zhong)* means "middle" or "central." Notice how it looks like a box or cake cut through the middle. The second character *(guo)* means "country" or "kingdom." The outside square is the wall of defense for the country. So China is the Middle Kingdom, the kingdom located at the most central position.

The very name of the country imparts an idea of centrality. China has seen itself as central to the world, in terms of both looking up and looking out. The Chinese worldview placed the emperor at the connection between heaven and earth. The emperor resided in the capital, at the center of the world, so it was natural that this should be the prime connecting place between land and sky. Around this center, other countries or dominions were far away in the periphery. Those faraway people were barbarians (Freeberne, 1992:149).

The name *China* comes from the first dynasty to unify China. The Qin (pronounced "chin") dynasty unified the country in 221 B.C.E. The Chinese people of that time named their country after that dynasty (Borthwick, 1998). The ancient Greeks knew of China as Seres, the land of silk. Silk was part of the trade across the vastness of Eurasia on the "Silk Road." Another name for China is Cathay. This comes from Khitai, an ethnic group that occupied northern China in the eleventh century. Marco Polo wrote about Cathay. People in Slavic-speaking areas still call China Khitai (Fairbank, Reischauer, and Craig, 1973:123).

The Chinese people call themselves Han, after the Han dynasty, which immediately succeeded the Qin, and adopted Confucian policies as its base. The Han are the dominant group in China. Although they loosely share some common physical features, their looks and average height vary from region to region, and they come from many distinct lineages. They are united by their common acceptance of the Confucian cultural norms that emerged during the Han dynasty (Cannon and Jenkins, 1990:67). Chapters 3 and 12 discuss this further.

According to Confucius, you should look carefully at the name of a person to understand what that person's role is (Fairbank, Reischauer, and Craig, 1973:44). The same can be said for the name of a country. China or *Zhong guo,* Qin dynasty or Middle Kingdom, these two names describe a country that is unified and located at the center of civilization. Its people, the Han, grant the country loyalty on the basis of traditional values.

▓ Challenging the Middle Kingdom

China and its very view of itself were both fundamentally challenged when the Pacific Ocean was opened to the fleets of Europe. China itself had sent ships as far as the Indian Ocean. But once European ships entered the Pacific in numbers, China became vulnerable militarily, culturally, and economically (Sivin, 1988:84–89). Chapters 3, 6, and 7 all have much more to say about this. When China found it could not resist those onslaughts, many in China began to question whether they could any longer identify themselves by the names they had been using, the people of Han traditions living in the center of the civilized world. Their space had been invaded.

■ Regions

China is a land of enormous internal contrasts. It is slightly larger than the United States (Pannell and Ma, 1983:1). If a map of China were superimposed on one of Europe, China would stretch from the North Sea south to the southern edge of the Sahara, east from Portugal to as far as the Ural Mountains. As

the United States or Europe vary regionally, so does China. It is easy to
approach this subject by focusing on two major divisions, east-west and
north-south.

■ East and West

A historical division is between China Proper and the Frontier (Leeming,
1993). This is a distinction between the east and the west. China Proper is east
of a line from Yunnan in the southwest looping around Beijing and Hebei to
the sea (see Map 2.2). As Map 2.3 helps you quickly comprehend, this region
has the heaviest population densities; 90 percent of the country's population
lives here. Most of those people are Han and live in a Confucian society. Much
of this area is suitable for agriculture in river basins and China also focused its
industrial might here. The people who live within China Proper consider themselves the center of China's civilization (Leeming, 1993:12–13).

The Frontier is west of that line bisecting the country. Western China
includes Inner Mongolia, Heilongjiang, Jilin, Liaoning, Ningxia, Gansu, western Sichuan, Tibet, Qinghai, and Xinjiang (see Map 2.2). Western China has
far fewer people. Much of the population—including Mongols, Tibetans, and
Uygurs—does not consider itself Han. Most of them adhere to Islam or Lama
Buddhism. This region consists of mountains and deserts and has low rainfall.

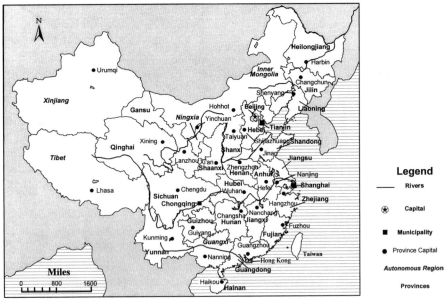

Geographic Information Systems Lab, Miami University, 1997 M.A.

Map 2.2 Provincial Map of China

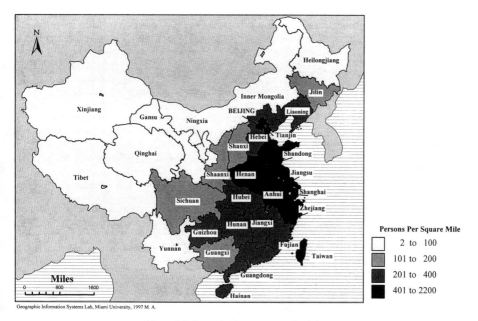

Map 2.3 Population Map of China

Traditionally, people were nomadic herders or farmed in oases. There is still very little industry here, even though this is one of China's richest sources for oil and coal (Cannon and Jenkins, 1990:65–67; Goodman, 1989:164).

Northeast and Southeast

Another regional difference exists within China Proper. A line following just north of the Yangtze River separates the northern and southern portions of China Proper (Borthwick, 1998). The Yellow River waters northern China (see Map 2.4). This is the cultural heart of China. Rainfall is adequate for agriculture. People raise wheat, which they eat in the form of noodles or steamed bread. Much of China's heavy industry is in the north because of the coal and oil here. The northern Mandarin dialect is the basis for the standard language (Leeming, 1993:12).

The Yangtze River and West River are the lifelines of the southern region (Map 2.4). Southern China is lush compared with the north. Paddy (wet-field) agriculture is practiced here, and rice is the main food crop. Tea is grown in the hillsides. The south focuses on light industry such as textiles; it has few fuel resources. Southern dialects of the standard language, such as Cantonese, are spoken here (Leeming, 1993:13).

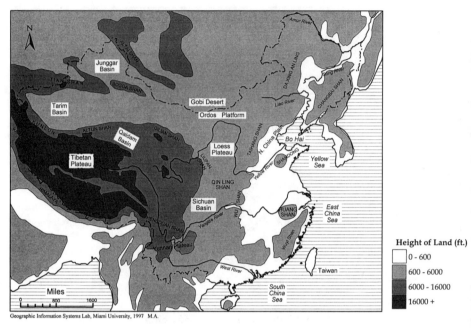

Geographic Information Systems Lab, Miami University, 1997 M.A.

Map 2.4 Physical Features of China

Part of this regionalization is expressed in the food styles of China. Cantonese style in the Guangdong province has a delicate flavor and sensibility, a more subtle approach. Sichuan food is spicy hot and numbing because of the combination of peppercorns used in preparation. Food from Hunan, Mao's home province, is the spiciest. Shanghai style makes liberal use of seafoods and is slightly sweet. Northern China style is plainer, using onions, garlic, and cabbage but few other vegetables. Beijing style is exceptional because of the imperial dishes like Beijing duck. In the north, noodles are the staple food for people, whereas rice is the staple in the south. Except in Muslim areas, pork is the main meat all over China. In northwestern China, rice pilaf, spicy noodles, and lamb kebabs are common. In Tibet, roasted barley flour is the staple, supplemented by some yak meat. All over China, tea is the preferred beverage (Sivin, 1988:120–121; Evans, 1992). Chinese love food and savor the specialties of their regions.

How different are the dialects? They are as different as the foods of China. *I love you* is expressed in these three characters:

我爱你

The first character means "I," the second "love," and the third "you." Anyone who can read Chinese characters knows this. But they do not all pronounce the words in the same ways. Although the Chinese use these same characters everywhere, in the north people say *wo ai ni* in Mandarin dialect. Cantonese living in Guangdong province to the south say *ngoh oi lei* in Cantonese dialect—quite a difference. Eventually, people have to write love notes to understand each other. A Cantonese writing these three characters to a lover in the north would immediately convey the meaning on paper, even though the words sound entirely different when spoken (Pannell and Ma, 1983:63–64). In Uygur, a Turkic language spoken in northwest China, *men sizni yahxi koremen* means "I love you"—quite different indeed. But since Uygur has its own written language, communication with outsiders becomes more complicated than it is among literate Chinese who can read the same characters but speak different dialects.

The regions of China are different in climate, culture, topography, agriculture, and industry (Toops and Andrus, 1993). Not only regional differences but regional identities are important. When you meet other people in China, you ask where they are from. In this fashion, identity is set up: "I am a Beijing person." "I am a Sichuan person." Regional identities are strong (Cannon and Jenkins, 1990:62).

■ The Natural Landscape

China's regional differences have their roots in physical geography. China is a land of extremes, of diverse topographies and varied landscapes. The highest point, Mt. Everest (Qomolangma) at 29,029 feet (8,848 meters) is on the border of Tibet and Nepal. The lowest point, the Turpan Depression at 505 feet (154 meters) below sea level, is in the far west of China (Hsieh and Hsieh, 1996). The Chinese people have been working this land for 4,000 years, constantly shaping and forming it. The terraces and waterworks are a good example of this. The Chinese have sculpted the landscape, but they are not masters of it. Floods and droughts still plague China. The Chinese have not transformed fierce and austere mountains and deserts into fields of grain (Tuan, 1969:1).

The Chinese have a phrase, "vast in territory and rich in resources" *(di da wu bo)*. One perception of China is of unlimited land and resources. Another perspective of Chinese reality is that "the land is scarce and the people are many" *(di shao ren zhong)* (Leeming, 1993). Ten percent of China's vast territory is cultivated (Zhao Songqiao, 1994:34); 90 percent of its 1.2 billion people live on terrain about the size of the United States to the east of the Mississippi River.

▓ Three Tiers

It is easiest to approach China's physical geography by visualizing the country in three parts. As Map 2.4 shows, nature orders this landscape in three tiers, ranging from mountains to floodplains (Zhao Songqiao, 1994:15). Powerful rivers have their origins high in the mountains of western China and then flow east to the sea. The rivers run through several tiers of mountains, hills, and then basins. Over two-thirds of China is mountainous, hilly, or high plateaus. This mountainous nature is a major constraint on human use of the land (Hsieh and Hsieh, 1996).

The highest tier is the mountains, shown on Map 2.4 with the two darkest gradations of shading, representing land ranging from 6,000 to 29,029 feet (1,829 to 8,848 meters) in elevation. Tibet lies in the heart of this region, but it also extends into Qinghai, Xinjiang, Sichuan, Gansu, and Guizhou provinces (see Map 2.2). The Himalaya range, at the southern end of this system, contains the world's highest mountains, Everest and K2. *Shan* means "mountain." You will notice several other ranges on Map 2.4 that are less familiar to you. The intermediate shading represents altitudes from 6,000 to 16,000 feet (1,829 to 4,877 meters); keep in mind that (except for 20,320-foot Mt. McKinley) the highest mountains of North America are under 15,000 feet. All the major rivers of China have their origins in these regions. Altitude is a major constraint on the habitation of people, plants, and animals (Cannon and Jenkins, 1990:85).

The middle tier is the hilly area, represented in the lightest shading—a broad expanse of basins, hills, and plateaus between 600 and 6,000 feet (183 and 1,829 meters). To the north are the Tarim and Junggar Basins and the Ordos Platform (Mongolian Plateau). Population in the northern portions of this tier (Tarim and Mongolia) is quite sparse because it is so dry. The deserts and the mountains combine to form effective barriers to the outside. Below them is the Loess Plateau, and east of Tibet are the Sichuan Basin and the Yunnan Plateau (south of the Hengduan Shan). Here there is more rainfall. The southern portion of this tier (Sichuan and Yunnan) has a dense population. Along the coast rise four ranges of hills—Changbai, Shandong, Huang, and Wuyi. Hainan Island to the south contains another range (Zhao Songqiao, 1994:15).

The lowest tier (without shading), with floodplains and lowlands, is both the smallest and the most populous. Notice from comparing Maps 2.3 and 2.4 how this portion of China supports the highest population densities—the land is scarce and the people are many. This segment following the coast lies below 600 feet (183 meters). The North China Plain follows the path of the Yellow River, while the Yangtze River and the combined paths of the Liao and Song Rivers form plains to the south and north. These plains with their many people are the agricultural and industrial heart of China. The North China Plain has less water, and the plain formed by the Liao and Song Rivers is quite cold in winter; as one moves south toward the delta of the West River, the warm, wet, fertile plains provide the principal basis for China's rich agricultural output (Pannell and Ma, 1983:119).

The two highest tiers are the result of tectonic activity, the moving of the earth's plates. The Himalayas are still growing; earthquakes strike China regularly. Basins are usually not vulnerable, but the tectonic boundaries (fault lines) between plateaus and the mountain ranges have earthquakes fairly often. The most disastrous earthquakes have been those in populated areas. In 1976 an earthquake in Tianjin, near Beijing, killed over 250,000 people (Cannon and Jenkins, 1990:87–89).

■ The Rivers Linking China

The mountains and deserts may divide China, but the river basins link it together. The natural landscape of China sometimes is summed up as *Huang He Chang Jiang,* the names for the two largest rivers, the Yellow and the Yangtze. These river systems connect the three physiographic tiers just discussed. Over long spans of time, the rivers flowed through the mountains and plateaus, carrying eroded material that washed into the sea to form and then build up the lowlands; they still break through dams and dikes during flood seasons to lay down more silt from upstream, contributing to the fertility of the soils in eastern China (Cannon and Jenkins, 1990:84).

The river of greatest historical importance is the Yellow River, since imperial China had its origins along its banks and those of its tributaries (see Chapter 3). As Map 2.4 shows, the Yellow River *(Huang He)* starts in the high mountain areas, runs north, cuts south through the Loess Plateau, and flows into the Bo Sea *(Bo Hai)* and out to the Yellow Sea *(Huang Hai).* The Yellow River and Yellow Sea gained their names from the fine fertile loess (yellow-brown soil) that the river carries in its muddy waters. When the Chinese speak of "the River," it is this one. The Yellow River is also called "China's Sorrow." According to Chinese historical records, it has changed its course twenty-six times in the past 4,000 years. Since the North China Plain is very flat, people have built dikes and then more dikes to control it. Over the years, it has deposited much silt on its bottom, raising the riverbed. People in turn raised the dikes to hold up the banks. Now the riverbed is higher than the surrounding plain. When dikes break, the flood carries for miles. This is the sorrow. The river also brings joy by irrigating fields along its floodplain. When the ancient Chinese organized to build the dikes and irrigation channels, their agricultural surplus increased, and Chinese civilization developed (Pannell and Ma, 1983:27).

The longest river in China and the third longest in the world is the Long River *(Chang Jiang).* This river is also known as the Yangtze *(Yangzi* in *pinyin);* technically, this refers only to the estuary (mouth) of the river, but Europeans and Americans who were introduced to it when arriving from the ocean adopted that name—which we use in this book—to describe the whole river. As you can see on Map 2.4, the Yangtze starts in the high mountain areas not far from the headwaters of the Yellow River, but the rivers take different paths to the sea. Out of Tibet, the Yangtze passes through Sichuan and then goes through the narrow Three Gorges in Wu Shan before coming out into the Yangtze Plain. Unlike the Yellow River, the Yangtze is very important for transportation, linking the interior to the East China Sea (Zhao Songqiao, 1994:110).

The Yangtze is also prone to flooding that affects millions of people, especially since this area receives plenty of rainfall. The government has built large dams and reservoirs to lessen flood damage and to generate hydroelectricity. Now the government is building the Three Gorges Dam, which will be the world's largest dam. The reservoir will fill much of the spectacular Three Gorges (Edmonds, 2000), and many people are concerned about the impact of such a dam on the environment (see Chapter 9).

The West River *(Xi Jiang)* drains southern China. As you can see from Map 2.4, this river rises out of the Yunnan Plateau and cuts through the South China Hills before it reaches the South China Sea. The Pearl River delta, the estuary of the West River, has been an important economic area for China. Hong Kong is located there. The area is hilly, but peasants have built terraces over the years for paddy agriculture. This southern section of China has more than adequate moisture for wet-rice fields, and the hillsides are also good for tea. The Chinese have a saying, "when you drink water, think of the source" *(yin shui si yuan).* These rivers are very important for China. Without water, the land is worth little (Pannell and Ma, 1983:141).

■ Climate, Soil, and Vegetation

The monsoon controls China's climate. The winter monsoon blows dry, cold air out of the northern Siberian steppes, bringing no moisture. The summer monsoon blows in hot and humid air masses from the South and East China Seas (see Map 2.4); by the time these air masses reach the interior, they have rained themselves out but are still hot. This north-south monsoon mechanism drives the climate process in China. It keeps south China warm and wet, whereas the north is cold and dry—relieved only by the Yellow River flowing from the south and winds from the East China Sea and Sea of Japan (Hsieh and Hsieh, 1996).

The Chinese designate their soils by color. Red soil is in the southeast, and the marshy areas of the south are blue. The loess of the north is yellow-brown, and the northeast has black soil. The deserts of the west have white soil. No soils anywhere in the world have fed so many people for so many generations (Tuan, 1969:23–31). Because of China's size and diversity, it helps to examine each region of the country to understand the linkage among climate, soils, and vegetation (Zhao Songqiao, 1994:30).

The southeast, the wettest part of China, receives over 60 inches (152.4 centimeters) of rain (sometimes nearly 80 inches [203.2 centimeters]), most in the summer. The southeast portion of the United States, by comparison, has a similar climate but receives 40–60 inches (101.6–152.4 centimeters) of rain. China's southeast is subject to typhoons in the summer. Summers are extremely hot and sticky, with daily highs above 87 degrees Fahrenheit (30 degrees Celsius). Winters are cool and damp, with daily averages around 50 degrees Fahrenheit (10 degrees Celsuis). In much of this part of China, people do not have heating, so the winter feels cold. Since the growing season is quite long, it is common to cultivate two crops of rice a year. On Hainan (see Map 2.2), a tropical isle, three crops of rice a year are possible (Sivin, 1988:48).

Soils in the southeast are thick and sticky. This area was originally covered by broadleaf evergreen forests. Now much of the region grows rice, on fields immersed in water to nourish the young paddy shoots, and the sticky soils hold the roots firmly. They have been farmed for a long time and have been leached of much of their nutrients, but the farmers add "night soil" (human waste from outhouses and buckets) to provide humus (Pannell and Ma, 1983:33).

North of the Yangtze, the climate begins to change. The North China Plain (see Map 2.4) gains enough precipitation for crops. The yearly variability of precipitation is marked; some years may not see 20 inches (50.8 centimeters), whereas others see closer to 40 inches (101.6 centimeters). Wheat, rather than rice, dominates. Water is at a premium; some have suggested diverting part of the Yangtze's flow northward. Summers are hot, with highs usually more than 80 degrees Fahrenheit (27 degrees Celsius); winters are quite cold, with lows down to 15 degrees Fahrenheit (-10 degrees Celsius). In the winter, dust storms sometimes come off the Gobi Desert, blanketing Beijing with a fine dust. Heilongjiang and Jilin (see Map 2.2) are cold indeed, especially in the long winter when lows can drop to 40 degrees below zero Fahrenheit (-40 degrees Celsius). Summers are short but warm with highs of 70 degrees Fahrenheit (22 degrees Celsius) and enough moisture for crops such as corn and soybeans (Pannell and Ma, 1983:41).

The sediment left by river flooding in the North China Plain is quite fertile, though dry. This area was originally covered by forest, although now fields of wheat are most common. Some of the soils have been irrigated so much that they have become salty. Wet-field paddy cannot be formed in the dry fields of the north, and so less rice can be grown here. Heilongjiang, Jilin, and Liaoning (see Map 2.2) have poor soils except in the floodplains of the Song and Liao Rivers. Conifer forests still cover much of the mountain region.

Aridity (lack of rainfall) begins to increase in the interior of the country; half of China's territory receives less than 20 inches (50.8 centimeters) of rainfall a year (Cannon and Jenkins, 1990:82). The Loess Plateau and Mongolian Plateau (Ordos Platform), shown on Map 2.4, are part of the 20 percent of China that is semiarid, with 10–20 inches (25.4–50.8 centimeters) of rainfall a year. Wheat and some corn and millet are grown here with irrigation from the Yellow River. Summers are very warm and dry, with highs above 80 degrees Fahrenheit (27 degrees Celsius), and winters are quite cold and dry, with average daily temperatures around 32 degrees Fahrenheit (0 degrees Celsius). The loess (the brownish-yellow soil that gives the Loess Plateau its name) is very deep and fertile, but erosion is a major problem in this area. The original vegetation was grassland and shrub; much that remains is overgrazed by cattle, and most has been plowed into fields. When the rains come, they fall hard and fast. Much of the surface loess ends up in the Yellow River (Pannell and Ma, 1983:36).

Over 30 percent of China is almost completely arid, with under 10 inches (25.4 centimeters) of rainfall a year (Cannon and Jenkins, 1990:82). The Takla Makan Desert in the Tarim Basin (Map 2.4) is the most extreme case, with less than 1 inch (2.54 centimeters) of rain per year. Turpan has recorded temperatures up to 118 degrees Fahrenheit (48 degrees Celsius). In this dry stretch of land, only the snowmelt from the mountains can give any water for sustenance. Even though the temperature is running high at 87 degrees Fahrenheit (30 degrees Celsius), it is not humid, so the summers are bearable. Because Siberia, where the winter monsoons blow in, is immediately to the north, winters are severely cold, averaging 15 degrees Fahrenheit (-10 degrees Celsuis), with lows of 20 degrees below zero Fahrenheit (-28 degrees Celsius). The many oases make the desert livable; they are highly productive, growing specialty crops such as melons, grapes, and cotton. In the northern portions of this arid area, steppe grasslands afford livestock grazing. The mountains have conifer forests also (Pannell and Ma, 1983:43).

The Tibetan Plateau (Map 2.4) has a unique and harsh climate. Altitude and location on the interior of a continent combine for a dry, cold climate, much like the polar extremes. Every month has temperatures below freezing; the long winters average only 20 degrees Fahrenheit (-7 degrees Celsius). The interior of the area receives less than 4 inches (10.2 centimeters) of precipitation per year. The summer is quite short, but temperatures in the sun are warm, with highs of 70 degrees Fahrenheit (22 degrees Celsius). Soils are poor in Tibet because there is not much plant life to decay into humus. Barley is grown in the south. The yaks, sheep, goats, and *dzo* (a cross between a yak and an ox) are the only livestock in this harsh climate. The yaks provide meat, milk, and hides for the Tibetans (Goldstein and Beall, 1990). They also keep donkeys and horses, and wild asses roam the countryside.

China's 1.2 billion people have many challenges. Only 10 percent of the land will grow crops. Deserts and mountains make up much of western China.

Northern China does not have enough water. Only the southeast has a climate that provides an abundance of food. Raising the economic well-being of the people will require careful management of the natural resources.

▓ Economic Resources

When Marco Polo came to China, he found the Chinese burning "black rocks"; the abundance of coal and other fuel has long contributed to China's high economic output. China has several sources for energy. In the rural areas, the energy of the sun and of plants is the major source for most peasants. The burning of coal and oil provides energy for most urban areas. In areas with great rivers, hydroelectric power contributes increasing amounts of electricity (Smith, 2000; Donald and Benewick, 2000).

Peasants use minimal amounts of oil. Coal is the fuel in the north, and people also burn rice straw, wheat straw, cornstalks, and cotton stalks to cook food and boil water. It takes a lot of straw to boil water. Since this material is burned, it is not plowed back into the ground to enrich the soil. Peasants scour the countryside looking for sticks, twigs, bark, and grass to use as fuel because so much of the natural landscape is overcut. This loss of natural cover causes the hill slopes to erode. Manure piles are often used to generate methane gas for cooking and lighting. Small-scale hydroelectric power plants provide enough electricity for lighting in many homes (Pannell and Ma, 1983:116).

In the city a different pattern emerges. Coal supplies much energy, both for industrial and for residential use. China has the world's largest coal reserves, located mainly in northern China. Coal is processed into charcoal for cooking in urban households, and China's heavy industry relies largely on coal. Because northern China has water shortages, much of the coal is unwashed and thus burns less efficiently. Shipment of coal to other areas is a major difficulty for China. As China's industrialization increases, it will burn more coal, adding to air and water pollution (Leeming, 1993:21–23; Veeck, 1991:125). See Chapter 9 for a discussion of these problems.

China is a major producer of oil, but uses most of its oil for its own industry. Much of the oil is in northeastern China; newer sites include the Bo Hai region in the northeast (Map 2.4) and Hainan Island in the southeast (Map 2.2). The biggest potential lies in the Tarim Basin of the northwest. Exploration of this desert area has been a major focus. These sites are far from industrial areas, however, so transporting the oil is a problem. As China increases its use of cars, the demand for oil products will also increase (Cannon and Jenkins, 1990:181–183; Li and Tang, 2000).

Another energy source is hydroelectric power. Strong potential exists for electricity production on rivers of the south such as the Yangtze. Here the problems lie in moving people and in flooding large farmland areas. This power, however, will serve the needs of industry and the urban population (Cannon and Jenkins, 1990:186; Hsieh and Lu, 2003).

China's iron ore reserves lie mostly to the north and northeast. The Chinese have mined iron for thousands of years, and many mining operations are small scale and locally run. The reserves should be adequate in coming years if used more efficiently. China is looking for more minerals in western regions as it advances into the twenty-first century. Many of them are in out-of-the-way places to the north and west, so transportation to the heavy industry located in the north will be a problem (Zhao Songqiao, 1994:45).

With better soils, water supplies, transportation, and terrain, the eastern portion of China has been more hospitable for living and economic production than the west. The northeast is well suited for heavy industry, and the southeast is ideal for agricultural production. Hence the economy of China Proper to the east has far surpassed that of Frontier China to the west. In Chapter 3 we observe that this disparity goes far back in time, and in Chapters 4 and 5 we discuss whether it might be reduced in the future. The Yangtze River can play a pivotal role in helping to move economic growth westward. The Chinese like to view the coast as a bow and the Yangtze River as an arrow that can shoot industry and economic reforms into China's interior. After all, as discussed in the next chapter, it was the Yellow River that shot China's imperial civilization out to the coast (Cannon and Jenkins, 1990:29).

■ Bibliography

Blunden, Caroline, and Mark Elvin. 1998. *Cultural Atlas of China.* New York: Checkmark Books.

Borthwick, Mark. 1998. *Pacific Century: The Emergence of Modern Pacific Asia.* Boulder: Westview Press.

Buchanan, Keith. 1970. *The Transformation of the Chinese Earth: Perspectives on Modern China.* London: G. Bell and Sons.

Cannon, Terry (ed.). 2000. *China's Economic Growth: The Impact on Regions, Migration, and the Environment.* New York: St. Martin's Press.

Cannon, Terry, and Alan Jenkins (eds.). 1990. *The Geography of Contemporary China: The Impact of Deng Xiaoping's Decade.* London: Routledge.

Cheung, Peter T. Y., Jae Ho Chung, and David S. G. Goodman (eds.). 1996. "The 1995 Statistical Yearbook in Provincial Perspective." *Provincial China* 1:34–68.

Donald, Stephanie, and Robert Benewick. 2000. *The State of China Atlas.* London: Penguin.

Edmonds, Richard Louis. 2000. "Recent Developments and Prospects for the Sanxia (Three Gorges) Dam." Pp. 161–183 in Terry Cannon (ed.), *China's Economic Growth: The Impact on Regions, Migration, and the Environment.* New York: St. Martin's Press.

Europa Publications. 2002. *The Territories of the People's Republic of China.* London: Taylor and Francis.

Evans, John C. 1992. *Tea in China: The History of China's National Drink.* New York: Greenwood Press.

Fairbank, John King, Edwin O. Reischauer, and Albert M. Craig. 1973. *East Asia: Tradition and Transformation.* Boston: Houghton Mifflin.

Freeberne, Michael. 1992. "The Changing Geography of the People's Republic of China." Pp. 122–159 in Graham Chapman and Kathleen Baker (eds.), *The Changing Geography of Asia.* London and New York: Routledge.

Geelan, Peter J. M., and Denis C. Twitchett (eds.). 1974. *The Times Atlas of China.* London: Times.

Goldstein, Melvyn C., and Cynthia Beall. 1990. *Nomads of Western Tibet: The Survival of a Way of Life.* Berkeley: University of California Press.

Goodman, David S. G. (ed.). 1989. *China's Regional Development.* London: Routledge.

Hsieh, Chiao-min, and Jean Kan Hsieh (eds.). 1996. *China: A Provincial Atlas.* New York: Macmillan.

Hsieh, Chiao-min, and Max Lu (eds.). 2003. *Changing China: A Geographical Appraisal.* Boulder: Westview Press.

Institute of Geography, Chinese Academy of Sciences. 1994. *The National Economic Atlas of China.* Oxford: Oxford University Press.

Kolb, Albert. 1971. *East Asia: Geography of a Cultural Region.* London: Methuen.

Leeming, Frank. 1993. *The Changing Geography of China.* Oxford: Blackwell.

Li, Chengrui (ed.). 1987. *The Population Atlas of China.* Hong Kong: Oxford University Press.

Li, Siming, and Tang Wingshing. 2000. *China's Regions, Polity, and Economy: A Study of Spatial Transformation in the Post-Reform Era.* Hong Kong: Chinese University Press.

Linge, Godfrey J. R., and Dean K. Forbes (eds.). 1993. *China's Spatial Economy.* Hong Kong: Oxford University Press.

Murphey, Rhoads. 1992. *A History of Asia.* New York: HarperCollins.

Pannell, Clifton, and Laurence J. C. Ma. 1983. *China: The Geography of Development and Modernization.* New York: John Wiley.

Sivin, Nathan (ed.). 1988. *The Contemporary Atlas of China.* London: Weidenfeld and Nicolson.

Smith, Christopher. 2000. *China in the Post Utopian Age.* Boulder: Westview Press.

Toops, Stanley W., and Simone Andrus. 1993. "Social Intelligence in China." *Journal of Economic and Social Intelligence* 3(1):3–20.

Tuan, Yi-fu. 1969. *China.* Chicago: Aldine.

Veeck, Gregory (ed.). 1991. *The Uneven Landscape: Geographical Studies in Post Reform China.* Baton Rouge: Lousiana State University Press.

World Bank. 1992. *World Development Report 1992: Development and the Environment.* New York: Oxford University Press.

Zhao Songqiao. 1994. *Geography of China: Environment, Resources, Population, and Development.* New York: John Wiley.

The Historical Context

Rhoads Murphey

In Chapter 2, Stanley Toops showed how China is situated within Asia and how its people blend into the three tiers of its natural landscape. He also introduced some of the cultural diversity that has resulted from the blending. In this chapter, too, I will emphasize how nature both limits and encourages human occupancy of the land, but now the focus is on the history of human settlement, conquest, and government in China. As we begin half a million years ago and move forward to the present, another kind of blending becomes evident: China's isolation from much of the rest of the planet let it develop a unique culture that contributed extensively to civilizations elsewhere. At the same time, this culture was able to absorb conquests, technology, migrations, and religions from outside without losing its own identity. Even periods of disunity and conquests by Europeans and Japanese during the past two centuries have left China's unique culture and institutions fundamentally intact.

Chapter 2 introduced you to the distinction between Frontier China and China Proper and between southeastern and northeastern China. As we review the histories of China's imperial dynasties in this chapter, it will quickly become evident that China's imperial civilization began in Frontier China (see Map 3.1) but has its base in the valley and floodplain of the Yellow River (see Map 2.4). Periodically, parts of northern China have been conquered by groups of invaders coming in from the Frontier, and the Mongols (briefly) and the Manchus (more enduringly) conquered the whole country. Yet those invaders themselves soon adopted the habits and institutions of China Proper. And China Proper itself has a long historical division; southeastern China's culture is as old and solid as that of the northeast. Those in the northeast conquered those in the southeast. That conquest has not been forgotten.

This chapter introduces a number of other themes that, like those in the prior two paragraphs, are treated more fully in subsequent chapters. China experienced feudalism and developed a centralized state long before those social and political processes came to Europe. It developed some unique relationships between government officials and merchants that often pitted south against north and region against region yet encouraged agriculture, commerce, and the early growth of cities. It repeatedly tried to conquer and control people in adjoining territories. It has sometimes welcomed traders from around the world and sometimes kept them more at arm's length. The early parts of new dynasties often brought exciting growth and innovation; the latter parts often brought decline and stagnation. When the European powers first tested the empire with the 1839 Opium War, the empire was in a period of decline. That war exposed China's technological backwardness and resistance to change and opened up a century of conquest and humiliation by outside powers. Yet China has once again found the strength to rebound as it seeks to bring its technology to world levels.

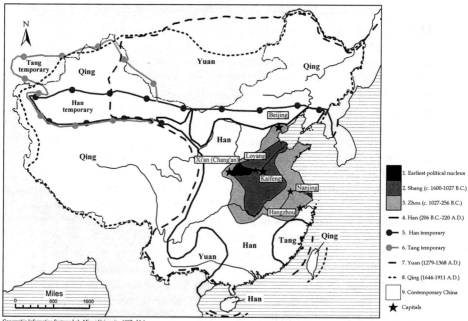

Geographic Information Systems Lab, Miami University, 1997 M.A.

Note: Although the Zhou dynasty did not fall until 221 B.C.E., its territory was significantly decreased in 256 B.C.E. by the barbarian invasion.

Map 3.1 Historical Boundaries of China

■ The Peopling of China

▓ Early Inhabitants

As far as we know, the ancestors of the Chinese have lived for the past half-million years in the area now covered by the modern provinces of China Proper. China Proper is—as Chapter 2 explained—the area south of the Great Wall (which is just north of Beijing) and east of the Tibetan massif (the uplifted highlands with the two darkest shadings on Map 2.4). The earliest remains of *Homo erectus* found in China Proper are of Peking (Beijing) Man, dated approximately 500,000 B.C.E.; since they are fossilized, it is hard to differentiate physical characteristics from those of fossilized *Homo erectus* remains discovered elsewhere in the world. There is, however, some evidence that by about 200,000 B.C.E., after *Homo erectus* had merged with other humanoid species, the population, at least of northern China, had developed certain physical features associated with modern Chinese. The handheld stone choppers and knives these people fashioned were similar to those at other Paleolithic sites in East Asia but different from the stone tools made in Paleolithic Europe, India, and Africa (Chang, 1986:22–70; Gernet, 1968:19–39; Watson, 1961:22–55; Howells, 1983). This suggests that China had by then become quite isolated within its mountain and desert borders. China was to remain largely isolated from areas and cultures to the west until Portuguese adventurers arrived by sea in the sixteenth century and British naval guns finally opened China's ports to residence by foreigners in the nineteenth century. Though isolated, the Chinese borrowed extensively from neighboring regions, developed many inventions of their own, and united large populations and regions while Central Asian and European states and empires rose and fell (Lattimore, 1940:27–39).

The Chinese have always been very conscious and proud of their long and glorious past. That consciousness and pride remain true today, and one really cannot understand contemporary China without considerable knowledge of its history.

▓ North and South

China covers a huge area, larger than the United States if one includes Tibet (Xizang), Xinjiang, Inner Mongolia, and Manchuria (Heilongjiang, Jilin, and Liaoning), where cultures and physical types remain basically different from those of China Proper (Lattimore, 1940:53–80; Cheng, 1966; Pulleyblank, 1983). Even the provinces within China Proper (which itself originally contained a wide but closely related variety of cultures and physical types) cover territory large enough to hold most of the countries of western

Europe. In the third century B.C.E., with the creation of empire under the Qin dynasty (221 B.C.E.), the people and culture of northern China conquered the central and southern regions of China Proper. Soon they were spreading their culture and then themselves southward.

From the time of the Han dynasty (202 B.C.E.–C.E. 220) and its consolidation of empire, the inhabitants called themselves "people of Han." Map 3.1 shows you how the Han dynasty moved into territory farther south and west than previous dynasties. The southernmost people conquered by the Han were distantly related to but distinct from them. Qin and Han expansion also took place at the expense of the several more closely related but distinct peoples and cultures of central and southern China. Some of these southerners had almost certainly created what we may call "civilization"—settled agriculture, metals, writing, and cities—at least as early as or earlier than these developments in the north, where in the dry climate the evidence is better preserved (Chang, 1986:95–106, 192–242, 368–408; Li, 1985:189–221). Such early developments in the south would be a logical result of its proximity to the original sources of cultivated rice, pigs, chickens, water buffaloes, and early making of bronze (Linduff, Han, and Sun, 2000), all in adjacent Southeast Asia (northern Vietnam and northern Thailand), probably well before they appeared in what is now China. Transmittal was easy, and there was probably also some movement of peoples. Before the Qin conquest forcibly united all Chinese into a single empire, the Guangdong (see Map 2.2) area was joined in a single state with what is now northern Vietnam, the state of Yueh, which spoke a common language (Meacham, 1983). But it is hard to imagine historical China without even one of the key elements derived from Southeast Asia—buffaloes for plowing the soil, rice and pigs as staples in the diet (Te-Tzu Chang, 1983:70–77), and bronze for casting (Li, 1985:265–314; Barnard, 1983; Franklin, 1983). In time, these presumably spread into central and northern China, but the north was generally too dry for rice and buffaloes and only marginally hospitable for pigs and chickens.

In the course of the Qin and Han conquests, a single written language was imposed as well as a common spoken language, the ancestor of modern standard spoken Chinese, for the officials who administered the empire. Originally, northern culture overlaid the widely different cultures of the south. With the fall of the Han dynasty in C.E. 220 began the long migration of northerners southward over some 2,000 years, which of course added further pressures toward a national mode, in addition to the northern troops and administrators who had been operating in the south since the third century B.C.E. Distinct traces of different regional cultures and speech patterns remain among Han Chinese in the south, including differences in diet and cuisine as well as strong provincial identity amounting almost to clannishness. But the southward wave of Han Chinese conquest and settlement has taken all of the good

Pigs have long been domesticated in Southeast Asia and south China

Laurel Bossen

agricultural land and greatly reduced the original non-Han population, who now live only in mountainous areas mainly unfit for agriculture, to which they have been driven by Han pressures. In a few subprovincial areas of this sort they constitute a majority, yet their numbers are small, and they are divided among themselves by cultural and linguistic differences. Some 91 percent of China's people are Han, with the remainder widely scattered and fragmented. As Chapter 8 explains, these percentages are somewhat inaccurate because many Han in recent years have married non-Han or asserted non-Han identity to avoid the one-child policy of the government, which does not apply to non-Han. Over the centuries since the Qin and Han conquest of the south, there has been widespread intermarriage as well as pressures for cultural conformity, so that the many originally quite separate and distinct cultures of central and southern China have been overlaid by a common imperial stamp. Traces of the originally wide variety of physical types as well as aspects of local or regional culture continue to be apparent beneath that stamp. Chapter 4 will tell you more about these divisions.

■ The Outer Areas

The outer areas—the Frontier—are a separate case, originally inhabited by people only slightly related to the Han Chinese (Lattimore, 1940:255–279; "Mysterious," 1998). The clearest cases are the Tibetans, Mongols, and Uygurs, the latter the dominant inhabitants of Xinjiang. Since 1950 the Chinese government has not only forcibly occupied these areas but promoted large-scale settlement there of Han Chinese as administrators and technicians, who now constitute the largest portion of the population of Xinjiang and a growing proportion of the population of Tibet. Outer Mongolia (Lattimore, 1940:489–510), north of the Gobi Desert, declared its independence from China in 1921 as the Mongolian Peoples' Republic, but Inner Mongolia, along the steppe frontier, was heavily occupied by Han Chinese, mainly as farmers dependent on new irrigation and road and rail lines. They now outnumber the remaining Mongols by about twenty to one, and the distinct Mongol culture is fading; significant numbers of Han Chinese have also settled in Outer Mongolia as technicians. Manchuria (Lattimore, 1940:103–150), known in China simply as "the Northeast" in an effort to soft-pedal the area's contended history as a target of Russian and Japanese ambitions (see Chapter 7), has been overwhelmed by mass Han Chinese migration since the late nineteenth century. This immigration has almost obliterated the original Tungusic, Manchu, and Mongol population as the northeast received refugees from overcrowded and drought-ridden northern China and developed its own surplus agricultural system and the largest heavy industrial complex in East Asia, thanks to its major resources of coal, iron, oil, and hydro (water) power.

The Chinese government's "solution" to the problem of non-Han minorities was to establish autonomous areas in the few pockets in the south where non-Han peoples remained a majority, and in Tibet, Xinjiang, and Inner Mongolia. "Autonomous" is a bad joke, since the ruling hand of the Chinese state is omnipresent, and nearly all positions of authority are held by Han or by collaborators. In Tibet (as Chapter 6 explains), the Chinese state has tried to eradicate a separate Tibetan identity and so viciously repressed Tibetan efforts to assert it or to seek a voice in their own affairs that China has been repeatedly accused of genocide. The "autonomous" formula has convinced no one and in Chinese parlance is best referred to as "great Han chauvinism." Since minorities are such an increasingly fragmented percentage of the total population, often occupying strategically sensitive borders where neighboring states like to play on their discontent, the Chinese state feels free to ride roughshod over them and their interests.

■ Political Patterns of the Past

▓ Feudalism

China's recorded history begins with the Shang dynasty (ca. 1600–1027 B.C.E.; see Map 3.1 and Table 3.1), whose authenticity was questioned by Western scholars until excavations in the 1920s uncovered the remains of the last Shang capital, Anyang, and a great number of inscriptions giving the names of Shang kings. Later excavations (Keightley, 1983) rounded out the picture of the Shang as being dependent upon slaves captured in chronic wars with surrounding groups, already referred to as "barbarians," and as managing a productive agricultural system on the fertile loess (wind-laid, yellow-brown soil) of northern China. The chief Shang crop was millet, probably native to northern China, slowly supplemented by rice as rice moved northward. The major technological achievement of the Shang was in the working of bronze, producing objects whose technical perfection has never been equaled (Cheng, 1960; Gernet, 1968:43–66; Watson, 1961:57–101). Excavations in central and southern China, where high temperatures and humidity have tended to obliterate much of the evidence, have nevertheless made it clear, as hinted at earlier, that Shang achievements were paralleled, perhaps even preceded, farther south, where writing, bronze, and a surplus-producing agriculture based mainly on rice were used (Chang, 1980; Hsu, 1995:1–32).

The Shang built large and ornate palaces whose remains can tell us a good deal about the wealth generated by agricultural surpluses, including the richly decorated chariots that were buried in the royal tombs with their horses and large numbers of followers or slaves. Writing, clearly the ancestor of modern written Chinese, slowly evolved and expanded to include abstractions; many of the characters can still be read, and the system was inherited by the next dynasty, the Zhou (Te-Tzu Chang, 1983:81–94, 107–129; Chang, 1986:295–307; Li, 1985:442–459). The Zhou's successor, the Qin dynasty, would impose this northern script on all of China, replacing the different scripts already in use farther south.

In about 1027 B.C.E., a great slave revolt was joined by one of the Shang feudal vassals, the Zhou who guarded the western frontiers (Hsu, 1995:33–67). Originally a "barbarian" group, the Zhou had acquired most of Shang culture and technology and used what became the traditional Chinese justification for rebellion, citing the injustices and oppression of the Shang rulers and declaring that "heaven commands us to destroy it" (Te-Tzu Chang, 1983:44–55; Hsu, 1995:68–111). The last Shang king, alleged to have been a monster of depravity, died in the flames of his palace.

The Shang had ruled from successive capitals, which were frequently moved, in the central Yellow River valley, including the site of modern

Table 3.1 China's Imperial Dynasties and Beyond

Dynasty	In China	In the Rest of the World
Xia 2100–1600 B.C.E. (?)	Chinese characters developed.	2700 B.C.E. Egyptians build Great Pyramid.
Shang 1600–1027 B.C.E. (?)	Advanced bronze casting.	1250 B.C.E. Moses and the exodus from Egypt. 1200 B.C.E. Trojan War.
Zhou 1027–211 B.C.E. Western Zhou 1027–771 B.C.E. Eastern Zhou 771–221 B.C.E.	Feudalism. Emperors called "Sons of Heaven." Spring and Autumn Period 771–476 B.C.E. Confucius 551–479 B.C.E. Warring States Period 476–221 B.C.E.	753 B.C.E. Rome founded. 560–483 B.C.E. Buddha in India. 399 B.C.E. Death of Socrates. 336–323 B.C.E. Alexander the Great.
Qin 221–206 B.C.E.	China unified. Great Wall unified.	
Han 202 B.C.E.–C.E. 220 Western Han 206 B.C.E.–C.E. 9 Eastern Han C.E. 25–220	Confucianism adopted. Silk Road opens. Buddhism to China. Paper invented.	54 B.C.E. Caesar invades Britain.
Three Kingdoms C.E. 220–280	Period of disunity.	
Eight Dynasties C.E. 265–589	Invasion and more division.	451 C.E. Attila the Hun defeated. 476 C.E. Fall of Rome.
Sui C.E. 589–618	Grand Canal built.	

continues

Dynasty	In China	In the Rest of the World
Tang C.E. 618–907	Expanding trade. First printed book.	Dark Ages in Europe. C.E. 742–814 Charlemagne.
Five Dynasties C.E. 907–960	Period of disunity.	
Qidan C.E. 936–1122	Rule northern China.	C.E. 1096 First Crusade.
Jin C.E. 1115–1234		
Song C.E. 960–1279 Northern Song C.E. 960–1126 Southern Song C.E. 1127–1279	Rule southern China. Capital in Kaifeng. Capitals in Nanjing, Hangzhou.	Medieval Europe. C.E. 1215 Magna Carta.
Yuan C.E. 1279–1368	Genghis and Kublai Khan invade from Mongolia.	C.E. 1300 Renaissance. C.E. 1347–1351 Black Death.
Ming C.E. 1368–1644	Return to rule by Chinese.	C.E. 1450 Printing in Europe. C.E. 1492 Columbus reaches America. C.E. 1517 Reformation. C.E. 1637 First British trade with Canton.
Qing C.E. 1644–1911	Manchu rulers.	C.E. 1776 American Revolution. C.E. 1789 French Revolution.
Republic C.E. 1912–1949	KMT Nationalist rule.	C.E. 1917 Russia's communist revolution. C.E. 1939–1945 World War II.
People's Republic 1949–	Communist rule.	

Zhengzhou, capital of Henan province (see Map 2.2). This was the heartland of early agriculture, but the Zhou established their new capital near modern Xi'an (see Map 3.1 and Shaanxi province on Map 2.2), their old base. Warfare continued with other groups around the fringes of the Zhou domains and periodically with groups to the south, all still called "barbarians."

The Zhou adopted the feudal solution used by the Shang, a network of supposed vassals owing loyalty to the Zhou king (Li, 1985:460–476; Hsu, 1995:112–257). This resembled the system in medieval Europe, whereby a central state with pretensions to wider power but without the means to enforce it made alliances with local and regional groups, symbolized by ritual homage, provision of troops, and periodic gifts, in exchange for their control over their regional lands as fiefs granted by the king. For perhaps the first two or three centuries of Zhou rule, this system seemed to work reasonably well (Watson, 1961:109–146; Chang, 1986:339–360). But China was changing as regional vassals increased their power and ambitions beyond the ability of the central state to control.

■ The Decline of Feudalism

More basically, the spread of iron tools greatly increased farm production, hastened the clearing of remaining forests with iron axes as well as with fire, expedited new irrigation systems, and taken together supported a major increase in population, from perhaps 5 or 10 million under the late Shang to perhaps 20 million by mid-Zhou, spurred by rising food output, which also provided surpluses to be exchanged in trade (Li, 1985:16–58). Towns and cities began to dot the plain and the Yangtze Valley, and a merchant class of some size emerged.

As in medieval Europe, none of this fit well with the feudal system based on fixed serfdom and the dominance of a hereditary aristocracy. Serfs could escape to the new towns and begin a new life. We don't know much about the life of the common people in the first few centuries of Zhou rule, but it may be revealing that the arrangement mentioned by Mencius much later (third century B.C.E.), which he called the "well field system," included a checkerboard plan with a well in the central plot. Serfs were supposed to give priority to irrigating and cultivating that plot, which belonged to the feudal lord, and only after that could work on the outer plots assigned to them. Serfs were bound to the lord and to his land for life, and on the lord's death could not leave but became serfs to his heir. As the economy altered and agricultural surpluses offered new opportunities for merchants and town dwellers to live and make money, such a system became increasingly hard to maintain (Li, 1985:477–490).

By this time, most writing was done with brush and ink, as in all subsequent centuries, on silk or on strips of bamboo. It was thus that the main body of the Chinese classics was originally written under the mid-Zhou: the *I-ching,* or *Classic of Change* (*Yijing*—a cryptic handbook for diviners), the *Book of Songs,* the *Book of Rituals,* and collections of historical documents (see Chapter 12).

New agricultural productivity freed increasing numbers from farm labor to serve as artisans, scribes, transport workers, soldiers, officials, scholars, and merchants. Towns and cities became more important as trade centers than as centers of feudal control. At the same time, many of the original Zhou vassals were evolving toward separate statedom, as in late medieval Europe, each with its own distinctive culture. After some four centuries of Zhou rule, the political, economic, and social structure began to show strains, and eventually it disintegrated.

In 771 B.C.E. (the first authenticated date in Chinese history) the Zhou capital, near Xi'an, was sacked by rebels, and though it was rebuilt, the capital was moved to Loyang—shown on Map 3.1—in the central Yellow River valley so as to better control the Zhou domains. It was to be a vain hope, as the feudal structure continued to break up, and vassals, now emerging states, increasingly ignored Zhou authority and fought each other for dominance. The old Zhou base in the Wei valley near modern Xi'an was given as a fief to a supposedly loyal noble of the Qin clan, the new guardians of the frontier. Five centuries later, the Qin were to sweep away the crumbling remnants of Zhou pretension to found the first all-China empire (Gernet, 1968:69–84).

◼ Toward a Centralized State

The Qin were, in fact, the smallest and weakest of the major contenders among the former Zhou vassals, at least to begin with (Li, 1985:222–239). The other rivals were various northern and central states as well as the state of Qu in the Yangtze valley and Yueh in the far south. It is still too early to speak of any of them, or of the Zhou, as "China"; each was culturally, linguistically, and politically distinct, and for some time there were also minor racial differences (Li, 1985:59–188). The 500 final years of feudalism over which they presided are known as the Spring and Autumn Period and the Warring States Period. Though they shared technology, no one state dominated until the Qin conquest in 221 B.C.E. (Gernet, 1968:87–108; Hsu, 1995: 258–287). The state of Qu provides a good example of the differences, in that its base along the central portion of the Yangtze River led to rapid development of trade and of towns and cities. But Qu was ultimately defeated by a coalition of northern states in 632 B.C.E. and again in 301 B.C.E. This may have been one of those contests that changes the course of history, giving the future to a peasant-based authoritarian empire, beginning with the Qin, rather than to a state where trade and merchants were prominent.

Increasing food production made it possible to field large armies of men who could be spared from farming for at least parts of the year and could be fed on surpluses. Warfare became larger in scale and more ruthless, no longer the earlier chivalric contests between aristocrats but efforts at wholesale conquest and fights for survival. The crossbow with a trigger mechanism, developed by or before this time, greatly increased firepower, range, and accuracy, and by the fourth century B.C.E., foot soldiers were supported by armed cavalry. All this undermined the earlier dominance of hereditary aristocrats, their chariots, and their personal retinues. Bronze and copper coins were minted by each state, standing armies proliferated, and bureaucracies began to appear. These changes offered a new range of opportunities for able commoners. For many it was a positive and welcome change, but for others the passing of the old order and the disruptions of warfare offered only chaos and moral confusion. Confucius, who lived in the Spring and Autumn Period (see Table 3.1), made it clear that his prescriptions were an effort to reestablish order and what he referred to as "harmony" following the values of an earlier "golden age." As fighting continued, the Qin exterminated the remnant of Zhou power in 256 B.C.E., with no ceremony, and went on a generation later to overwhelm all the other states in a series of lightning campaigns ending in 221 B.C.E. China derives its name from the word *Qin* (*Ch'in* in Wade-Giles transliteration).

The chaos of the Warring States led to the growth of formulas for restoring order, like that of Confucius (551–479 B.C.E.) and his later disciple Mencius (372–289 B.C.E.), which stressed the need for order within a social hierarchy (de Bary, Chan, and Watson, 1960:17–35, 100–111, 256–266; Waley, 1939). The most important of these, after Confucianism, was Daoism, which through its cryptic text, the *Dao de jing,* or "Classic of the Way," represented a different approach to the troubles of the time (de Bary, Chan, and Watson, 1960:50–87). The supposed author, Laozi, whose name means simply "the old one," is a shadowy figure who was a contemporary of Confucius. Where Confucius emphasized the importance of rules for human behavior and gave advice to rulers, Daoism urged believers to relax, go with the flow, and use nature as the pattern, especially water, which flows around obstructions and seeks the lowest places. Whatever exists is natural and hence good. In practice, both Confucianism and Daoism had an appeal for most Chinese, who tended to follow both at different times: Daoism in retirement or when things went badly and Confucianism when in office; or, as has been said, they were workday Confucians and weekend Daoists. Other later philosophical schools, especially under the Qin, adopted the doctrines called Legalism, which emphasized harsh laws to control behavior instead of Confucianism's dependence on morality (Schwartz, 1985; de Bary, Chan, and Watson, 1960:136–158; Gernet, 1968:111–125). Chapter 12 discusses these thinkers in greater depth.

The Qin conquest in 221 B.C.E. imposed stern measures to ensure conformity within the new empire. Primogeniture, whereby the eldest son inherits all of his father's property and status, was abolished, as a possible basis for power that might threaten the state. Land was now privately owned and freely bought and sold, which completed the end of the former feudal system. Walls had been built before to discourage raids along the northern steppe border, but these were consolidated and rebuilt under the Qin as the Great Wall, which runs east and west approximately along a line between areas to the south where normal rainfall is enough for farming and those to the north that are too dry. The Great Wall and the system of imperial roads and canals were built by forced labor, levied as part of taxes (corvée), which caused much suffering. Those who asked questions, the intellectuals, were suppressed by the new totalitarian state. Empire building is a rough business anywhere, but for all its excesses the Qin laid the groundwork for the dynasties that followed and for the modern state. These moves were doubtless popular, but the oppressively heavy set of state controls led to revolts that toppled the Qin in only fifteen years and burned the emperor's magnificent palace as rebels occupied the capital near modern-day Xi'an in 206 B.C.E. (Lattimore, 1940:429–446).

By 202 B.C.E. a new rebel leader emerged out of the civil war, Liu Bang, who founded a new dynasty, which he called Han. He placed his capital on the site of modern-day Xi'an (see Maps 2.2 and 3.1). The harsher aspects of Qin rule were softened by the more humane morality of Confucianism, but many of the empire-building systems of the Qin were retained. The new dynasty emphasized the Confucian precept that government exists to serve the people and that unjust rulers must forfeit the support of the ruled while encouraging educated men to serve the state (de Bary, Chan, and Watson, 1960:172–199; Li, 1985:240–262; Wang, 1982; Loewe, 1994).

What remains of the glory of the Qin was rediscovered near Xi'an in the 1970s as excavations were begun at the massive tomb of the Qin emperor, Qin Shihuang, revealing a terra cotta (pottery) army, each of the thousands of life-size figures individually portrayed and set to guard the tomb's entrance. The idea of empire is contagious, and the Han extended their boundaries still farther. In 111 B.C.E., the emperor Han Wudi reclaimed the Qin conquests of Guangdong and into northern Vietnam and added southern Manchuria and northern Korea to the empire in 109–108 B.C.E. (see Maps 2.2 and 3.1). Earlier he had conquered the desert of Xinjiang, mainly to guard the "Silk Roads" westward (Map 2.1), and built watchtowers and garrison posts along it while mounting several successful campaigns against the ancestors of the Mongols in Inner Mongolia.

Silk caravans crossed the desert of Xinjiang by any one of three main routes and then handed over the silk to a series of Central Asian groups, who carried it to the shores of the Mediterranean, whence it went by ship to Rome, the biggest market, which paid for it in gold, since the Romans had nothing to offer in exchange that the Chinese wanted. Tibet remained outside the empire. Wudi's endless campaigns and the burdens they imposed nearly caused a revolt, but following the advice of the imperial censors, he issued a famous penitential edict promising to be a better and less oppressive ruler. Han rule was briefly broken by a palace coup in C.E. 9 when the empress's nephew Wang Mang declared himself emperor of a new dynasty, but he was overthrown in C.E. 23 and the Han reestablished itself in C.E. 25, now as the Eastern Han, with its capital at Loyang (Map 3.1), where most of the dynasty's former grandeur was continued. But no political order lasts forever, and in the face of rebellion the last Han ruler abdicated in C.E. 220.

■ The Move South

There followed a confused and confusing period sometimes called the Six Dynasties, when originally "barbarian" groups ruled most of the north, while the south was contested among a number of Chinese rivals. Buddhism had come in from India during the Han, and now, in this "time of troubles," it spread widely and for a time eclipsed Confucianism while at the folk level merging with Daoism (de Bary, Chan, and Watson, 1960:279–410). But the model of a unified empire established by the Han remained in people's minds, and after three and a half centuries of fragmentation, a new all-China dynasty, the Sui, re-created the empire of the Han. The fall of the Han dynasty had stimulated a mass movement southward of Chinese fleeing trouble in the north, a major new wave in the Han people's occupation of the south, driving most of the original non-Han inhabitants up into the mountains as the Han took the good agricultural land. This process was to continue cumulatively over the next 1,500 years or more and included the incorporation of Fujian both within the Chinese sphere and into the empires of Sui and Tang. Fujian is mountainous, and its easiest communications are by sea from the coast; its people were among the first to develop trade with Taiwan and Southeast Asia. The language of Fujian people remains different from standard Chinese but essentially the same as Taiwanese, since most of the people of Taiwan migrated from coastal Fujian beginning after C.E. 1600.

The move south meant a series of adjustments to a very different environment from that in the north, where most Han had previously lived (Lattimore, 1940:469–471). New tools suited to wet-rice agriculture were developed, including the endless chain of paddles driven by two men pushing pedals on a crank, designed to move water efficiently from one paddy level to another. Rice, the dominant crop, was now transplanted from seedbeds to irrigated fields, and in the warmer and wetter southern climate yields greatly increased as a result, and two or even three crops a year became possible. Irrigation, intensive cultivation, and the creation of more or less level paddies by terracing on slopes required huge amounts of labor, provided by a growing population sustained by increased food output. In this period also began the use of human manure, or "night soil," to build the nitrogen levels that boosted yields and increased in supply as the population grew. Perhaps the clearest and most potentially destructive impact of the rising southern population was, however, the removal of most of the original forest cover to clear land for farming. As the population continued to rise, steeper and steeper slopes were invaded by terraces and the area covered by trees was greatly reduced, producing, as in the north where deforestation was much older, erosion, siltation of stream and irrigation channels, and flooding. But forests harbored wild beasts such as tigers and also offered refuge for bandits, both used as peasant reasons for destroying them, often by fire.

By about the eighth century C.E., half or more of the population lived in the south, which also provided most of the imperial revenue and the food supply to feed the capital (still retained in the north because of tradition) and to guard the threatened area of the northern and northwestern frontier. But the north, the cradle of empire, had become a marginal area economically, or at least agriculturally, as the progressive removal of the forest since before Shang times led to massive erosion, siltation of streams and irrigation systems, and consequent severe and chronic flooding, especially of the silt-laden Yellow River but also of all the other streams in the north. Irrigated and cultivated land shrank disastrously, and much of the north could no longer feed itself and had to depend on southern imports of rice. The Grand Canal was built to link the north with the south for such transport.

In the south, the wetter and warmer climate meant that forest or second growth could more easily reestablish itself, especially if it was left alone, but as the population continued to increase that became less and less common, and large areas reverted to grass and brush, much less effective in retarding erosion. The growing population not only cleared more land to farm but cut from all hillsides twigs and grass for use as fuel or as fodder for penned animals. Trade, along both rivers and the sea coast, flourished in the south and supported a growing number of cities. Most places could be reached by cheap water transport, sometimes in no other way, whereas in the north most streams (including the heavily silted Yellow River) were not navigable, and goods had to be transported by pack animal, cart, and human porters at far greater cost.

The south also benefited from overseas trade in far greater volume than before, and port cities, especially along the coast from the mouth of the Yangtze River south, multiplied and prospered on the trade with Taiwan and Southeast Asia. Permanent colonies of Chinese merchants were established in the Philippines, Vietnam, Java, and elsewhere, and there was a great advance in shipbuilding, drawing its wood from near-coastal southern forests, especially in mountainous Fujian. Such developments tended to reemphasize the cultural differences of Cantonese and Fujianese from the main body of Chinese, and such differences remain. Canton (Guangzhou) and ports north of it such as Swatow (Shantou) and Amoy (Xiamen) joined Fuzhou and other Fujianese ports in generating a maritime, mercantile, seagoing world that contrasted with the inward-centered and agricultural world of the rest of China, with its imperial capital far inland and its revenue heavily dependent on the land tax. The Cantonese and Fujianese (Min) spoken languages remain distinct from standard Chinese, not mutually intelligible with it, and there is a prejudice among most other Chinese against the Cantonese, especially, as wily traders communicating with each other in their own spoken language and practicing clannishness and sharp dealing. Even their food and other customs are different. The Cantonese return the compliment by stereotyping northerners as slow-witted peasants or interfering bureaucrats. But there was a growing north-south trade as well, especially in tea, which had been adopted as the national drink during the Tang dynasty and was grown mainly in the misty hills of the south, in the mountains south of the Yangtze River, where it did not compete with rice for land and profited from the ample rainfall. To serve both domestic and overseas trade, the Chinese developed instruments of long-distance credit called "flying money" and, finally in the tenth century, paper money.

■ Rebellion, Radiance, and More Rebellion

The Sui dynasty, which reunified China in C.E. 589, did so by harsh methods and hence is often compared with the Qin (Graff, 2001). The Sui rebuilt the Great Wall and constructed the first Grand Canal, all with forced (corvée) labor. Rebellion soon spread, as in the last years of the Qin, and out of the fighting emerged a new dynasty, the Tang, which presided over an even greater empire than the Han. The Tang is considered by most Chinese the high point of their history. Elite culture flourished, and poetry achieved new richness, especially in the work of Li Bai and Du Fu, still thought to be China's greatest poets (see Chapter 13). The Tang capital, now named Chang'an (which means "Long Peace"; see Map 3.1), was again in the Wei valley on the site of modern Xi'an, which carried the aura of a great tradition because the first capital of the Han dynasty had been located there. It was a highly cosmopolitan place to which merchants and travelers came from as far as the eastern Roman empire and from most of Asia in between: Nestorian Christians (see Chapter 12), Jews, Muslims, Turks, Indians, Persians, and others thronged the streets of the capital. Tang conquests reached far into Central Asia, where they acquired horses for the imperial stables. Perhaps the best-known aspect of Tang art is their mass production of glazed porcelain figures and paintings of their beloved horses. Under Tang rule, the development of the south continued apace as more land was cleared for farming by northern migrants and as trade flourished. Renewed contacts westward revealed, as in Han times, no other civilization that could rival the Celestial Empire, and Tang China was clearly the zenith of power and sophistication. Did not all other people the Chinese encountered acknowledge this, by tribute, praise, and imitation of Chinese culture, and is that not the sincerest form of flattery?

Like the Han, Tang rule was briefly broken by rebellion in the mid–eighth century, and although the imperial order was restored, regional commanders continued to build their power, while rich landed families managed to slip off the tax rolls (Peterson, 1979:464–560). The civil service system begun under the Han was reestablished and strengthened, but was increasingly undermined by the rich and powerful. In the mid–ninth century, the state moved against the Buddhist establishment (Weinstein, 1987) as a potential rival, confiscating the extensive temple and monastery lands and their wealth, but this was not enough to turn the tide. Total revenues fell by the end of the century, accompanied by spreading rebellion. In 907 one of the rebels usurped the throne and declared the Tang at an end, but fighting continued until 960, when one of the contending generals announced a new dynasty, the Song. The Song have been criticized by Chinese scholars because they gave up the wasteful and unprofitable building of empire and were ultimately overwhelmed by the hated Mongols. But the Song decision to avoid the endless wars of empire was wise and concentrated the state's energies on the provinces south of the Great Wall and east of the deserts and mountains of the west, the most productive and profitable area. The chronic struggle to hold Vietnam, Korea, Mongolia, Tibet, and Xinjiang was abandoned; these conquests had never even begun to pay their way, and the state now controlled the richest land and enterprises.

▓ Southern Strategies

The Song capital was fixed at Kaifeng, on the great bend of the Yellow River (see Map 3.1), where the rebuilt Grand Canal could bring to it the rice surpluses of the Yangtze valley and where it could better administer the south, now the heart of the economy. Kaifeng became a major industrial center with a greater production of iron and steel than the whole of Europe would have in the eighteenth century and used coal as metallurgical fuel and for heating houses seven centuries before the West. China's total population passed 100 million for the first time, and Kaifeng contained over 1 million people. The carved wooden blocks used since the Han dynasty for printing were supplemented by movable type, which was pressed onto paper, also invented in the Han dynasty, to produce books. Literacy grew, and popular literature boomed. Paper currency issued by the state served the needs of an expanded commerce. Government officials distributed printed pamphlets to promote improved agricultural techniques; there were also ingenious new metal tools and proto-machines and new, improved crop strains. It was an age of good government, with the rich landed families and regional commanders under central control for the time and revenues correspondingly healthy.

An important reason for the Song success was the re-creation of the civil service and its strengthening to new heights. Most officials were selected from among those who passed the imperial examinations (whose history is

discussed in Chapter 4); imperial relatives, a plague in the past, were barred
from taking those exams. Once in power, officials were regularly rated for
merit and promoted or passed over accordingly. Lists of successful candidates
from this time include nearly half from families who had never before produced an official—a remarkable degree of mobility and opportunity whatever
one's birth. This largely civilian government tended to have a low opinion of
the military, and the army did not match the efficiency of the civil service.
Soldiers were recruited largely from the poorer classes, and they faced formidable opponents in the mounted warriors from the steppe, who progressively
detached much of the northwest and the northeastern borderland, marginal
areas to be sure, but traditionally part of the empire. There were efforts at
reforming and beefing up the military, but these failed due to the rigid opposition of conservatives at the capital.

The price was high: the siege and capture of Kaifeng in 1126 by a
mounted nomad group originally from Manchuria, the ancestors of the
Manchus. The Song army regrouped and pushed the nomads north of the
Yangtze but were obliged to shift their capital south to Nanjing for four years,
and then to Hangzhou (see Map 3.1), where they presided over continued
flourishing in the arts and technology, building on advances in the Kaifeng
period, now known as Northern Song (the Hangzhou period is called Southern Song). This is thought to be the greatest period of Chinese landscape and
nature painting, which together with vernacular literature and drama, blos-
somed in the rich urban culture of Hangzhou, which was dominated by the
growing merchant group but increasingly shared with city dwellers there and
in many other large southern cities. Cut off from normal trade routes through
the northwest, the Song turned in earnest to developing more sea routes to
Southeast Asia and India. Ports on the southeast coast flourished and became
home to large numbers of resident foreign merchants, mostly Arabs. Foreign
accounts agree that these were the world's largest port cities of the time.

There was a striking advance in the size and design of oceangoing ships,
some of which could carry over 600 people as well as cargo, far larger than
anywhere else until modern times. The earlier Chinese invention of the compass was a vital navigational aid, and these ships used multiple masts, separate watertight compartments (not known elsewhere until much later), and the
stern-post rudder. In all of this, Song ships predated modern ships by many
centuries. Ironically, they helped make it possible for Europeans much later,
after they adopted much of Chinese ship technology, to make the sea voyage
to Asia, also using the gunpowder invented in China to subdue those they visited. Hangzhou itself had a population over 1.5 million, but there were some
six large cities within 300 miles and a network of smaller ones, depending like
Hangzhou on the intricate system of waterways that crisscrossed the Yangtze
Delta and adjacent areas. Marco Polo, who actually saw Hangzhou only later
under Mongol rule, marveled at its size and wealth and called it the greatest

city in the world, a judgment confirmed by several other Western travelers of his period (Gernet, 1962). Chapter 8 discusses China's urban history in greater depth.

The Southern Song was also an exciting time of technological innovation and even of what seem like early steps toward the emergence of modern science. Confucian scholars like Zhu Xi pursued what they called "the investigation of things" (de Bary, Chan, and Watson, 1960:489–490), and in agriculture, manufacturing, and transport a variety of new machines and tools were developed—cultivators and threshers, pumps for lifting water, machines to card and spin and weave textile fibers, windlasses, inclined planes, canal locks, water clocks, and water-powered mills. It all looked like eighteenth-century Europe, with commercialization, urbanization, a widening market (including overseas), rising demand, and hence both the incentive and the capital to pursue mechanical invention and other measures to increase production. Would these developments have led to a true industrial revolution in thirteenth-century China, with all its profound consequences? We will never know, because the final Mongol onslaught cut them off, and later dynasties failed to replicate the details of the Song pattern. But it is tempting to think that if the Song had had just a little longer, China might have continued to lead the world, and the rise of modern Europe might not have happened as it did.

The Southern Song dynasty was far wealthier than the Northern Song and had a booming economy. Unfortunately, this did not make it immune to the administrative and financial problems it inherited, but it kept functioning reasonably well until the end. Overseas trade, now a major source of revenue, was far larger than in Europe as late as the nineteenth century. Porcelain, perfected under the Tang, joined silk and lacquer as exports, and the finest pieces, called celadon, mostly made for the imperial court, have never been equaled, with their subtle bluish green or shades of white and gray glazes, exquisitely shaped. Government and private schools multiplied, to educate both the sons of the rich and the able sons of the less well-to-do (Chaffee, 1995). The explosion of printing and publication led to the spread of libraries and book shops and the appearance of anthologies and encyclopedias, as well as maps of the empire based on a grid of coordinates. Chapter 12 discusses dynamic resurgence of philosophical and religious thinking under the Song. Mathematics was further developed, including the appearance of algebra and the use of the zero. So why did the Song succumb?

The Song were overrun in the end because the Mongols were formidable fighters who had already conquered the world's largest empire, extending even into Europe, and because of some drastic Song errors. In 1222 the Song foolishly made an alliance with the Mongols and within two years reoccupied Kaifeng, but a year later they were desperately defending their gains. For forty years the fighting raged in the north, where the heavily fortified Chinese cities were both defended and attacked with the help of explosive weapons, including cannons, which the Mongols had learned about from their great neighbor. Song naval ships on the Yangtze mounted cannons and mortars and helped to hold back the Mongol tide, all before this devastating new technology spread to Europe, where it was quickly copied. But the Song were chronically weakened by factionalism at court, divided counsels, and inconsistent, often faulty, strategy (Murphey, 1996:113–122).

■ Unity and Cultural Continuity

By 1273 the Mongols had triumphed in the north and soon poured south, where Hangzhou surrendered in 1276. One false move against an opponent like the Mongols was usually all it took. But the Song put up a longer and more effective resistance to them than any of their other opponents—and the Mongols could never have won without the help of Chinese technicians, artillery experts, and siege engineers (de Hartog, 2000; Ratchnevsky, 1991). Their rule in China, to which they gave the dynastic title of Yuan (see Map 3.1), lasted much less than a century and depended on many thousands of Chinese collaborators to administer the empire (Langlois, 1981; Hoang, 2001; Bulog, 2002; de Francis, 1993; de Hartog, 2000). They also employed many foreigners, including Marco Polo, who served as a minor Yuan official from 1275 to 1292. His account of his experience has been dismissed by many, but on his deathbed he told his confessor, "I have not told the half of what I saw." Richard Lister (1976), Marco Polo (1982), and John Larner (2000) provide readable accounts of his travels; Frances Wood (1998) disputes his tale, but Jonathan Spence (1996b) points out reasons to believe it.

Kublai Khan, the Mongol ruler whom Marco Polo served, fixed his new capital at Beijing and became almost entirely Chinese culturally, though the welcome he extended to travelers and innovations from all over the world and the many rewards he gave to his fellow Mongols disturbed his subjects (Rossabi, 1988). His successors were far less able, and the empire began to fall apart soon after Kublai's death in 1294, torn by rivalries among Mongol commanders and by widespread revolts among the Chinese against the exploitative Mongol rule (Murphey, 1996:121–122). By the end of the 1330s, most of China was in rebellion, and by 1350 control of the vital Yangtze Valley was lost. A peasant rebel leader welded together Chinese forces, chased the remaining Mongols back into the steppe north of the Great Wall, and founded a new dynasty, the Ming, which was to restore Chinese pride and grandeur, from a new capital first at Nanjing and then at Beijing (Andrew and Rapp, 2000).

The imperial capital thus moved progressively eastward, from the Wei Valley and Chang'an where the Zhou, Han, Sui, and Tang had ruled, to Loyang in the later Han and Tang, to Kaifeng and Hangzhou under the Song, and finally north to Beijing (see Map 3.1). This migration reflected the eastward movement of the main area of threat to the imperial frontiers, from the nomads of the northwestern steppe in the Han to the Turkish tribes in the Tang to those who harried the Northern Song, then to the Mongols, and finally to the Manchus of Manchuria and their predecessors. But these northern capitals were increasingly unable to feed themselves, as the north declined ecologically and economically; hence the Grand Canal was extended to Beijing by the Mongols to bring food up from the south. Putting the capital on the exposed frontier (Beijing is only some 40 miles from the borders of Inner Mongolia) made less sense economically than establishing one in the growing southern heart of the country, such as Nanjing. The imperial tradition of locating the capital close to frontier threats exerted too strong a pull, however, and even obliged the Ming to move to Beijing from Nanjing.

Chinese history readily divides into dynastic periods and into what is called the dynastic cycle. Most post-Qin dynasties (but not the Yuan) lasted about three centuries, sometimes preceded by a brief whirlwind period of empire building such as the Qin or the Sui. The first century of a new dynasty would be one of vigor, expansion, and efficiency; the second would build on or consolidate what the first had achieved; and in the third vigor and efficiency would wane, corruption would mount, banditry and rebellion would multiply, and the dynasty would ultimately fall. A new group coming to power (again with the exception of the Mongols) would rarely attempt to change the system, only its management. Culture was continuous, even during interdynastic periods of chaos. By Tang times, most of the elements of modern Chinese culture were present. Irrigated rice was supplemented or replaced in the more arid parts of the north by wheat noodles (said to have been brought to Europe by Marco Polo or others along the Silk Roads as the origin of spaghetti) and steamed bread, or for poorer people by millet and *gaoliang* (a sorghum introduced from Central Asia and, like millet, tolerant of drought).

Food was eaten with chopsticks since at least the Zhou dynasty, a model adopted early by Korea, Vietnam, and Japan, although the rest of the world ate with fingers. The Chinese cuisine is justly famous, including as it does such a wide variety of ingredients (the Chinese have few dietary inhibitions), flavors, and sauces. What went on the rice—vegetable or animal—was sliced small so that its flavors were maximized and distributed and also so it could cook quickly over a hot but brief fire. There was an increasing shortage of fuel as the rising population cut down the forests and people were reduced to twigs, leaves, and dried grasses for cooking. The universal cooking utensil was the thin cast-iron saucer-shaped pot (*wok* in Cantonese, the dialect of Guangzhou) still in use, which heats quickly but holds the heat and distributes it evenly, the technique we now call "stir-frying." Not only Cantonese words like *wok* but much of the Chinese food served in restaurants in this country and elsewhere betray their Cantonese origins, since Cantonese are the great majority of all overseas Chinese and, like many other immigrant groups, have used their native cuisine as a means of livelihood.

The Chinese landscape became converted more and more into an artificial one of irrigated and terraced rice paddies, fish and duck ponds, villages, and market towns where the peasants sold their surplus products or exchanged them for salt, cloth, tools, or other necessities not produced in all villages. Teahouses became the common centers for socializing, relaxation, and gossip and for the negotiation of business or marriage contracts. Fortune-tellers, scribes, book-sellers, itinerant peddlers, actors or jugglers, and storytellers enlivened the market towns and cities and the periodic markets held on a smaller scale in most villages at regular intervals (see Chapter 13). All this made it less necessary for people to travel far from their native places, and most never went beyond the nearest market town. Beyond it they would have found for the most part only more villages and towns like those they knew, except for the provincial capital and, of course, the imperial capital. In the dry north and the mountains of the south, many goods moved by human porter. The wheelbarrow and the flexible bamboo carrying pole were early Chinese inventions that greatly enhanced the ability to transport heavy weights, balanced as they were by each design (wheelbarrows had their single wheel in the middle, more efficient than the Western copy) and hence enabling porters to wheel or trot all day with loads far exceeding their unaided capacity. Most of these and many other aspects of Chinese culture have remained essentially unchanged today, as has the deep Chinese sense of history and of the great tradition to which they are heir.

Robert Gamer

An early Chinese invention, the carrying pole,
is still commonly used in China

■ The Rise and Fall of Ming

The Ming dynasty, officially founded in 1368, fit the dynastic pattern of a first century of vigor and expansion, a second of complacency, and a third of decline and fall. Probably the most spectacular aspect of the first century was the expeditionary voyages of Admiral Zheng He, seven altogether between 1405 and 1433, from ports on the southeast coast with fleets of up to sixty ships (Levathes, 1994; Mote and Twitchett, 1988; Marks, 2002). They toured most of Southeast Asia, the east and west coasts of India (where Vasco da Gama ninety years later was to make his first Asian landfall), Ceylon (now Sri Lanka), the Persian Gulf, Aden, Jidda (from where seven Chinese went to Mecca), and on to eastern Africa. Some ships may have gone as far as the Cape of Good Hope or even around it. They brought back giraffes, zebras, and ostriches to amaze the court, and tributary agreements from a host of newly contacted states. The ships carried export goods, mainly silks and porcelains, and brought back foreign luxuries such as spices and tropical woods. The economic motive for these huge ventures may have been important, but the chief aim was probably political, to show the flag and command respect for the empire. Chapter 7 discusses these missions in more detail.

Despite their size, Zheng He's ships were fast with their four decks, large crews, and large cargo capacities, faster than the Spanish galleons or Portuguese caravels of a century or two later. Their rig was designed to take advantage of the monsoonal wind patterns; properly timed voyages could count on sailing with the wind for about half the year as far as Africa, and returning with the opposite monsoon in the other half. Like Song ships, they were built with separate watertight compartments, and despite their many encounters with storms, few were ever lost. Such exploits of seamanship and exploration were unprecedented in the world. Their grand scale was an expression of new imperial pride, but they contributed little to the Ming economy and made no lasting impression on the minds of Chinese, who continued to think of theirs as the only civilized empire and had little curiosity about foreign places. The expeditions were very expensive and, perhaps mainly for that reason, were stopped after 1433. The emperor may have felt he had made his imperial point, and it seems unlikely that trade profits even began to cover the costs. Another factor was the decision to move the capital from Nanjing to Beijing in 1421 to better command the chronically troubled northern frontier, where there was an attempted revival of Mongol power.

But the abandonment of the expeditions, like the move to Beijing, was a symptom of the Ming's basic conservatism and traditionalism. China's relations by sea had always been given a far lower priority than its land frontiers. Zheng He's explorations and contacts were not followed up. The Ming turned inward, rebuilt the Great Wall in the form we see today in the few parts near

Beijing that have been restored, and reasserted the Chinese style in everything, partly as a reaction against the hated Mongol conquest. They devoted
their energies to the development of their home base, which since Shang times
they had called the Middle Kingdom, meaning not only the center of the
world but one that combined the advantages of a golden mean, avoiding the
extremes of desert, jungle, mountains, or cold around its borders. In whatever
direction one went from China, the physical environment worsened: north
(too cold), south (too hot and jungly), west (too mountainous and dry), or east
into a vast and, in cultural or economic terms, empty ocean. The Chinese
attributed the lack of civilization they noted in all "barbarians" to their far less
favorable environment as well as to their distance from the only center of
enlightenment. China was indeed the most productive area of comparable size
anywhere in the world, bigger than all of Europe, more populous, and with a
far greater volume of trade, domestic and foreign. The Chinese saw their
interests as best served by further embellishing their home base rather than by
pursuing less rewarding foreign contacts.

For some time this worked well. Prosperity increased, and with it population, trade, and cities, continuing the developments under the Song. Rice
yields rose with the introduction of more productive and earlier-ripening
varieties introduced from Vietnam and actively promoted by the state. In the
sixteenth century, new crops from the New World, most importantly maize
(corn), potatoes, and peanuts, came in via the Spanish connection in the
Philippines. New irrigation and better application of manure swelled total
output further, and there was a boom in silk production as well as in cotton,
introduced from India and soon the basic material of clothing for all but the
rich, who often wore silk. New supplies of silver came in to pay for the
exports of silk, tea, porcelain, lacquerware, and other goods, and more and
more of the economy was commercialized. Merchant guilds acquired new,
though unofficial, power in the growing cities and followed the luxurious
lifestyle of the elite. Right through the last century of the Ming, despite political decay, technological innovation continued on Song foundations, including the development of mechanical looms. Popular literature and drama
flourished, and fine porcelains, including the famous Ming blue-and-white
pattern, spread beyond the court and were found in many merchant houses.
Beijing was rebuilt on its Mongol foundations and filled with gorgeous
palaces. The civil service system inherited from the Song also worked well
until the final collapse. It was a confident and prosperous time (Struve, 1984;
Chan, 1982).

But by the end of the sixteenth century, there was a clear decline in
administrative effectiveness, made worse by a succession of weak emperors
and the rise of palace eunuchs to power (see Chapter 4). Banditry and piracy
multiplied as government efficiency declined and poorer areas suffered
increasing distress. Increased population, probably by now about 130 million,

The Great Wall at Simitai, northwest of Beijing

was not accompanied by a commensurate increase in the number of officials, who were thus overworked and less effective, as well as prone to bribery to maintain their incomes. Famine and rebellion spread, and the Manchus, waiting on the northeastern border, took their opportunity to establish their own dynasty, the Qing, in 1644 (Huang, 1981).

Multiple sawblades
cut marble into table-
tops and tiles, adapt-
ing centuries-old
technology

Robert Gamer

■ The Rise and Fall of Qing

Unlike the Mongols, the Qing successfully reproduced the Chinese pattern in all ways, and their control rested on widespread Chinese collaboration; Chinese filled about 90 percent of all official posts. The dynasty was fortunate in producing three successive able emperors, who presided over the reconquest of all of the empire and even added Tibet for the first time (see Chapter 6). The "barbarian" invaders on the steppe to the west were finally crushed for good, and Taiwan was conquered and added to the empire. The peace and order provided by the Qing and its efficient administration led to new heights of prosperity, trade, and urbanization, far beyond Ming levels, and also to a population that probably tripled between 1620 and the dynasty's end in 1911, gained another 100 million by 1950, and doubled again between 1950 and 1983 to over 1 billion (Chao, 1987:41). By the end of the eighteenth century, production was no longer keeping pace, and in the course of the nineteenth century China fell gradually into poverty and rebellion, as Europe and the

United States rode a wave of new prosperity and technological/industrial revolution. Chinese technology had long been superior, but now it fell disastrously behind, to its great loss. Yet until as late as 1850, foreigners described China as prosperous, orderly, and admirable for its Confucian-based civil service that was open to any young man with the skill to pass the imperial examinations.

We know more about China at this period than at any before it, not only from the voluminous Chinese records but also from the numerous foreign accounts, which are generally highly positive and, among other things, noted that China's foreign trade as late as the 1830s was probably larger than England's, whereas its domestic trade was many times larger. Portuguese traders had arrived at Guangzhou (Canton) early in the sixteenth century, and Jesuit missionaries were shortly thereafter at work even in Beijing. By the eighteenth century, the British became the dominant traders with China, buying silk and tea that they paid for in silver, accompanied by French, Dutch, and other European merchants and finally by Americans. From the mid–eighteenth century, all foreign traders were restricted to Guangzhou, the chief port for foreign trade, a condition they found increasingly irritating as British and European power grew while their merchants at Guangzhou continued to be treated like minor barbarians. A party sent by King George in 1793 to request wider trade privileges and diplomatic representation at Beijing was haughtily rebuffed (see Chapter 7), as was a subsequent mission in 1816.

But despite the grand exterior, all was not well domestically, as population continued to outrun production in the absence of major technological change. As under the Ming, the number of administrator-officials stayed the same while the population rapidly expanded, and both efficiency and honesty suffered. China continued to protect itself against the disruptions of institutional and technological change, looking backward to its great tradition rather than forward, and was especially opposed to any ideas or innovations of foreign origin. As China declined in the nineteenth century and was wracked by increasing rebellions (Perry, 1980; Fairbank and Goldman, 1998:187–232), the Qing had entered its third century. There might have been a different response from a new and vigorous administration, but the Qing were now old, rigid, fearful of change, and as alien conquerors originally, anxious not to depart in any way from their role as guardians of the ancient Chinese way in all things. The emperor Qianlong, who reigned from 1735 to 1799, was a great patron of art and rebuilt or refurbished the imperial capital inherited from the Ming in essentially the same form one can see today. There he and other emperors received "tribute missions" from "barbarian chieftains," who knelt abjectly before the throne. China was slow to recognize that external threat now came from the "sea barbarians" instead of from its landward frontiers and looked down on them as inferior, despite their clear technological and military superiority.

Matters came to a head in 1839 over opium, which the British and Americans had begun to export from India and Persia to China in exchange for silver. The resulting drain of silver from China was worrying, and in any case the opium trade had been declared illegal. Chinese efforts to destroy the opium stored at Guangzhou led to war in which the Chinese army and navy were totally humiliated by modern British weapons. The Treaty of Nanjing, signed in 1842, granted the access the foreigners had long sought and the right to reside and trade at several coastal ports, the "treaty ports" (Fairbank, 1978). Such humiliations were destined to continue and grow in scope for over a century. A war in 1858–1860 extended foreign privileges further and opened the interior to missionaries and the rivers to foreign shipping. The empire had the help of volunteer foreign troops to put down the Taiping (see Spence, 1996a; Chin, 2000) and Nian rebellions that took over extensive territory in southern China (Elleman, 2001). The Taiping rebels ruled much of Jiangsu, Anhui, and Zhejiang provinces (see Map 2.2) for eleven years. The fighting and radical social experiments (see Chapters 11 and 12) left well over 20 million casualties and formerly lush fields as barren wasteland. The Qing emperor found himself at the mercy of the foreigners and regional warlords who helped squelch the rebellions; his treasury was depleted. Foreign Christian missionaries sought converts without the traditional supervision always imposed on such activities in the past. Powerful landlords raised their own armies and collected their own taxes. In an effort to catch up, mathematics, science, and foreign languages were made part of school curricula, and sons of prominent Chinese were sent abroad for study. Still, China suffered humiliating defeat in the Sino-Japanese War of 1894–1895. Reform efforts in 1898 to improve the navy, railroads, banking, agriculture, and industry were cut short when the young emperor who endorsed them was arrested by his aunt, who took over as empress dowager. Chapters 6 and 7 discuss these matters further.

But China's decline into poverty was primarily the result of its own internal problems, as summarized earlier, and indeed one can argue that the foreign traders helped China, by widening the market and introducing railways, telegraph lines, and other aspects of "modernization," much more than they harmed it, although the psychological hurt to Chinese pride was deep.

■ **Beyond the Dynasties**

In 1911 the dynasty toppled or fell of its own weight; a republic was inaugurated under Sun Yat-sen, the nationalist leader, but China was soon torn by fighting among regional warlords and was partially unified only in 1927 under Chiang Kai-shek, with its new capital at Nanjing (Fairbank, 1992:279–293). There was some progress in the short decade before the Japanese attacked, burning Nanjing in 1937; killing perhaps 300,000 unarmed men, women, and children; and raping and torturing 100,000 women (Chang, 1997; Honda,

1999; Fogel and Maier, 2000; Zhang, 2000). The long war against Japan that followed, from a refugee capital in Chongqing in Sichuan, exhausted Chiang's Nationalist (Kuomintang, or KMT) government while it built the strength of the Chinese communists, who waged a guerrilla war in the north and captured the leadership of Chinese nationalism. Resumed civil war after the defeat of Japan ended in a total communist victory in 1949, and Chiang and his government fled to Taiwan, where his successors remain in power. Beijing was again made the capital to realign the country with imperial tradition.

Hong Kong, ceded to Britain in 1841, joined the treaty ports as a major center of foreign trade and an entrepôt for trade with the rest of China; it remained a British colony until its return to China in 1997. Cut off from its hinterland in 1949, it built a profitable new structure of light industry and banking and successfully housed and employed the stream of refugees from the rest of China. Hong Kong's example of economic development was important to China as it pursued its own development, and the areas of the southeast near Hong Kong shared in its prosperity, producing goods for export as well as for domestic consumption. New industrial cities multiplied in every province, led by Shanghai, China's biggest city since about 1900, which still supports an economic and industrial boom and supplies technicians and skilled labor to other growing cities. To this extent, the semicolonial foreign period, with its example of "modernization" in the treaty ports, has provided a model for developing modern China, whatever its imperialist nature and its denunciation by communists and Nationalists alike (see Chapters 6, 7, and 10 for more detail).

Manchuria (the "Northeast"), its industrial plant built by the Japanese after 1905 when they wrested control from the Russians and built a dense railway network, remains the chief center of heavy industry, but many other new ones have arisen in the provinces south of the Great Wall. As one result, China is now probably the most polluted country in the world and has been stripped of forests to supply wood for its huge and still growing population, now over 1.2 billion; this has drastically increased erosion, siltation, and flooding (see Chapter 9).

■ Chinese Attitudes and Ours About China

Most Chinese still feel a deep pride in their country, not only in its modern achievements but also in the long record of Chinese superiority. The record of Chinese firsts is impressive: paper and printing, porcelain, the compass, gunpowder and cannons, lacquer, distillation (during the Han, many centuries ahead of Europe), ship design, the wheelbarrow, the double-acting piston bellows, the square pallet chain pump for raising water, iron suspension bridges, canal locks, water clocks, discovery of the circulation of the blood (also during the Han, 2,000 years before Europe), breakthroughs in metallurgy, and much more (Needham, 1981). Unfortunately for later centuries, these discoveries or innovations were not followed up by thoughts about how to put them to new practical uses outside the confines of low-technology agriculture. Except for the early Zhou dynasty and some later periods like the Song, there really was not a group in China who could be called "scientists"; most innovations were worked out by artisans, who were often illiterate, whereas philosophers, who dealt in abstractions, looked down on manual workers and manual work. Chinese intellectuals generally did not speculate about how changes in technology might affect society and commerce and the natural environment or devise experiments to observe the workings of the forces of nature—a key factor in the much later Western successes during the scientific revolution. They preferred to observe and speculate about human behavior and values. The general mind-set of the Confucian power-holders against change as disruptive doubtless also retarded the kind of scientific inquiry that led to the industrial revolution in Europe.

China did develop astronomy very early, noting and recording eclipses and sunspots in Zhou times and devising an accurate calendar. Early achievements in mathematics, mechanics, physics, and biology tended to lapse in later centuries, as did the development of instruments for predicting earthquakes, remarkable in their time. Some intellectuals in the Southern Song dynasty revived a brief interest in science, and under the Mongol Yuan dynasty Chinese scientists resumed work in mathematics and also built a large array of instruments and structures for astronomical observations. But by the time the Jesuits, carriers of the latest scientific advances in Europe, arrived at the Ming court with great curiosity about these Yuan instruments, the Chinese said they had forgotten how to use them and the mathematics that went with them. The response of the court astronomers to their realization that the ancient calculations predicting the movement of the heavenly bodies no longer fit observable reality was not that the theory needed revision but that "the heavens are out of order." Such a response could never have happened in Europe after 1600; those scientists would have sought to revise the theory so it would accord with empirical reality.

Despite such blind spots and the overriding importance of technology and science in the modern world, one cannot dismiss imperial China in any sense as a failure. For some 2,000 years it led the world in technology as in the art of government, in power as well as in sophistication, as all who encountered the Middle Kingdom acknowledged. It is difficult to measure economic well-being in the past, as it is now, but it seems likely that for most of their history until perhaps 1850, most Chinese were better off materially than most people elsewhere. As for that elusive quality we call happiness, who really knows, but China's rich literature certainly gives a picture of a generally contented populace with a strong sense of humor and a love of life. Indeed, the Chinese still value long life as the greatest of all goals, some testimony to their enjoyment of living and its pleasures. Family, and next to that food, remain the biggest values, as they have been for thousands of years. All these things are surely worth something, perhaps even more than modern technological leadership.

As Chapter 8 explains further, China has long produced more cities, and larger ones, than the rest of the world, and its urban experience is rich. European observers were impressed by it and by the huge streams of trade flowing along all China's rivers, lakes, and canals as well as in and out of its coastal ports. For all its growing technological backwardness as the nineteenth century wore on, China remained vibrantly alive; since the 1950s and the death of Mao in 1976, with his irrational utopian ideas that cost heavily in retarding economic progress as well as in lives lost, China has concentrated on maximizing its economic development and raising its technological levels toward world standards. It developed national identity and unity long before Europe and other parts of the world. Its chief failure is in denying its people anything approaching free expression, let alone a genuine democracy. It is a police state pure and simple, where all dissent is suppressed and where non-Han like the Tibetans are cruelly oppressed. It is just possible—but unlikely—that more scope may be allowed for individual freedom and initiative and for the aspirations of the many subject minorities. When one adds the record of environmental destruction since 1950 (He, 1992), what is the best way to judge China's "success"? That depends, like so many things, on one's point of view and the topics about which one asks questions. As you read the rest of this book, with its discussion of many realms of Chinese life, this question will come to your mind more than once: What are the most important questions to ask about China's success or failure?

■ Bibliography

Andrew, Anita M., and John A. Rapp. 2000. *Autocracy and China's Rebel Founding Emperors: Comparing Chairman Mao and Ming Taizu.* Lanham, MD: Rowman and Littlefield.

Barnard, Noel. 1983. "Further Evidence to Support the Hypothesis of Indigenous Origins of Metallurgy in Ancient China." Pp. 237–277 in David N. Keightley (ed.), *The Origins of Chinese Civilization.* Berkeley: University of California Press.

Blunden, Caroline, and Mark Elvin. 1998. *Cultural Atlas of China.* New York: Checkmark Books.

Brandauer, Frederick P., and Chun-chieh Huang (eds.). 1994. *Imperial Rulership and Cultural Change in Traditional China.* Seattle: University of Washington Press.

Brook, Timothy. 1998. *The Confusions of Pleasure: Commerce and Culture in Ming China.* Berkeley: University of California Press.

Bulog, Uradyn E. 2002. *The Mongols at China's Edge: History and Politics of National Unity.* Lanham, MD: Rowman and Littlefield.

Chaffee, John W. 1995. *The Thorny Gates of Learning: Examinations in Sung China.* Albany: State University of New York Press.

Chan, Albert. 1982. *The Glory and Fall of the Ming Dynasty.* Norman: University of Oklahoma Press.

Chang, Iris. 1997. *The Rape of Nanking: The Forgotten Holocaust of World War II.* New York: HarperCollins.

Chang, Kwang Chih. 1980. *Shang Civilization.* New Haven: Yale University Press.

———. 1983. *Art, Myth, and Ritual: The Path to Political Authority in Ancient China.* Cambridge: Harvard University Press.

———. 1986. *The Archaeology of Ancient China.* 4th ed. New Haven: Yale University Press.

Chang, Te-Tzu. 1983. "The Origins of Early Cultures of the Cereal Grains and Food Legumes." Pp. 65–94 in David N. Keightley (ed.), *The Origins of Chinese Civilization.* Berkeley: University of California Press.

Chao, Kang. 1987. *Man and Land in Chinese History: An Economic Analysis.* Stanford: Stanford University Press.

Cheng, Te K'un. 1960. *Archaeology in China: Shang China.* 3 vols. Cambridge: W. Heffer.

———. 1966. *New Light on Prehistoric China.* Cambridge: W. Heffer.

Cheung, Kwong-Yue. 1983. "Recent Archaeological Evidence Relating to the Origin of Chinese Characters." Pp. 323–391 in David N. Keightley (ed.), *The Origins of Chinese Civilization.* Berkeley: University of California Press.

Chin, Shunshin. 2000. *The Taiping Rebellion.* Trans. Joshua A. Fogel. Armonk, NY: M. E. Sharpe.

Cohen, Paul A. 1997. *Discovering History in China: American Historical Writing on the Recent Chinese Past.* 2nd ed. New York: Columbia University Press.

———. 1998. *History in Three Keys: The Boxers as Event, Experience, and Myth.* New York: Columbia University Press.

Cohen, Warren I. 2001. *East Asia at the Center: Four Thousand Years of Engagement with the World.* New York: Columbia University Press.

Connery, Christopher Leigh. 1999. *The Empire of the Text: Writing and Authority in Early Imperial China.* Lanham, MD: Rowman and Littlefield.

Dardess, John W. 1997. *A Ming Society: Tiai-ho County, Kiangsi, Fourteenth to Seventeenth Centuries.* Berkeley: University of California Press.

de Bary, William Theodore, Irene Bloom, and Joseph Adler (eds.). 2000. *Sources of Chinese Tradition: From Earliest Times to 1600.* 2nd ed., vol. 1. New York: Columbia University Press.

de Bary, William Theodore, Wing-Tsit Chan, and Burton Watson (eds.). 1960. *Sources of Chinese Tradition.* 2 vols. New York: Columbia University Press.

de Bary, William Theodore, and Richard Lufrano. 1999. *Sources of Chinese Tradition: 1600 Through the Twentieth Century.* 2nd ed., vol. 2. New York: Columbia University Press.

de Francis, John. 1993. *In the Footsteps of Genghis Khan.* Honolulu: University of Hawaii Press.

de Hartog, Leo. 1999. *The Cambridge Illustrated History of China.* Cambridge: Cambridge University Press.

———. 2000. *Genghis Khan: Conqueror of the World.* New York: I. B. Tauris.

Dillon, Michael (ed.). 1998. *China: A Cultural and Historical Dictionary.* London: Curzon Press.

Ebrey, Patricia Buckley. 1993. *Chinese Civilization: A Sourcebook.* 2nd ed. New York: Free Press.

Elleman, Bruce. 2001. *Modern Chinese Warfare*. London: Routledge.

Elvin, Mark. 1996. *Another History: Essays on China from a European Perspective*. Honolulu: University of Hawaii Press.

Fairbank, John King. 1978. "The Creation of the Treaty System." Pp. 213–263 in John King Fairbank (ed.), *The Cambridge History of China: Late Ching 1800–1911*, vol. 10, pt. 1. Cambridge: Cambridge University Press.

———. 1987. *The Great Chinese Revolution, 1800–1985*. New York: Perennial.

Fairbank, John King, and Merle Goldman. 1998. *China: A New History*. Cambridge: Belknap Press of Harvard University Press.

Fairbank, John King, Edwin O. Reischauer, and Albert M. Craig. 1973. *East Asia: Tradition and Transformation*. Boston: Houghton Mifflin.

Fogel, Joshua A., and Charles S. Maier (eds.). 2000. *The Nanjing Massacre in History and Historiography*. Berkeley: University of California Press.

Franklin, Ursula Martins. 1983. "On Bronze and Other Metals in Early China." Pp. 279–296 in David N. Keightley (ed.), *The Origins of Chinese Civilization*. Berkeley: University of California Press.

Gernet, Jacques. 1962. *Daily Life in China on the Eve of the Mongol Invasion, 1250–1276*. London: Macmillan.

———. 1968. *Ancient China: From the Beginnings to the Empire*. London: Faber and Faber.

———. 1996. *A History of Chinese Civilization*. 2nd ed. Trans. John R. Foster. Cambridge: Cambridge University Press.

Graff, David A. 2001. *Medieval Chinese Warfare, 300–900*. London: Routledge.

Grasso, June, Jay Corrin, and Michael Kort. 1997. *Modernization and Revolution in China*. Armonk, NY: M. E. Sharpe.

Hansen, Valerie. 1995. *Negotiating Daily Life in Traditional China: How Ordinary People Used Contracts, 600–1400*. New Haven: Yale University Press.

Hardy, Grant. 1999. *Worlds of Bronze and Bamboo: Sima Qian's Conquest of History*. New York: Columbia University Press.

Harrell, Stevan. 1995. *Cultural Encounters on China's Ethnic Frontiers*. Seattle: University of Washington Press.

He, Bochuan. 1992. *China on the Edge: The Crisis of Ecology*. San Francisco: China Books.

Henriot, Christian, and Wen-hsin Yeh. 2003. *Shanghai Under Japanese Occupation*. Cambridge: Cambridge University Press.

Hoang, Michel. 2001. *Genghis Khan*. New York: Palgrave.

Honda, Katsuichi. 1999. *The Nanjing Massacre: A Japanese Journalist Confronts Japan's National Shame*. Armonk, NY: M. E. Sharpe.

Howells, W. W. 1983. "Origins of the Chinese People: Interpretations of the Recent Evidence." Pp. 297–319 in David N. Keightley (ed.), *The Origins of Chinese Civilization*. Berkeley: University of California Press.

Hsu, Immanuel Cho Yun. 1980. *Han Agriculture: The Formation of the Early Chinese Agrarian Economy (206 B.C.–A.D. 220)*. Ed. Jack L. Dull. Seattle: University of Washington Press.

———. 1995. *The Rise of Modern China*. Oxford: Oxford University Press.

Hsu, Immanuel Cho Yun, and Katheryn M. Linduff. 1989. *Western Chou Civilization*. New Haven: Yale University Press.

Huang, Ray. 1981. *1587: A Year of No Significance—The Ming Dynasty in Decline*. New Haven: Yale University Press.

———. 1997. *China: A Macro History*. Rev. ed. Armonk, NY: M. E. Sharpe.

————. 1999. *Broadening the Horizons of Chinese History: Discourses, Syntheses, and Comparisons.* Armonk, NY: M. E. Sharpe.

Jenks, Robert D. 1994. *Insurgency and Social Disorder in Guizhou: The "Miao" Rebellion, 1854–1873.* Honolulu: University of Hawaii Press.

Keightley, David N. 1983. "The Late Shang State: When, Where, What?" Pp. 523–564 in David N. Keightley (ed.), *The Origins of Chinese Civilization.* Berkeley: University of California Press.

Kuhn, Philip A. 2002. *Origins of the Modern Chinese State.* Stanford: Stanford University Press.

Langlois, John D., Jr. 1981. *China Under Mongol Rule.* Princeton: Princeton University Press.

Larner, John. 2000. *Marco Polo: Discoverer of the World.* New Haven: Yale University Press.

Lattimore, Owen. 1940. *The Inner Asian Frontiers of China.* New York: American Geographical Society.

————. 1947. *China: A Short History.* New York: Norton.

Levathes, Louise. 1994. *When China Ruled the Seas: The Treasure Fleet of the Dragon Throne, 1405–1433.* New York: Simon and Schuster.

Li, Xueqin. 1985. *Eastern Zhou and Qin Civilizations.* New Haven: Yale University Press.

Linduff, Katheryn M., Han Rubin, and Sun Shuyun (eds.). 2000. *The Beginnings of Metallurgy in China.* Lewiston, NY: Edwin Mellen Press.

Lister, Richard Percival. 1976. *Marco Polo's Travels in Zanadu with Kublai Khan.* New York: Macmillan.

Loewe, Michael. 1994. *Divination, Mythology, and Monarchy in Han China.* New York: Cambridge University Press.

Loewe, Michael, and Edward L. Shaughnessy (eds.). 1999. *The Cambridge History of Ancient China: From the Origins of Civilization to 221 B.C.* Cambridge: Cambridge University Press.

Lufrano, Richard John. 1997. *Honorable Merchants: Commerce and Self-Cultivation in Late Imperial China.* Honolulu: University of Hawaii Press.

Marks, Robert B. 2002. *The Origins of the Modern World: A Global and Ecological Narrative.* Lanham, MD: Rowman and Littlefield.

Meacham, William. 1983. "Origins and Development of Yüeh Coastal Neolithic: A Microcosm of Culture Change in the Mainland of East Asia." Pp. 147–175 in David N. Keightley (ed.), *The Origins of Chinese Civilization.* Berkeley: University of California Press.

Meyer, Milton W. 1994. *China: A Concise History.* 2nd ed. Lanham, MD: Rowman and Littlefield.

Michael, Franz. 1986. *China Through the Ages: History of a Civilization.* Boulder: Westview Press.

Mote, Frederick W. 1999. *Imperial China 900–1800.* Cambridge: Harvard University Press.

Mote, Frederick W., and Denis Twitchett (eds.). 1988 and 1998. *The Cambridge History of China: The Ming Dynasty 1368–1644.* Vol. 7, pts. 1–2. Cambridge: Cambridge University Press.

Mungello, D. E. 1999. *The Great Encounter of China and the West, 1500–1800.* Lanham, MD: Rowman and Littlefield.

Murphey, Rhoads. 1996. *A History of Asia.* New York: HarperCollins.

————. 1997. *East Asia: A New History.* New York: Addison Wesley Longman.

"Mysterious Mummies of China." 1998. *NOVA.* PBS 2501. January 20.

Nathan, Andrew. 1990. *China's Crisis.* New York: Columbia University Press.

Needham, Joseph. 1965–1986. *Science and Civilisation in China.* 6 vols. Cambridge: Cambridge University Press.

———. 1981. *Science in Traditional China.* Cambridge: Cambridge University Press.

Pan Ku. 1974. *Courtier and Commoner in Ancient China: Selections of the History of Pan Ku.* Trans. Burton Watson. New York: Columbia University Press.

Perry, Elizabeth J. 1980. *Rebels and Revolutionaries in North China, 1845–1945.* Stanford: Stanford University Press.

Peterson, C. A. 1979. "Court and Province in Mid and Late T'ang." Pp. 464–560 in Denis Twitchett (ed.), *The Cambridge History of China: Sui and T'ang China, 589–906,* vol. 3. Cambridge: Cambridge University Press.

Polo, Marco. 1982. *The Travels of Marco Polo.* Trans. Ronald Latham. New York: Abaris Books.

Pomeranz, Kenneth. 2002. *The Great Divergence: China, Europe, and the Making of the Modern World Economy.* Princeton: Princeton University Press.

Prazniak, Roxann. 1996. *Dialogues Across Civilizations: Allegorical Sketches in World History from the Chinese and European Experiences.* Boulder: Westview Press.

Pulleyblank, E. G. 1983. "The Chinese and Their Neighbors in Prehistoric and Early Historic Times." Pp. 411–466 in David N. Keightley (ed.), *The Origins of Chinese Civilization.* Berkeley: University of California Press.

Ratchnevsky, Paul. 1991. *Genghis Khan: His Life and Legacy.* New York: Blackwell.

Rawski, Evelyn S. 1998. *The Last Emperors: A Social History of Qing Imperial Institutions.* Berkeley: University of California Press.

Roberts, J. A. G. 1999. *A Concise History of China.* Cambridge: Harvard University Press.

Rossabi, Morris. 1988. *Khubilai Khan: His Life and Times.* Berkeley: University of California Press.

Schlyter, Birgit N., and Mirja Juntunen (eds.). 1998. *Re-entering the Silk Routes: Current Scandinavian Research on Central Asia.* New York: Columbia University Press.

Schoppa, Keith B. 2000. *The Columbia Guide to Modern Chinese History.* New York: Columbia University Press.

Schwartz, B. I. 1985. *The World of Thought in Ancient China.* Cambridge: Harvard University Press.

Smith, Richard J. 1994. *China's Cultural Heritage: The Qing Dynasty, 1644–1912.* 2nd ed. Boulder: Westview Press.

Soled, Debra E. (ed.). 1995. *China: A Nation in Transition.* Washington, DC: Congressional Quarterly Press.

Spence, Jonathan. 1996a. *God's Chinese Son: The Taiping Heavenly Kingdom of Hong Xiuquan.* New York: Norton.

———. 1996b. "Marco Polo: Did He Go to China?" *Far Eastern Economic Review* 159 (August 22): 37–45.

———. 1999. *The Search for Modern China.* 2nd ed. New York: Norton.

Struve, Lynn. 1984. *The Southern Ming, 1644–1662.* New Haven: Yale University Press.

Twitchett, Denis (ed.). 1986. *The Cambridge History of China.* Vol. 1: *Ch'in and Han.* Cambridge: Cambridge University Press.

VonGlahn, Richard. 1997. *Fountain of Fortune: Money and Monetary Policy, Tenth to Seventeenth Centuries.* Berkeley: University of California Press.

Wakeman, Frederic E. 1981. *The Fall of Imperial China.* New York: Free Press.

————. 1985. *The Great Enterprise: The Manchu Reconstruction.* Berkeley: University of California Press.

————. 1997. *Strangers at the Gate: Social Disorder in South China, 1839–1861.* Berkeley: University of California Press.

Waley, Arthur. 1939. *Three Ways of Thought in Ancient China.* Stanford: Stanford University Press.

————. 1958. *The Opium War Through Chinese Eyes.* Stanford: Stanford University Press.

Wang, Zhangshu. 1982. *Han Civilization.* New Haven: Yale University Press.

Watson, William. 1961. *China Before the Han Dynasty.* New York: Praeger.

Weinstein, Stanley. 1987. *Buddhism Under the T'ang.* Cambridge: Cambridge University Press.

Whitfield, Susan. 2000. *Life Along the Silk Road.* Berkeley: University of California Press.

Wilkinson, Endymion. 2000. *Chinese History: A Manual, Revised and Enlarged.* Cambridge: Harvard University Press.

Wood, Frances. 1998. *Did Marco Polo Go to China?* Boulder: Westview Press.

Wright, Arthur F. 1978. *The Sui Dynasty.* New York: Knopf.

Zhang, Kaiyuan (ed.). 2000. *Eyewitness Accounts of the Nanjing Massacre: American Missionaries Bear Witness to Japanese Atrocities.* Armonk, NY: M. E. Sharpe.

Zurndorfer, Harriet T. 1999. *China Bibliography: A Research Guide to Reference Works About China Past and Present.* Honolulu: University of Hawaii Press.

Chinese Politics

Robert E. Gamer

China has the world's oldest political system. As Rhoads Murphey explained in Chapter 3, its cultural dominance of the regions it now occupies began during the second century B.C.E. Its habits of governance extend to that period as well. For two millennia, those habits helped it ward off or absorb invasions from the societies that occupied Central Asia. They proved vulnerable, however, when challenged during the past two centuries by the technology and institutions of Europe and a modernizing Japan.

What are China's political traditions? What has it absorbed from communism and the West? How much must China's political system change to remain unified and sustain economic growth? Can it achieve those goals? These are the questions with which this chapter deals.

First, we will briefly examine some of China's political and economic traditions. In the second section, we will look at the changes that took place in China's politics between the 1839 Opium War and World War II. Third, we will examine how and why the communists took over China. Their consolidation of power was followed by three periods of major economic and political change; in the fourth section we will try to sort out the changes that worked from those that did not. Fifth, we will look at the principal challenges facing China's contemporary leaders and their chances of surmounting them. In the last two sections, we will explore further adaptations that China is likely to absorb.

■ A Legacy of Unity and Economic Achievement

In Chapter 3, Rhoads Murphey explained how the Qin first unified China in 221 B.C.E. and how the subsequent Han dynasty consolidated that conquest.

One of the most significant and enduring achievements of the Han was the adoption of Confucianism, a philosophy also discussed in Chapters 3 and 12. Confucian traditions would have a strong influence on China's subsequent ability to maintain unity and prosperity.

Confucius contended that stable governance derives from the proper performance of social obligations. The most fundamental obligation, called filial piety, is obedience of sons to fathers. Likewise, wives obey husbands, younger brothers defer to their older brothers, and subjects obey rulers. In turn, those being obeyed are to treat their cohorts with sincerity, affection, or respect, demonstrated through rituals of speech and behavior. Individuals who fail to carry out these mutual obligations disgrace themselves and those to whom they owe these obligations and destroy the foundations of the state. Citizens cannot expect to live in a stable country when they themselves fail to carry out their most basic social obligations within their families. When individual freedom or political theories conflict with one's obligation to one's family and state authorities, they must be rejected. Expressing an opinion or taking an action that shows disrespect for these mutual obligations and rituals actually destroys your own essence; you must rectify this by apologizing and changing your behavior, in order to restore your good name and come to grips with who you really are. To be true to yourself you must carry out your ritual obligations to others; to do so bonds state and society.

Furthermore, in Confucian philosophy, society is divided into greater and lesser orders. The emperor and his assistants hold the highest position, yet the social hierarchy limits both them and those with wealth. Directly below the emperor in this hierarchy are the peasants and artisans, who produce the goods and whose families cleared the land and created the farms that set apart Chinese civilization from the "barbarian" cultures of wandering hunters and herders. Merchants, who produce nothing yet profit from the toil of others, occupy the lowest rung on the social order of Chinese civilization. All this creates a harmonious society, with emperors naturally chosen to rule, and even wealthy subjects predisposed to obey. That obedience ends only when peace and prosperity are supplanted by war, bad harvests, and natural disasters, proving that Heaven's Mandate to the emperor to govern has been withdrawn. Then a challenger may rouse popular support to overthrow the emperor. The Han dynasty itself was founded by a peasant who led such a revolt against the excesses of the Qin dynasty.

Four other customs evolved that also help keep the emperor and those with wealth in line while still investing them with the power to rule and engage in business:

1. The system of choosing emperors and their wives. To reduce the role of the noble families that had dominated before the Qin dynasty, the sons of emperors married daughters of peasants, who were taken away from their families when they were very young. These heirs to the throne might take several wives. Sons of the first wife were thought to have more right to the throne, but emperors had some choice in designating a successor. During most dynasties, when the emperor died, his wives and their other children would return to an obscure existence, rather than become titled nobility. Although this reduced the prestige and power of those related to the emperor, it made the stakes surrounding succession into an all-or-nothing game. That created much intrigue around the court. Many an emperor or designated heir was murdered by the mother of another heir, who might rule as an empress dowager while her young son grew up (see Fu, 1994).

2. Eunuchs. To ensure loyalty and see to it that only the emperor had sexual access to his wives, males working within the compound of the palace were recruited at a young age from villages, castrated, and removed from their families. These eunuchs ran the compound and took care of the emperor, his wives, and their children. The eunuchs were often involved in the murders and intrigues. Public officials had to access the emperor through the eunuchs. The number and power of eunuchs grew greatly during the Ming dynasty; the Qing dynasty sought to limit their power, but it continued. (For more on their role, see Mitamura, 1970.)

3. The system of choosing public officials. To choose its top officials, the empire held regular competitive examinations open to all boys. These exams tested the candidates' ability to write Chinese characters and their knowledge of the Confucian classics. Those who passed became "literati," or Confucian scholar-officials. They were selected and transferred as needed by the emperor to preside over justice and administration in all the regions of China. Most who passed these exams, which required extensive education and preparation, were the sons of scholar-officials, larger landowners, or wealthy merchants. But the system moving them from post to post ensured that control of administration and of a region could not automatically stay within the hands of the same local notables, as had been the case under feudalism. Sometimes a village or lineage group would help one of their brightest children prepare for these exams, allowing him to rise from the family of a humble peasant into the highest realms of the state. Ichisada Miyazaki (1981) gives an extensive introduction to this unique—and often terrifying—system for selecting public officials.

These officials had the power to regulate commerce. They sought to ensure that agriculture remained prosperous by keeping the complex system of waterways and irrigation canals working, maintaining marketplaces where goods could be bartered, and protecting private property. They also collected taxes and presided over the civil and criminal courts and local administrators.

During the twelfth century, in the Southern Song dynasty (see Chapters 3 and 5), foreign and domestic trade began to flourish. Large numbers of people engaged in the manufacture of porcelain, textiles, alcoholic beverages, ships, and other goods. Because Confucian philosophy sees agriculture as the provider of food and the supporter of the family units on which Chinese civilization is built, the scholar-officials had always encouraged invention, trade, the buying and selling of land, and other commercial pursuits that supported agriculture. These new trends disturbed them. Young people were leaving their families to seek work in the towns and cities. People were making large amounts of money creating frivolous luxuries that competed with cloth and handicrafts once produced on the farms. The richest of them could travel between regions to escape the jurisdiction of individual literati. Scholar-officials had often used their power and income to buy large amounts of land and thus ensure their high social and economic stature. Now people without land or official status, who ranked at the bottom of the Confucian social hierarchy, were in a position to become the richest in the realm.

Song Confucian philosophers thought hard about these problems. Their neo-Confucianism (see Chapter 12) created checks on the power of merchant acquisition by placing new emphasis on the extended family. Clans should stick together in the same villages, whose property would remain under the control of their leaders. People should be punished for moving away to set up independent households. To prevent monopolies, officials should regulate the number of looms or production facilities one person could own as well as the market prices. And the state would manufacture or distribute some important goods and resources. This would slow down investment in capitalist production and discourage the creation of an independent middle class. It would also encourage community leaders to assist those less fortunate in their communities (for an insightful overview, see Gates, 1996:42–61).

4. The five Confucian relationships, guanxi. As in the past, however, these new powers for officials were softened by *guanxi* (King, 1991; Yang, 1994; Yan, 1996; Kipnis, 1997). In Confucian thinking, a man's most important relationships are as father and son, as husband, as brother, as subject of the ruler, and with certain selected neighbors, kinsmen, classmates, or other associates with whom he chooses to have special long-term relationships. These individuals exchange special favors and gifts, called *renqing* (literally, benevolence that two people owe each other; more about this in Chapter 12). This exchange affirms that these individuals have "connections." Literati and merchants had always created such connections with one another; that is how many literati had acquired land. As commerce grew, these relationships helped merchants escape from overregulation and receive clearance to engage in new business activities. Connections helped individuals make money, while ensuring that it circulated back to the community. They also continued to divert investment capital into unproductive gifts.

As China approached the nineteenth century, it looked back on a long tradition of political and cultural unification combined with a vibrant market economy. It was presided over by a government that both encouraged and limited capitalist enterprise and that was itself limited by the expectations of its people that its reign bring social order and bountiful agriculture. The chief restraints on governments and citizenry lay in the expectation that people should live up to their social obligations. Communities placed limits on their own members; entrepreneurs were expected to adapt to the needs of the community. International capitalism wants social peace, but it also resists social and political restraints that hold back individual initiative. The stage was set for conflict.

■ A Century of Turmoil

The year 1839 ushered in a century of profound challenge to these Chinese traditions (Table 4.1). In retaliation against Chinese efforts to regulate the trade in opium, British forces invaded China and forced the government to sign a treaty, which was soon followed by many others (discussed in Chapters 3, 6, and 7). Foreigners gained the right to establish settlements and businesses partially free from Chinese regulation. Workers in their factories oper-

Table 4.1   Important Dates in Modern Chinese History

1839	Beginning of first Opium War
1911	Founding of republic
1919	Founding of May Fourth Movement
1921	Founding of Communist Party
1927	KMT-communist split
1932	Japan occupies Manchuria
1934	Long March
1936	KMT-communist United Front
1937	Japan attacks China
1945	End of World War II
1949	Founding of People's Republic
1950	Collectivization of agriculture
1953	Start of First Five-Year Plan
1957	Hundred Flowers
1958	Great Leap Forward
1963	Socialist education campaign
1966	Start of Cultural Revolution
1976	Arrest of "Gang of Four"
1978	Deng Xiaoping starts four modernizations
1989	Bloody recapture of Tiananmen Square
1992	Deng calls for expanded economic liberalization

ated outside traditional associations, and their goods competed with those manufactured in Chinese workshops. They were entitled to bypass established Chinese business groups when making deals and built railways to link their coastal commerce with inland regions. Their commerce was hard for Chinese officials or local clan leaders to regulate.

In 1894 a Guangzhou native named Sun Yat-sen, who had studied in Japan and Hawaii, founded the Revive China Society (Wei, Myers, and Gillin, 1994; Bergere, 1998). It advocated constitutional government for China, as did a commission created by the empress dowager. Following her death in 1908, under urging from Sun Yat-sen's movement, the imperial leaders let the provinces elect assemblies. After a series of army mutinies in 1911, China held elections for a new premier (for a survey of that dramatic year of change, see Eto and Schiffrin, 1994). Sun, the winner, returned to China from abroad to assume this post. He soon was nudged aside by Yuan Shikai, a regional leader in Beijing who had once advised the empress dowager. Sun's National People's Party, also called the Nationalist Party or Kuomintang (KMT), won the elections Yuan promised in 1913, but their victorious candidate was killed as he stepped off the train upon his arrival in Beijing. Yuan would not step down. His troops battled KMT troops, and Sun returned to exile. After Yuan's death in 1916, his successor called back Sun and the assemblies. But Yuan's successor was soon overthrown by a military coup, and Beijing's power collapsed. China fell under the control of regional warlords (for case studies, see Duara, 1988). Because the examination system was now abolished, the old literati were no longer around to help maintain the civil bureaucracy. To make matters even worse, the 1919 Versailles Conference awarded part of the Shandong peninsula (see Map 2.2 and Chapter 7) to Japan, as a reward for its support of the Allies in World War I. That began the May Fourth Movement, which Charles Laughlin introduces colorfully in Chapter 13.

In 1921, Sun met with representatives of Russia's new government, the Soviet Union, to procure help in reuniting China. That same year a small group of men (including Mao) founded the Chinese Communist Party. While they were organizing miners and textile workers into unions, Sun was using aid from the Soviet Union to create a military academy at Whampoa, just below Guangzhou (see Map 2.2). He sent his associate Chiang Kai-shek to Moscow for training, while Zhou Enlai took over as Whampoa's director. Meanwhile, Mao Zedong led KMT efforts to organize peasants.

After Sun's death in 1925, this cozy alliance dissolved. He left leadership of the KMT to Chiang Kai-shek. After defeating warlords who controlled the region around Guangzhou, Chiang recruited their troops to help attack other warlords. Soon the KMT controlled the territory of seven provinces. But now the communists and Kuomintang disagreed on strategy for the next move.

Chiang wanted to turn the offensive along the Yangtze River and up the coast to converge on Shanghai. The communist leaders preferred to head farther north, making alliances with warlords friendly to them there. After that they would join forces against the two most powerful warlords of the north. By then, Chiang might be pushed from leadership of the movement. The Russian advisers sided with the communists on this. In addition, many of Chiang's supporters were landlords and industrialists who feared communist demands for peasant and worker rights. Communists led powerful worker organizations in Guangzhou, Shanghai, and Wuhan (see Map 2.2; Perry, 1993; Honig, 1986). In the spring of 1927, Chiang (now leading the KMT and about to marry the sister of Sun's widow—see Seagrave, 1987) made a secret deal with Zhang Zuolin, one of the northern warlords the communists planned to attack. Early on the morning of April 12, Chiang's men began killing all the communists they could find in Shanghai. Meanwhile, Zhang carried out a similar mission in Beijing. By year's end, the communists in Wuhan and Guangzhou had been defeated as well, but the price was heavy for the Kuomintang. Warlord forces defeated some of their troops. Out of money, Chiang used triad society (organized crime) gangs to extort money from merchants in the foreign concession areas of Shanghai.

The following year, Chiang Kai-shek broke his alliance with Zhang and headed north to defeat Zhang's armies around Beijing. The Japanese, occupying the Shandong peninsula just south of Beijing, also had designs on Zhang's territory. They blew up a train he was riding on, and he was succeeded by his son, Zhang Xueliang, who retained control of Manchuria but ceded Beijing to Chiang's KMT Nationalists. By 1931 this position had been reversed; the Japanese controlled Manchuria, and Zhang Xueliang operated from Beijing as an ally of the Nationalists. Meanwhile, Mao Zedong was organizing peasants in rural areas to the north of Guangzhou, experimenting with policies, strategies, and institutions that would improve living standards and attract followers. Having consolidated his position in the cities, Chiang sent his troops to wipe out this last remaining communist stronghold. In 1934 these communists began a Long March on foot to escape Chiang's forces; 370 days, numerous pitched battles, and 6,000 miles later, 8,000 of them (they started out with 80,000) arrived at a new base area in the hills to the north of Xi'an. Some had been members—often with little military training—of the Red Army, while others were civilian members of the Communist Party. Now, in this adversity, those lines were blurred, fitting Mao's notion that the army should be the masses directly serving the masses. Mao used the organizational methods he had pioneered farther south to help his troops aid peasants in taking control of their region, setting up farming, and patrolling the perimeters (Hinton, 1970; Snow, 1938; Thomas, 1996, on Snow). By this time, Zhang controlled Xi'an, and the Japanese in Manchuria were threatening further hostilities. Chiang

Kai-shek urged Zhang to wipe out Mao's new stronghold, but Zhang was convinced that the time had come for the KMT Nationalists and the communists to make a truce and unite against the Japanese. When Chiang flew to Xi'an in 1936, he was in for a surprise. Zhang arrested him and demanded he declare a united front with the communists. Chiang did so. Six months later, Japan attacked China.

The war against Japan was long and bloody. The Japanese troops swept from Beijing almost to Guangzhou and pushed Chiang Kai-shek's headquarters inland to Chongqing, behind the Three Gorges on the Yangtze River. Mao's forces gradually expanded their hold over the territory to the west of the Yellow River. Life was horrendous in all three areas:

- Though they refused to go along with racial extermination policies of their ally Hitler and estimates by experts vary widely, the Japanese may have killed as many as 35 million Chinese by war's end (see, for example, figures in Spence, 1999:422–425, 439, 452–453; Chang, 1997; Honda, 1999; Fogel and Maier, 2000; Zhang, 2000). They used many people for slave labor in farms and factories and wiped out entire villages in their "three-alls" ("kill all, burn all, destroy all") campaigns.

- Warlords controlled much of the remaining territory. Impoverished peasants on their lands worked long hours producing crops to be sold elsewhere, while local people starved. In areas administered by the Kuomintang, lineage leaders often dominated their entire community, or absentee landlords exploited poor tenants. Unions were banned in the cities, and people worked for low wages under harsh conditions.

- In contrast, the communists worked with landlords to reduce their rents. They paid peasants for food and supplies used by their troops and warned their troops not to molest women. They created producer cooperatives, helped peasants pool their labor to build up fields and irrigation, and developed local industries (see Hinton, 1970, 1997). As a result their numbers grew rapidly, and many students left the universities to help. Peasants in Japanese or KMT areas were eager to bring their regions into communist hands or to escape into communist-held territory. By 1941, communist and Kuomintang forces were fighting one another. In 1942 Mao initiated the first of many rectification campaigns (based on the Confucian notion of rectifying your good name when you have shamed it, by apologizing and correcting your behavior), forcing people to stand before their neighbors and admit their mistakes in an effort to enforce political solidarity. The communists started letting peasants settle old scores by killing their landlords. If the land fell back into KMT control, landlords would in turn shoot peasants; the Japanese would kill them all and burn their villages. Fighting and recrimination among the three sides grew increasingly bloody.

■ Unity Nearly Restored

At war's end in 1945, much of China's countryside had been ravaged by war, deforestation, erosion, floods, and exploitative landlords. Many of its industries had been dismantled. The communists had personnel trained and eager to tackle such problems and peasants willing to work long hours to restore fields and factories. In the communist areas, inflation was low and production quickly resumed. Furthermore, Soviet leader Joseph Stalin left Manchuria to the communist forces. Many warlords and KMT leaders had their attention focused on other matters, and morale among their laborers was low. A portion of food that cost U.S.$1 in KMT cities in mid-1947 cost over U.S.$500 by the beginning of 1949, but strikes for higher wages were forbidden (see Spence, 1999:474–480). Against that background, KMT Nationalists battled communist forces for control of China. Morale also was low among many KMT troops, especially those who had not been paid. Even during the fight against Japan, U.S. General Joseph Stilwell was "horrified at the campaigns of enforced conscription carried out by the Kuomintang armies, and at the sight of ragged, barefooted men being led to the front roped together, already weakened almost to death by beriberi or malnutrition" (Spence, 1999:453). Many officers fled to Taiwan before battles with communist forces ended. After Japan's surrender, Stalin occupied Manchuria and then left it to the Red Army, and the communists already occupied large pieces of terrain in northern China. Toward the end of 1948, the Red Army engaged the demoralized KMT troops to seize the railway connections linking the cities, which (except for Harbin) were still under KMT control. In January 1949, after capturing nearby Tianjin in a focused assault, the Red Army persuaded the heavily outnumbered KMT troops guarding Beijing to surrender that city, and ten days later Chiang Kai-shek resigned as president. The Red Army swept southward to take strategic cities there; by year's end, the KMT regime had retreated to Taiwan. On October 1, 1949, Mao declared formation of the People's Republic of China.

China was ready for a restoration of order. That required curbing inflation, restoring land to the peasants, rebuilding heavy industry, and creating a stable administrative structure. To accomplish this, the communists needed the skills of landlords, managers, technicians, and able civil servants. Many Chinese returned from abroad to help with the reconstruction. In 1950 the regime seized and redistributed about 40 percent of cultivable land and may have killed over 2 million landlords (Dietrich, 1994:69); many friendly landlords were spared and allowed to keep their land. The government vigorously cracked down on the secret triad societies, whose corruption had been keeping urban fiscal and civil order at bay. Repeating a tactic pioneered during the Han dynasty, foreign and domestic business owners were forced to sell out for "back taxes" but then were hired to manage their former firms if they stayed. The country was divided into six military/administrative districts, each under separate command of officers of the Red Army, now renamed the People's Liberation Army (PLA). These commanders supervised both military and civil activities in their districts. The Communist Party was the "leading element" in the country but needed coordination with these military units and the civilian bureaucracy to rule. The party's top organs, the Central Committee and Politburo (see below) contained many military officers. Extending the Qing dynasty's *baojia* approach (households grouped together under a leader; see Chapter 5), all factories, offices, schools, and other places of employment were organized into work units that reported the activities of their members to those authorities (*danwei;* see Walder, 1986). A common currency was created for the entire country, and government spending was brought under tight control. Inflation declined rapidly.

The next challenge was to root out opponents of the new regime and inspire the citizenry to set aside personal gain so as to restore the nation's vitality. The animosities surrounding the Korean War (see Chapter 7), which lasted from 1950 to 1953, provided a backdrop to these efforts. As the U.S. Seventh Fleet patrolled the waters between Taiwan (whose regime was asserting its right to take back the mainland by force) and the mainland, and U.S. aid helped Taiwan rearm and rebuild, the communist government began a series of rectification campaigns. It wanted to be sure its citizens did not side with Taiwan and that they gave their all to promote national development and a new communist society that would be free from exploitation and that sought to better the lives of everyone rather than a select few (see Chapter 12). The 1951 "counterrevolutionary" campaign forced people to stand before their neighbors and confess that they had been disloyal to the new regime; tens of thousands of them were executed. Then the "three anti" campaign brought managers and bureaucrats before their work units to confess waste, corruption, and activities that obstructed development. The 1952 "five anti" campaign was aimed at foreign and domestic capitalists engaged in tax evasion, bribery, theft of state property, fraud on government contracts, and theft of state economic information. The government needed their production for the Korean War and civil development and even helped pay many of their fines— making them more subservient and cautious about such practices. Few were killed. The campaigns attacked foreign enemies and called for patriotism and determination to rout those holding back China's development (for discussion of these campaigns, see Liu, 1996; and Teiwes, 1993).

The Korean War also brought a trade blockade of China and removed it from access to foreign capital. The Soviet Union supplied capital and technical assistance for China's First Five-Year Plan (discussed further in Chapter 5). The separate military-political units of the country were abandoned, and planning was centralized to promote frugality and growth. Government agencies were placed on tight budgets, and resources were carefully targeted. Between 1953 and 1957, agencies invested extensively in state-operated heavy industries, spread throughout the country, and in hydroelectric plants, railroads, and urban housing. Production focused on military hardware and then increasingly on machinery, construction materials, and basic consumer goods. Wages were kept low, and workers had to "contribute" heavy taxes and savings bond investments to the state, but employment was guaranteed. Little was spent on education or social welfare, but citizens were recruited for drives to wipe out pests, improve sanitation, combat common diseases, and promote literacy. Peasants were organized into mutual aid teams composed of six or seven (later, fifty) families who kept title to their land while pooling their resources. They sold the government a fourth of their grain at low prices; the government, in turn, sold flour, rice, and cooking oil to urban workers for low prices (keeping inflation low). Wealthy peasants were excluded from these teams. Agricultural output rose, but not enough to keep pace with industrial production. People's diets steadily improved, but they could buy little beyond food.

Up to that point, the government's efforts had some historical precedents in China's long history of encouraging but regulating capitalist enterprises in a successful effort to restore social and economic stability. Many people had, in fact, been pleased to see individual excesses brought under control. But now the government was ready to move beyond that, testing dangerous new waters in its efforts to ratchet up agricultural production. Capitalism would be banned, not just reformed; the state and peasant organizations would own all production enterprises. By 1955, many mutual aid teams were being incorporated into cooperatives containing 200 to 300 families, and credit was being withheld from richer families. Much of the cooperatives' land was being farmed in common, though each family retained a private plot of land.

China had pulled itself together and left the war years behind, but it was facing a baffling dilemma it still cannot solve. The Chinese people are prepared to give support to strong leaders, especially when they remember periods of disarray. They have long experience at investing in and developing farms and businesses and will devote long hours to work. But they feel strongly about carrying out their *guanxi* obligations to their own families and others with whom they have special relationships. In the 1950s, they were being asked to sacrifice living standards for their own families when they knew others were passing favors to their friends. Given a choice to spend their efforts on common fields or on their own plots, many members of cooperatives chose the latter and then lied to the tax authorities about the income they derived from selling their own livestock and vegetables (and about how small the harvest was on the common land). The most fervent communists saw this emphasis on one's own land and on jobs like hauling or hawking to earn extra money as putting capitalist family interests above those of the whole community. Communists also disliked religious practices that helped bond the community because they held back material progress by wasting resources on extravagant funerals and weddings. The communists had returned the land to the peasants but were imposing rules that ran counter to their traditional culture.

The year 1956 began on a hopeful note (see Macfarquar, 1974). According to the often-inflated reports, agricultural output seemed to be rising, so China's leaders followed Mao Zedong's guidance and rapidly pushed greater numbers of mutual aid teams into the larger cooperatives. Soviet premier Nikita Khrushchev was secretly denouncing Stalin (who had died in 1953) in the Soviet Union's party congress and openly called for peaceful coexistence. Mao and others within China's ruling circle (hoping for reconciliation with Taiwan) secretly discussed allowing greater intellectual freedom and encouraging more openness to foreigners and minorities. Some of their colleagues strongly resisted such accommodation with bourgeois elements, but this debate was short-lived. The summer brought a severe drought and disastrous harvest. Peasants resisted the imposition of the badly managed large cooperatives. In the fall, the Hungarians rose against the Soviet Union, Tibetans rioted against Chinese rule (see Chapter 6), and the Chinese communists held their first party congress since taking over China. The congress abruptly stopped converting mutual aid teams into cooperatives, called for greater central control of the economy, supported those who opposed a Khrushchev-style united front with bourgeois elements, and challenged Mao's leadership. For a time, neither the Soviet Union nor China suffered from a "cult of personality."

Mao had been ostracized from inner party circles before (for interesting biographies, see Spence, 2000; Schram, 1966; Cheek and Saich, 2002; Terrill, 1999; Karnow, 1972; and Li, 1994). Among the party's founders, he was the only one who came from a peasant background and had not studied in Europe. The others tended to associate with intellectuals and attempted to organize among workers in the cities where they lived, whereas Mao moved into the countryside to organize peasants. His work was largely ignored by his urban comrades. In 1927, after the Kuomintang attack on the communists, Mao tried to lead a peasant uprising. The KMT quickly squelched it, and the Communist Party removed him from the Central Committee. While the KMT suppressed urban branches of the party, Mao simply continued organizing the peasants—thus providing the basis for the 1934 Long March. The survivors of that march formed the core group who would take over China. Mao was their natural leader—not the urban intellectuals.

Removed once again in 1956 from the inner circle, Mao returned to the source of his power, the peasants and workers. Early in 1957 he publicly delivered a speech drawing on one he had made privately the previous year, calling for greater intellectual freedom so that "a hundred flowers" could bloom and "a hundred schools of thought contend" (Karnow, 1972:87–90; Spence, 1999:539–543). He said the country was now so united it could benefit from such a debate. The press, a natural ally in such an initiative, hesitated at first to print his words. When they did, criticism rushed forth. Mao had hoped the press and citizens would attack his adversaries leading the party and support his reforms. Instead, the students at Beijing University started a "Democracy Wall" and filled it with posters denouncing a wide range of Communist Party policies and even the right of the communists to rule. People around the country joined in; many were critical of Mao himself. Within weeks, Mao backed down and joined the inner circle in calling for a crackdown on the campaign and severe punishment of those making the criticisms. The antirightist rectification campaign that ensued led to 300,000 intellectuals (branded as "rightists") losing their jobs without hope of finding other employment and sent many of them into exile on farms. Their numbers included many of the youths who had been most zealous in supporting the initial rise to power of the communists. They would not forget this humiliation.

■ Two Decades of Turmoil

In 1957, agricultural production moved to center stage as the primary concern of China's leaders. Industrial production had been growing far more rapidly than grain production, and the income of rural workers had outpaced that of peasants. Left once again to their own devices, peasants had focused on more profitable vegetables and livestock, leaving the country with inadequate flour, rice, and cooking oil to feed its burgeoning population. Mao was determined to end this lethargy and propel China into a communist utopia by increasing agricultural and industrial output to improve the lives of everyone and surpass the capitalist West. Late in 1957 the party mobilized millions of peasants into work gangs to irrigate and terrace millions of acres of new cropland. The effort was carried out through a mass rectification campaign; units outdid themselves to show their all-out commitment to pure "red" communism by reporting huge increases in production. Encouraged by these wildly inflated figures, the following year the party announced the Great Leap Forward (for alarming close-ups, see Macfarquar, 1983; Bachman, 1991; Domenach, 1995; and Yang, 1996; for an overview, see Dietrich, 1994:110–150). Private plots were abolished. Mutual-aid teams and cooperatives were amalgamated into gigantic communes. Families were absorbed into large crews who worked in the fields and made their meals together. These crews were even mobilized to help develop an atomic bomb and increase steel production by melting scrap metal in backyard ovens, based on Mao's ideas that committed peasants could enhance industrial output more effectively than professionals working with central planners.

In the long run, the Great Leap Forward opened much new land for agricultural production and brought new industry and agricultural capabilities to

This sculpture outside Mao's Tomb on Tiananmen Square depicts herioc workers and peasants

Robert Gamer

formerly remote regions (for an account of how the Great Leap Forward improved life in one small village, after a period of great pain, see Chan, Madsen, and Unger, 1984:213–220). And it enlarged local militias, which competed with the PLA. In the short run—due to bad weather, diversion of labor to other projects, increased exports of grain to the Soviet Union based on the exaggerated output claims, layoff of skilled civil servants during the antirightist campaigns, and other mismanagement—agricultural production fell below even the disastrous levels of the prior two years. Millions of people were starving; over 20 million died (see Yang, 1996; Spence, 1999:553). Yet grain exports to the Soviet Union in payment for its aid in developing industry were increasing. Once again, the party leadership called off the campaign and removed Mao as head of state in 1959. Registration in the *danwei* was intensified to pull people back to the countryside. Private plots began to be distributed again, communes were divided among private production brigades, and rural markets reopened. Many inefficient rural industries and state enterprises were closed. Gradually, agricultural production and private entrepreneurship began to revive.

Meanwhile, the United States had begun supplying Taiwan with missiles. The Soviet Union, talking of "peaceful coexistence" with the capitalist nations, showed no signs of helping China develop an atomic bomb. Khrushchev had sent no assistance to the Great Leap Forward, which differed from his own new initiatives to provide workers with economic incentives. While China was having foreign policy disputes with India and Indonesia (discussed in Chapters 6 and 7), Khrushchev was warming relations with them. In 1960, the Soviet Union called home its technical advisers and cut off aid to China, bringing a halt to many projects.

The debate within China's inner circle of top Communist Party leaders defies simple summation. They decried the excesses that resulted from suppressing capitalist enterprises yet did not want capitalism to return. They all largely agreed that Khrushchev's policy of accommodation with capitalists was the wrong tack for China and that China's peasants and workers needed more discipline, but they disagreed on how to achieve that discipline. Mao preferred those who were "red" (a true devotee of the communist cause) to those who were simply trained experts. As evidence mounted that the efforts to instill "redness" by organizing great communes and putting peasants and workers in charge was a disaster threatening their positions as leaders of government and party organs and popular support for Communist Party rule, the leaders struggled for a way out. They chose, at this point, to restore the use of expert bureaucrats, managers, and technicians in central bureaucracy to plan allocation of resources, direct what should be grown and produced, and assist with distribution of finished products; meanwhile, they sought to give people more chance to profit from their output. Some in the party leadership felt China needed more technical expertise from the outside but feared that exposure to bourgeois capitalism would weaken people's resolve to serve their whole community.

To ensure that the renewed opportunities for profit were not at the expense of the community, national party leaders initiated a "socialist education campaign" in 1963, which attempted to reduce fraud both in accounting for grain and property and in distributing incentive pay to those who worked harder. The campaign, however, was carried out by local party leaders who themselves might have been guilty of those offenses. The communist leaders of communes, cooperatives, work teams, and state enterprises were made responsible for judging how to proceed and determining who among their own ranks was cheating; they were to discipline themselves (for an account of how local leaders found themselves involved in such national projects, see Siu, 1999). Thus local leaders could cheat without getting caught, but ordinary people were closely supervised, without assurance of extra rewards for hard work.

To challenge his opponents within the party leadership, Mao took advantage of citizens' resentment over leaders' abuses of power. He applauded his model village of Dazhai for increasing production through "red" ideological fervor rather than supervision by experts, even though a party inspection team found its production was down and many of its inhabitants were undernourished. He called once again for more open debate, to let the masses—not the local party leaders—ferret out the corruption among their leaders. His position gained support among troops within the People's Liberation Army who felt that their own power was being eclipsed by the party's civilian leaders, who were calling for stricter discipline and professionalism, and by the militias, who had grown in strength since the Great Leap Forward. And Mao had the ear of some groups who, ironically, were suffering from his own efforts: city people from "bourgeois" or former Kuomintang families who had lost university admissions, jobs, and party posts to individuals from the countryside who had more humble (and therefore presumably more "red") origins. He also gained support from many unemployed youth who had fled to the cities during the agricultural downturn Mao had helped create and now had been returned to the farms, where they were not always well received. Finally, the current batch of university students worried about their prospects in the wake of all the recent cataclysms.

Mao preached to these politically alienated listeners that they should assert themselves against their leaders, and they listened. In 1965 the PLA abandoned all ranks and insignia on their uniforms; officers and enlisted soldiers would be "equal" and share all work assignments. By the spring of 1966, Mao had stirred leading university campuses into protest, and protesting students began calling themselves "Red Guards." Soon they were joined by students and other supporters from throughout the country. By fall, they were dragging political leaders, teachers, bureaucrats, and others into the streets and making them confess crimes before kangaroo courts. Schools were closed, workers were stealing property from their factories, historic buildings and monuments were being destroyed, production was grinding to a halt. The Great Proletarian Cultural Revolution had begun (Macfarquar, 1999; Feng, 1996; Perry and Li, 1996; Schoenhals, 1996; White, 1989; Yuan, 1987; Karnow, 1972; Dietrich, 1994: 205–234; Wang, 1995; Chang, 1991; Yan and Gao, 1996; Xiguang Yang, 1997; Jun, 1997).

Mao had hoped to regain control of China's leadership and keep China's people focused on the good of the whole community. Instead, once again, he had roused (together with millions of people acting out of pure idealistic fervor) the anticommunist, anarchist, and disaffected citizens in the country to attack authority and seek their own personal gain—or at least disrupt community life. By February 1967, Mao was supporting efforts by the party leaders and the army to restore order. This time, it would take ten years. By the late 1960s, schools were beginning to reopen, and Mao was seeking ties with the United States. Many more students had been sent to work in the country-side alongside those sent there earlier in the 1960s; slowly they returned to the cities, bitter over their forced exile and long-disrupted education. Because the party's membership had expanded to include many Red Guards, a series of rectification campaigns first attacked those leading the Cultural Revolution and then those trying to bring it under control. Even top leaders of the party were subjected to beatings and imprisonment, and many were humiliated to the point of suicide.

In 1976, Zhou Enlai (who had led the restoration of party control) and Mao died. Mao's successor, Hua Guofeng, promptly arrested the "Gang of Four," four of the most prominent leaders of the Cultural Revolution; in their trial, they were blamed for all the excesses of that era. A new era had begun. Within four years, Deng Xiaoping (for biographies, see Goodman, 1994; Shambaugh, 1995; and Yang, 1997) had overcome strong challenges from his rivals to take control of the party, and the United States had extended diplo-matic recognition to the People's Republic. Mao had paved the way for reforms more in keeping with tradition—such as encouraging limited capital-ism—by weakening the central bureaucracies, returning land to the peasants, and helping even small communities develop consumer industries. The United States made reforms possible by helping Hong Kong, Taiwan, Japan, and Southeast Asian countries develop strong economies and currencies to invest in China; for more on this, see Chapter 6.

■ Into the World Economy

After Mao's era ended, China was free to pursue the added elements of economic strength that had eluded it before: foreign capital, technology, and markets (Baum, 1996; Dittmer, 1994; Shirk, 1993). China's attempt to mod-ernize its economy without changing its political system would confuse those in the West and would burden China with new social problems, but it would also bring China the broadest prosperity it had ever experienced.

To implement reform, Deng called for four modernizations—of agricul-ture, industry, defense, and science and technology—and initiated new eco-nomic policies, which are discussed in more detail in Chapter 5. The household responsibility system allowed peasants to lease plots of land and sell their crops for profit. Groups of individuals or entire villages and townships could form cooperative enterprises to manufacture, transport, and sell goods (some-times hiring workers from villages farther inland, for low pay). In addition, foreign firms could create joint ventures with firms in China. Special economic zones were created where foreign businesses could buy land and get special breaks on taxes and regulations. And state industries were authorized to fire workers, give incentive pay, and sell shares of stock to Chinese investors.

These reforms have brought China continuous economic growth at a rate surpassing 10 percent a year. By 1999 its gross national income had become the seventh largest in the world, though on a per capita basis it ranked only 146th (World Bank, 2001:12).

▇ Meeting the Challenges of Reform

The three groups initially most helped by Deng's reforms were the peasants, party bureaucrats in coastal provinces, and urban workers who could form cooperatives. The groups most harmed were students, intellectuals, urban youth still trapped in the countryside, central planners, and workers in state industries. To achieve power after Mao's death, Deng had to win support from factions with adherents in all these camps. Deng's successor, Jiang Zemin, faced that same challenge. This created a dynamic in modern Chinese politics that both calls for and limits openness to the outside world.

Mao's reforms allowed the land to be returned to peasant producers; Deng's responsibility system and cooperatives gave them the incentive to produce. They rapidly began bringing home profits. Intellectuals, bureaucrats, and skilled blue-collar workers with assigned jobs and fixed salaries found themselves making less than uneducated peasants and laborers. Rural workers used their incomes to build large new houses, whereas urban dwellers were crowded into small, dingy apartments. Many urban youths who had been sent to the countryside during the Cultural Revolution still could not get permission to return to the cities yet were not entitled to land or jobs where they were. The government had little money to invest in universities; students studied on drab campuses with few laboratory or library facilities, ate food ladled from buckets of gruel onto metal plates, and lived with six people in dorm rooms meant for two, without heat or air conditioning. Even graduates of the leading universities anticipated assigned jobs paying less than the income of a bicycle repairperson on a street corner or someone gathering scrap cardboard in a cart and selling it to a wholesaler. Many students had marched in demonstrations and hung posters on the "Democracy Wall" in 1976 and 1978 to help bring Deng to power and felt both unrewarded and betrayed by the arrest of Wei Jingsheng and others who had led those demonstrations (see Black and Munro, 1993; Ding, 1994; Wasserstrom and Perry, 1994).

By 1986, students were marching again, against rigged elections, their poor living conditions, low pay for university graduates, the growth in inflation and the corruption of officials who were hiring their own children and diverting resources into the pockets of their factional cohorts. In the spring of 1989, students marched once more, to raise these concerns. This time the foreign media was in Beijing to cover the historic reopening of relations with the Soviet Union as Mikhail Gorbachev flew in for a state visit, and reporters saw the students occupy and refuse to leave Tiananmen Square at the center of Beijing.

The 1989 demonstrations took place for several weeks in cities all over China. Hanzhou saw daily scenes like this.

Some of the leaders felt it was time to take a more tolerant view than had ever been taken in the past toward demonstrations and suggested inviting the leaders into public dialogue about the issues the demonstrations had raised. Most, however, worried that they might get out of hand like those during the prior two decades; the students' complaints about corruption and economic disparities and their ties to political factions within the party were reminiscent of the Red Guards, who had started the Cultural Revolution with similar demonstrations (for interviews with participants in such demonstrations going back to 1942, see Benton and Hunter, 1995). That approach prevailed, and the government responded with a bloody recapture of Tiananmen Square, arrests of and long prison sentences for demonstration leaders, a rectification campaign condemning the action, and requirements that students should serve stints in the army to remind them of the need for discipline (for inside reports, see Zhang, Nathan, and Link, 2001; Liu, Ming, and Xu, 1989; Gamer, 1989; Ogden, Hartford, Sullivan, and Zweig, 1991; Unger, 1991; Lin, 1992; Black and Munro, 1993; Gordon and Hinton, 1995; Sullivan, 1995; Feigon, 1999; Zhao, 2001; and Fewsmith, 2001).

The government then took steps to defuse the anger that lay behind the demonstrations. Part of this strategy focused on the PLA. The units who ran the tanks into the square were from inland rural areas that had not benefited from the reforms; they feared and distrusted the students, who lived better than they did and were taking actions country youths would not dream of.

Some soldiers lost their lives on the square, raising the level of distrust and envy. When Deng came to power he had sought to reduce the power of the PLA, which had greatly expanded during the Cultural Revolution, by separating police units from the PLA, reducing the size of military forces and budgets, and removing officers from top party posts. Now he restored officers to some of these posts and gradually increased military spending (Soled, 1995:263–282). The PLA was given rights to set up numerous joint ventures and sell arms abroad, which helped improve life on the bases (Mulvenon, 2000). Later in the 1990s it would be forced to divest itself of those assets, but a large increase in its budget to procure weaponry served to keep it quiet.

Universities were mandated to start businesses (a policy since abandoned), charge wealthier students tuition, and raise money in other creative ways. University campuses acquired new gardens, paint, furniture, buildings, and equipment. Mess halls began serving a variety of foods. Occupancy of dorm rooms was reduced, and more buildings were heated and air-conditioned. Later in the 1990s some key universities received large grants from the government to give large raises to instructors, construct new buildings, and increase the size of their student bodies.

Rather than being assigned to low-paying, government jobs as in the past, students were now free to seek jobs with joint ventures after graduation. In 1992 Deng called for an expansion of economic liberalization. This set off a wave of construction; new housing, roads, public buildings, factories, airports, dams, and electrical power stations brought jobs and better living all over the country. Censors began to wink at the proliferation of pornography, foreign fiction, and rock music (in Chapter 13, Charles Laughlin elaborates on these developments).

These changes, in turn, disadvantage other groups. Peasants are upset because the government is levying higher taxes and purchasing fewer goods from them at much lower prices as it weans urban workers off food vouchers. At the same time, both peasants and workers are paying more for purchases. This combination especially harms villagers in remote areas, whose income depends on grain sales. Village leaders control the distribution of leased land, which they increasingly confiscate and sell to urban institutions as urban growth creates demands for more land (Jiang, 2002). These leaders sometimes lead newly revived temple sects and lineage organizations, which promote conflicts with other communities (Jun, 1997). These groups are tied together in networks that owe each other *guanxi* (Huang, 2000). Many state factories, now competing with joint ventures and private enterprises, cannot afford to give pay increases sufficient to compensate for inflation; increasingly, they are going out of business altogether. Inland provinces lag behind those on the coast. Millions of itinerant workers are unwelcome in the cities where they had taken temporary residence (see Chapter 8); they and many workers in cooperatives and small businesses are without social services. Health and education services falter, while AIDS spreads rapidly in central and western provinces.

Toward the end of the 1990s, governments were encouraging rural communities to create village and township enterprises at a faster pace. Inhabitants from those regions were hired to work in factories of those enterprises. Yet with all the emphasis on urban development, the countryside continues to decline. Many of the enterprises are faltering. By 2000 the price of vegetables had plummeted, lowering rural incomes. Local officials raised taxes even higher while eliminating all subsidies and spending little to help the rural infrastructure or provide agricultural extension services. Inland drought and lowering of water tables was reducing wheat crops. Now a member of the World Trade Organization (WTO, discussed below and in Chapter 5), China is likely to use the same loopholes used by Europeans and Americans to protect its grain farmers from imports while encouraging exports of its fruit, nuts, vegetables, flowers, and shrimp (Lardy, 2002). That is a holding action; new means to revive the countryside are needed.

▪ New Political Challenges

Economic development requires decentralization of control, but also national unity. It widens the gap between the rich and the poor; bridging that gap requires help from the central government. Development not only requires some democratic reforms but also depends on some traditional social ties that interfere with democratic reforms. Economic development needs the help of foreign traders and investors; every group is likely to agree on that. But not every group can benefit from economic development at the same time. This is where disagreements arise.

Chapter 5 surveys some of the principal economic challenges with which China's leaders must grapple: inflation and deflation, inefficient state industries and township and village enterprises, environmental degradation, rising unemployment, banking reform, the shrinking social safety net, widespread corruption, maintenance of peasant incomes.

People complain about the lack of legal reforms to stop corruption, yet many benefit directly or indirectly from the money that changes hands outside official channels (on corruption, see Oi, 1989; Kwong, 1997; and Lu, 2000). They know the absence of such reforms slows growth, but although they may want to let that fresh air in, they also want to keep out anything that interferes with cultural reciprocities. Reforms like tightening legal procedures and allowing groups to register complaints threaten the very relationships that have allowed some to advance, or may be used by unions and cadres to block further reform. Premier Zhu Rongji led a campaign against corruption, with some high-level officials and businessmen condemned to death for corruption, yet charges of corruption have crept close to the top leaders themselves, a widespread problem. The wife of Jia Qinglin, one of the new Politburo members (discussed below), was protected by Jiang against charges that she was involved in a major smuggling scandal. An internal party document says that 78 percent of fraud cases over U.S.$600,000 involve senior officials, and that 98 percent of them have relatives in key business or government posts. Some economists estimate that 14 percent of China's gross domestic product (GDP) is bled into corruption (Liu, 2002; Wang, Hu, and Ding, 2002). Chinese media reports that 200,000 officials have been prosecuted since 1998.

The Confucian scholars living during the Song dynasty recognized the danger a free economy can pose to the rural communities, on which China's citizens depend as a source of jobs, sustenance, and social reciprocities. Contemporary Chinese are learning that free land sales, market competition, and access to modern technology can destroy communities and render many peasants and workers jobless.

■ Maintaining Unity

The decentralization accompanying economic reform has given new freedoms to China's provincial leaders. These freedoms have largely been made possible because China is once again unified, accorded diplomatic recognition by other governments, able to ensure political stability, and able to move people and resources from one region to another for manufacturing and marketing. In 2002 China was admitted into the WTO, making it a regular part of the world trading community. Beijing has been chosen as the site of the 2008 Olympics. All this gives political leaders incentive to work together to achieve continuing economic growth; provinces cannot achieve these objectives on their own. At the same time, it gives provinces control over a lot of money and resources. Municipalities, townships, and provinces allied with foreign multinational corporations have become the main recipients of investment capital. They collect most tax revenues as well, including internal tariffs on goods crossing their boundaries. Cities pass "health" and "quality control" laws banning goods from other provinces. Over 1,000 disputes over internal boundary lines have sometimes led to bloodshed, as two provinces make claims on the same mines or timber. In addition, the country is divided into seven military regions whose boundaries do not correspond with provincial lines; though the central government frequently moves around senior officers, their troops have strong regional loyalties. New cars demand new roads, which often ended at the city limit. Hence the central government has initiated a vast program to build new freeways linking all the major cities, more electric generating capacity, numerous modern airfields, and other infrastructure. Still, large areas of the country do not have access to these amenities. In fact, large numbers of people do not have access to this newly accumulating wealth, because they may not be included in the informal channels where that money accumulates.

One's ethnic background also helps determine access to those resources. Chapter 6 discusses Tibet. On Tibet's eastern border, many Tibetans and other inhabitants of Sichuan and Yunnan provinces share in the religion and customs of Tibet and of areas in Southeast Asia. The regions to the north and east of Tibet—now the provinces of Xinjiang, Qinghai, and Gansu (see Map 2.2)—were occasionally penetrated by Chinese armies (see Map 3.1). Tang dynasty conquests brought in Chinese culture that local people continued to absorb even after military withdrawals. The "Silk Roads" (Map 2.1) made these provinces a meeting place for many cultures and of all the world's great religions. Many of their people are Muslim and share religious and family customs far different from those of the Han.

During the Cultural Revolution, acting on communist ideological convictions that nationality traits must be removed if bourgeois society is to wither away and the dictatorship of the proletariat flourish, Red Guard activists aggressively sought to destroy places of worship, languages, clothing, music, and all other manifestations of these cultures. During the earlier years of the People's Republic and again since the Cultural Revolution, China's communist regime has sought to retain such expressions of cultural differences, while at the same time bringing modernization to these regions. Whole provinces like Tibet, as well as individual prefectures, counties, and townships, are designated autonomous areas; they cover nearly two-thirds of China's territory (generally the least populous). Their legislatures have the right to create laws protecting local customs. In addition, citizens registered as cultural minorities have many special privileges unavailable to those officially classified as Han. They are exempt from family planning limits (see Chapter 8) and can gain admission to higher education and cadre posts with lower qualifications.

Today, Beijing sends large numbers of Han to Tibet and cities in the outer northern arc and the southwest in the belief that it is spreading modernization and civilization, but also to develop the vast natural resources in those regions (which some there would prefer to exploit themselves). Han sent to these regions often feel exiled from the best schools, housing, and food and resent the special privileges enjoyed by inhabitants there. And local inhabitants deeply resent their destruction of old neighborhoods, hundreds of monasteries, and hillsides of timber; murders of religious leaders; insistence on communicating in Chinese rather than their native languages; cultural arrogance; and growing numbers. Non-Han residents of autonomous areas often have lower incomes and rates of literacy than their Han compatriots; some of the nation's worst pockets of poverty are to be found among them. During the 1990s, numerous civil rebellions broke out in Tibet, Xinjiang, and Inner Mongolia. These regions border on countries, and movements like Al-Qaida, that may even stir up unrest to help them seize disputed territories (see Chapter 7); consequently the Chinese authorities are determined to squelch the resistance. Since the September 11, 2001, attack on New York's World Trade Center, they have increased the intensity of their efforts to round up and execute individuals engaged in such resistance. All the while, the non-Han peoples in these regions fall behind in sharing China's growing prosperity, and the growing cross-border trading increases contacts among radical groups fomenting cultural and religious separation.

■ Binding Together

The Communist Party has about 66 million members, with about 2 million primary organizations meeting in villages, urban neighborhoods, *danwei,* and military divisions. These local branches elect a local secretary, a local party committee, and other officers, who select individuals to serve on the county and provincial party congresses. Those bodies send about 1,500 delegates to a National Party Congress, which meets every five years; about 300 of those delegates form the Party Congress's Central Committee. Fifteen to twenty-four of the Central Committee's members constitute its Politburo, seven to nine of whom belong to the Standing Committee of the Politburo, which meets regularly. That body wields the highest authority in the land.

The Standing Committee of the Politburo works closely with the party's Military Affairs Commission—the top body directing the armed forces—and with leading government ministers in the State Council. A number of individuals hold posts on more than one of these bodies: both Deng Xiaoping and Jiang Zemin held the posts of general secretary of the party (its highest-ranking member), as head of both the Standing Committee and the Military Affairs Commission. During Jiang's tenure, Premier Zhu Rongji headed the State Council and Li Peng led the National People's Congress. At the Sixteenth Party Congress, held in 2002, all the members of the Standing Committee resigned, except for fifty-nine-year-old Hu Jintao, who had become a member of the Standing Committee in 1992 and vice president in 1998. Hu, a former hydraulic engineer who had long been groomed for a leadership position, then replaced Jiang as general secretary of the Communist Party, and the other eight posts in the Standing Committee were filled with new individuals (ranging in age from fifty-eight to sixty-seven, all engineers). Zhu Rongji's former deputy and close associate, Wen Jiabao, became premier. Meanwhile, half of the members of the Central Committee were replaced, leaving a fifth of its members under the age of fifty. This move had been planned for several years to allow for a peaceful succession of power to a younger generation (see Cheng, 2001). There are about 4 million central government bureaucrats, along with 4 million party cadres. And about 3.2 million people serve as delegates to the 48,000 people's congresses ranging from the township level to the National

People's Congress. Thus the Communist Party, the government, and the armed forces intersect to govern China.

The party's cadres, including the party secretaries, are paid functionaries of the party charged with supervising the work of the government bureaucracy (including provincial governors, and mayors), the armed forces, and other elements of government and society. Many party members and cadres were chosen during the Cultural Revolution and often had little education. In 1992 Deng Xiaoping made a number of the older cadres retire (Lieberthal, 1997: 230–239), and that process has continued, especially accelerated again in 2002. There is still tension between the older-style cadres with less education and the new elite with advanced degrees from universities in the United States and Europe. Party secretaries at the provincial, county, municipal, and township levels hold the highest power there and are served by dual government and party bureaucracies at those levels (J. Wang, 2001; Lieberthal, 1997: 159–218; Shirk, 1993:55–128; Blecher and Shue, 1996; Saich, 2001; Chen, 1999; Mengin and Rocca, 2002; Shambaugh, 2000b; Zhao, 2002). There is no government bureaucracy at the village level, but cadres and village committees serve there. Even today, it is easier for the most highly educated individuals to rise high in the ranks of government than it is for them to become a high party leader (Bo, 2002). Only about 10 percent of judges have graduate degrees, holding back judicial reform; many local judges have been appointed unlawfully and a number have been convicted on corruption charges (Fong, 2002).

Local leaders help choose candidates for elections to party congresses and to people's congresses. *Danwei,* neighborhoods, and military and cultural groups hold elections to select delegates for the local government councils and some of their own leaders; sometimes delegates are selected from among eight small parties, which operate mostly among older city intellectuals who cooperated with the Communist Party before World War II. Usually the voters are presented with only one candidate. In contrast, China's 600,000 villages are encouraged by the central government to hold elections with rival candidates competing to head the village council. An uncertain number are doing so, though the nomination process tends to be carefully controlled (O'Brien, 2001; O'Brien and Li, 2000; Pastor and Tan, 2000; Pomfret, 2002; Zhong and Chen, 2002; Shi, 1999; Li, 1999, 2001, 2002; Kennedy, 2002; Kelliher, 1997). In addition, some villages are electing their local party leader in competitive elections (Hutzler, 2002). Efforts to extend competitive elections to the township level have been strongly resisted by the central government. These moves are in response to a rising level of unrest in rural China—discussed below—over corruption by local officials, tepid economic growth, high taxes, and other issues (Bernstein, 2000; Bernstein and Lu, 2000; Li and O'Brien, 1996).

Each year, meetings of the National People's Congress (the national legislature, whose Standing Committee enforces martial law during domestic disturbances) and the national meeting of the People's Political Consultative Conference (chosen from among the 32,025 members of these conferences from the county level on up) showcase diversity. Though the main purpose of the week-long meetings is to rubber-stamp government programs, in recent years they have engaged in some lively debates about some of the divisive issues just discussed. The controversial Three Gorges Dam project barely passed the People's Congress with a majority vote. Most of the time, the debate takes place behind the scenes. Many factions develop among these individuals, tying them and others together through *guanxi*. Kenneth Lieberthal and Michel Oksenberg (1988:138–168) explain how these connections, in turn, link the regions of the country with the center and one another. Lieberthal also makes a counterargument that people develop loyalty to their own *danwei,* whose leaders report to multiple bosses, causing the leaders to resist cooperation that might harm their own local interests; this results in "fragmented authoritarianism," with individual units living in "economic, social, and political cocoons" (1997:120, 169, 217–218). In recent years, instances of local and provincial people's congresses taking issue with government policies or appointments have increased.

Relations between the People's Liberation Army, with its 2.5 million personnel, and the government are more complex than most. Civilian ministries report directly to the State Council, which is the highest body of the government, and also are supervised by the Communist Party. In contrast, the PLA reports directly to the Military Affairs Commission of the Communist Party; Deng Xiaoping held on to that post after he retired from his other posts, as did Jiang Zemin. The Military Affairs Commission does not report to the State Council. The Ministry of Defense under the State Council has little real control over the military. So the armed forces are supervised by the party, but not by the government. PLA members serve on the party's Politburo and Central Committee, and they are well connected with party leaders at provincial and local levels as well. Many of those connections have been with the old guard, who developed close ties with the military in the early years of the revolutionary struggle; in 2002, at the Party Congress, all the top posts in the PLA were also passed to younger individuals who had entered the military since the PRC came into being and were closely allied to Jiang Zemin.

Imperial China sought a new ruler only after the prior one died. Communist China has kept that tradition. Mao was no longer in control of China's government when he died in 1976, but the struggle to succeed him did not begin until after his death. Though Deng Xiaoping finally gave up all his formal titles during the 1980s, the mantle of rule could not fall on anyone until his death more than a decade later. Jiang Zemin, the former leader of Shanghai, became the general secretary of the Standing Committee of the Communist Party after his predecessor was removed over the 1989 demonstrations; though he was head of the Military Affairs Commission, he was not able to visit the headquarters of the PLA without direct permission from Deng (Lieberthal, 1997:189). He worked to strengthen his position by gaining support of various elements of the army, party, and bureaucracy in all areas of the country. To do that he had to widen the spread of economic reforms while controlling the problems that arose along with them. He also had to show the networks that he was not selling out China to foreigners in any moves reminiscent of the period of foreign domination (see Chapter 7). Jiang's successor, Hu Jintao, must do the same. Like Deng before him, Jiang Zemin will likely remain a power behind the throne. The combination of six members of the new Politburo being Jiang's strong allies (including his close ally, Zeng Qinghong, who retains considerable control over patronage and appointments as the new vice president and as secretary of the party's Central Committee; Jia Qinglin, reportedly best man at Jiang's wedding; and Wu Bangguo, former Shanghai party secretary, who succeeds Li Peng as head of the National People's Congress), together with his continuing leadership of the Military Affairs Commission, gives him strong leverage. Though he is vice chair of the Military Affairs Commission, Hu has little connection with the military, and none of the new top military commanders are in the new Politburo. Lieberthal (Ruwitch, 2002) says: "There is a possibility—I stress possibility, not certainty—that Jiang's ongoing effort to exert influence will prove disruptive and perhaps a source of tension rather than the steadying force that I think he would see it as being."

The new economic freedoms and the general disillusionment with the Cultural Revolution by people who had initially supported its ideology without question have lessened the value of communism as a unifying ideology (see Ding, 1994; Unger, 1996). Jiang turned instead to nationalism (Unger, 1996) and Confucian values (see the "Religion and Chinese Society" section in Chapter 12) as unifying themes—first in the form of his 1996 "spiritual civilization" campaign and then in his incorporation of the "three representatives" into the constitution in 2002: "the people's interests, modern productive forces, and advanced civilization." China's greatness derives from its unique culture, which gives it both unity and dynamic drive. Jiang wants China to become powerful in the world without outside challenges to its core values. He wants it to combine concerns like environmental protection, appreciation for the arts, and family morality with an economic system that both addresses basic needs and promotes affluence. China's Communist Party has quietly developed close ties with social democratic parties in Europe. At the 16th Party Congress in 2002, businessmen were for the first time admitted to party membership.

The annexation of Hong Kong in 1997 fits these themes. China's system would remain the same, while Hong Kong keeps its own political system with greater freedoms. Chinese leaders see this as a model for the eventual inclusion of Taiwan in a "one country with three systems" policy. Combining their advanced growth with China's, they reason, can move China to the forefront among the world's economies and powers, while still resisting foreign influences that weaken it. How far Hong Kong can move toward full democracy in this process, not to mention China, remains a big question. An even bigger question is whether China has the capacity to expand market integration and a modern economy across its length and breadth.

▓ Pulling Apart

These unifying institutions and ideological strands must counter some broader historical economic and cultural rifts. Those rifts developed traditions of resistance to authority, especially among rural people and inhabitants of outlying cities.

In Chapter 3, Rhoads Murphey pointed to numerous differences between the cultures of north and south China and the conquests of the south by the north. During the seventeenth century, the Manchus, to the northeast of China above Korea (now the eastern part of Inner Mongolia, Heilongjiang, Jilin, and Liaoning; see Map 2.2), crossed the Great Wall to conquer China; their rulers adopted the Confucian system but kept separate administrative units for Manchus. Although they told the Han people they were imposing Confucian customs on people in the periphery, they in fact allowed those peoples much leeway in carrying out their own cultural traditions (Rawski, 1996). In 1911, much support for ending the empire came from southern Chinese who were tired of being ruled by these alien Manchus (see earlier in this chapter, and Chapter 6). Once they took power, they tried to impose their laws and customs more rigidly on those in the periphery, including the Manchus. These peoples have strongly resisted that imposition, seeking to preserve old customs. Rank-and-file Manchus, who now constitute less than 10 percent of the populace in Jilin and Heilongjiang provinces, often failed to adopt Chinese ways. Thousands of Mongols were tortured and killed during the Cultural Revolution on suspicion that they were foreign agents (Friedman, 1995:49, 77).

Chapter 3 also discussed the numerous peasant revolts in China's history. Many began on the Shandong peninsula at the mouth of the Yellow River, just across the Yellow Sea from Korea (Map 2.4). This has given Shandong residents a streak of independence, though they combine it with longer attachment to farming and Confucian values than their neighbors to the north. Other areas developed some independence as well. Over succeeding centuries, the inhabitants of Guangdong, Fujian, and Zhejiang (see Map 2.1) used their access to the sea to develop trading relations with peoples throughout Southeast Asia. Many were pirates, taking advantage of the many islands that dot the south China sea to evade central authorities.

In past centuries, peasants who moved south to escape the poverty of the north became known as Hakkas; Mao and Deng Xiaoping came from Hakka families. Southern inhabitants came to resent these new residents with strange habits and no land; their communities became hotbeds for secret societies and rebel groups. They also added to suspicions between urban and rural folk. During the nineteenth century, Shanghai burgeoned in size as a treaty port; many of its immigrants came from the south. They are surrounded by northern peasants, whose culture is very different (Honig, 1992). Hangzhou, the old capital, speaks dialects left over from the Southern Song dynasty period that are very different from those spoken by rural neighbors. The same is true of cities like Beijing and Tianjin in the north. The natural suspicions that separate city from countryside were enhanced in the 1980s, when housing and incomes were improving faster in rural than in urban areas, and then during the 1990s, when this trend was reversed. Urbanites who have descended from families of intellectuals or merchants, who traditionally did not do manual labor and may have been sent to the countryside for this purpose during the Cultural Revolution, may feel this gulf to an especially great degree. But most important, today's urban growth is leaving rural areas far behind; the resistance there is mounting. If China is to become an integrated modern economy, it must devise new measures to spread prosperity to those areas. It is having great trouble devising such measures. Hu Jintao, China's new leader, has repeatedly pledged to make that quest a high priority.

■ What Will Endure and What Will Change?

China has a long tradition of limited, small-scale capitalism (Gates, 1996). Households produced crops and goods for their own use and to exchange with relatives and neighbors. They could also hire labor to produce surpluses sold in small markets or through brokers. The state taxed and regulated that trade. By combining resources of small producers, brokers could prevent large producers from monopolizing trade. Public officials could regulate the brokers and prevent the large producers from adopting technology they deemed inappropriate for maintaining the rural communities, who are the ideological backbone for Confucian social relations. The introduction of guilds also gave small craftspeople the power to hold back technical innovations that might threaten their jobs. State firms produced some goods needed by other components of the economy. The *baojia* system later allowed for the organization of larger groups of people. Leaders and members of each of these units developed special relationships and exchanged favors to get others to cooperate. The basic social unit, the family, relied on the cooperation of all its members to carry out their obligations in providing labor and distributing output. Even the wealthy accepted the governmental controls that helped keep alive a peaceful and orderly business climate, let them dominate the labor force, maintained the waterways, and operated the marketplaces. They could use their wealth to help their sons become officials and respectable members of the community.

Modern China has been able to draw upon the dynamics of this system and allow the size of some of the enterprises to grow. State firms mining coal, casting steel, building locomotives, or grinding cement often employed hundreds or thousands of workers on one site using simple technology. The parts of bicycles could be produced in thousands of homes or small workshops and then collected for final assembly in a manufacturing plant. State bureaucrats and private middlemen collected crops from small farmers for distribution in urban stores and markets. Families readily grasp opportunities for their members to earn extra income; parents ensure that the members of their household work hard, if need be, to make money. Households are frugal in their expenditures and invest savings in productive activities. They will also spend large amounts of money for weddings, funerals, and special occasions—thus providing work for many small craftspeople.

The new economic reforms in 1978 initially expanded that system further. Joint ventures set up large shop floors where young women at sewing machines produced designer-label shoes, caps, shirts, and dresses. Small assembly lines fit together transistors and other simple components into television sets to be sold as "price leaders" in discount stores around the world. Auto plants built stripped-down versions of prior-model cars. The plants themselves often have scraps lying around and resemble overgrown backyard workshops.

But as modern capitalism makes greater inroads within China, the features of China's society that initially created growth can become impediments to further development. The newest plants, many of them now privately owned by large corporations, are bringing with them the newest technology. Plants in Shanghai's Pudong special economic zone and other of the latest-developed areas are clean and modern; they increasingly need workers with advanced technical skills. These large firms produce economical and tempting products whose design and sophistication make them competitive with goods produced by many of the smaller firms, as well as with inefficient state firms. Indeed, they are wiping out many of these firms and the jobs of many workers. China's entry into the WTO in 2002 accelerates that competition. However, major impediments to such market dominance include the regulations that surround the older forms of capitalist enterprise and a judicial system that still protects the old special arrangements; the government is passing many new laws designed to attack those problems, but the big test will come with implementing them. An even greater impediment to more modern capitalism is the lack of an independent middle class.

The industrial revolution in Europe created a new middle class there separate from the old dominating nobility; the former used political revolution to overthrow the political ascendancy of the latter. In contrast, China's entrepreneurs have not had to free themselves from wealthy landowning families with titles of nobility, whose dominance ended there over 2,000 years ago when the Qin dynasty overthrew the feudal system of the Zhou dynasty (see Chapter 3). Today's business and political leaders have in fact descended from the same social orders who ruled imperial China (and also include in their ranks individuals from the "Red Guard" era, who moved from being peasants to bureaucrats before becoming involved in economic enterprises). The leaders of today's joint ventures have experience as Communist Party cadres devoted to instilling loyalty among the populace and periodically suppressing capitalist pursuits. Starting in 2002, the party and its Central Committee are open to private entrepreneurs, large and small, as well; only 1 of the 350 members of the Central Committee chosen at the 2002 meeting is a private entrepreneur, however. If this is a crossing over from the old to the new economy, it represents a very small and fragile one. Unlike its counterpart in the French Revolution, this China-style middle class brings with it the attitudes of the "old regime," rather than providing a radical alternative to it. Its members are more comfortable with the old capitalism than with the new (Dickenson, 2003). While the distance between China's old and new economy is not as great as Europe's was, it is nonetheless real. The two economies cannot simply blend; they are in competition with one another. Each economy must make concessions to adapt to the other's needs. If the new simply wipes out the old, or one holds back the other, China will not have achieved economic and political integration. And many could be without jobs.

The latest generation of technically trained university graduates are taking jobs in private firms and joint ventures that pay several times what jobs in government and state enterprises offer. This gives them access to the latest consumer goods but not to great amounts of capital. To keep their jobs, they must remain loyal to their firms and the government. Those who venture into cooperatives find the same restraints that held back such enterprises in the traditional system. Many are investing in the stock market, but treacherous fluctuations in its prices make it a risky bet. The leading independent businesspeople are the business leaders in Taiwan and Hong Kong. They know that full political independence for Taiwan would endanger all their business dealings in China, so they offer support to Beijing's government in resisting that (see Chapter 6). Those businesspeople and foreign firms want to introduce enforceable civil law and open exchange of currency. But they recognize the limits on China's ability to extend such reforms even as they push for them. They seldom advocate political reforms beyond that, especially when they threaten political stability.

Fewer than 2 percent of China's youth receive higher education (the government is aggressively expanding the size of university student bodies, but that percentage will rise very slowly), and political activism does not increase one's chances for admission. China's people have been in the habit of obeying those who lead the units to which they belong. They have a long tradition of saying in public what the officials want to hear and reserving their complaints for private conversations; this conforms with the Confucian tradition that correct ritual behavior requires a socially responsible person to publicly support official ideology regardless of what one thinks of it. This tradition is a useful way to keep the public in line, but it is a powerful barrier to the organization of interest groups or to the government's learning what the public really thinks (Link, 1992).

The emperors' Mandate of Heaven was endangered by a breakdown of order and prosperity. Today, both rapid economic growth and potential economic slump threaten those conditions. The inflation, deflation, and other side effects of rapid growth can endanger the economic well-being of many groups. An economic slump would endanger the prosperity of nearly all groups. Either can lead to civil unrest. China must steer a course in between, alternately heating up and cooling down the economy, with constant attention to accommodating the problems of the groups disadvantaged by each swerve. If recent decades are any indicators, it will not always be successful, and then it will seek correction. Those maneuvers, giving waxing and waning influence to different groups and factions, help hold together the political structure and dampen economic excesses.

However, as the modern economy grows it becomes increasingly difficult to keep that process going. It is hard to devise policies that stop the current economic slide and official corruption in the countryside. That provokes resistance. Workers and peasants in Hunan, Jiangxi, Shaanxi, Fujian, Sichuan, and other provinces hold frequent strikes and demonstrations, while Xinjiang has experienced periodic rioting; the Hong Kong Center for Democracy and Human Rights estimated there were 100,000 such actions in 2000, and sources close to Beijing's security establishment said that several million peasants took part (Lam, 2000).

The government meets such activities with large numbers of police and arrest of leaders afterward. Between 1997 and 1998, the number of armed police nearly doubled and a new Office on Maintaining Social Stability was created, which continues to grow. Falun Gong, a group that promotes *qigong* exercises but also recruits people for demonstrations against the government (Madsen, 2000) has been effective in using the Internet to reach large numbers of peasants and workers. The government has responded with a crackdown, arresting members of that group both for demonstrating and for using the Internet to communicate. It has worked with a number of U.S. companies to develop a firewall on the Internet to keep out political content of all sorts the government finds objectionable, and Amnesty International asserts that thirty-three prisoners face trial for using the Internet to transmit information the government deems unsuitable (Lee, 2002; Bodeen, 2002). Many members of unregistered churches (see Chapter 12) have also been arrested. Andrew

Standing guard (top) and marching before
Mao's Tomb (bottom) in Tiananmen Square, 2000

Nathan and Bruce Gilley (2002), citing secret party files, assert that between 1998 and 2001 over 60,000 Chinese were executed, died in custody, or were shot by police while fleeing.

Today's radical economic and social transformation requires radical political transformation as well. To keep up the growth it needs to avoid civil

Chinese tourists at
the entrance to the
Forbidden City, 2000

Robert Gamer

unrest, China must become a major global economic player. It cannot simply be a multiplicity of "Hong Kongs," conjoined or separated, economically dynamic or stagnant, surrounded by a poverty-stricken and hostile country-side. The rural populace has resisted such tendencies in the past, and is even more likely to do so with its modern communication venues and public aware-ness. And without additional innovations in civil law, banking, election processes, and administrative procedures, the cities will not be able to sustain a vibrant role in the world economy.

For the immediate future, most elements of China's society will be seek-ing stable governance. Leaders know that China's security depends on con-tinuing high economic growth and adjusting to the social, economic, and eco-logical problems that growth has produced. This requires political liberalization, somehow suited to China. In 1989, during the brief period of greater press freedom that was brutally suppressed on and after June 4, intel-lectuals talked about the possibilities of a "new authoritarianism" that would be firm but more open to modern society (Gamer, 1994). In 1998 ("Hayek's

Children," 1998), a new debate ensued, focusing on the "civil society" concepts of German thinker Friedrich Hayek (1994)—"spontaneous order" emerging within society from the bottom up rather than through planning by government. By the year 2000 an intense interest in Europe's social democratic parties ensued.

China has 200,000 "mass organizations" registered with the government, representing everything from economic interests to environmental groups. In addition, Matt Forney (1998) believes there may be an equal number of nongovernmental organizations (NGOs) that have failed to register with the government; they shelter abused wives, give physical therapy rehabilitation, network divorcees and homosexuals, help the poor, stand up for women and migrant workers, try to preserve historic homes (Becker, 2001a), help evicted tenants, and provide other educational and philanthropic services. Press reports increasingly focus on bureaucratic corruption and misbehavior, environmental degradation, and other ills, and Zhu Rongji encouraged submission of petitions to the government. Internet usage is expanding rapidly (the number of people online in China, currently 54 million, is likely to surpass the number in the United States by 2006), as is viewership of foreign films and television programs. Two hundred million people have cell phones. Computer-based accounting makes fraud more difficult.

Conceivably, a combination of those innovations and social changes could transform China into a pluralist democracy, but this process would probably take a long time (Zheng, 1998; Zhao, 2002; Nathan, 1990; Friedman, 1995; Friedman and McCormick, 2000). Meanwhile, the government's handling of rural development, unemployment and social services, corruption, village and township elections, investigative reporting, access to the Internet, NGOs, ethnic conflict, and labor and peasant protest will provide clues as to how far liberalization, and China's efforts to remain a leading player in the world economy, can proceed. So will a continuance of Beijing's present policy of refraining from overt interference in Hong Kong's and Taiwan's policy and encouraging enforcement of higher productivity, a modern bureaucracy, responsible banking and stock markets, intellectual property rights, and refined contract and bankruptcy law procedures.

■ **Bibliography**

Alpermann, Bjorn. 2001. "The Post-Election Administration of Chinese Villages." *China Journal* 46 (July): 45–67.

Angle, Stephen C., and Marina Svensson (eds.). 2001. *The Chinese Human Rights Reader: Documents and Commentary, 1900–2000.* Armonk, NY: M. E. Sharpe.

Bachman, David M. 1991. *Bureaucracy, Economy, and Leadership in China: The Institutional Origins of the Great Leap Forward.* New York: Cambridge University Press.

Barnet, A. Doak. 1994. *China's Far West: Four Decades of Change.* Boulder: West-view Press.

Baum, Richard. 1996. *Burying Mao: Chinese Politics in the Age of Deng Xiaoping.* Princeton: Princeton University Press.

Becker, Jasper. 1997. *Hungry Ghosts: Mao's Secret Famine.* New York: Henry Holt.

———. 2001a. "At Vanishing Point." *South China Morning Post,* February 10.

———. 2001b. *The Chinese.* New York: Free Press.

Benewick, Robert, and Stephanie Donald. 1999. *The State of China Atlas.* New York: Penguin.

Benton, Gregor, and Alan Hunter (eds.). 1995. *Wild Lily, Prairie Fire: China's Road to Democracy, Yan'an to Tian'anmen, 1942–1989.* Princeton: Princeton University Press.

Bergere, Marie-Claire. 1998. *Sun Yat-sen.* Trans. Janet Lloyd. Stanford: Stanford University Press.

Bernstein, Thomas P. 2000. "Instability in Rural China?" Pp. 95–111 in David Shambaugh (ed.), *Is China Unstable? Assessing the Factors.* Armonk, NY: M. E. Sharpe.

Bernstein, Thomas P., and Xiaobu Lu. 2000. "Taxation Without Representation: Peasants, the Central and the Local State in Reform China." *China Quarterly* 163 (September): 742–752.

———. 2003. *Taxation Without Representation in Contemporary Rural China.* Cambridge: Cambridge University Press.

Black, George, and Robin Munro. 1993. *Black Hands of Beijing: Lives of Defiance in China's Democracy Movement.* New York: Wiley.

Blecher, Marc, and Vivienne Shue. 1996. *Tethered Deer: Government and Economy in a Chinese County.* Stanford: Stanford University Press.

Bo, Zhiyue. 2002. *Chinese Provincial Leaders: Economic Performance and Political Mobility Since 1949.* Armonk, NY: M. E. Sharpe.

Bodeen, Christopher. 2002. "Rights Group Condemns China's Internet Muzzle." *Seattle Post-Intelligencer,* November 27.

Brook, Timothy, and B. Michael Frolic (eds.). 1997. *Civil Society in China.* Armonk, NY: M. E. Sharpe.

Brugger, Bill, and Stephen Reglar. 1994. *Politics, Economy, and Society in Contemporary China.* Stanford: Stanford University Press.

Cao, Chien-min, and Bruce J. Dickson (eds.). 2001. *Remaking the Chinese State: Strategies, Society, and Security.* London: Routledge.

Chai, Joseph C. H. 1997. *China: Transition to a Market Economy.* Oxford: Clarendon.

Chan, Anita, Benedict J. Tria Kerkvliet, and Jonathan Unger. 1999. *Transforming Asian Socialism: China and Vietnam Compared.* Lanham, MD: Rowman and Littlefield.

Chan, Anita, Richard Madsen, and Jonathan Unger. 1984. *Chen Village: The Recent History of a Peasant Community in Mao's China.* Berkeley: University of California Press.

Chan, Anita, Stanley Rosen, and Jonathan Unger (eds.). 1985. *On Socialist Democracy and the Chinese Legal System: The Li Yizhe Debates.* Armonk, NY: M. E. Sharpe.

Chan, Anita, Richard Madsen, and Jonathan Unger. 1992. *Chen Village Under Mao and Deng.* Expanded and updated. Berkeley: University of California Press.

Chang, Iris. 1997. *The Rape of Nanking: The Forgotten Holocaust of World War II.* New York: HarperCollins.

Chang, Jung. 1991. *Wild Swans: Three Daughters of China.* New York: Simon and Schuster.

Cheek, Timothy, and Tony Saich (eds.). 1997. *New Perspectives on State Socialism in China*. Armonk, NY: M. E. Sharpe.

———. (eds.). 2002. *Mao Zedong and China's Revolutions: A Brief History with Documents*. New York: Palgrave.

Chen, An. 1999. *Restructuring Political Power in China: Alliances and Opposition, 1978–1998*. Boulder: Lynne Rienner.

Chen, Feng. 1995. *Economic Transition and Political Legitimacy in Post-Mao China*. Albany: State University of New York Press.

Cheng, Li. 1997. *Rediscovering China: Dynamics and Dilemmas of Reform*. Lanham, MD: Rowman and Littlefield.

———. 2001. *China's Leaders: The New Generation*. Lanham, MD: Rowman and Littlefield.

Chun, Lin (ed.). 2000. *China*. 3 vols. Burlington, VT: Ashgate.

Dickson, Bruce J. 2003. *Red Capitalists in China: The Party, Private Entrepreneurs, and Prospects for Political Change*. Cambridge: Cambridge University Press.

Dietrich, Craig. 1994. *People's China: A Brief History*. 2nd ed. New York: Oxford University Press.

Dikotter, Frank. 2002. *Crime, Punishment, and the Prison in Modern China, 1895–1949*. New York: Columbia University Press.

Ding, X. L. 1994. *The Decline of Communism in China: Legitimacy Crisis, 1977–1989*. Cambridge: Cambridge University Press.

Ding, Yijiang. 2002. *Chinese Democracy After Tiananmen*. New York: Columbia University Press.

Dittmer, Lowell. 1994. *China Under Reform*. Boulder: Westview Press.

Domenach, Jean-Luc. 1995. *The Origins of the Great Leap Forward: The Case of One Chinese Province*. Boulder: Westview Press.

Dong, Stella. 2001. *Shanghai: The Rise and Fall of a Decadent City, 1842–1949*. New York: HarperPerennial.

Dreyer, June Teufel. 1999. *China's Political System: Modernization and Tradition*. 3rd ed. Boston: Allyn and Bacon.

Duara, Prasenjit. 1988. *Culture, Power, and the State: Rural North China, 1900–1942*. Stanford: Stanford University Press.

Dutton, Michael (ed.). 1999. *Streetlife China*. Cambridge: Cambridge University Press.

Eastman, Lloyd. 1990. *The Nationalist Era in China*. Cambridge: Cambridge University Press.

Edmonds, Richard Louis (ed.). 2000. *The People's Republic of China After Fifty Years*. Oxford: Oxford University Press.

Elvin, Mark. 1973. *The Pattern of the Chinese Past*. Stanford: Stanford University Press.

Eto, Shinkichi, and Harold Z. Schiffrin. 1994. *China's Republican Revolution*. New York: Columbia University Press.

Feigon, Lee. 1999. *China Rising: The Meaning of Tiananmen*. Lanham, MD: Rowman and Littlefield.

Feng, Jicai. 1996. *Ten Years of Madness: Oral Histories of China's Cultural Revolution*. San Francisco: China Books.

Fewsmith, Joseph. 2000. *Elite Politics in Contemporary China*. Armonk, NY: M. E. Sharpe.

———. 2001. *China Since Tiananmen: The Politics of Transition*. Cambridge: Cambridge University Press.

Finkelstein, David M., and Maryanne Kiviehan (eds.). 2002. *Chinese Leadership in the Twenty-First Century.* Armonk, NY: M. E. Sharpe.

Fitzgerald, C. P. 1964. *The Birth of Communist China.* Baltimore: Penguin.

Fitzgerald, John. 1996. *Awakening China: Politics, Culture, and Class in the Nationalist Revolution.* Stanford: Stanford University Press.

Fogel, Joshua A., and Charles S. Maier (eds.). 2000. *The Nanjing Massacre in History and Historiography.* Berkeley: University of California Press.

Fong, Tak-ho. 2002. "Law to Root Out the Corrupt and Unfit Who Sit in Judgment." *South China Morning Post,* January 2.

Forney, Matt. 1998. "Voice of the People." *Far Eastern Economic Review* 161(19) (May 7).

Friedman, Edward. 1995. *National Identity and Democratic Prospects in Socialist China.* Armonk, NY: M. E. Sharpe.

Friedman, Edward, and Barrett L. McCormick (eds.). 2000. *What If China Doesn't Democratize? Implications for War and Peace.* Armonk, NY: M. E. Sharpe.

Friedman, Edward, Paul G. Pickowicz, and Mark Selden. 1991. *Chinese Village, Socialist State.* New Haven: Yale University Press.

Fu, Zhengyuan. 1994. *Autocratic Tradition and Chinese Politics.* Cambridge: Cambridge University Press.

———. 1996. *China's Legalists: The Earliest Totalitarians and Their Art of Ruling.* Armonk, NY: M. E. Sharpe.

Gamer, Robert E. 1989. "From Zig-Zag to Confrontation at Tiananmen: Tradition and Politics in China." *University Field Staff Reports* 10 (November):1–11.

———. 1991. "Helping History Find Its Way: Liberalization in China." *Crossroads: A Socio-Political Journal* (Jerusalem) 32:54–67.

———. 1994. "Modernization and Democracy in China: Samuel P. Huntington and the 'Neo-Authoritarian' Debate." *Asian Journal of Political Science* 2(1) (June):32–63.

———. 1995. "The Changing Political Economy of China." Pp. 187–219 in Manochehr Dorraj and Albert Harris (eds.), *The Changing Political Economy of the Third World.* Boulder: Lynne Rienner.

Gates, Hill. 1996. *China's Motor: A Thousand Years of Petty Capitalism.* Ithaca: Cornell University Press.

Gilley, Bruce. 2001. *Model Rebels: The Rise and Fall of China's Richest Village.* Berkeley: University of California Press.

Goldman, Merle, and Roderick Macfarquhar (eds.). 1999. *The Paradox of China's Post-Mao Reforms.* Cambridge: Harvard University Press.

Goodman, David S. G. 1994. *Deng Xiaoping and the Chinese Revolution: A Political Biography.* London: Routledge.

Goodman, David S. G., and Gerald Segal. 1994. *China Deconstructs: Politics, Trade, and Regionalism.* London: Routledge.

Gordon, Richard, and Carma Hinton. 1995. "The Gate of Heavenly Peace." Brookline, MA: Long Bow Group. Videorecording.

Grasso, June, Jay Corrin, and Michael Kort. 1997. *Modernization and Revolution in China.* Rev. ed. Armonk, NY: M. E. Sharpe.

Grousset, René. 1959. *The Rise and Splendour of the Chinese Empire.* Berkeley: University of California Press.

Hayek, Friedrich A. 1994. *The Road to Serfdom.* Chicago: University of Chicago Press.

"Hayek's Children." 1998. *Far Eastern Economic Review* 161(20) (May 14): 82.

He, Baogang, and Yingjie Guo. 2000. *Nationalism, National Identity, and Democratization in China.* Burlington, VT: Ashgate.

Hershatter, Gail. 1986. *The Workers of Tianjin, 1900–1949.* Stanford: Stanford University Press.

Hinton, William. 1970. *Iron Oxen: A Documentary of Revolution in Chinese Farming.* New York: Vintage.

———. 1997. *Fanshen: A Documentary of Revolution in a Chinese Village.* Berkeley: University of California Press.

Honda, Katsuichi. 1999. *The Nanjing Massacre: A Japanese Journalist Confronts Japan's National Shame.* Armonk, NY: M. E. Sharpe.

Honig, Emily. 1986. *Women in the Shanghai Cotton Mills, 1919–1949.* Stanford: Stanford University Press.

———. 1992. *Creating Chinese Ethnicity: Subei People in Shanghai, 1850–1980.* New Haven: Yale University Press.

Hook, Brian. 1997. *The Individual and the State in China.* Oxford: Oxford University Press.

Hu, Shaohua. 2000. *Explaining Chinese Democratization.* Westport, CT: Praeger.

Hua, Shiping. 2001. *Chinese Political Culture, 1989–2000.* Armonk, NY: M. E. Sharpe.

Huang, Jing. 2000. *Factionalism in Chinese Communist Politics.* Cambridge: Cambridge University Press.

Huang, Philip C. C. 1985. *The Peasant Economy and Social Change in North China.* Stanford: Stanford University Press.

———. 1990. *The Peasant Family and Rural Development in the Yangzi Delta, 1350–1988.* Stanford: Stanford University Press.

———. 1997. *Civil Justice in China: Representation and Practice in the Qing.* Stanford: Stanford University Press.

Huang, Ray. 1996. *China: A Macro History.* Armonk, NY: M. E. Sharpe.

Huang, Shu-min. 1989. *The Spiral Road: Change in a Chinese Village Through the Eyes of a Communist Party Leader.* Boulder: Westview Press.

Hutzler, Charles. 2002. "Winding Road to Reform." *Far Eastern Economic Review* 165(35) (September 5): 28–31.

Itoh, Fumio (ed.). 1997. *China in the Twenty-First Century: Politics, Economy, and Society.* Washington, DC: Brookings Institution.

Jennings, Kent. 1997. "Political Participation in the Chinese Countryside." *American Political Science Review* 91(2) (June): 361–373.

Jiang, Xuebin. 2002. "Stealing the Land." *Far Eastern Economic Review* 165(5) (February 7): 56–59.

Jun, Jing. 1997. *The Temple of Memories: History, Power, and Morality in a Chinese Village.* Stanford: Stanford University Press.

Karnow, Stanley. 1972. *Mao and China: From Revolution to Revolution.* New York: Vintage.

Kelliher, Daniel. 1997. "The Chinese Debates over Villager Self-Government." *China Journal* 37 (January): 63–86.

Kennedy, John. 2002. "The Face of 'Grassroots Democracy' in Rural China: Real Versus Cosmetic Elections." *Asian Survey* 42(3) (May–June): 456–482.

Kent, Ann E. 1994. *Between Freedom and Subsistence: China and Human Rights.* New York: Oxford University Press.

King, Ambrose Y. C. 1991. "Kuan-hsi and Network Building: A Sociological Interpretation." *Daedalus* (spring): 63–83.

Kipnis, Andrew B. 1997. *Producing Guanxi: Sentiment, Self, and Subculture in a North China Village.* Chapel Hill, NC: Duke University Press.

Kristof, Nicholas, and Sheryl WuDunn. 1994. *China Wakes: The Struggle for the Soul of a Rising Power.* New York: Random House.

Kwong, Julia. 1997. *The Political Economy of Corruption in China.* Armonk, NY: M. E. Sharpe.

Lam, Willy Wo-Lap. 2000. "A Matter of Window Dressing." *South China Morning Post,* September 6.

Lardy, Nicholas. 2002. *Integrating China into the Global Economy.* Washington, DC: Brookings Institution.

Lawrance, Alan. 1998. *China Under Communism.* London: Routledge.

Lee, David. 2002. "Multinationals Making a Mint from China's Great Firewall." *South China Morning Post,* October 2.

Li, Lianjiang. 1999. "The Two-Ballot System in Shanxi Province: Subjecting Village Party Secretaries to a Popular Vote." *China Journal* 42:103–118.

———. 2001. "Elections and Popular Resistance in Contemporary China." *China Information* 15(2):1–19.

———. 2002. "The Politics of Introducing Direct Township Elections in China." *China Quarterly* 171 (September): 704–723.

Li, Lianjiang, and Kevin J. O'Brien. 1996. "Villagers and Popular Resistance in Contemporary China." *Modern China* 22(1) (January): 28–61.

Li, Zhisui. 1994. *The Private Life of Chairman Mao: The Inside Story of the Man Who Made Modern China.* London: Chatto and Windus.

Lieberthal, Kenneth. 1997. *Governing China: From Revolution Through Reform.* New York: Norton.

Lieberthal, Kenneth, and Michel Oksenberg (eds.). 1988. *Policy Making in China: Leaders, Structures, and Processes.* Princeton: Princeton University Press.

Lin, Nan. 1992. *The Struggle for Tiananmen: Anatomy of the 1989 Mass Movement.* New York: Praeger.

Link, E. Perry, Jr. 1992. *Evening Chats in Beijing: Probing China's Predicament.* New York: W. W. Norton.

Liu, Alan P. 1996. *Mass Politics in the People's Republic: State and Society in Contemporary China.* Boulder: Westview Press.

Liu, Binyan, Ruan Ming, and Xu Gang. 1989. *"Tell the World": What Happened in China and Why.* Trans. Henry Epstein. New York: Pantheon Books.

Liu, Melinda. 2002. "Party Time in Beijing." *Newsweek,* November 25.

Liu, Xin. 2000. *In One's Own Shadow: An Ethnographic Account of the Condition of Post-Reform Rural China.* Berkeley: University of California Press.

Lu, Xiaobo. 2000. *Cadres and Corruption: The Organizational Involution of the Chinese Communist Party.* Cambridge: Cambridge University Press.

Lubman, Stanley B. 2001. *Legal Reform in China After Mao.* Stanford: Stanford University Press.

Lupher, Mark. 1996. *Power Restructuring in China and Russia.* Boulder: Westview Press.

Lyons, Thomas P. 1994. *Poverty and Growth in a South China County: Anxi, Fujian, 1949–1992.* Ithaca: Cornell University Press.

Lyons, Thomas P., and Victor Need (eds.). 1994. *The Economic Transformation of South China: Reform and Development in the Post-Mao Era.* Ithaca: Cornell University Press.

Ma, Stephen K. 1996. *Administrative Reform in Post-Mao China: Efficiency or Ethics?* Lanham, MD: University Press of America.

Macfarquhar, Roderick. 1974. *The Origins of the Cultural Revolution: Contradictions Among the People, 1956–1957.* Vol. 1. New York: Columbia University Press.
———. 1983. *The Origins of the Cultural Revolution: The Great Leap Forward, 1958–1960.* Vol. 2. New York: Columbia University Press.
——— (ed.). 1997. *The Politics of China: The Eras of Mao and Deng.* 2nd ed. Cambridge: Cambridge University Press.
———. 1999. *The Origins of the Cultural Revolution: The Coming of the Cataclysm, 1961–1966.* New York: Columbia University Press.
Madsen, Richard. 2000. "Understanding Falun Gong." *Current History* 99(638) (September): 243–247.
Manion, Melanie. 1996. "The Electoral Connection in the Chinese Countryside." *American Political Science Review* 90(4) (December): 736–748.
Mengin, Françoise, and Jean-Louis Rocca (eds.). 2002. *Politics in China: Moving Frontiers.* New York: Palgrave.
Misra, Kalpana. 1998. *From Post-Maoism to Post-Marxism: The Erosion of Official Ideology in Deng's China.* London: Routledge.
Mitamura, Taisuke. 1970. *Chinese Eunuchs: The Structure of Intimate Politics.* Rutland, VT: Charles E. Tuttle.
Miyazaki, Ichisada. 1981. *China's Examination Hell: The Civil Service Examinations in Imperial China.* New Haven: Yale University Press.
Mulvenon, James Charles. 2000. *Soldiers of Fortune: The Rise and Fall of the Chinese Military-Business Complex, 1978–1998.* Santa Monica, CA: RAND.
Nathan, Andrew J. 1990. *China's Crisis: Dilemmas of Reform and Prospects for Democracy.* New York: Columbia University Press.
———. 1998. *China's Transition.* New York: Columbia University Press.
Nathan, Andrew J., and Bruce Gilley. 2002. *China's New Rulers: The Secret Files.* New York: New York Review of Books.
Nathan, Andrew J., Zhaohui Hong, and Steven R. Smith (eds.). 1999. *Dilemmas of Reform in Jiang Zemin's China.* Boulder: Lynne Rienner.
O'Brien, Kevin J. 2001. "Villagers, Elections, and Citizenship in Contemporary China." *Modern China* 27(4) (October): 407–436.
O'Brien, Kevin J., and Lianjiang Li. 1995. "The Politics of Lodging Complaints in Rural China." *China Quarterly* 143 (September): 756–783.
———. 2000. "Accommodating 'Democracy' in a One-Party State: Introducing Village Elections in China." *China Quarterly* 162 (June): 465–489.
Ogden, Suzanne, Kathleen Hartford, Lawrence Sullivan, and David Zweig (eds.). 1991. *China's Search for Democracy: The Student and Mass Movement of 1989.* Armonk, NY: M. E. Sharpe.
Oi, Jean C. 1989. "Market Reforms and Corruption in Rural China." *Studies in Comparative Communism* 22 (summer–autumn): 221–233.
———. 1991. *State and Peasant in Contemporary China: The Political Economy of Village Government.* Berkeley: University of California Press.
———. 1995. "The Role of the Local State in China's Transitional Economy." *China Quarterly* 144 (December): 1132–1150.
———. 1999. *Rural China Takes Off: Institutional Foundations of Economic Reform.* Berkeley: University of California Press.
Oi, Jean C., and Scott Rozelle. 2000. "Elections and Power: The Locus of Decision-Making in Chinese Villages." *China Quarterly* 162 (June): 513–542.
Park, Nancy E. 1997. "Corruption in Eighteenth-Century China." *Journal of Asian Studies* 56(4) (November): 967–1005.

Pastor, Robert, and Qingshan Tan. 2000. "The Meaning of China's Village Elections." *China Quarterly* 162 (June): 490–512.

Peerenboom, Randall. 2002. *China's Long March Toward Rule of Law.* Cambridge: Cambridge University Press.

Pepper, Suzanne. 1999. *Civil War in China: The Political Struggle, 1945–1949.* 2nd ed. Lanham, MD: Rowman and Littlefield.

Perry, Elizabeth J. 1993. *Shanghai on Strike: The Politics of Chinese Labor.* Stanford: Stanford University Press.

———. 2001. *Challenging the Mandate of Heaven: Social Protest and State Power in China.* Armonk, NY: M. E. Sharpe.

Perry, Elizabeth J., and Xun Li. 1996. *Proletarian Power: Shanghai in the Cultural Revolution.* Boulder: Westview Press.

Perry, Elizabeth J., and Mark Selden (eds.). 2000. *Chinese Society: Change, Conflict, and Resistance.* London: Routledge.

Phillips, Richard T. 1996. *China Since 1911.* New York: St. Martin's Press.

Pomfret, John. 2002. "Bringing Revolution to China's Villages." *Washington Post,* September 15.

Radchnevsky, Paul. 1993. *Genghis Khan: His Life and Legacy.* London: Blackwell.

Rawski, Evelyn S. 1996. "Reenvisioning the Qing: The Significance of the Qing Period in Chinese History." *Journal of Asian Studies* 55(4) (November): 829–850.

Rosemarin, Arno (ed.). 2001. *China Human Development Report 2001/2002: Transition and the State.* Oxford: Oxford University Press.

Rowe, William T. 1989. *Hankow: Conflict and Community in a Chinese City, 1796–1895.* Stanford: Stanford University Press.

Ruwitch, John. 2002. "China Reshuffle Brings in Military Young Blood." Reuters, November 20.

Saich, Tony. 2000. "Negotiating the State: The Development of Social Organizations in China." *China Quarterly* 161 (March): 124–141.

———. 2001. *Governance and Politics of China.* New York: Palgrave.

Saich, Tony, and Hans van de Ven (eds.). 1997. *New Perspectives on the Chinese Communist Revolution.*

Sargeson, Sally, and Jian Zhang. 1999. "Reassessing the Role of the Local State: A Case Study of Local Government Interventions in Property Rights Reform in a Hangzhou District." *China Journal* 42 (July): 77–99.

Schoenhals, Michael (ed.). 1996. *China's Cultural Revolution, 1966–1969: Not a Dinner Party.* Armonk, NY: M. E. Sharpe.

Schram, Stuart. 1966. *Mao Tse-Tung.* New York: Simon and Schuster.

Seagrave, Sterling. 1987. *The Soong Dynasty.* New York: HarperPerennial.

———. 1995. *Lords of the Rim: The Invisible Empire of the Overseas Chinese.* New York: G. P. Putnam.

Seybolt, Peter J. 1996. *"Throwing the Emperor from His Horse": Portrait of a Village Leader in China, 1923–1995.* Boulder: Westview Press.

Seymour, James D., and Richard Anderson. 1998. *New Ghosts, Old Ghosts: Prisons and Labor Reform Camps in China.* Armonk, NY: M. E. Sharpe.

Shambaugh, David. 1995. *Deng Xiaoping: Portrait of a Chinese Statesman.* Oxford: Oxford University Press.

——— (ed.). 2000a. *Is China Unstable? Assessing the Factors.* Armonk, NY: M. E. Sharpe.

——— (ed.). 2000b. *The Modern Chinese State.* Cambridge: Cambridge University Press.

Shaw, Victor. 1996. *Social Control in China: A Study of Chinese Work Units.* Westport, CT: Praeger.

Shi, Tianjian. 1997. *Political Participation in Beijing.* Cambridge: Harvard University Press.

———. 1999. "Economic Development and Village Elections in Rural China." *Journal of Contemporary China* 8(22) (November): 425–442.

Shirk, Susan. 1993. *The Political Logic of Economic Reform in China.* Berkeley: University of California Press.

Shue, Vivienne. 1988. *The Reach of the State: Sketches of the Chinese Body Politic.* Stanford: Stanford University Press.

Siu, Helen F. 1999. *Agents and Victims in South China: Accomplices in Rural Revolution.* New Haven: Yale University Press.

Snow, Edgar. 1938. *Red Star over China.* New York: Random House.

Soled, Debra E. (ed.). 1995. *China: A Nation in Transition.* Washington, DC: Congressional Quarterly.

Spence, Jonathan. 1999. *The Search for Modern China.* 2nd ed. New York: W. W. Norton.

———. 2000. *Mao Zedong.* New York: Penguin.

Stranahan, Patricia. 1998. *Underground: The Shanghai Communist Party and the Politics of Survival, 1927–1937.* Lanham, MD: Rowman and Littlefield.

Sullivan, Lawrence R. (ed.). 1995. *China Since Tiananmen: Political, Economic, and Social Conflicts.* Armonk, NY: M. E. Sharpe.

Svensson, Marina. 2002. *Debating Human Rights in China: A Conceptual and Political History.* Lanham, MD: Rowman and Littlefield.

Teiwes, Frederick C. 1993. *Politics and Purges in China: Rectification and the Decline of Party Norms, 1950–1965.* Armonk, NY: M. E. Sharpe.

Terrill, Ross. 1992. *China in Our Time: The Epic Saga of the People's Republic, from the Communist Victory to Tiananmen Square and Beyond.* New York: Simon and Schuster.

———. 1997. *Madame Mao: The White-Boned Demon.* Rev. ed. Stanford: Stanford University Press.

———. 1999. *Mao: A Biography.* Rev. ed. Stanford: Stanford University Press.

Thaxton, Ralph A., Jr. 1997. *Salt of the Earth: The Political Origins of Peasant Protest and Communist Revolution in China.* Berkeley: University of California Press.

Thomas, Bernard S. 1996. *Season of High Adventure: Edgar Snow in China.* Berkeley: University of California Press.

Tien, Hung-mao, and Yun-han Chu. 2000. *China Under Jiang Zemin.* Boulder: Lynne Rienner.

Tong, Yanqi. 1997. *Transitions from State Socialism: Economic and Political Change in China and Hungary.* Lanham, MD: Rowman and Littlefield.

Tsai, Lily Lee. 2002. "Cadres, Temple and Lineage Institutions, and Governance in Rural China." *China Journal* 48 (July): 1–27.

Tyson, James, Jr., and Ann Scott Tyson. 1995. *Chinese Awakenings: Life Stories from the Unofficial China.* Boulder: Westview Press.

Unger, Jonathan (ed.). 1991. *The Pro-Democracy Protests in China: Reports from the Provinces.* Armonk, NY: M. E. Sharpe.

——— (ed.). 1996. *Chinese Nationalism.* Armonk, NY: M. E. Sharpe.

——— (ed.). 2002a. *The Nature of Chinese Politics: From Mao to Jiang.* Armonk, NY: M. E. Sharpe.

———. 2002b. *The Transformation of Rural China.* Armonk, NY: M. E. Sharpe.

Unger, Jonathan, and Anita Chan. 1999. "Inheritors of the Boom: Private Enterprise and the Role of Local Government in a Rural South China Township." *China Journal* 42 (July): 45–74.

Vermeer, Eduard B., Frank N. Pike, and W. L. Cheng (eds.). 1998. *Cooperative and Collective in China's Rural Development: Between State and Private Interests.* Armonk, NY: M. E. Sharpe.

Wakeman, Frederick, and Richard Louis Edmonds (eds.). 2000. *Reappraising Republican China.* Oxford: Oxford University Press.

Walder, Andrew George. 1986. *Communist Neo-Traditionalism: Work and Authority in Chinese Industry.* Berkeley: University of California Press.

———— (ed.). 1995. *The Waning of the Communist State: Economic Origins of Political Decline in China and Hungary.* Berkeley: University of California Press.

———— (ed.). 1998. *Zouping in Transition: The Process of Reform in Rural North China.* Cambridge: Harvard University Press.

Wang, Gungwu, and John Wang (eds.). 1999. *China: Two Decades of Reform and Change.* Singapore: World Scientific and Singapore University Press.

Wang, Gungwu, and Zheng Yongnian (eds.). 2001. *Reform, Legitimacy, and Dilemmas: China's Politics and Society.* Singapore: World Scientific.

Wang, James C. F. 2001. *Contemporary Chinese Politics: An Introduction.* 7th ed. Englewood Cliffs: Prentice Hall.

Wang, Shaoguang. 1995. *Failure of Charisma: The Cultural Revolution in Wuhan.* Oxford: Oxford University Press.

Wang, Shaoguang, Hu Angang, and Ding Yuanzhu. 2002. "Behind China's Wealth Gap." *South China Morning Post,* October 31.

Wank, David L. 1999. *Commodifying Communism: Business, Trust, and Politics in a Chinese City.* Cambridge: Cambridge University Press.

Wasserstrom, Jeffrey N., and Elizabeth Perry (eds.). 1994. *Popular Protest and Political Culture in Modern China.* 2nd ed. Boulder: Westview Press.

Wedeman, Andrew H. 2003. *From Mao to Market: Rent Seeking, Local Protectionism, and Marketization in China.* Cambridge: Cambridge University Press.

Wei, Julie Lee, Ramon H. Myers, and Donald G. Gillin. 1994. *Prescriptions for Saving China: Selected Writings of Sun Yat-sen.* Stanford: Hoover Institution Press.

Wei, Pan. 1998. *The Politics of Marketization in Rural China.* Lanham, MD: Rowman and Littlefield.

White, Gordon, Hsiao-yuan Shang, Shang Xiaoyuan, Howell Xiaoyuan White, and Jude A. Howell. 1997. *In Search of Civil Society: Market Reform and Social Change in Contemporary China.* Oxford: Oxford University Press.

White, Lynn T., III. 1989. *Policies of Chaos: The Organizational Causes of Violence in China's Cultural Revolution.* Princeton: Princeton University Press.

————. 1998 and 1999. *Unstately Power: Local Causes of China's Intellectual, Legal, and Governmental Reforms.* Vols. 1–2. Armonk, NY: M. E. Sharpe.

White, Tyrene (ed.). 2000. *China Briefing 2000: The Continuing Transformation.* Armonk, NY: M. E. Sharpe.

Winckler, Edwin A. 1999. *Transition from Communism in China: Institutional and Comparative Analysis.* Boulder: Lynne Rienner.

Wood, Alan T. 1995. *Limits to Autocracy: From Sung Neo-Confucianism to a Doctrine of Political Rights.* Honolulu: University of Hawaii Press.

World Bank. 2001. *World Development Indicators 2001.* Washington, DC: World Bank.

Wright, Mary C. (ed.). 1971. *China in Revolution: The First Phase, 1900–1913.* New Haven: Yale University Press.

Wright, Teresa. 2001. *The Perils of Protests: State Repression and Student Activism in China and Taiwan.* Honolulu: University of Hawaii Press.

Yan, Jiaqi, and Gao Gao. 1996. *Turbulent Decade: A History of the Cultural Revolution.* Trans. D. W. Y. Kwok. Honolulu: University of Hawaii Press.

Yan, Yunxiang. 1996. *The Flow of Gifts: Reciprocity and Social Networks in a Chinese Village.* Stanford: Stanford University Press.

Yang, Benjamin. 1997. *Deng: A Political Biography.* Armonk, NY: M. E. Sharpe.

Yang, Dali L. 1996. *Calamity and Reform in China: State, Rural Society, and Institutional Change Since the Great Leap Famine.* Stanford: Stanford University Press.

Yang, Mayfair Mei-hui. 1994. *Gifts, Favors, and Banquets: The Art of Social Relationships in China.* Ithaca: Cornell University Press.

Yang, Xiguang. 1997. *Captive Spirits: Prisoners of the Cultural Revolution.* Oxford: Oxford University Press.

Yuan, Gao. 1987. *Born Red: A Chronicle of the Cultural Revolution.* Stanford: Stanford University Press.

Zhang, Kaiyuan (ed.). 2000. *Eyewitness Accounts of the Nanjing Massacre: American Missionaries Bear Witness to Japanese Atrocities.* Armonk, NY: M. E. Sharpe.

Zhang, Liang, Andrew J. Nathan, and Perry Link (eds.). 2001. *The Tiananman Papers: The Chinese Leadership's Decision to Use Force Against Their Own People.* New York: PublicAffairs.

Zhang, Wei-wei. 1996. *Ideology and Economic Reform Under Deng Xiaoping, 1978–1993.* New York: Columbia University.

———. 2000. *Transforming China: Economic Reform and Its Political Implications.* New York: St. Martin's Press.

Zhao, Dingzin. 2001. *The Power of Tiananmen: State-Society Relations and the 1989 Student Movement.* Chicago: University Press of Chicago.

Zhao, Hongwei. 2002. *Political Regime of Contemporary China.* Lanham, MD: University Press of America.

Zhao, Suisheng (ed.). 2000. *China and Democracy: Reconsidering the Prospects for a Democratic China.* London: Routledge.

Zheng, Shiping. 1997. *Party vs. State in Post-1949 China: The Institutional Dilemma.* Cambridge: Cambridge University Press.

Zheng, Yongnian. 1998. "Will China Become More Democratic? A Realistic View of China's Democratisation." Pp. 167–190 in Wang Gungwu and John Wong (eds.), *China's Political Economy.* Singapore: University of Singapore Press.

Zhong, Yang, and Jie Chen. 2002. "To Vote or Not to Vote: An Analysis of Peasants' Participation in Chinese Village Elections." *Comparative Political Studies* 35(6) (August): 686–712.

5

China's Economy

John Wong

Prior chapters have referred to the amazing speed at which China's economy has been growing. It is now time to explore in greater detail the extent of that growth, what has led up to it, and whether it can be expected to continue. The easiest way to comprehend the full extent of this phenomenon is to look at several sets of rather dramatic numbers. Then we shall briefly examine China's economic history and look at some of the problems facing its economy.

■ China's Dynamic Growth in Perspective

The Chinese economy has experienced spectacular growth since it started economic reform and its open-door policy some twenty years ago. Real growth during 1979–2000 was at an annual rate of 9.6 percent. The 1997 Asian financial crisis brought down many Asian economies. China's economy, however, was hardly affected; it continued to grow at 8.8 percent in 1997 and 7.8 percent in 1998. More recently, while economic growth in most of Asia was falling to low or negative growth and the world economy at large crept into recession, China's economy alone was still steaming ahead with strong growth. In 2001, China still chalked up 7.3 percent growth (see Figure 5.1). Growth for 2002 was 7.5 percent.[1]

China's economy is much less affected by the global economic downturn, mainly because of its large size and population: about 80 percent of its growth is generated by domestic demand. However, this does not mean that external demand (i.e., exports of goods and services) is not important for China's economic growth. In fact, China's economy is becoming more dependent for its

Figure 5.1 China's Economic Growth, 1978–2002

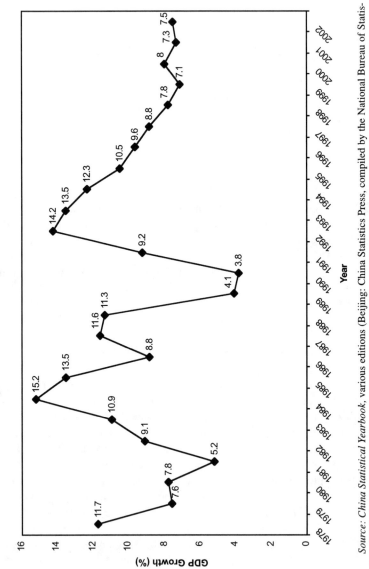

Source: China Statistical Yearbook, various editions (Beijing: China Statistics Press, compiled by the National Bureau of Statistics of China).

growth on exports, which have been growing at an annual rate of 15 percent (or more than twice the world average) for the past two decades, from U.S.$9.8 billion in 1978 to U.S.$326 billion in 2002 (see Figure 5.2). By 2002, China became the world's sixth largest exporting nation. While many Asian economies currently find their exports plunging, China's export machine is still going fairly strong, up by 22 percent by 2002. Exports as a source of growth for the Chinese economy are far more important than its nominal share of 20 percent because of the higher multiplier effect of the export sector.

As a result of its rapid export growth, China's export structure has experienced far-reaching changes over the past two decades. When China embarked on its open-door policy in 1978, primary commodities (i.e., agricultural products and natural resources such as coal and petroleum) constituted 55 percent of its total exports. In 2001, manufactured products made up 90 percent of China's total exports, reflecting China's extensive industrialization progress.[2] Even more dramatically, the export structure has undergone another radical transformation. In the early 1990s, China's exports were dominated by labor-intensive manufactured products, particularly textiles, clothing, footwear, and toys. In the second half of the 1990s, these traditional labor-intensive manufactures were overtaken by nontraditional items like electronics and machinery, whose share in total exports rose to 42 percent in 2000. In other words, along with China's successful industrial upgrading, Chinese exports today are no longer confined to low-technology and low value-added products.[3]

For foreign direct investment (FDI), China has become the world's most-favored destination among all developing countries for foreign capital since 1993 (Wong, 2001). From 1988 to 2001, as shown in Figure 5.3, China's realized FDI grew at an average rate of 30 percent per annum; and by the end of 2002 the accumulated FDI in China reached a total of U.S.$446 billion. In recent years, China has regularly captured about half of all FDI in Asia, in addition to around 20 percent for Hong Kong, which will eventually end up in China (see Figure 5.4). In fact, 80 percent of the world's 500 companies have now set up their businesses in China.[4] As a result of such a large influx of FDI, coupled with its persistent trade surplus, China's foreign exchange reserves by mid-2002 stood at the staggering level of U.S.$250 billion, the world's second largest after Japan. At the same time, China's foreign debt by the end of 2001 amounted to only U.S.$150 billion, with 80 percent of it being long-term debt. Among all the former socialist economies ("transitional economies"), China arguably has the strongest external balance so much so that in recent years the Chinese *renminbi* (the "people's currency"), despite its fixed exchange rate regime, is under pressure to appreciate.

Economic growth means increases in gross domestic product (GDP) and it works like compounding interest rates. When an economy grows at 7 per-

Figure 5.2 China's Exports, 1980–2001

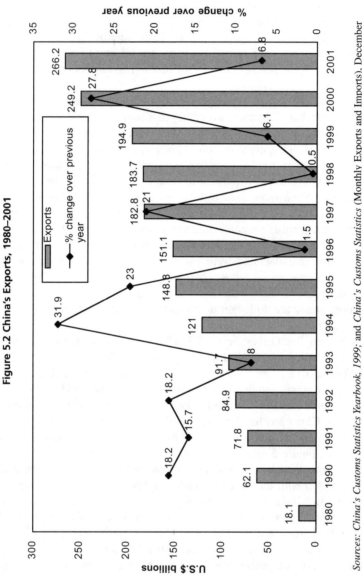

Sources: China's Customs Statistics Yearbook, 1999; and China's Customs Statistics (Monthly Exports and Imports), December 2000 and March 2002 issues.

Figure 5.3 China's Foreign Direct Investment, 1988–2001

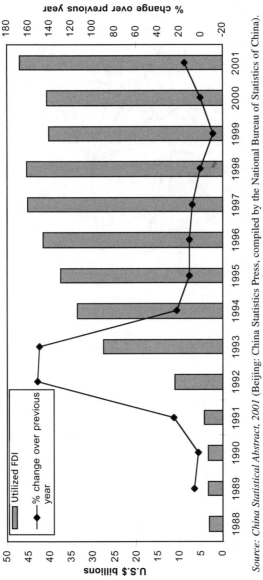

Source: China Statistical Abstract, 2001 (Beijing: China Statistics Press, compiled by the National Bureau of Statistics of China).
Note: In 2001, China's official FDI intake was a record total of U.S.$47 billion.

Figure 5.4   Regional Distribution of FDI, 1998 and 2002

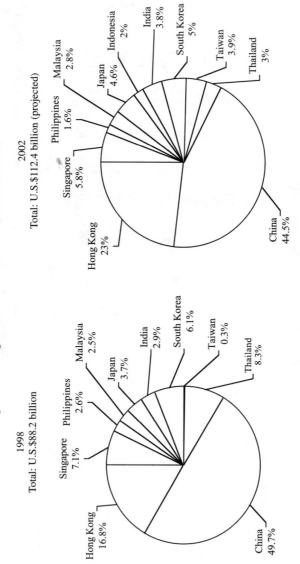

1998
Total: U.S.$88.2 billion

Singapore
7.1%
Philippines
2.6%
Malaysia
2.5%
Japan
3.7%
India
2.9%
South Korea
6.1%
Taiwan
0.3%
Thailand
8.3%
Hong Kong
16.8%
China
49.7%

2002
Total: U.S.$112.4 billion (projected)

Malaysia
2.8%
Indonesia
2%
Japan
4.6%
India
3.8%
South Korea
5%
Taiwan
3.9%
Thailand
3%
Philippines
1.6%
Singapore
5.8%
Hong Kong
23%
China
44.5%

Source: Economic Intelligence Unit, "Business China," April 2002.

cent, it doubles its GDP in ten years. As a result of sustained high economic growth, China's nominal GDP increased from 362 billion yuan in 1978 (when it started economic reform) to 9,435 billion yuan in 2001.[5] In all, China's total GDP in 2001 translated into U.S.$1.1 trillion, ranking China the world's seventh largest economy. In terms of purchasing power parity (PPP), the Chinese economy in 1999 was the world's second largest after the United States—one needs, of course, to be aware of the problem of overstating China's real GDP by the PPP measure.[6]

However, China's current per capita GNP, at about just U.S.$900, remains low on account of its large population base. There is considerable variation of per capita GNP among provinces and cities. As can be expected, the more developed and the more open provinces and cities along its coast have per capita incomes above the national average while those in the interior and the western region have per capita incomes below the average national level. Specifically, the per capita incomes of Shenzhen, Guangzhou, Shanghai, and Beijing, ranging between U.S.$4,000 and U.S.$5,000, reach the level of what the World Bank has classified as upper-middle-income economies.

Beyond the rise in GDP, China's high rates of economic growth are clearly reflected in its industrial statistics. In 2001, China's manufacturing sector accounted for 45 percent of its total GDP, a proportion that is much higher than the average for the developing world. Accordingly, China in 2001 was able to produce 1,107 million tons of coal, 153 million tons of steel, 40 million color television sets, 13.5 million refrigerators, 23 million air-conditioners, 25 million cell phones, 7.5 million personal computers, and 2.3 million automobiles.[7] Indeed, as a result of its rapid industrialization progress, China is fast becoming the world's foremost manufacturing base. In 2001, China passed the United States as the world's largest mobile phone market. China is also overtaking Japan as Asia's largest manufacturer of personal computers.[8] By the end of 2002, China's registered Internet users had exceeded 59 million to become the world's second largest "Web population."[9]

Not surprisingly, the meteoric rise of China's economy has suddenly become a hot topic in international and regional media. It has also become a real concern to many Asian countries.[10] Many commentators saw the emergence of China to be a disruptive force for the Asian economies. In particular, Japan has grown increasingly apprehensive about the rise of China as a manufacturing powerhouse.[11] As shown in Figure 5.5, by the end of 2001, about one in two of the world's motorcycles, one in three of the world's air-conditioners, and one in four of the world's color televisions were manufactured in China.

On the other hand, a number of Western journalists and scholars take issue with Chinese official statistics, arguing that the official numbers are grossly inaccurate and therefore exaggerate China's economic performance.[12] Interestingly, this Western argument stands in sharp contrast to the "China's

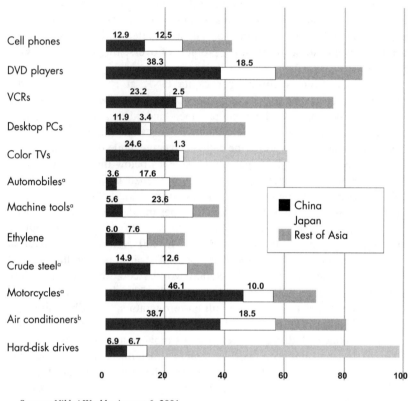

Figure 5.5   China's Shares of World Production of
Key Commodities, 2001 (percentage)

Source: Nikkei Weekly, August 6, 2001.
Notes: a. 2000.
b. 1999.

economic threat" thesis, which is circulating in Japan and other Asian countries. When pushed to its extreme, the Western thesis culminates in the recent popular book *The Coming Collapse of China* (2001) by the American Chinese lawyer Gordon Chang, which brings out every possible negative façade of China's development.

How reliable are official Chinese statistics? Every modern China scholar has to confront this important question, just as every Sovietologist had to do for the former Soviet Union. During the Cold War period it was commonly believed that because governments of the communist countries were prone to control information and use official statistics for propaganda purposes, their numbers should not be trusted. Technically speaking, central planning involves setting targets for enterprises to fulfill, and thereby puts pressure on the underperforming production units to make false reports.

In the case of China, public confidence in its official statistics had indeed been dented by official revelations of exaggerated reports of falsified figures by local authorities, especially during the Great Leap Forward period in the late 1950s.[13] Nonetheless, for five decades since the formation of the People's Republic, successive generations of China scholars, after their consistency checks, have found no evidence that Beijing has ever deliberately fabricated statistical information. Official mendacity is simply impossible because (1) it is technically and politically difficult for any government to systematically manufacture false economic and social statistics on a large scale, year after year (for consistency); (2) deliberate falsification of official statistics would entail the mammoth administrative complications of keeping two or more separate sets of books all the way from the central down to local levels; and (3) many economic data such as wages and prices cannot be faked, as they can be easily checked by people based on their own personal experience, while other data like foreign trade and foreign investment involve foreign countries.[14]

With the emergence of the "socialist market economy," China's National Bureau of Statistics (NBS) is under no political and ideological pressures to produce inflated numbers. In fact, as the Chinese government is becoming more technocratic, it demands for itself more accurate figures from the NBS for effective macroeconomic management. Since under the market system Chinese enterprises are no longer made to fulfill production targets, there is also no incentive for enterprise managers to exaggerate output figures— which will actually lead to higher taxes on their enterprises. Furthermore, the NBS today has become a modern organization, run by professionals and employing modern methodologies (e.g., undertaking frequent sample surveys as counterchecks) and up-to-date computation and communication facilities (e.g., using fax and Internet technologies for reporting) (Wong, 2001b).

All this does not mean that Chinese official statistics are automatically accurate. Quality remains a major issue, due to the deficiencies in the data compilation, mainly caused by underqualified statistical officers at the local levels. In a sense, Chinese statistics should be no better or no worse than those from other large developing economies like India and Indonesia. In China, market reform has brought about a different form of statistical abuse. Some enterprises underreport output and profits to evade taxes while others hide their losses for different reasons. Also for different reasons, some underreport imports while others overreport exports. But these kinds of "statistical abuses" do not constitute a real problem as long as the authorities do not countenance such practices. In principle, the mathematical law of large numbers can normally take care of such discrepancies, with overreporting being balanced by underreporting so that the final macroeconomic data at the national level are not compromised by local irregularities. This explains why international organizations and most China scholars have continued to use official figures, particularly those related to trade, investment, and GDP. Some even argue that in view of the existence of a large underground economy and widespread activities of smuggling and capital flight, China's official GDP figures, if anything, actually tend to underestimate rather than overestimate the true size of its economy.

However, the controversy was rekindled by a recent study by China scholar Thomas Rawski, who observed that increases in China's GDP and industrial production since 1998 were negatively correlated with a decline in energy use. He therefore took the view that the actual GDP growth for China could range from negative numbers in 1998 to 2–3 percent growth in 2000— a far cry from the official growth figures of 7–8 percent growth (Rawski, 2001). Rawski's argument was soon widely picked up by Western media because of its sensational nature.

A number of Chinese scholars and official statisticians have since refuted Rawski's argument as being "groundless."[15] Chinese economists argue that with the growth of the service sector in China and the shift of its industrial structure from the previous smoke-stacked heavy industries to light and high-tech industries, it would be unrealistic for Rawski to expect any close correlation between growth in industrial production and growth in energy consumption. In most industrial economies, economic growth is actually accompanied by a decline in energy consumption. As shown earlier, the growth industries in China in recent years are the light and high-tech industries such as electronics and electrical machinery, which are not energy intensive. There should be no permanent causal relationship between GDP growth and energy consumption.[16]

Economics Nobel Laureate Lawrence Klein and his associate, employing a more comprehensive test of the relations between China's GDP and fifteen other major indicators (not just energy, but also electricity, grain, steel, freight, civil aviation, long-distance phone, and so on) for the entire period of 1980–2000, confirm that the movements of these major economic components "are consistent with the movements of real GDP as officially estimated." Klein has qualified that their study has not "proved" the Chinese official GDP measure correct, as no one knows the "correct estimate."[17] But this is sufficient to discount Rawski's simplistic argument.

The "China Collapse" school serves a useful function in highlighting the many structural problems that the Chinese economy is presently confronted with. But China's dynamic economy is not about to easily collapse as its distracters might wish. China today is a fairly open country, which in 2001 received 11 million foreign tourists (in addition to 73 million visits—some daily—from ethnic Chinese in Hong Kong and Taiwan) and allowed 12 million of its own citizens to tour overseas. Any foreign tourist can see for him- or herself the hectic economic activities, including the incessant construction of roads, skyscrapers, and houses, not just in big cities like Shanghai and

Guangzhou, but also in numerous regional cities formerly classified as rural county towns. A tourist can also see the massive industrial sprawl, along with the smog and suffocating traffic congestion, not just in the Pearl River Delta and the Yangtze Delta, but also in many other locations (Lyons and Need, 1994; Marton, 2000). Certainly all this does not add up to the kind of 3–4 percent low-growth economy as suggested by Rawski.

In fact, China's high economic growth of the past two decades as reflected in its official GDP statistics, though very impressive, is actually not exceptional in the historical context of many high-performance East Asian economies. As shown in Table 5.1, Japan had double-digit rates of growth in the 1960s. The four newly industrialized economies (NIEs) of South Korea, Taiwan, Hong Kong, and Singapore had similar high growth for more than three decades, the 1960s through the 1980s, while several economies of the Association of Southeast Asian Nations (ASEAN) also experienced high growth performance in the 1970s and the 1980s.

China is a much larger country than its East Asian neighbors. China should have much more internal dynamics to sustain an even longer period of high growth, as China has virtually a whole continent to develop for itself. Empirically speaking, the skeptical views of China's economy by Rawski and others are therefore not consistent with the historical experiences of other East Asian economies.

■ China's Presocialist Traditional Mixed Economy

China's economy has long involved, and eluded, state planning. From the earliest dynasties, it has centered around agriculture (Chao, 1987; Kamachi, 1990; Perdue, 1987). Already during the Qin and Han dynasties (see Table 3.1), feudalism, with serfs working the land of nobles, came to an end. Until the Song dynasty, however, large landowners controlled much of the land, expecting their tenants to furnish them with labor and loyalty; this dominance receded slowly in later centuries (see Elvin, 1973). The land produced little surplus; much of this went to enrich landowners and public officials and pay taxes. Agricultural workers were also required to devote long hours in forced corvée labor to fulfill their tax obligations to the state. The state created large factories, mines, franchises, and monopolies to produce and distribute salt, porcelain, armaments, bricks, timber, coal, gold, and copper (Wagner, 2002). Periodically, reforming emperors would attempt to redistribute land or regulate interest rates; those reforms were short-lived. Merchants bought and sold goods largely for sale to public officials and wealthy landowners (Lufrano, 1997; Shiba, 1969; Mann, 1987).

The introduction of two and three crops of rice a year during the Song dynasty, made possible by new rice strains from Southeast Asia, enabled

Table 5.1 China's Economic Performance Indicators in East Asian Context

	Population (millions) 2000	GNP per Capita (U.S.$) 2000	PPP Estimates of GNP per Capita (U.S.$) 2000	Growth of GDP (%)								Annual Export Growth (%), 1990–2000	Manu-facturing Exports as % of Total Exports, 1999	Exports as % of GDP, 2000
				1960–1970	1970–1980	1980–1990	1990–2000	1998	1999	2000	2001			
China	1261	840	3,940	5.2	5.5	10.1	10.3	7.8	7.1	8.0	7.3	15.6	88	26
Japan	127	34,210	26,460	10.9	4.3	4.0	1.3	-1.1	0.8	1.5	-0.4	4.6	94	10.8
NIEs														
South Korea	47	8,910	17,340	8.6	10.1	9.4	5.7	-6.7	10.9	9.3	3.0	16	91	45
Taiwan	22	14,188	n.a.	9.2	9.7	7.9	6.3	4.6	5.4	5.9	-1.9	7.9	n.a.	55
Hong Kong	7	25,950	25,660	10.0	9.3	6.9	4.0	-5.3	3.0	10.5	0.1	8.4	95	150[a]
Singapore	4	24,740	24,970	8.8	8.3	6.6	7.8	0.3	6.9	10.3	-2.0	11.2	86	179[a]
ASEAN-4														
Indonesia	210	570	2,840	3.9	7.2	6.1	4.2	-13.2	0.9	4.8	3.3	5.4	54	39
Malaysia	23	3,380	8,360	6.5	7.9	5.3	7.0	-7.4	6.1	8.3	0.4	12	80	125[a]
Philippines	76	1,040	4,220	5.1	6.0	1.0	3.3	-0.6	3.4	4.0	3.4	7.3	41	56
Thailand	61	2,010	6,330	8.4	7.1	7.6	4.2	-10.8	4.4	4.6	1.8	9.5	74	66

Sources: World Bank, *World Development Report 2000/2001*, *World Development Report 2002*; World Bank website, www.worldbank.org/data; *World Bank Half-Yearly Report on East Asia*, April 2002; Taiwan Ministry of Economic Affairs, www.moea.gov.tw; *Asian Development Outlook 2002*; *EIU DataServices*; *Statistical Yearbook of the Republic of China*, 2001.

Notes: GDP growth rates from 1998–2001 extracted from *Asian Development Outlook 2002*. Per capita GNP figure for Taiwan from *Statistical Yearbook of the Republic of China*, 2001. Average annual GDP figures for Taiwan from 1980–1990 and 1990–2000 from *Statistical Yearbook of ROC*, 2001. GDP growth rates for Japan from 1998–2001 represent real GDP growth rates. Average annual export growth for Singapore calculated from data provided by *EIU*; that of Taiwan from Ministry of Economic Affairs website.

a. Includes entrepôt re-exports of goods produced elsewhere.

China to support a much larger population and paved the way for major economic and social changes. Gradually the large estates gave way to smaller owner-occupied plots suitable for intensive agricultural cultivation. Greater agricultural surpluses allowed for an expanded market economy (see Shiba, 1969). Already during the Song, a fifth of China's population had moved to towns and cities, which began to produce a great variety of household products on which ordinary people came to depend (see Ma Rong's discussion in Chapter 8, and Chao, 1987:56; Shiba, 1969). Many such goods were produced by family groups who regulated sales and set up apprenticeships open to new residents. In the countryside, large numbers of agricultural families sent some of their members to work in cottage industries producing silk, cotton, and other textiles.

The state issued franchises to brokers, who were authorized to witness all wholesale transactions in agricultural commodities, cotton, and silk. This allowed them to ensure that prices were not fixed by large extended families who came to control such trade in their regions and that proper taxes were paid. These brokers, the holders of franchises for state monopolies, and the public officials to whom taxes were paid, were in a position to accumulate wealth along with the many new merchants and heads of extended agricultural families. They formed a market for a growing array of luxury consumer goods. They could use their surplus capital to extend credit at high interest rates or to run pawnshops, but they failed to invest in new technologies that would spur an industrial revolution. Much of the capital was distributed among merchants and officials as *renqing*—special favors to fulfill the reciprocal obligations owed to family, officials, and special friends (see Chapters 4 and 12). As a result, life did not improve for most members of the populace.

Northern China had been under control of the Mongols since the tenth century; they had reduced a portion of the rural populace there to virtual serfs living on the estates of Mongol nobles. Under Kublai Khan (see Chapter 3), they tried to extend this system southward. By the seventeenth century, large landowning lineages were running their own schools and charities and keeping much (though gradually declining portions) of the rural populace tied to the land as virtual serfs (Elvin, 1973:235–267; Kamachi, 1990; Huang, 1985:85–87; Naquin, 1987:146). But private urban businesses kept growing, still within a controlled atmosphere (Gates, 1996; Deng, 1999; Redding, 1990). Artisans in state-directed, guild-controlled small workshops produced an array of consumer goods. They defended themselves against excessive demands from officials and fixed wages and prices (see Rowe, 1989; Fewsmith, 1983). Nicholas Kristof and Sheryl WuDunn (1994:321) cite evidence that they also discouraged the introduction of inventions that might displace their jobs. Pawnshops and brokers extended loans and credit. As Manchu conquerors founded the Qing dynasty, they kept the Confucian system in place but added an important new social and political resource, the *baojia* system.

All households were grouped together under the supervision of a headperson, who reported their activities to the authorities and organized them for activities like building dikes. All members of a *bao* were responsible if one of their members committed a criminal activity.

During the nineteenth century, the Europeans built modern infrastructure in China's treaty ports, which in turn led to the establishment of some modern factories. But this did not spark off the industrial revolution. Modern factories were too few, and some actually had the effect of disrupting the rural economy. Peasants started to leave farms to work in coastal factories for low pay. Cheap new factory-made textiles competed with textiles made in villages and thus depressed local economies (Rowe, 1984; Honig, 1986; Bell, 1999; Feuerwerker, 1996b). Regions came under control of warlords who siphoned off taxes from the new enterprises for their own use. Clan leaders and absentee landlords often sold goods outside their regions, where they could get higher prices. Whole regions were increasingly ravaged by warfare, often paid for by high taxes on agriculture (Prazniak, 1999). The state granaries, established during the Song dynasty (Will, 1991) to provide peasants with grain during times of hardship, as well as irrigation facilities, waterways, and other public services, were often not maintained. Soil exhaustion, erosion, deforestation, floods, and droughts added to the problems (Perkins, 1969; Perdue, 1987). The new republic established in 1911 tried to address these problems but, as Robert Gamer discussed in Chapter 4, found it hard to take back control from regional warlords and foreign powers and in addition found itself confronting Japanese invaders.

After the 1934 Long March, Mao Zedong led his dwindling communist forces to establish a small base in Yenan in the arid region of China's northwest. The Japanese invasion of China touched off a strong nationalism, which provided Mao a good opportunity to recoup and expand. Mao promised land to the peasants and he carried out land reform in areas occupied by the communist forces. In effect, this enabled Mao to enlist the support of the peasant masses, to fight first the Japanese invaders and subsequently the Kuomintang. After the Japanese surrender, the urban areas occupied by the Kuomintang were suffering from strikes, social unrest, hyperinflation, and desperate shortages of agricultural and manufactured goods. Such economic and social instability hastened the demise of the Kuomintang regime.

■ From Revolution to Reform

When Mao Zedong formally declared the formation of the People's Republic of China on October 1, 1949, he found himself taking over an economy poorly adapted to modernization and much ravaged by a long period of war and internal strife. In the cities, his first order of business was to bring down high inflation and reestablish production and distribution of manufactured goods (for a clear introduction to this period, see Spence, 1999:473–480; and Eckstein, 1977). He set in place a disciplined bureaucracy and fiscal measures that curbed inflation, and he worked with factory owners whose plants he had seized to start up production. In 1953, as the economy had completed this stage of rehabilitation, the government launched the First Five-Year Plan (FFYP), which was a typical replica of the Soviet industrialization strategy under Joseph Stalin, putting strong emphasis on the development of some key capital-intensive industries like iron and steel, railroad trains, and agricultural equipment. Large state-owned industries were created throughout China to manufacture these, employing large numbers of workers who would be housed and offered social services and lifetime employment by their employers (guarantees now dubbed the "iron rice bowl") (Frazier, 2002).

The FFYP was a great success, with the economy growing at the average annual rate of 8.5 percent during the plan period. But Mao was unhappy. He saw inherent "contradictions" in the Soviet development strategy, which was biased against small industry and labor-intensive technology as well as rural development. In Mao's view, the Soviet development strategy was fundamentally at odds with China's basic development conditions and resource endowment, because China had started off as a much more backward economy with a huge population and a lower level of technological development.

Hence Mao started to experiment with his own developmental model. In the rural areas, after land reform, he organized the peasants first into small production teams and agricultural cooperatives, and then collectives. Subsequently, he transformed the collectives into the people's communes (Eckstein, 1977:66–76; Rawski, 1972; Wong, 1973). The height of this collectivization came during the Great Leap Forward in 1958–1960, which called for a simultaneous development of both agriculture and industry, both small and large industry—what Mao propagandists called "walking on two legs." The "people's communes" mobilized peasants en masse for large-scale capital construction projects like building dams and irrigation systems as well as making iron and steel by native methods (the so-called backyard furnaces). Not just wasteful of resources, these mass activities also resulted in a serious neglect of farming and cultivation (Tiewes and Sun, 1998; Yong, 1996).

The Great Leap Forward collapsed in 1959 with disastrous economic consequences, particularly a dive in agricultural production and widespread food shortages in the countryside (Chang, Madsen, and Unger, 1984; Tiewes and Sun, 1998; Yang, 1996). The other party leaders tried to return to more traditional production methods, making industrial goods in factories and producing food on collectivized farms, but Mao was undaunted and unconvinced. As Chapter 4 explained, in 1966 he tried again by starting the Great Proletarian Cultural Revolution, which he also used as a means of getting rid of his dissenting senior party colleagues, who were considered to be revisionist.

Thus, millions of students were organized as Red Guards to attack the country's power structures, including government and party establishments. Virtually all senior party leaders except Zhou Enlai had been attacked or were purged at one time or another by the Red Guards. The excesses of the Cultural Revolution are now made known to the public for the first time.

Unlike the Great Leap Forward, the Cultural Revolution was primarily political in nature. In the economic arena, it merely emphasized certain ideological attributes in the overall economic development strategy such as "self-reliance," "ideology and politics to take precedence over economics," or "ideological incentive to be a substitute for material incentive." Consequently, the Cultural Revolution brought much less direct disruption to economic production, particularly in the rural areas, though it resulted in long-term economic damage to government administration and factory management as well as the country's education system (Riskin, 1987).

However, the Cultural Revolution did leave behind at least one positive legacy. Many old guards, like Deng Xiaoping, emerged from this nightmare to finally realize that political and social stability is most crucial to economic development, whereas incessant class struggle and ideological contention were inimical to economic growth. Thus, when Deng finally regained power, he was determined to open a new chapter in China's modern economic history, which he did by launching economic reform and the open-door policy in December 1978 (Wong, 1993).

■ Successful Transition to a Market Economy

China's transition to the market system since the late 1970s has been immensely successful, especially compared to the dismal performance of the economic reform programs of the former Soviet Union and Eastern European countries. Numerous books and articles have been written about the different reform experiences of China and Eastern Europe.[18] Most discussion is focused on the gradual and incremental strategy adopted by China, versus the "Big Bang" approach in Eastern Europe, where major political and economic reforms were initiated side by side. It has also been argued that the initial conditions on the eve of their respective reforms were much more favorable for China than for Russia or other Eastern European countries; China was less industrialized, its economy was much less tightly planned, and its people had a long history of individual entrepreneurship (Woo, 1996; Wu, 1994; McCormick and Unger, 1995; Wank, 1999; Lin, Cai, and Li, 2001).

In a more concrete sense, the Chinese success was the product of its unique reform strategies, which were carried out with great flexibility ("taking two steps forward and—if in trouble—one step back") and great pragmatism. (Deng's well-known adage is, "It does not matter if the color of the cat is black or white so long as she can catch mice.") It can also be argued that China's past reform success owes a great deal to its entrepreneurial style, as opposed to the largely bureaucratic reform process characteristic of the Eastern European approach (Wong, 1995b; Sheff, 2002; Cheung, 2002; Liu, 2001; Skoggard, 1996; Tsai, 2002).

From the start, Chinese reformers recognized that there would be no textbooks to teach them how to go about "unplanning" a socialist economy. China's reform process was therefore open-ended, not accompanied by any detailed plans or complicated blueprints. Since reforming a socialist economy inevitably involves a great deal of risk and uncertainty, the best strategy for Chinese reformers was to grope their way around with a gradual trial-and-error approach and then to exploit opportunity for reform breakthroughs, much like true entrepreneurs making their business decisions.

Furthermore, China owed its smooth progress to the right sequencing of reform policies to suit its economic and institutional conditions. Thus China chose to start with agricultural reform first, by instituting the "household responsibility system" (Garnaut, Shutian, and Guonan, 1996; Kelliher, 1992; Zweig, 1997; Lyons, 1994; Oi, 1999). The communes returned the control of land to the townships, which in turn leased it to community members (see Oi, 1989b:155–226; Zhou, 1996). They would initially sell a portion of their crops to state marketing agencies, which in turn sold basic grains and oils to urban dwellers at much lower prices (with the government subsidizing the difference). The rest they could sell privately in farmers' markets. For the first time in decades, Chinese peasants had the incentive to produce more. The reform impact was almost immediate: a rapid growth of agricultural productivity and rural incomes. This in turn led to the mushrooming of township and village enterprises (TVEs), which soon became the driving force for China's economic growth (see Yabuki and Harner, 1999; Zhou, 1996; Wei, 1998; Yang, 1996; Wong, Ma, and Yang, 1995; Gore, 1999; Vermeer, Pieke, and Chong, 1997; White, 1998). These unique nonstate businesses created new jobs, provided many cheap consumer products to meet the rising demand, and contributed to regional development. By the late 1990s the TVEs had accomplished their development objectives, and thus most were subsequently privatized.

In retrospect, the Chinese reform strategy based on trial and error had worked well in the initial phases. But many critical macroeconomic reform measures like taxation, banking, finance, and foreign exchange did not effectively lend themselves to the gradualist approach by experimentation (Chen, Dietrich, and Fang, 1999; Deyo, Doner, Hershberg, 2001; Kim, 2000; Young, 1995; Wang and Hu, 2001; Tam, 1995; Oi and Walder, 1999). All these reform measures are interrelated, and they have to be dealt with in one blow rather than the piecemeal strategy of the earlier phase. The recognition of this fact

A young worker in a village plastic factory

actually paved the way for the Third Party Plenum in November 1993 to adopt the fifty-article "Decision" for a comprehensive reform of China's economic structure, which is, in a way, the Chinese equivalent of the "Big Bang" approach to economic reform (Yabuki, 1995:235–237).

Overall, in putting economic liberalization ahead of political liberalization and phasing in reform changes gradually, China was better able to interface political changes with economic reform. Basically, China has followed closely the East Asian tradition of "economic growth first and political changes later" (for an overview of this approach, see Wade, 1990). Successful economic reform is used to boost the legitimacy of the political leadership, which is in turn under strong pressures to achieve good economic performance. In contrast, Russia put *glasnost* (political reform) before *perestroika* (economic reform). As a result, its vital reform measures were delayed and often bogged down by politics and polemics.

Since the Eighth National People's Congress in March 1993, China has officially become a "socialist market economy," which is conceptually devoid of meaning or just as contradictory as the journalistic term "red capitalism." But such semantics are rather insignificant. China's "socialist market economy" increasingly looks like a conventional mixed economy; government controls big industries while leaving many light and consumer-oriented economic activities to a competitive marketplace. In 1994 the prices of over 90 percent of China's consumer goods, 80 percent of raw materials, and 79 percent of agricultural produce were no longer fixed by the state but set by market forces.[19] This, along with the rapid decline of the state sector, has actually rendered the Chinese economy more and more capitalistic in operation.

When Deng started economic reform in the late 1970s (Ash and Kueh, 1996), state-owned industry accounted for over 70 percent of China's gross industrial output; by 2000 the proportion came down to only 24 percent, with the state ownership mainly confined to the large strategic industries. In terms of operational units, by the end of 1999 state enterprises accounted for 9.7 percent, collective enterprises (i.e., TVEs) 23.5 percent, private *(siying)* and individual *(getihu)* enterprises 21.9 percent, shareholder enterprises 32.5 percent, and others 12.4 percent (Guiheux, 2002).

It is not so much the relative decline of the state sector but rather the rapid expansion of the private sector in the Chinese economy that is the most important. For ideological reasons, "privately managed" enterprises *(siying qiye)* first appeared in the party document only in 1987. The Thirteenth Party Congress in October 1987 recognized the need to encourage the development of the private economy in order to supplement the growth of the state sector. It was only after the Fourteenth Party Congress in 1992 (which adopted the "socialist market economy") that the private economy in China was able to develop and expand freely without political hindrances. In September 1997, at the Fifteenth Party Congress, private enterprises were formally legitimized as an "important element" of China's socialist economy, and this was subsequently written into the modified constitution in 1999. At the eightieth anniversary celebration of the Chinese Communist Party (CCP) on July 1, 2001, Jiang Zemin went a step further by calling on the party to admit into its ranks capitalists ("outstanding elements" of society such as private entrepreneurs, professionals, technical and managerial personnel from nonstate firms and multinational corporations [MNCs]). Jiang's move to embrace capitalists partly represents his efforts to strengthen the party by ensuring that it can adapt itself to changing economic and social needs (see Chapter 4). It is also partly designed to leave his own ideological legacies (based on his "Three Represents") to the younger fourth-generation leaders under Hu Jintao (Wong and Zheng, 2001). Thus, in his keynote address at the Sixteenth Party Congress on November 8, 2002, Jiang urged all ranking party members to "keep pace with the times" by embracing his new theory of Three Represents for broadening the social base of the party by admitting the capitalists.[20] In short, China has politically and economically gone a long way in developing its own brand of "socialism" (Guthrie, 2002; Hamilton, 2002; Ikels, 1996; Lin, 2000; Sheff, 2002; Brodsgaard and Young, 2001).

Back in October 1995, the Fifth Plenary Session of the Fourteenth Central Committee of the Chinese Communist Party adopted the Ninth Five-Year Plan (1996–2000) and the Long-Term Vision of China's Economic and Social Development for 2010. It was envisaged that China's real per capita GNP (total economic output divided by the number of people) by the year 2000 would have quadrupled from the 1980 level, despite the addition of over 300 million more people. China would then have reached the moderately affluent *(xiao-kang)* level of development, for having basically eliminated poverty and satisfied the basic needs of its people (see Wong, 1998b; Yabuki, 1995:229–235). From 2000 to 2010, China expects to double its per capita income so that within fifteen years it will have developed into a moderately affluent middle-income economy.[21] At the Sixteenth Party Congress in November 2002, Jiang Zemin reiterated that "China would concentrate on building a well-off society (i.e., *xiao-kang*) of a higher standard in an all-round way in the first 20 years of this century." [22] This means that China's 2000 GDP would be doubled and doubled again by 2020.

Traditionally, a five-year plan has been regarded as an integral part of a command communist economy. With the growth of the market since economic reform, the Chinese economy is no longer taking to mandatory central planning. This is very much evidenced by the grossly reduced economic role of the government over the years (Lin, 2002; Leong, 1998). The share of government expenditure declined from 32 percent of GDP in 1979 to 19 percent in 2001; and the proportion of industrial production from the state sector similarly declined from 73 percent to 24 percent.[23] This, along with the inevitable uncertainty that accompanies an increasingly market-oriented Chinese economy, has rendered central planning irrelevant. At best, a five-year plan is to serve only as a kind of "perspective plan," or as a rough indicator of government policy direction. The last few five-year plans have already functioned much like indicative plans as found in other mixed economies. One would not be surprised if China's current Tenth Five-Year Plan (2000–2005) could well be the last one launched by the CCP.

■ **Is High Growth Sustainable?**

It is sufficiently clear that China has become the world's most successful "transitional economy" in terms of both dynamic growth and the reform of its economic systems. The next question can then be posed: Is China's dynamic economic growth sustainable?

Following four consecutive years of double-digit rates of growth during 1992–1995, the Chinese economy became overheated, with inflation (measured by the consumer price index) rising to a 27 percent record high in 1994 and then down to 14.8 percent in mid-1995. In 1995, Premier Zhu Rongji, dubbed China's "economic czar," was charged with the task of bringing down the rampant inflation. Zhu introduced a number of tough macroeconomic stabilization measures, including a credit squeeze and the reimposition of control on prices of certain essential commodities. By November 1997, inflation was brought down to 1.1 percent, with only a small reduction in economic growth, which was still 9 percent for 1997 (Wong, 1997a). In common economic parlance, the Chinese economy achieved a "soft landing."

However, since the middle of 1997 (when many Southeast Asian economies were struck by the Asian financial crisis; see Garran, 1998) deflation started to set in, lasting to 2001. As can be seen from Figure 5.1, China's economic growth rates have been sliding down from the peak of 14.2 percent in 1992 to just 7.3 percent in 2001. This calls to question if China's past high economic growth is coming to an end. True, economic downturn had hit other Southeast Asian economies even more severely, with their economic growth plunging to even lower levels. In the case of China, the government had to counter the sluggish domestic consumption demand by artificially priming the economy with a vigorous program of domestic fixed investment. Can one still take China's high growth for granted?

It may be noted that even before the reform, the Chinese economy still grew at a rather fast rate of 5.7 percent (during 1952–1978), despite all its

Carrying merchandise to a retail store in Xiamen

Robert Gamer

inherent socialist economic inefficiencies and the disruptions caused by Mao's numerous political campaigns.[24] The reform has set free the latent dynamic economic and social forces to fuel China's further economic growth. This expansion can be easily analyzed from both demand and supply sides.

To give a technical explanation, China's high economic growth on the demand side stems from its high levels of domestic investment, which are matched by equally high levels of domestic savings. According to the World Bank, China's gross domestic investment during 1990–1999 grew at 12.8 percent per year, and this gave rise to GDP growth of 10.7 percent per year for the same period. In 1999, China's gross domestic savings as a proportion of its GDP was 42 percent while its gross domestic investment was 40 percent. Thus, China's domestic investment and domestic savings levels are among the highest in the world.[25] High investment and high savings creates what may be called the "virtuous circle of growth": high savings, high investment, high export growth, high GDP growth, and then high savings. It provides the simplest explanation of the arithmetic of China's high economic growth. The past high growth of Hong Kong, Taiwan, South Korea, and Singapore was similarly due to their high levels of savings and investment (Brodsgaard and Young, 2001; Deyo, Doner, and Hershberg, 2001).

Still very much a developing economy, China certainly has enormous need for infrastructural investment in transportation, communications, ports, airports, and power plants. Figure 5.3 captures the major sources of China's growth for the period 1988–2001. External demand comes from exports, which play a relatively minor role in China's economic growth. For domestic demand, fixed investment is most crucial for the early period. During the heady years of double-digit rates of growth in the early 1990s, fixed asset investment increased by 50–60 percent a year. In recent years, however, China's economic growth has become less investment-driven while exports and personal consumption are becoming increasingly more important. However, the government still depends critically on fixed investment as the main lever to stimulate economic growth when exports and domestic consumption come down.

Apart from fixed investment, China still has a lot of room for increasing domestic consumption as a source of its future growth, particularly in the rural areas and small towns, where millions of peasants are in need of basic household consumer durables like televisions, refrigerators, and cell phones. In the more developed coastal region, economic affluence has created a burgeoning middle class, whose consumption of those basic consumer durables has by and large been satisfied. However, the affluent urban middle class are now shifting their consumption patterns toward residential housing, household goods, and automobiles, which can be a new source of consumption demand growth (Davis, 1999; Robison and Goodman, 1996). Apart from the consumption of goods, demand for services such as education and vacation has also been fast rising in recent years. The government has in fact actively promoted domestic tourism by encouraging people to take extended leave for the Chinese New Year (February), Labor Day (May), and National Day (October) periods in order to boost the so-called holiday economy. Total domestic tourists rose from 524 million in 1994 to 784 million in 2001.[26]

In the long run, the Chinese economy has to grow mainly by relying on domestic demand (i.e., both personal consumption and fixed investment), quite unlike its smaller Asian neighbors, whose economic growth can be mainly propelled by export growth or external demand. Since economic reform began in 1978, as mentioned earlier, China's exports have been growing at the average annual rate of 15 percent, and this provides additional impetus for China's economic growth. However, the world market simply cannot continue to absorb such a massive onslaught of manufactured goods from China. It is therefore fortunate for China that its sheer size and diversity can provide sufficient internal dynamics to generate its own growth in the long run.

Viewed from the supply side, China's economic growth can also be sustained on its own by a growing labor force and increasing productivity. As has happened to Japan and South Korea before, growth in productivity is associated with the shift of labor from low-productivity agriculture to high-productivity manufacturing. In China, the rural sector is a huge reservoir of millions of underemployed laborers (commonly known among economists as "rural disguised unemployment"), which can be a source of economic growth for a long time to come.

The key element on the supply side of economic growth lies in productivity growth. Clearly, continuing high economic growth cannot be sustained by just dumping more and more capital (i.e., more fixed investment) into an increasingly large labor force. What is more crucial to the process of sustained economic growth is the condition of technological progress resulting from the acquisition of knowledge. Such is the "endogenous growth theory," which emphasizes improvement in productivity through investment in human capital.

Paul Krugman has argued that East Asian growth has been based exclusively on the accumulation of capital per worker rather than increases in output per worker, that is, productivity growth. Accordingly, he argued that East Asian growth could be a flawed strategy of growth without total factor productivity (TFP)—the amount of measured overall growth that cannot be explained by such factors as capital or labor—and would eventually bring about a collapse in growth as in the former Soviet Union (Krugman, 1994). His observation has since stirred up a lively debate among economists and commentators. Several researchers have since argued that Krugman has exaggerated the TFP problem of East Asia, and that many East Asian economies have in fact experienced real TFP growth.[27]

Productivity or technological progress is admittedly a nebulous concept, which is also empirically difficult to measure or quantify. In the case of China, for instance, its high growth during the last twenty years has indeed been accompanied by substantial productivity gains. In accounting for China's 9.4 percent growth between 1978 and 1995, the World Bank has identified 8.8 percent (elasticity: 0.4) for physical capital growth, 2.7 percent (elasticity: 0.3) for human capital growth measured by years of education per worker, and 2.4 percent (elasticity: 0.3) for labor force increases, leaving the unexplained share of growth at 46 percent. This means that of China's 9.4 percent GDP growth, 4.3 percent is the unexplained residue, which is unusually large, compared to South Korea and Japan for the appropriate periods. A substantial part of the residual portion could be the TFP, which was generated from economic reform and the open-door policy.[28] In other words, China's high growth for the past two decades has actually been sustained by a productivity boom.

The argument runs as follows. High savings and high investment alone would not have generated such sustained high growth for China. Operating under socialist planning before 1978, China also had relatively high savings and high investment by controlling consumption. But China's average annual growth during 1952–1978 was only 5.7 percent, which was achieved with gross inefficiency coupled with a great deal of fluctuation. After 1978, with the introduction of economic reform and the open-door policy, China's economy started to take off by consistently chalking up near double-digit rates of growth. Economic reform, by introducing market forces to economic decisionmaking, had brought about greater allocative efficiency. The open-door policy, by reintegrating China into the global economy, had also exposed China to greater external competitive pressures. Hence higher TFP for China.[29]

All in all, we can be justifiably optimistic about the overall growth prospects of China's economy over the medium and long run. The Chinese economy is in many ways developing in a manner similar to the past growth pattern of the other high-performance East Asian economies. But unlike them, China is a vast country with a huge resource base and a huge domestic market. At present, most growth has been concentrated on the coastal region, which stood to gain the most from Deng's open-door policy. China's new frontiers of growth can come from its interior.

The turning point in the strategy came in 1999. Faced with overinvestment and overproduction in the coastal region, Chinese policymakers realized the need to spread development into the country's less developed interior so as to cultivate new sources of economic growth. The western region, comprising the ten provinces of Xinjiang, Gansu, Qinghai, Ningxia, Shaanxi, Tibet, Sichuan, Yunnan, Guizhou, and Chongqing, occupies 57 percent of China's total area, but accounts for only 23 percent of China's total population and about only 15 percent of China's total GDP. Furthermore, the whole western region in 1999 absorbed only 12 percent of the country's total domestic investment and 3 percent of the country's total FDI.[30] Clearly economic development has bypassed the western region. Viewed from a different angle, the western region provides new growth opportunities.

In January 2000, the State Council set up a high-level interministerial Western Development Committee, headed by Premier Zhu Rongji. The committee is charged with the mission of planning long-term development strategies to guide China's western development over the next fifteen years. The involvement of Premier Zhu underscores China's determination to develop its western region as China's new frontier for future development.[31] Clearly, it will take a long time for China to exhaust its total development potential.

■ Overcoming Problems and Constraints

▒ Human Resource Development

The favorable progrowth scenario described previously has to be qualified by two considerations. First, China's population growth has been slowing down considerably from the average natural growth rate of 1.5 percent during 1980–1990 to 0.9 percent in 1999 as a result of the successful implementation of its "one-child policy" (discussed in Chapter 8). Accordingly, China's total fertility rate came down from 2.5 in 1980 to 1.7 in recent years, which is well below the replacement level of fertility (Wong, 2002). This also means that China's population is not just slowing down in growth but could eventually reach zero growth after a certain time lag. But before this, the population will become rapidly aging, during the first decade of the twenty-first century. This will change its labor force structure and pose an ultimate constraint on industrial development in the longer run.

Second, as shown in Table 5.2, China's human resource development is among the weakest in East Asia. China's adult illiteracy in 1999 stood at 16.6 percent, which translates into some 200 million people who cannot read and write. In the same year, only 7.5 percent of the relevant age group in China were receiving tertiary education, compared to 71.7 percent in South Korea, 56 percent in Taiwan, and 43.8 percent in Singapore. Furthermore, about two-thirds of the 300,000 or so Chinese students sent abroad for studies have not returned to China. This will in time constrain attempts to restructure and upgrade the Chinese economy into more skill-intensive and higher value-added activities. In short, China's manpower gaps, in quantitative as well as in qualitative terms, could well operate to moderate its long-term growth potential (see Watson, 1992).

Table 5.2 China's Social Indicators in East Asian Context

	GNP per Capita (U.S.$) 2000	Total Fertility Rate (%) 2000	Life Expectancy at Birth (years) 2000	Infant Mortality Rate (per 1,000 births) 2000	Population per Doctor, 2001	Adult Illiteracy Rate (%) 1999	Percentage of Age Group Enrolled in School 1999			Human Development Index (1998)	
							Primary	Secondary	Tertiary	HDI[a]	World Ranking
China	840	1.9	70.3	32.0	1,034	16.6	106.4[b]	62.8	7.5	0.718	87
Japan	34,210	1.4	80.7	3.8	522	1.0	101.3[b]	102.1	46.0	0.928	9
NIEs											
South Korea	8,910	1.4	73.2	8.2	855	2.4	98.6	97.4	71.7	0.854	27
Taiwan	12,916	1.7	72.7	7.0	807	5.0	101.0[b]	99.0	56.0	—	—
Hong Kong	25,950	1.0	79.8	2.9	772	6.8	96.0	75.0	—	0.880	24
Singapore	24,740	1.5	77.7	2.9	667	8.0	79.8	—	43.8	0.876	26
ASEAN - 4											
Indonesia	570	2.5	66.0	40.9	6,786	13.8	107.9[b]	54.9	11.3	0.677	102
Malaysia	3,380	3.0	72.5	7.9	1,477	13.2	101.4[b]	98.8	23.3	0.774	56
Philippines	1,040	3.4	69.3	30.7	1,016	5.0	113.2[b]	75.9	29.5	0.749	70
Thailand	2,010	1.9	68.8	27.9	4,361	4.8	93.5	79.0	31.9	0.757	66
Average of low-income countries	420	3.1[c]	59.4[d]	80.0[d]	—	31.0	96.0	42.0	—	0.549	—
Average of middle-income countries	1,970	2.5[c]	69.5[d]	32.0[d]	—	12.6	111.0[b]	67.0	12.0	0.740	—

Sources: World Development Report 2000/2001; World Development Indicators 2002; World Bank website, www.worldbank.org/countrydata; Asian Development Bank, Key Indicators of Developing Asian and Pacific Countries 2000; Human Development Report 2001; Taiwan Statistical Data Book 2002; Statistical Yearbook of ROC 2001; Asiaweek, April 20, 2001, and national sources.

Notes: Data for enrollment rate ratio for primary, secondary, and tertiary is updated to the most recent data estimate. Data for group average of lower-middle income countries is 1998.

a. Human Development Index combines life expectancy, educational attainment, and income indicators to give a composite measure of human development.
b. Due to the inclusion of some overaged children in the primary school stream, these figures are more than 100 percent.
c. Denotes 1998 data.
d. Denotes 1999 data.

■ WTO and Globalization

On December 11, 2001, China was formally and finally admitted into the World Trade Organization (WTO) as its 143rd member, thus ending China's fifteen years of efforts to join this multilateral trading body. China's WTO membership has been highly politicized from the outset. Few WTO members have gone through such a protracted process of negotiation and experienced so many political twists and turns as China has. China's WTO membership will speed up its integration into the global economy. To meet such globalization challenges, China needs to step up efforts to accomplish the unfinished business of its economic reform. There will be both opportunities and risks. China's medium-term growth scenario is therefore very much dependent on how well it can respond to global economic challenges brought about by its WTO membership (Cass, Williams, and Barker, 2003; Panitchpakti and Clifford, 2002; Moore, 2002; Zweig, 2002).

In anticipation of China's imminent WTO membership, foreign firms from Taiwan, South Korea, and Japan, as well as from Western countries, flocked to China to set up "beachheads" (Bramson, 2000; Mann, 1997; Studwell, 2002; Luo, 2001; Gibbons, 1997; Ambler and Witzel, 2000; Blackman, 2001). In 2001, FDI to China surged to an all-time high of U.S.$47 billion (see Figure 5.3). Many foreign businesses saw this as a good opportunity for establishing a stronghold in the China market. Starting from January 1, 2002, China is to reduce its average tariff rate to 12 percent from the then-existing 15.3 percent. By 2005, the average tariff level will be 9.6 percent. At the same time, many foreign and Chinese commentators are concerned about the disruptive WTO effects: How can China's ailing state-owned enterprises (SOEs) and inefficient financial sector survive foreign competition? What will be the fate of millions of small businessmen and small farmers?

However, the Chinese leadership in Beijing appears highly confident of its ability to cope with the adverse WTO impact. Many have come to realize that, with or without WTO membership, China's economy would still have to continue with its reform and restructuring, and would still be moving in the same direction. Perhaps, the long process of negotiation (fifteen years) has helped China to be psychologically prepared for such eventuality. China had a grace period of three to five years to adjust itself before the full implementation of the WTO regulations. Various trade and investment liberalization measures are to be phased in gradually in a progressive manner.

More important, as indicated earlier in this chapter, the external balance of the Chinese economy has been exceptionally strong: (1) for many years in a row, China has continued to chalk up a huge trade surplus, though its size has been slightly decreasing; (2) the influx of FDI has continued unabated, and will continue for at least a few more years; and (3) China's total foreign exchange reserves have kept on rising. Not surprisingly, Beijing was able to take its first year of WTO adjustment in full confidence.

The general economic impact of WTO membership is well known to the Chinese government. Accession to the WTO represents a new phase in China's open-door policy, often referred to as the third wave of China's opening up to the world. Previously, China's open-door policy was based on selective and unilateral liberalization; but from now on, it will be comprehensive and rule-based liberalization. Such extensive liberalization will promote China's overall economic efficiency through greater competition and technological progress. Chinese exports will have easier access to world markets and many Chinese products will not be subjected to unfair treatment or discrimination in some markets. A case in point is the granting to China by the United States of permanent normal trade relations (PNTR) status. At the same time, as China's economic door is thrown widely open, many Chinese industries, particularly those SOEs in less competitive sectors such as chemicals, automobiles, pharmaceuticals, and agriculture, will face fierce competition; many of these SOEs may not survive. Service industries such as banking, insurance, and telecommunications, which used to be highly protected, will be particularly vulnerable. This means that China must urgently deal with the remaining reform problems in connection with its SOEs and state banks (Chen, Dietrich, and Feng, 1999).

Until recently, progress on reforming China's SOEs and the financial sector had been slow. Efforts to reform state enterprises were initially directed at improving their efficiency by restructuring management, including measures to define enterprise rights under law and to free management from government supervision. This culminated in the promulgation on July 1, 1994, of a new Company Law, which provides the needed legal framework for the formation of "shareholding companies," the Chinese method of privatization (Oi and Walder, 1999). However, mere focus on ownership reform cannot ensure the efficiency and profitability of state enterprises, which eventually have to go through a fundamental management reform in order to learn how to behave like true profit-maximizing enterprises (Yi and Ye, 2003; Moore, 2002). In other words, state enterprises would ultimately have to operate under "hard budget constraints." Hopelessly unprofitable state enterprises would have to be shut down. China passed a bankruptcy law as early as 1986; but before 1997 the government was extremely reluctant to allow the ailing state enterprises to fold up for fear of social instability that would result from the massive *xiagang* (layoffs).

Since 1997, Beijing's basic strategy for reform of state enterprises has been the *zhua-da fang-xiao* (freeing up smaller state enterprises first while hanging on to large ones), which enabled the government to get rid of many nonstrategic small to medium-sized SOEs (Lin, 2000). In preparing China's accession to the WTO, the government did put a lot of pressures for SOEs, particularly the state banks, to accelerate their reform process.

For historical reasons, the state-owned commercial banks have incurred a high proportion of nonperforming loans (NPLs) because of the political pressures to lend out to SOEs (the so-called policy lending) (Wong, 2001a; Huang, 2001). In fact, NPLs of China's four state banks increased from 21.4 percent in 1995 to 29.2 percent in 2000. To cope with rising NPLs, the government set up four assets management corporations in 2000 and introduced the "debt-equity" swap scheme. By 2001, the level of NPLs was brought down to 25.4 percent. In August 2002 the People's Bank governor confirmed that China's total NPLs still amounted to 18 percent of its GDP.[32] However, some Western credit-rating agencies gave much higher estimates.[33] Nobody actually knows the exact level of China's NPLs because of its different standards of accounting and financial valuation. But the problem of bad loans in China's banking system is certainly mounting. The government can take comfort from the fact that Chinese people are big savers, leaving huge deposits in the banking system— total private savings deposits in banks amounted to 8 trillion yuan, almost the same size as China's total GDP.[34] As long as the economy can keep growing at 7 percent a year, the bad loans will be gradually digested.

While strengthening the state sector, the weakest link of China's economy, may help China better weather the adverse effects of increased global competition, it is actually very difficult at this initial stage to pinpoint precisely how or which industry or sector will fare under the initial or full impact of the WTO. Apart from the shortage of reliable data, the winners and losers simply cannot be surmised with any certainty, with much depending on how a particular industry will restructure or position itself for WTO challenges. It is generally expected by China scholars that the actual operating environment of China's post-WTO economy will not change overnight in one way or the other. Many new opportunities do present themselves to foreign firms, but risks still abound. Similarly, some Chinese SOEs would fold up under mounting foreign competition; but most of them would manage to survive, as they should continue to enjoy many of the existing "native" competitive advantages (Tsai, 2002).

■ Rising Unemployment

The most serious challenge to Beijing in the immediate WTO aftermath is the growing structural unemployment. As the economy is undergoing more vigorous macroeconomic reform and as businesses are forced to restructure for greater efficiency in order to meet WTO challenges, there will be more layoffs (Bian, 1995; Chan, 2001). Rising unemployment, therefore, will become the burning social issue in the years ahead.

Since 1997 as Premier Zhu Rongji stepped up SOE reform, about 7–8 million urban workers have been laid off every year under the *xiagang* scheme (actually a disguised form of laying off redundant workers). By mid-2002, about 24 million workers had been laid off as their SOEs were restructured. At the same time, about 8 million new jobs have been created every year since 1997, which, however, is inadequate to meet the rising number of new entrants to the labor force (roughly about 10 million a year), not to mention the numerous underemployed rural laborers ("disguised unemployment"). For years, the official "registered" urban unemployment rate stayed at a very low level, edging up from 1.8 percent in 1985 to 3.6 percent in 2001; it increased to 4.4 percent by the end of 2002.[35] However, China's actual urban unemployment rate realistically should be more like 7–8 percent if the past laid-off workers from SOEs are included. Indeed, China's labor and social security minister recently admitted, for the first time, that China's open urban unemployment was currently about 7 percent.[36] But this still leaves out the millions of rural migrants *(liudong renkou)* on odd jobs.

Besides such open urban unemployment, there is also growing rural underemployment or disguised rural unemployment, which will be aggravated by China's WTO membership. Many small farmers in China will suffer as a result of greater competition from the world's more efficient agricultural producers. In recent years, rural discontent has been rising in many areas due to widening rural-urban income inequalities, increasing tax burdens, and local misgovernment. WTO membership may increase the incidence of rural unrest

Heading to work in Beijing, 2001

(discussed below and in Chapter 4). The swelling ranks of the unemployed will be roaming around in China's urban areas, posing a serious threat to social stability, as manifested in the recent spate of labor protests (Cannon, 2000). In a sense, China has started paying the social price of its WTO membership.

The Chinese government has started to pay attention to human resource development programs, including job retraining. But its efforts are by far inadequate. The government has also stepped up its social security reform; but it will take many years to put the new social safety net in place. In the final analysis, the government still depends on sustaining high economic growth to ameliorate the unemployment problem. Not surprisingly, the government will always stand ready to prime the economy through massive spending on infrastructural investment whenever signs of economic slowdown appear. Herein also lies the social imperative of maintaining high economic growth in China, with or without the WTO.

▨ Social Constraints

China's rapid economic growth in recent years has given rise to many negative social externalities, from rising social expectations to rising crime and rising superstition, including the spread of the quasi-religious sect Falun Gong, which has started to worry the Chinese leadership. As a result of the unprecedented growth of materialism, a sense of a general "moral crisis" is sweeping China, as Chapter 12 attests. To what extent does all this represent a transitional phenomenon? Will it go away by itself once the economy and society develop further?

Most China scholars take the view that many of those negative social externalities may create frictions in the economic growth process, but they will not, on their own, be serious enough to disrupt the development process. The Chinese authorities understandably place a high priority on maintaining social order, which is crucial for economic growth and economic reform. It is often the case that the best way to deal with the by-products of rapid economic growth is to continue with rapid economic growth, which will generate more resources to deal with social problems.

However, there are other critical problems that will create strains in Chinese society even with continuing high economic growth. First, the leadership must mobilize all its institutional resources to combat corruption, which is rampant in China today (Wank, 2001; Kwong, 1997; Oi, 1989a). Economic reform in all transitional economies generates opportunities for extortion, profiteering, and open graft and corruption. The problem is becoming so serious that it threatens to undermine the social fabric of the country as well as the moral authority of the CCP. More than a mere social evil, corruption hampers economic growth by increasing transaction costs and reducing efficiency

(Kwong, 1997; Zweig, 2002; Hughes, 2002). Rampant corruption also slows trade and investment (Luo, 2000). Excessive use of *guanxi* (see Chapters 4 and 12) retards business operations. So far there has been a lot of rhetoric about corruption from the Chinese leaders, who have yet to demonstrate a sufficiently strong political will and effective measures to address this problem.

A second macro social issue with serious economic and political consequences is the growing income disparity between urban and rural areas, or between industrial and agricultural sectors (Wei, 2000). Between 1978 and 2001, average rural household income increased from 134 yuan to 2,366 yuan, or by a factor of 17.7. In the same period, average urban household income increased from 343 yuan to 6,860 yuan, or by a factor of 20.[37] At the start of economic reform in 1978, the rural-urban gap was 1 to 2.6. By 2001, the gap increased to 1 to 2.9, implying that China's pattern of economic growth for the past few years has been blatantly urban-biased.

The economic plight of the rural people is actually much worse than indicated by the aggregate official statistics (Riskin, Zhao, and Li, 2001). First, the rural household income is not "net cash income" as for the urban dwellers, but only "gross income," including "imputed elements" of food and livestock as well as working capital like payment for seed and fertilizer for the next production period. Second, during the past five years, while the average income of urban households continued to grow, variously from 5 percent to 12 percent, that of rural households experienced increases of only 1–2 percent, thereby further widening the existing income gaps. Third, unlike urban households, rural households receive no state welfare from education to housing and medical care.[38] Worse still, the rural population are subjected to burdensome levies and taxes, both lawful and unlawful, as so widely reported in the Chinese press.[39]

In short, while China's high economic growth during the past twenty years has brought about a perceptible measure of material affluence to the urban sector, particularly to the middle class in the many large coastal cities, the same is not true for the masses in the rural areas; and rural income growth for the past few years has actually stagnated (Riskin, Zhao, and Li, 2001; Wei, 2000). To escape poverty, some 50 to 100 million young peasants have flocked to the urban areas to seek nonfarm employment as migrant labor, constituting the *liudong renkou* ("floating population") (Zhang, 2001; Cannon, 2000; Murphy, 2002). However, instead of economically and socially absorbing the surplus rural labor as in other industrial countries during their industrialization process, the Chinese urban sector has continued to use the old practice of *hukou* (household registration) to discriminate against rural migrant labor (see Chapter 8). Hence the aggravation of the rural problem.

Not surprisingly, the rural problem has become a hotly debated subject in China today, with top leaders and intellectuals all making statements to stress its socioeconomic importance as well as its wide political implications. Most Chinese discussion of the rural problem involves three complicated aspects (the *san-nong* issue): the agricultural problem, or *nongye;* the village problem, or *nongcun;* and the peasant problem, or *nongmin*. The agricultural problem is mainly an economic issue involving food production and agricultural trade, while the village problem is largely caused by the rapid deterioration of the overall economic and social conditions in the countryside as a result of China's rapid economic modernization. The peasants also have a problem, basically because their income is not rising fast enough to keep pace with their increasing output.

China today has by and large resolved its food production problem. As a result of rising agricultural productivity brought about by rapid technological progress, China has developed the capacity to feed itself, despite its growing population and shrinking cultivated acreage. Ironically, increased agricultural productivity has rendered many rural laborers redundant, so they must leave their village for nonfarm employment. At the same time, because of the income-inelasticity nature of agricultural products, higher output actually tends to depress the farmer's income. Furthermore, in the process of industrialization (which takes place in urban areas), the terms of trade will always work against the agricultural sector so as to effect the transfer of agricultural surplus for industrial development. In other words, industrialization will inevitably bring about drastic transformation of the rural sector, which is manifested in the rapidly declining share of agricultural activity in employment, GDP, and exports. Hence the inexorable decline of the rural sector in the long run.

In a nutshell, the whole rural problem is basically a development problem. Many of the economic and social problems in the rural areas can only be resolved by further development of the nonfarm sectors. In the short run, however, the government can devise more effective policy measures to manage the rural decline without squeezing the peasants too hard and too fast. The government can also channel some resources back to the rural areas for the building of social infrastructure such as schools and health care facilities, not just to relieve rural poverty but also to prepare the young peasants for future nonfarm employment.

In reality, the present Chinese leadership has done precious little to help the peasants (Cheung, Chung, and Lin, 1998). Mao and most of his Long-March comrades were either peasants in origin or highly experienced in working with the peasants. China's younger generation of leaders, in contrast, were basically urban intellectuals, with little or no rural background in their previous careers. If the new leadership should continue to neglect the rural problem, they would have to deal with the consequences of increasing rural unrest, which could in turn endanger China's economic growth.

■ Notes

1. "China's Economy Grew 8 Percent in 2002," *China Daily,* January 15, 2003.

2. *China Statistical Abstract 2002* (Beijing: China Statistical Press, 2002).

3. John Wong and Sarah Chan, "China's Emergence as a Global Manufacturing Center: Implications for ASEAN," *Asia Pacific Business Review* 9(1) (fall 2002).

4. *The Standard* (Hong Kong), July 12, 2002.

5. *China Statistical Abstract 2002.*

6. World Bank, *World Development Report 2000/2001* (New York: Oxford University Press, 2001).

7. *China Statistical Abstract 2002.*

8. "China Becomes the World's No. 2 Web, PC Market," *China Daily,* August 19, 2002; Mary Hennock, "Who's Online in China?" BBC News Online, September 26, 2002.

9. "Internet Brings Sweeping Changes in China," *Xinhua News,* November 11, 2002.

10. "Analysing China's Economy: Is China a Threat?" *Journal of Japanese Trade and Industry* (Tokyo), September–October 2002.

11. "China's Rise Threatens Japanese Industry," *Nikkei Weekly* (Japan), August 19, 2002.

12. Brian Palmer, "China by the Numbers," *Fortune,* December 6, 1999; "Beijing Has HK$54 b Chasm in Key Data," *South China Morning Post,* July 24, 2000; and "Why China Cooks the Books?" *Newsweek,* April 1, 2002.

13. Dwight H. Perkins, *Market Control and Planning in Communist China* (Cambridge: Harvard University Press, 1966).

14. Nai-Ruenn Chen, "An Assessment of Chinese Economic Data: Availability, Reliability, and Usability," in Joint Economic Committee, U.S. Congress, *China: A Reassessment of the Economy* (Washington, DC: U.S. Government Printing Office, 1985).

15. "China's Data, Open and Credible," *China Daily,* August 9, 2002.

16. Shi Liangping, "China's GDP Statistics Are Credible," *Beijing Review,* July 4, 2002.

17. L. R. Klein and S. Ozmucur, "The Estimation of China's Economic Growth Rate," seminar paper presented at the Singapore Management University, May 2002.

18. See, for example, the June 1994 issue of the *Journal of Comparative Economics,* "Experiences in the Transition to a Market Economy," with Jeffrey Sachs and Wing Thye Woo as guest editors. For a more recent analysis, see Rawski, 1995.

19. *China Price Yearbook 1995* (Beijing).

20. "Keep Pace with Times, Jiang Urges Party Forum," *International Herald Tribune,* November 9–10, 2002.

21. For the full text of the plan in English, see Xinhua News Agency (Beijing), October 4, 1995, 0702 GMT.

22. "Congress Draws Nation's Blueprint," *China Daily,* November 9, 2002.

23. State Statistical Bureau, *Statistical Yearbook of China 2001* (Hong Kong: Economic Information Agency, 2001).

24. This official growth rate tends to overstate China's actual growth as it was estimated by revaluing Chinese GDP at 1980 prices rather than at earlier-year prices and hence inflates the contribution of industry to GDP growth. A more realistic average growth should be around 4.5–5.0 percent, which is still quite a respectable growth performance.

25. World Bank, *World Development Report 2000/2001.*

26. *China Statistical Abstract 2002.*
27. See, for example, Alwyn Young, "The Tyranny of Numbers: Confronting the Statistical Realities of the East Asian Growth Experience," *Quarterly Journal of Economics* 110, no. 3 (1995): 641–680; and Barry Bosworth, Susan Collins, and Yu-Chin Chen, *Accounting for Differences in Economic Growth,* Brookings Discussion Papers in International Economics no. 115 (Washington, DC: Brookings Institute, 1995).
28. World Bank, *China 2020: Development Challenges in the New Century* (Washington, DC: World Bank, 1997).
29. See Hu Zuliu and Mohsin Khan, *Why Is China Growing So Fast?* Economic Issues no. 8 (Washington, DC: International Monetary Fund, 1997).
30. *Statistical Yearbook of China 2000.*
31. See Tian Xiaowen, "China's Drive to Develop Its Western Region (I) and (II)," pp. 237–272 in John Wong and Lu Ding (eds.), *China's Economy into the New Century: Structural Issues and Problems* (Singapore: Singapore University Press and World Scientific, 2002).
32. *Beijing Review,* August 29, 2002.
33. "On the Road to Ruin," *Far Eastern Economic Review,* November 14, 2002.
34. *Mingpao,* November 13, 2002.
35. "China to Maintain Unemployment Rate Within 4.5 Percent in 2003," *People's Daily,* February 13, 2003.
36. "Beijing Tally of Jobless Far Too Low, Aide Admits," *International Herald Tribune,* November 12, 2002.
37. *China Statistical Abstract 2002.*
38. "Low Rural Income Threatens the Whole Economy," *Xinbao* (Hong Kong), July 15, 2002.
39. "Reform to Lift Tax Yoke off Farmers," *China Daily,* September 5, 2002.

■ Bibliography

Alford, William P. 1995. *To Steal a Book Is an Elegant Offense: Intellectual Property Law in Chinese Civilization.* Stanford: Stanford University Press.
Allee, Mark A. 1995. *Law and Local Society in Late Imperial China: Northern Taiwan in the Nineteenth Century.* Stanford: Stanford University Press.
Ambler, Tim, and Morgen Witzel. 2000. *Doing Business in China.* London: Routledge.
Ash, Robert, and Y. Y. Kueh (eds.). 1996. *The Chinese Economy Under Deng Xiaoping.* Oxford: Oxford University Press.
Bell, Lynda S. 1999. *One Industry, Two Chinas: Silk Filatures and Peasant-Family Production in Wuxi County, 1865–1937.* Stanford: Stanford University Press.
Berger, Mark, and Douglas Borer. 1997. *The Rise of East Asia: Critical Visions of the Pacific Century.* London: Routledge.
Bernhardt, Kathryn, and Philip C. C. Huang (eds.). 1994. *Civil Law in Qing and Republican China.* Stanford: Stanford University Press.
Bhalla, A. S. 1995. *Uneven Development in the Third World: A Study of India and China.* 2nd ed. New York: St. Martin's Press.
Bian, Yanjie. 1995. *Work and Inequality in Urban China.* Albany: State University of New York Press.
Blackman, Carolyn. 2001. *China Business: The Rules of the Game.* London: Allen and Unwin.

Blecher, Marc, and Vivienne Shue. 1996. *Tethered Deer: Government and Economy in a Chinese County.* Stanford: Stanford University Press.

Bramson, Christopher Bo. 2000. *Open Doors: Vilhelm Meyer and the Establishment of General Electric in China.* London: Curzon Press.

Brodsgaard, Kjeld Erik, and Susan Young (eds.). 2001. *State Capacity in East Asia: China, Taiwan, Vietnam, and Japan.* Oxford: Oxford University Press.

Brook, Timothy. 1989. *The Asiatic Mode of Production in China.* Armonk, NY: M. E. Sharpe.

Cannon, Terry (ed.). 2000. *China's Economic Growth: The Impacts of Regions, Migration, and the Environment.* New York: St. Martin's Press.

Cass, Deborah Z., Brett Gerard Williams, and George Barker (eds.). 2003. *China and the World Trading System: Entering the New Millennium.* Cambridge: Cambridge University Press.

Chan, Anita. 2001. *China's Workers Under Assault: The Exploitation of Labor in a Globalizing Economy.* Armonk, NY: M. E. Sharpe.

Chan, Anita, Benedict J. Tria Kerkvliet, and Jonathan Unger (eds.). 1999. *Transforming Asian Socialism: China and Vietnam Compared.* Lanham, MD: Rowman and Littlefield.

Chan, Anita, Richard Madsen, and Jonathan Unger. 1984. *Chen Village: The Recent History of a Peasant Community in Mao's China.* Berkeley: University of California Press.

Chang, Gordon. 2001. *The Coming Collapse of China.* New York: Random House.

Chao, Kang. 1987. *Man and Land in Chinese History: An Economic Analysis.* Stanford: Stanford University Press.

Chen, Baizhu, J. Kimball Dietrich, and Yi Feng. 1999. *Financial Market Reform in China: Progress, Problems, and Prospects.* Boulder: Westview Press.

Chen, Min, and Winston Pan. 1993. *Understanding the Process of Doing Business in China, Taiwan, and Hong Kong.* Lewiston, NY: Edward Mellen Press.

Cheng, Li. 1997. *Rediscovering China: Dynamics and Dilemmas of Reform.* Lanham, MD: Rowman and Littlefield.

Cheung, Peter T. Y., Jae Ho Chung, and Zhimin Lin (eds.). 1998. *Provincial Strategies of Economic Reform in Post-Mao China: Leadership, Politics, and Implementation.* Armonk, NY: M. E. Sharpe.

Cheung, Tai Ming. 2002. *China's Entrepreneurial Army.* Oxford: Oxford University Press.

Child, John. 1994. *Management in China During the Age of Reform.* Cambridge: Cambridge University Press.

Chung, Jae Ho (ed.). 1999. *Cities in China: Recipes for Economic Development in the Reform Era.* London: Routledge.

Cook, Sarah, Shujie Yao, and Juzhong Zhuang (eds.). 2000. *The Chinese Economy Under Transition.* New York: Palgrave.

Croll, Elisabeth. 1994. *From Heaven to Earth: Images and Experiences of Development in China.* London: Routledge.

Davis, Deborah S. (ed.). 1999. *The Consumer Revolution in Urban China.* Berkeley: University of California Press.

de Trenck, Charles (ed.). 1998. *Red Chips and the Globalization of China's Enterprises.* Seattle: University of Washington Press.

Deng, Gang. 1999. *The Premodern Chinese Economy: Structural Equilibrium and Capitalist Sterility.* London: Routledge.

Deyo, Frederick C., Richard F. Doner, and Eric Hershberg (eds.). 2001. *Economic Governance and the Challenge of Flexibility in East Asia.* Lanham, MD: Rowman and Littlefield.

Ding, Lu, and John Wong (eds.). 2001. *China's Economy into the New Century: Structural Issues and Problems.* Singapore: Singapore University Press and World Scientific.

Eckstein, Alexander. 1977. *China's Economic Revolution.* Cambridge: Cambridge University Press.

Elvin, Mark. 1973. *The Pattern of the Chinese Past.* Stanford: Stanford University Press.

Engholm, Christopher. 1994. *Doing Business in Asia's Booming "China Triangle": People's Republic of China, Taiwan, Hong Kong.* Englewood Cliffs: Prentice-Hall.

Feuerwerker, Albert. 1996a. *The Chinese Economy, 1870–1949.* Ann Arbor: University of Michigan Monographs in Chinese Studies.

———. 1996b. *Studies in the Economic History of Late Imperial China: Handicraft, Modern Industry, and the State.* Ann Arbor: University of Michigan Monographs in Chinese Studies.

Fewsmith, Joseph. 1983. "From Guild to Interest Group: The Transformation of Public and Private in Late Qing China." *Comparative Studies in Society and History* 25:617–640.

———. 1994. *Dilemmas of Reform in China: Political Conflict and Economic Debate.* Armonk, NY: M. E. Sharpe.

Forster, Keith. 1999. *Zhejiang Province in Reform.* Sydney: Wild Peony.

Frazier, Mark W. 2002. *The Making of the Chinese Industrial Workplace: State Revolution and Labor Management.* Cambridge: Cambridge University Press.

Friedman, Edward, Paul G. Pickowicz, and Mark Selden. 1991. *Chinese Village, Socialist State.* New Haven: Yale University Press.

Gamble, William. 2003. *Investing in China: Legal, Financial, and Regulatory Risk.* New York: Quorum Books.

Gao, Shangquan. 1999. *Two Decades of Reform in China.* Singapore: World Scientific.

———. 2000. *China's Economic Reform.* New York: Palgrave.

Gardella, Robert, Andrea McElderry, and Jane K. Leonard (eds.). 1999. *Chinese Business History: Interpretive Trends and Priorities for the Future.* Armonk, NY: M. E. Sharpe.

Garnaut, Ross, Guo Shutian, and Ma Guonan (eds.). 1996. *The Third Revolution in the Chinese Countryside.* Cambridge: Cambridge University Press.

Garnaut, Ross, Ligang Song, Yang Yao, and Xiaolu Wang. 2001. *Private Enterprise in China.* Canberra: Asia Pacific Press.

Garran, Robert. 1998. *Tigers Tamed: The End of the Asian Miracle.* Honolulu: University of Hawaii Press.

Gates, Hill. 1996. *China's Motor: A Thousand Years of Petty Capitalism.* Ithaca: Cornell University Press.

Gibbons, Russell. 1997. *Joint Ventures in China: A Guide for the Foreign Investor.* Melbourne: Macmillan.

Godement, François. 1997. *The New Asian Renaissance.* London: Routledge.

Goodman, David S. G. (ed.). 1997. *China's Provinces in Reform: Class, Community, and Political Culture.* London: Routledge.

Gore, Lance L. P. 1999. *Market Communism: The Institutional Foundation of China's Post-Mao Hyper-Growth.* Oxford: Oxford University Press.

Grub, Phillip Donald, and Lin Jian Hai. 1991. *Foreign Direct Investment in China.* New York: Quorum Books.

Guiheux, Gilles. 2002. "The Incomplete Crystallization of the Private Sector." *China Perspectives* 42 (July–August): 24–36

Guthrie, Doug. 2002. *Dragon in a Three-Piece Suit: The Emergence of Capitalism in China.* Princeton: Princeton University Press.

Hamilton, Gary (ed.). 2002. *Chinese Capitalism? The Organization of Chinese Economics.* London: Routledge.

Harvie, Charles (ed.). 2000. *Contemporary Developments and Issues in China's Economic Transition.* New York: Palgrave.

Ho, Samuel. 1978. *Economic Development of Taiwan, 1860–1970.* New Haven: Yale University Press.

Ho, Samuel, and Y. Y. Kueh. 2000. *Sustainable Development in South China.* New York: Palgrave.

Honig, Emily. 1986. *Sisters and Strangers: The Cotton Textile Workers of Shanghai.* Stanford: Stanford University Press.

Howell, Jude. 1993. *China Opens Its Doors: The Politics of Economic Transition.* Boulder: Lynne Rienner.

Huang, Philip C. C. 1985. *The Peasant Economy and Social Change in North China.* Stanford: Stanford University Press.

———. 1990. *The Peasant Family and Rural Development in the Yangzi Delta, 1350–1988.* Stanford: Stanford University Press.

Huang, Yasheng. 1996. *Inflation and Investment Controls in China: The Political Economy of Central-Local Relations During the Reform Era.* Cambridge: Cambridge University Press.

———. 2002. *Selling China: Foreign Direct Investment During the Reform Era.* Cambridge: Cambridge University Press.

Huang, Yiping. 2001. *China's Last Steps Across the River: Enterprise and Banking Reforms.* Canberra: Asia Pacific Press.

Hughes, Neil C. 2002. *China's Economic Challenge: Smashing the Iron Rice Bowl.* Armonk, NY: M. E. Sharpe.

Ikels, Charlotte. 1996. *The Return of the God of Wealth: The Transition to a Market Economy in Urban China.* Stanford: Stanford University Press.

Kamachi, Noriko. 1990. "Feudalism or Absolute Monarchism? Japanese Discourse on the Nature of State and Society in Later Imperial China." *Modern China* 87(3):330–370.

Keith, Ronald C. 1994. *China's Struggle for the Rule of Law.* New York: St. Martin's Press.

Kelliher, Daniel. 1992. *Peasant Power in China: The Era of Rural Reform, 1979–1989.* New Haven: Yale University Press.

Kim, Samuel S. (ed.). 2000. *East Asia and Globalization.* Lanham, MD: Rowman and Littlefield.

Kluver, Alan R. 1995. *Legitimating the Chinese Economic Reforms: A Rhetoric of Myth and Orthodoxy.* Albany: State University of New York Press.

Kristof, Nicholas, and Sheryl WuDunn. 1994. *China Wakes: The Struggle for the Soul of a Rising Power.* New York: Random House.

Krugman, Paul. 1994. "The Myth of Asia's Miracle." *Foreign Affairs* 73(6) (November–December): 62–75.

Kwong, Julia. 1997. *The Political Economy of Corruption in China.* Armonk, NY: M. E. Sharpe.

Lardy, Nicholas R. 1992. *Foreign Trade and Economic Reform in China.* Cambridge: Cambridge University Press.
―――. 1994. *China in the World Economy.* Washington, DC: Institute for International Economics.
―――. 1998. *China's Unfinished Economic Revolution.* Washington, DC: Brookings Institution.
―――. 2002. *Integrating China into the Global Economy.* Washington, DC: Brookings Institution.
Lee, James. 1990. *State and Economy in Southwest China.* Stanford: Stanford University Press.
Leong, Liew. 1998. *The Chinese Economy in Transition: From Plan to Market.* Cheltenham, England: Edward Elgar.
Lin, Justin Yifu, Fang Cai, and Zhou Li. 2001. *The China Miracle: Development Strategy and Economic Reform.* Rev. ed. Hong Kong: Chinese University Press.
Lin, Yi-min. 2000. *Between Politics and Markets: Firms, Competition, and Institutional Change in Post-Mao China.* Cambridge: Cambridge University Press.
Lindau, Juan D., and Timothy Cheek. 1998. *Market Economics and Political Change: Comparing China and Mexico.* Lanham, MD: Rowman and Littlefield.
Liu, Xiuwu R. 2001. *Jumping into the Sea: From Academics to Entrepreneurs in South China.* Lanham, MD: Rowman and Littlefield.
Lu, Aiguo. 1999. *China and the Global Economy Since 1840.* New York: St. Martin's Press.
Lu, Xiaobo, and Elizabeth J. Perry. 1997. *Danwei: The Changing Chinese Workplace in Historical and Comparative Perspective.* Armonk, NY: M. E. Sharpe.
Lufrano, Richard John. 1997. *Honorable Merchants: Commerce and Self-Cultivation in Late Imperial China.* New York: Columbia University Press.
Luo, Yadong. 2000. *Guanxi and Business.* Singapore: World Scientific.
―――. 2001. *How to Enter China: Choices and Lessons.* Ann Arbor: University of Michigan Press.
Lyons, Thomas P. 1994. *Poverty and Growth in a South China County: Anxi, Fujian, 1949–1992.* Ithaca: Cornell University Press.
Lyons, Thomas P., and Victor Need (eds.). 1994. *The Economic Transformation of South China: Reform and Development in the Post-Mao Era.* Ithaca: Cornell University Press.
Maddison, Angus. 1998. *Chinese Economic Performance in the Long Run.* Washington, DC: Organization for Economic Cooperation and Development.
Mann, Jim. 1997. *Beijing Jeep: A Case Study of Western Business in China.* Boulder: Westview Press.
Mann, Susan. 1987. *Local Merchants and the Chinese Bureaucracy, 1750–1950.* Stanford: Stanford University Press.
Marton, Andrew M. 2000. *China's Spatial Economic Development: Regional Transformation in the Lower Yangzi Delta.* London: Routledge.
Mastel, Greg. 1997. *The Rise of the Chinese Economy: The Middle Kingdom Emerges.* Armonk, NY: M. E. Sharpe.
McCormick, Barrett L., and Jonathan Unger (eds.). 1995. *China After Socialism: In the Footsteps of Eastern Europe or East Asia?* Armonk, NY: M. E. Sharpe.
Moore, Thomas G. 2002. *China in the World Market: Chinese Industry and International Sources of Reform in the Post-Mao Era.* Cambridge: Cambridge University Press.
Murphy, David J. 1996. *Plunder and Preservation: Cultural Property Law and Practice in the People's Republic of China.* Hong Kong: Oxford University Press.

Murphy, Rachel. 2002. *How Migrant Labor Is Changing Rural China.* Cambridge: Cambridge University Press.

Nann, Richard C. 1995. *Authority and Benevolence: Social Welfare in China.* New York: St. Martin's Press.

Naquin, Susan. 1987. *Chinese Society in the Eighteenth Century.* New Haven: Yale University Press.

Naughton, Barry. 1995. *Growing Out of the Plan: Chinese Economic Reform, 1978–1993.* Cambridge: Cambridge University Press.

Newman, William H. 1992. *Birth of a Successful Joint Venture.* Lanham, MD: University Press of America.

Nolan, Peter. 2001. *China and the Global Business Revolution.* New York: Palgrave.

Oi, Jean C. 1989a. "Market Reforms and Corruption in Rural China." *Studies in Comparative Communism* 22 (summer–autumn): 221–233.

————. 1989b. *State and Peasant in Contemporary China: The Political Economy of Village Government.* Berkeley: University of California Press.

————. 1999. *Rural China Takes Off: The Institutional Foundations of Economic Reform.* Berkeley: University of California Press.

Oi, Jean, and Andrew G. Walder (eds.). 1999. *Property Rights and Economic Reform in China.* Stanford: Stanford University Press.

O'Leary, Greg. 1997. *Adjusting to Capitalism: Chinese Workers and the State.* Armonk, NY: M. E. Sharpe.

Panitchpakti, Supachai, and Mark. L. Clifford. 2002. *China and the WTO: Changing China, Changing World Trade.* New York: John Wiley.

Pearson, Margaret M. 1997. *China's New Business Elite: The Political Consequences of Economic Reform.* Berkeley: University of California Press.

Perdue, Peter C. 1987. *Exhausting the Earth: State and Peasant in Hunan, 1500–1850.* Cambridge: Harvard University Press.

Perkins, Dwight. 1969. *Agricultural Development in China, 1368–1968.* Chicago: Aldine.

————. 1996. "China's Future: Economic and Social Development Scenarios for the Twenty-First Century." Paper presented at the OECD conference on "China in the Twenty-First Century: Long-Term Global Implications," Paris, January 8–9.

Pomeranz, Kenneth. 2000. *The Great Divergence: China, Europe, and the Making of the Modern World Economy.* Princeton: Princeton University Press.

Potter, Jack M. 1968. *Capitalism and the Chinese Peasant: Social and Economic Change in a Hong Kong Village.* Berkeley: University of California Press.

Powell, Simon. 1992. *Agricultural Reform in China: From Communes to Commodity Economy, 1978–1990.* Manchester: Manchester University Press.

Prazniak, Roxann. 1999. *Of Camels and Kings and Other Things: Rural Rebels Against Modernity in Late Imperial China.* Lanham, MD: Rowman and Littlefield.

Rawski, Evelyn Sakakida. 1972. *Agricultural Change and the Peasant Economy of South China.* Cambridge: Harvard University Press.

Rawski, Thomas G. 1995. *Implications of China's Reform Experience.* Pittsburgh: Department of Economics, University of Pittsburgh Working Paper no. 295.

————. 2001. "What Is Happening to China's GDP Statistics?" *China Economic Review* 12(4) (December):347–354.

Redding, S. Gordon. 1990. *The Spirit of Chinese Capitalism.* Berlin: Walter de Gruyter.

Richardson, Philip. 2000. *Economic Change in China, c. 1800–1950.* Cambridge: Cambridge University Press.

Rimmer, Peter J. 1997. *Pacific Rim Development: Integration and Globalisation in the Asia-Pacific Economy.* London: Allen and Unwin.

Riskin, Carl. 1987. *China's Political Economy: The Quest for Development Since 1949.* New York: Economics of the World Series.

Riskin, Carl, Renwei Zhao, and Shi Li (eds.). 2001. *China's Retreat from Equality: Income Distribution and Economic Transition.* Armonk, NY: M. E. Sharpe.

Robison, Richard, and David S. G. Goodman (eds.). 1996. *The New Rich in Asia: Mobile Phones, McDonalds, and Middle Class Revolution.* London: Routledge.

Rowe, William T. 1984. *Hankow: Commerce and Society in a Chinese City, 1796–1889.* Stanford: Stanford University Press.

———. 1989. *Hankow: Conflict and Community in a Chinese City, 1796–1895.* Stanford: Stanford University Press.

Sheff, David. 2002. *China Dawn: The Story of a Technology and Business Revolution.* New York: HarperBusiness.

Shiba, Yoshinobu. 1969. *Commerce and Society in Sung China.* Trans. Mark Elvin. Ann Arbor: University of Michigan Abstracts of Chinese and Japanese Works on Chinese History.

Shih, Chih-yu. 1995. *State and Society in China's Political Economy: The Cultural Dynamics of Socialist Reform.* Boulder: Lynne Rienner.

Shirk, Susan. 1993. *The Political Logic of Economic Reform in China.* Berkeley: University of California Press.

Skoggard, Ian A. 1996. *The Indigenous Dynamic in Taiwan's Postwar Development: The Religious and Historical Roots of Entrepreneurship.* Armonk, NY: M. E. Sharpe.

Solinger, Dorothy. 1993. *China's Transition from Socialism: Statist Legacies and Market Reforms.* Armonk, NY: M. E. Sharpe.

Spence, Jonathan. 1999. *The Search for Modern China.* New York: W. W. Norton.

Stross, Randall E. 1990. *Bulls in the China Shop and Other Sino-American Business Encounters.* New York: Pantheon.

Studwell, Joe. 2002. *The China Dream: The Quest for the Last Great Untapped Market on Earth.* New York: Atlantic Monthly Press.

Tam, On Kit. 1995. *Financial Reform in China.* London: Routledge.

Taylor, Robert. 1996. *Greater China and Japan: Prospects for Economic Partnership in East Asia.* London: Routledge.

Tiewes, Frederick C., and Warren Sun. 1998. *China's Road to Disaster: Mao, Central Politicians, and Provincial Leaders in the Unfolding of the Great Leap Forward, 1955–1959.* Armonk, NY: M. E. Sharpe.

Tipton, Frank B. 1998. *The Rise of Asia: Economics, Society, and Politics in Contemporary Asia.* Honolulu: University of Hawaii Press.

Tsai, Kellee S. 2002. *Back-Alley Banking: Private Entrepreneurs in China.* Ithaca: Cornell University Press.

UNDP (United Nations Development Programme). 1999. *China Human Development Report.* Oxford: Oxford University Press.

Vermeer, Eduard B., Frank N. Pieke, and Woei Lien Chong. 1997. *Cooperative and Collective in China's Rural Development.* Armonk, NY: M. E. Sharpe.

Wade, Robert. 1990. *Governing the Market: Economic Theory and the Role of Government in East Asian Industrialization.* Princeton: Princeton University Press.

Wagner, Donald B. 2002. *The State and the Iron Industry in Han China.* Oslo: Nordic Institute of Asian Studies.

Walder, Andrew G. 1986. *Communist Neo-Traditionalism: Work and Authority in Chinese Industry.* Berkeley: University of California Press.

———— (ed.). 1996. *China's Transitional Economy.* Oxford: Oxford University Press.

Wang, Hongying. 2001. *Weak State, Strong Networks: The Institutional Dynamics of Foreign Direct Investment in China.* Oxford: Oxford University Press.

Wang, Shaoguang, and Hu Angang. 1999. *The Political Economy of Uneven Development: The Case of China.* Armonk, NY: M. E. Sharpe.

————. 2001. *The Chinese Economy in Crisis: State Capacity and Tax Reform.* Armonk, NY: M. E. Sharpe.

Wank, David L. 1999. *Commodifying Communism: Business, Trust, and Politics in a Chinese City.* Cambridge: Cambridge University Press.

Watson, Andrew (ed.). 1992. *Economic Reform and Social Change in China.* London: Routledge.

Wei, Pan. 1998. *The Politics of Marketization in Rural China.* Lanham, MD: Rowman and Littlefield.

Wei, Yehua Dennis. 2000. *Regional Development in China: States, Globalization, and Inequality.* London: Routledge.

Weng, Eang Cheong. 1997. *The Hong Merchants of Canton: Chinese Merchants in Sino-Western Trade, 1684–1798.* London: Curzon Press.

White, Gordon. 1993. *The Politics of Economic Reform in Post-Mao China.* Stanford: Stanford University Press.

————. 1996. *In Search of Civil Society: Market Reform and Social Change in Contemporary China.* Oxford: Oxford University Press.

White, Lynn T., III. 1998. *Unstately Power: Local Causes of China's Economic Reform.* Vol. 1. Armonk, NY: M. E. Sharpe.

Will, Pierre-Etienne. 1991. *Nourish the People: The State Civilian Granary System in China, 1650–1850.* Ann Arbor: Center for Chinese Studies, University of Michigan.

Wong, John. 1973. *Land Reform in the People's Republic of China: Institutional Transformation of Agriculture.* New York: Praeger.

————. 1993. *Understanding China's Socialist Market Economy.* Singapore: Times Academic Press.

————. 1994. "Power and Market in Mainland China: The Danger of Increasing Government Involvement in Business." *Issues and Studies* (Taipei) 30(1) (January): 1–12.

————. 1995a. "Assessing China's Economic Reform Progress in 1994." *JETRO China Newsletter* (Tokyo) 112 (January–February).

————. 1995b. "China's Entrepreneurial Approach to Economic Reform." *IEAPE Internal Study Paper* (Singapore) 8 (February 16).

————. 1995c. "China's Ninth Five-Year Plan: Economic Agenda of the Fifth Party Plenum." *IEAPE Commentaries* (Singapore) 17 (October).

————. 1995d. "Why Is the Chinese Government So Concerned About Agriculture?" *IEAPE Background Brief* (Singapore) 87 (May 18).

————. 1996. "Promoting Confucianism for Socioeconomic Development: The Singapore Experience." Pp. 277–293 in Tu Wei-ming (ed.), *Confucian Traditions in East Asian Modernity.* Cambridge: Harvard University Press.

————. 1997a. "China's Economy in 1997." *EAI Background Brief* (Singapore) 6 (December 29).

————. 1997b. "Will China Be the Next Financial Domino?" *EAI Background Brief* 4 (December 11).

————. 1998a. "Interpreting Zhu Rongji's Strategies for the Chinese Economy." *EAI Background Brief* (Singapore) 11 (March 31).

———. 1998b. "Xiao-Kang: Deng Xiaoping's Socio-Economic Development Target for China." *Journal of Contemporary China* 7(17) (March):141–152.

———. 2001a. "China's Banking Reform and Financial Liberalization." *Review of Asian and Pacific Studies* 22:43–56.

———. 2001b. "Understanding Recent Changes in China's Statistical System." *China Perspective* 35 (May–June): 56–62.

———. 2002. "China's Sharply Declining Fertility Rate: Implications for Its Population Policy." *Issues and Studies* (May–June): 68–86.

Wong, John, Rong Ma, and Mu Yang. 1995. *China's Rural Entrepreneurs: Ten Case Studies.* Singapore: Times Academic Press.

Wong, John, and Zheng Yongnian. 2001. "Embracing the Capitalists: The Chinese Communist Party to Brace Itself for Far-Reaching Changes." *EAI Background Brief* (Singapore) 100 (September).

——— (eds.). 2001. *The Nanxun Legacy and China's Development in the Post-Deng Era.* Singapore: World Scientific.

Woo, Wing Thye, Stephen Parker, and Jeffrey Sachs (eds.). 1996. *Economies in Transition: Comparing Asia and Europe.* Cambridge: MIT Press.

World Bank. 1994. *China: International Market Development and Regulation.* Washington, DC: World Bank.

———. various years. *World Development Report.* New York: Oxford University Press.

Wu, Yanrui. 1996. *Productive Efficiency of Chinese Enterprises: An Empirical Study.* New York: St. Martin's Press.

Wu, Yu-Shan. 1994. *Comparative Economic Transformations: Mainland China, Hungary, the Soviet Union, and Taiwan.* Stanford: Stanford University Press.

Xia, Mei, Lin Jian Hai, and Phillip Donald Grub. 1992. *The Reemerging Securities Market in China.* New York: Quorum Books.

Yabuki, Susumu, and Stephen M. Harner. 1999. *China's New Political Economy: The Giant Awakes.* 2nd. ed. Boulder: Westview Press.

Yang, Dali L. 1996. *Calamity and Reform in China: Rural Society and Institutional Change Since the Great Leap Famine.* Stanford: Stanford University Press.

Yi, Gang. 1993. *Money, Banking, and Financial Markets in China.* Boulder: Westview Press.

Yi, Jeannie J., and Shawn X. Ye. 2003. *The Haier Way: The Making of a Chinese Business Leader and a Global Brand.* Dumont, NJ: Homa and Sekey Books.

Young, Susan. 1995. *Private Business and Economic Reform in China.* Armonk, NY: M. E. Sharpe.

Zhang, Li. 2001. *Strangers in the City: Reconfigurations of Space, Power, and Social Networks Within China's Floating Population.* Stanford: Stanford University Press.

Zhang, Wei. 1996. *Ideology and Economic Reform Under Deng, 1978–1993.* Geneva: Kegan Paul International.

Zhou, Kate Xiao. 1996. *How the Farmers Changed China: Power of the People.* Boulder: Westview Press.

Zhou, Kate Xiao, and Lynn T. White III. 1995. "Quiet Politics and Rural Enterprise in Reform China." *Journal of Developing Areas* 29 (July): 461–490.

Zweig, David. 1997. *Freeing China's Farmers: Rural Restructuring in the Reform Era.* Armonk, NY: M. E. Sharpe.

———. 2002. *Internationalizing China: Domestic Interests and Global Linkages.* Ithaca: Cornell University Press.

6

China Beyond the Heartland

Robert E. Gamer

H aving overviewed China's geography, history, politics, and economy, in this chapter we will take a closer look at four special topics: overseas Chinese, Hong Kong, Taiwan, and Tibet. These elements are all part of China, and yet not. They figure prominently in China's defense, foreign policy, economy, and culture. Even before reading this book, you were probably already aware that Hong Kong reverted to China in 1997, that Taiwan and China are engaged in vigorous diplomatic and military competition, and that Tibetans have resisted China's presence in their territory. The outcome of these issues will have enormous consequences in determining China's future. We will look at some historical background on each and then examine present and future trends. But we will begin with another topic, perhaps less familiar to you, that will help you comprehend China's extraordinary economic growth and some of the threads that tie together China, Hong Kong, and Taiwan: overseas Chinese. As Chapter 1 indicated, there are some 60 million Han who have left or whose ancestors left China, including those in Taiwan and Hong Kong. The richest among them control large amounts of investment capital. As you will see, most of China's foreign direct investment comes from them. How have they become so wealthy? How have they come to figure so prominently in China's affairs?

■ Overseas Chinese

For thousands of years, Chinese merchants have been trading in Indochina (Vietnam), Cambodia, Siam (Thailand), Malaya (mainland Malaysia), and Java (part of Indonesia)—all in Southeast Asia (see Map 2.1)—

and in Korea and Japan. Their trade brought great prosperity to China's leading families during the Tang, Song, Yuan, Ming, and Qing empires (see Table 3.1). Most simply traveled there on business trips; a few settled, married native women, and became absorbed into local society. When the Europeans arrived in the sixteenth century, they created or captured Macao (across the bay from Hong Kong), Manila in the Philippines (the big island group north of Indonesia; see Map 2.1), Melaka (Malacca) in Malaya, and Batavia (Jakarta) and other ports in Java, and encouraged Chinese merchants and artisans (largely from the southern provinces of Fujian, Guangdong, and Zhejiang; see Map 2.2) to move there. These settlers brought Chinese wives and established or expanded Chinese communities; many became prosperous from their trading activities (Wang, 1991; Reid, 2001). As China's population burgeoned during the nineteenth century, relatives from their home provinces and unemployed urban youth moved to those communities and to the newly founded ports of Penang and Singapore in Malaya. They filled jobs as laborers, miners, plantation workers, teachers, journalists, traditional opera performers, house servants, and retailers. Others went to the Americas and Australia to construct railroads and work on farms. Some settled in Tokyo, smaller Pacific islands, Sydney, Calcutta, Paris, London, San Francisco, Vancouver, the West Indies, and Lima. Those working on farms, plantations, mines, and railroads often experienced cruel treatment and harsh conditions. Those who did not perish or return home stayed to set up laundries or small shops or work for other Chinese in "Chinatowns," which began to emerge even in cities beyond the port of original entry into the country (Dirlik, 1998a).

The principal source of income for overseas Chinese communities was trade with China. The wealthiest families made their fortunes serving as middlemen in trade transactions between China and non-Chinese in Asia, Europe, or the Americas. They became patrons to Chinese-language schools, newspapers, temples, festivals, and other cultural activities; welfare and legal aid societies; and cemeteries. Siam and the Philippines encouraged Chinese to intermarry and mingle with indigenous people in places of work; elsewhere they met with greater wariness and prejudice. The British in Malaya and Singapore hired Chinese and other ethnic groups for some bureaucratic posts; most of the remaining Chinese in these settlements worked for themselves or for other Chinese. Most Chinese sent money home to poorer relatives in China.

In the second half of the nineteenth century, prominent Chinese families began sending some of their children abroad to study. Those students discovered that except in the Philippines, where the Spanish had established schools and universities for native inhabitants, few Chinese born overseas were studying outside their own communities. Most who attended school were taught in Chinese dialects. In contrast, U.S. missionary schools in China introduced their students to English and a modern Western curriculum; their best graduates were welcomed into leading U.S., British, and European colleges and universities. Japan, too, welcomed students from China. Upon their return home, many of these graduates became prominent in China's government, commerce, and cultural life. Their exposure to Japanese, U.S., and European languages and cultures was far deeper than that of most Chinese living abroad.

The Chinese studying abroad returned home wanting to introduce China to techniques and ideas they had learned on their sojourns—to change Chinese culture. In contrast, leaders of Chinese communities abroad wished to preserve Chinese traditions among their families, workers, and neighbors. In exchange for cash remitted to their families in China, they asked China's leaders for assistance in dealing with the governments and societies of their adopted lands. Both these responses were very new. Until the second half of the nineteenth century, educated Chinese did not venture abroad to study, and China did not concern itself with the needs of Chinese who had moved abroad. To control piracy and rebels, the Ming and Qing governments had forbidden emigration under penalty of death. The treaties imposed after the Opium Wars (discussed below and in Chapter 7) changed that. They forced the emperors to allow emigration, while giving China the right (as a new participant in European-created international law) to protect its subjects living abroad. For the first time, China sent ambassadors and consuls to foreign capitals and trading cities. There they discovered the great prosperity of the overseas Chinese. The Qing government began to support schools for Chinese in Southeast Asian countries and conferred citizenship on overseas Chinese and their children. Chinese consular officials were available to assist Chinese when they encountered problems in their adopted countries and to intercede against abuses of laborers. After centuries of being cut off from their homeland, under threat of the death penalty imposed since the Ming dynasty for being illegal emigrants, overseas Chinese were being treated as compatriots. In exchange, the Qing government encouraged them to send money home to relatives.

This created precedents that continue to affect China's foreign relations and the lives of overseas Chinese. It encouraged the predisposition of overseas Chinese to isolate themselves from the social and political life of their adopted lands and to interest themselves in the politics and economy of China. It reinforced the inclination of China's governments to treat the overseas Chinese as continuing subjects of China and the lands where some of them reside as part of China's domain. Most important, it also helped end the Qing dynasty. The Kuomintang (KMT) and the Republican movements were born among Chinese studying abroad and benefited from substantial financial contributions from overseas Chinese.

After the Qing dynasty was overthrown in 1911, all political factions in China sought financial and moral support among overseas Chinese, who helped set up schools for their children. The Kuomintang government promoted equal treatment for overseas Chinese in their countries of residence, helped them send their children to China for study, and gave special incentives to overseas Chinese for establishing businesses in China. It focused heavily on establishing schools, training teachers, and setting standards for the children of overseas Chinese and criticized the governments of those countries for "interfering" in this education, which was conducted entirely in the Chinese language, when they sought assurance that it would help integrate pupils into their adopted lands (Fitzgerald, 1972:8).

From 1921 to 1927, the communists and Nationalists cooperated in a "united front" in China; after that, they vied with each other and with the warlords for control of territories. All these factions sought financial and moral support from the overseas Chinese. In 1936, to counter the Japanese, they once again declared a united front, with both the Kuomintang and the communists proclaiming that overseas Chinese were included in their efforts to cooperate. By giving their attention and resources variously to the Kuomintang and the communists, overseas Chinese remained within China's orbit and roused suspicions among their new compatriots that they were not entirely loyal to their adopted lands. They also found themselves caught up in the ideological battle between communism and the Western democracies, even though many of them had thought little about such issues.

As you will see in Chapter 7, that problem of divided loyalties would continue after World War II. Both China and Taiwan, now ruled respectively by the communists and the Kuomintang Nationalists, would need the deep pockets and the economic connections of these overseas Chinese as they sought to spread their economic and political influence in the region. And an island that was barren when China sought to control the opium trade in 1839 would play a pivotal role in this. So we fit it into the story here.

■ Hong Kong

▨ Beginnings

In 1839 the Qing emperor appointed Lin Zexu as special commissioner in Guangzhou, the only port open to foreign trade (as Chapter 7 explains), and ordered him to stamp out the opium trade. Thus began China's humiliation by foreign powers. Guangzhou (Canton) is located near the Pearl River delta of the West River (see Maps 2.2 and 2.4), just upstream from the Portuguese-founded city of Macao. Lin sent troops to the foreign wharves where trading took place and refused to let anyone leave until they surrendered the opium inside and promised not to import more. Among those in attendance was Captain Charles Elliot, Britain's trade representative. After six weeks of standoff, Elliot surrendered 3 million pounds of opium to Lin, who had it flushed into the sea. Elliot retreated downstream to Macao, where the Portuguese did not

Lee, David Tawei. 2000. *The Making of the Taiwan Relations Act: Twenty Years in Retrospect*. Oxford: Oxford University Press.

Li, Kuo-Ting. 1995. *The Evolution of Policy Behind Taiwan's Development Success*. 2nd ed. Singapore: World Scientific.

Li, Xiabing, Xiabe Hu, and Yang Zhong. 1998. *Interpreting China-Taiwan Relations: China in the Post–Cold War Era*. Lanham, MD: University Press of America.

Maguire, Keith. 1998. *The Rise of Modern Taiwan: Government and Politics in the Republic of China*. Burlington, VT: Ashgate.

Marsh, Robert. 1996. *The Great Transformation: Social Change in Taipei, Taiwan, Since the 1960s*. Armonk, NY: M. E. Sharpe.

Metzler, John J. 1996. *Divided Dynamism: The Diplomacy of Separated Nations— Germany, Korea, and China*. Lanham, MD: University Press of America.

Rawnsley, Gary D. 2000. *Taiwan's Informal Diplomacy and Propaganda*. New York: St. Martin's Press.

The Republic of China Yearbook: Taiwan 2002. 2002. Taipei: Government Information Office.

Rigger, Shelley. 2001. *From Opposition to Power: Taiwan's Democratic Progressive Party*. Boulder: Lynne Rienner.

Rubinstein, Murray A. (ed.). 1994. *The Other Taiwan, 1945 to the Present*. Armonk, NY: M. E. Sharpe.

——— (ed.). 1999. *Taiwan: A New History*. Armonk, NY: M. E. Sharpe.

Sheng, Lijun. 2001. *China's Dilemma: The Taiwan Issue*. New York: Palgrave.

Simon, Denis F., and Michael Kau Ying-mao. 1992. *Taiwan Beyond the Economic Miracle*. Armonk, NY: M. E. Sharpe.

Skoggard, Ian A. 1996. *Dynamics in Taiwan's Postwar Development: The Religious and Historical Roots of Entrepreneurship*. Armonk, NY: M. E. Sharpe.

Stafford, Charles. 2000. *Separation and Reunion in Modern China*. Cambridge: Cambridge University Press.

Syu, Agnes. 1995. *From Economic Miracle to Privatization: Initial Stages of the Privatization Process in Two SOEs on Taiwan*. Lanham, MD: University Press of America.

Tan, Alexander, Steve Chan, and Calvin Jillson. 2001. *Taiwan's National Security: Dilemmas and Opportunities*. Burlington, VT: Ashgate.

Tien, Hung-mao. 1989. *The Great Transition*. Stanford: Hoover Institution Press.

——— (ed.). 1995. *Taiwan's Electoral Politics and Democratic Transition: Riding the Third Wave*. Armonk, NY: M. E. Sharpe.

Tsang, Steve (ed.). 1993. *In the Shadow of China: Political Developments in Taiwan Since 1949*. Honolulu: University of Hawaii Press.

Tsang, Steve, and Hung-Mao Tien. 1999. *Democratization in Taiwan: Implications for China*. New York: St. Martin's Press.

Tucker, Nancy Bernkopf. 1994. *Taiwan, Hong Kong, and the United States, 1945–1992*. New York: Maxwell Macmillan.

Wachman, Alan M. 1994. *Taiwan: National Identity and Democratization*. Armonk, NY: M. E. Sharpe.

Wang, Mei-ling T. 1999. *The Dust That Never Settles: The Taiwan Independence Campaign*. Lanham, MD: University Press of America.

Weller, Robert. 1999. *Alternative Civilities: Democracy and Culture in China and Taiwan*. Boulder: Westview Press.

Wu, Jausheih Joseph. 1995. *Taiwan's Democratization: Forces Behind the Momentum*. Oxford: Oxford University Press.

Yang, Maysing H. (ed.). 1997. *Taiwan's Expanding Role in the International Arena.* Armonk, NY: M. E. Sharpe.

Yu, Peter Kien-hong. 2002. *The Crab and Frog Motion Paradigm Shift: Decoding and Deciphering Taipei and Beijing's Dialectical Politics.* Lanham, MD: University Press of America.

■ Tibet

Avedon, John F. 1994. *In Exile from the Land of the Snows: The Definitive Account of the Dalai Lama and Tibet Since the Chinese Conquest.* New York: HarperPerennial.

Barnett, Robert (ed.). 1994. *Resistance and Reform in Tibet.* Bloomington: University of Indiana Press.

Batt, Herbert J. (ed.). 2001. *Tales of Tibet: Sky Burials, Prayer Wheels, and Wind Horses.* Lanham, MD: Rowman and Littlefield.

Beckwith, Christopher I. 1993. *The Tibetan Empire in Central Asia: A History of the Struggle for Great Power Among Tibetans, Turks, Arabs, and Chinese During the Early Middle Ages.* Princeton: Princeton University Press.

Bell, Charles. 1924. *Tibet, Past and Present.* Oxford: Clarendon Press.

Buescher, Hartmut, and Tarab Tulku. 2000. *Catalogue of Tibetan Manuscripts and Xylographs.* London: Curzon Press.

Candler, Edmund. 1987. *The Unveiling of Lhasa.* 3rd ed. New York: Snow Lion Graphics.

Cao, Changching, and James Seymour (eds.). 1997. *Tibet Through Dissident Chinese Eyes: Essay in Self-Determination.* Armonk, NY: M. E. Sharpe.

Carnahan, Sumner. 1995. *In the Presence of My Enemies: Memoirs of Tibetan Nobleman Tsipon Shuguba.* Santa Fe: Clear Light, 1995.

Carrasco, Pedro. 1959. *Land and Polity in Tibet.* Seattle: University of Washington Press.

Cassinelli, C. W., and Robert B. Ekvall. 1969. *A Tibetan Principality: The Political System of Sa sKya.* Ithaca: Cornell University Press.

Craig, Mary. 1997. *Kundun: A Biography of the Family of the Dalai Lama.* Washington, DC: Counterpoint.

———. 1999. *Tears of Blood: A Cry for Tibet.* Washington, DC: Counterpoint.

Dalai Lama. 1991. *Freedom in Exile: The Autobiography of the Dalai Lama.* San Francisco: HarperSanFrancisco.

Dalai Lama and Melissa Mathison Ford. 1997. *My Land and My People: The Original Autobiography of His Holiness the Dalai Lama of Tibet.* New York: Warner Books.

Dawa, Norbu. 1987. *Red Star over Tibet.* 2nd ed. New York: Envoy Press.

Epstein, Lawrence, and Richard Sherburne (eds.). 1990. *Reflections on Tibetan Culture: Essays in Honor of Turrell V. Wylie.* Lewiston, NY: Edwin Mellen Press.

Feigon, Lee. 1998. *Demystifying Tibet: Unlocking the Secrets of the Land of the Snows.* Chicago: Ivan. R. Dee.

French, Rebecca Redwood. 1995. *The Golden Yoke: The Legal Cosmology of Buddhist Tibet.* Ithaca: Cornell University Press.

Ginsburgs, George. 1964. *Communist China and Tibet: The First Dozen Years.* The Hague: M. Nijhoff.

Goldstein, Melvyn C. 1991. *A History of Modern Tibet, 1913–1951: The Demise of the Lamaist State.* Berkeley: University of California Press.

————. 1999. *The Snow Lion and the Dragon: China, Tibet, and the Dalai Lama.* Berkeley: University of California Press.

Goldstein, Melvyn C., and Cynthia Beall. 1990. *Nomads of Western Tibet: The Survival of a Way of Life.* Berkeley: University of California Press.

Goldstein, Melvyn C., Matthew Kapstein, and Orville Schell (eds.). 1998. *Buddhism in Contemporary Tibet: Religious Revival and Cultural Identity.* Berkeley: University of California Press.

Grunfeld, A. Tom. 1996. *The Making of Modern Tibet.* Rev. ed. Armonk, NY: M. E. Sharpe.

Gyatso, Palden. 1997. *The Autobiography of a Tibetan Monk.* New York: Grove Press.

Harrer, Heinrich. 1954. *Seven Years in Tibet.* Trans. Richard Graves. New York: E. P. Dutton.

————. 1997. *Lost Lhasa: Heinrich Harrer's Tibet.* New York: Harry N. Abrams.

————. 1998. *Return to Tibet: Tibet After the Chinese Occupation.* Trans. Ewald Osers. New York: J. P. Tarcher.

Hoffman, Helmut. 1971. *Tibet: A Handbook.* Bloomington, IN: Asian Studies Research Institute.

Hopkins, Jeffrey. 1999. *Emptiness in the Mind-Only School of Buddhism: Dynamic Responses to Dzong-ka-ba's* The Essence of Eloquence. Vol. 1. Berkeley: University of California Press.

Hopkirk, Peter. 1995. *Trespassers on the Roof of the World: The Secret Exploration of Tibet.* New York: Kodansha International.

Karan, Pradyumna P. 1976. *The Changing Face of Tibet.* Lexington: University Press of Kentucky.

Knaus, John Kenneth. 1999. *Orphans of the Cold War: America and the Tibetan Struggle for Survival.* Washington, DC: PublicAffairs.

Laird, Thomas. 2002. *Into Tibet: The CIA's First Atomic Spy and His Secret Expedition to Lhasa.* New York: Grove.

Lhalungpa, Lobsang P. 1983. *Tibet: The Sacred Realm: Photographs 1880–1950.* Millerton, NY: Aperture.

Lopez, Donald S., Jr. 1997. *Religions of Tibet in Practice.* Princeton: Princeton University Press.

McKay, Alex (ed.). 1997a. *Pilgrimage in Tibet.* London: Curzon Press.

————. 1997b. *Tibet and the British Raj: The Frontier Cadre, 1904–1947.* London: Curzon Press.

Moraes, Frances Robert. 1960. *The Revolt in Tibet.* New York: Macmillan.

Morrison, James, and Kenneth J. Conboy. 2002. *The CIA's Secret War in Tibet.* Lawrence: University of Kansas Press.

Novick, Rebecca McClen. 1999. *The Fundamentals of Tibetan Buddhism.* New York: Crossing Press.

Patt, David. 1992. *A Strange Liberation: Tibetan Lives in Chinese Hands.* Ithaca: Snow Lion.

Patterson, George N. 1960. *Tibet in Revolt.* London: Faber and Faber.

Perry, Art, and Robert A. F. Thurman. 1999. *The Tibetans: Photographs.* New York: Viking Press.

Powell, Andrew. 1995. *Living Buddhism.* Forward by His Holiness the Dalai Lama. Berkeley: University of California Press.

Rahul, Ram. 1969. *The Government and Politics of Tibet.* Delhi: Vikas.

Richardson, Hugh E. 1984. *Tibet and Its History.* 2nd ed. Boulder: Shambhala.

Rinpoche, Sogyal. 2000. *The Tibetan Book of Living and Dying.* Rev. ed. San Francisco: HarperSanFrancisco.

Schell, Orville. 2000. *Virtual Tibet: Searching for Shangri-La from the Himalayas to Hollywood.* New York: Henry Holt.
Schwartz, Ronald David. 1994. *Circle of Protest: Political Ritual in the Tibetan Uprising, 1987–92.* New York: Columbia University Press.
Shakabpa, Tsepon W. D. 1967. *Tibet: A Political History.* New Haven: Yale University Press.
Shakya, Tsering. 1999. *The Dragon in the Land of Snows: A History of Modern Tibet Since 1947.* New York: Columbia University Press.
Siebenschuh, William, Tashi Tsering, and Melvyn C. Goldstein. 2000. *The Struggle for Modern Tibet: The Autobiography of Tashi Tsering.* Armonk, NY: M. E Sharpe.
Smith, Warren W., Jr. 1997. *Tibetan Nation: A History of Tibetan Nationalism and Sino-Tibetan Relations.* Boulder: Westview Press.
Stein, R. A. 1995. *Tibetan Civilization.* Stanford: Stanford University Press.
Strong, Anna Louise. 1976. *When Serfs Stood Up in Tibet.* 2nd ed. San Francisco: Red Sun.
Thurman, Robert A. F. 1993. *The Tibetan Book of the Dead.* New York: Bantam Books.
Tucci, Giuseppe. 2000. *The Religions of Tibet.* Trans. Geoffrey Samuel. New York: Columbia University Press.
Tung, Rosemary Jones. 1996. *A Portrait of Lost Tibet.* Berkeley: University of California Press.
U.S. Department of State. 1996. *Foreign Relations of the United States, 1958–1960.* Vol. 19. Washington, DC: U.S. Government Printing Office.
Valli, Eric (director). 1999. *Himalaya.* Galatee Films, France.
Van Spengen, William. 1997. *Tibetan Border Worlds: A Geo-Analysis of Trade and Traders.* New York: Columbia University Press.
Waddell, L. Austine. 2001. *The Buddhism of Tibet, or Lamaism with Its Mystic Cults, Symbolism, and Mythology, and Its Relation to Indian Buddhism.* London: Curzon Press.
Wignall, Sidney. 2002. *Spy on the Roof of the World.* New York: Lyons Press.

International Relations

Robert E. Gamer

At the end of Chapter 6, I suggested that China is torn between its new desire to become a part of the world community and its traditional wishes to establish cultural and political dominance over its surrounding territories. The notion of being part of a world community composed of sovereign nations is something that has come into focus in China only during your lifetime. For most of its long history, China had little contact with the outside world. Its southern coastal communities developed trading contacts through the South China Sea. Its northern capitals sought to conquer, or protect themselves from conquest by, groups in the regions on China's borders. Abruptly and unexpectedly, all that changed in the nineteenth century when Beijing was brought to its knees by a small fleet of British ships. China spent the next century trying to free itself from domination by countries about which it had little prior knowledge and with which it had little prior contact. Then it spent three decades trying to reestablish rule without outside domination. Now, suddenly, during the last decades of the twentieth century, China has emerged as a premier participant in world trade and a player in regional crises of importance to the major powers; it is surrounded by small, newly independent nation-states dependent on its economic output and competes with Taiwan for seats on international bodies and the investments of enormously wealthy overseas Chinese families. It is scrambling to take full advantage of those opportunities while maintaining unity and stability at home. Those goals sometimes conflict, especially in a nation so recently thrust upon the world stage.

■ China's Foreign Relations Before the Opium Wars

Throughout most of its history, China's leaders had little contact with regions beyond those on the western borders. Largely isolated from the rest of the world, it had much reason to think of itself as the "Middle Kingdom" in the universe. But as Chapter 6 indicated, long before the Roman Empire, its merchants began trade with Java (in the Indonesian archipelago; see Map 2.1), Europe, India, and points between. In the twelfth century B.C.E., towns stretching from Guangzhou (Canton) to Fuzhou began extensive sea trade with Southeast Asia (see Maps 2.1, 2.2). In the fourth century B.C.E. a kingdom along China's southern coast, and during the third century B.C.E. the Qin dynasty (Chapter 3), sent out fleets of rafts full of settlers who might even have reached North America (Needham, 1971). Early in the Han dynasty, Chinese garrisons began to protect traders along the Silk Roads into inner Asia (Map 2.1). In the sixth century C.E., Arab, Jewish, Christian, and Turkish merchants started settling in China's coastal cities. Chinese ship captains (most notably, Admiral Zheng He's expedition into the Indian Ocean early in the fifteenth century, discussed in Chapter 3) accepted gifts from local rulers, which they passed on as tribute to Chinese emperors. Merchants coming overland brought the emperors tribute, as did emissaries from some kings of bordering states. As we saw in Chapter 6, China sought to control the administration of Tibet. Beyond this, China had no formal relations with foreign governments.

Like those of Siam (Thailand), Tibet, Japan, and Turkey, traditional Chinese leaders received tribute from lesser kingdoms around them. This solemnized their trade and foreign relations (Fairbank and Teng, 1941; Cohen, 2000). Emissaries or merchants from the lesser kingdoms brought gifts to the leader of the dominant one; the leader of the dominant kingdom reciprocated with gifts of greater value. China's emperors assumed these gifts were an indication that the kingdoms sending them recognized China's cultural superiority. To emphasize this, emissaries carrying the gifts were required to kneel before the emperor, hit their heads against the ground three times, and then lie flat (prostrate themselves) on the ground nine times. This was called the "kowtow." After that, the emperor would hold a banquet for the emissaries, give them gifts of greater value than those they had brought, and accord them the right to trade with China. The emperors interpreted this to mean that the barbarians who brought this tribute had "come to be transformed" and were recognizing China as the center of world civilization. The emperors believed any kingdom sending such gifts was a "vassal" recognizing China's "suzerainty" (dominance) over it. Korea, the kingdom of Melaka (Malacca) on the Strait of Malacca (near the southern tip of peninsular Malaysia; see Map 2.1), Siam (Thailand), Burma, and Vietnam (all in Southeast Asia; see Map 2.1), Japan, the Ryukyu Islands (stretching between Taiwan and Japan, containing Okinawa), and bordering kingdoms of Central Asia all sent emissaries to China's emperors bearing tribute; in exchange, China traded with them. Several ports were open for this trade; foreigners had to reside and stay within neighborhoods reserved for them. Ships came from as far as India and Arabia.

The sixteenth century brought major challenges to this system; new out-side forces, coming by sea, challenged China's suzerainty. In 1511 Portuguese ships took over one of China's vassal states, the kingdom of Melaka, and then established a fort on an island off southern China. The emissary they sent to Beijing was rebuffed and jailed. By 1557, in the Pearl River delta below Guangzhou (see Map 2.2), the Portuguese had established the colony of Macao, which was sending emissaries to Beijing with tribute in exchange for trading privileges. In 1555 Japanese pirates sacked the city of Nanjing, near the mouth of the Yangtze River (Map 2.2). In 1592 and 1597, the Japanese emperor Hideyoshi invaded China's vassal Korea and some Chinese ports; the threat subsided with Hideyoshi's sudden death. These provocations caused China's emperor to close most ports to trade. Macao became the principal port for China's trade with Japan, until Japan closed its ports to Portugal in 1639. In 1637 a British flotilla shot its way up the Pearl River toward Guangzhou, hoping to open the port. Then in 1685 China decided to open all its ports to foreign trade, and they remained open until 1757.

During the seventeenth century, the expanding Russian empire arrived at China's border; the Ming emperors granted trading rights. When the Mongols, whose territories had bordered those of Russia, took Beijing and established the Qing dynasty in 1644, they created the Lifan Yuan, an agency (staffed entirely by Manchus and Mongols) to deal with Russia. The Russian emper-ors were not comfortable having their embassies prostrate themselves before the Chinese emperors; they preferred a relationship between empires of equal stature. After some protracted wrangling over kowtowing and some border skirmishes, Jesuit court advisers helped the Lifan Yuan negotiate a treaty—China's first—to demarcate China's western boundaries and stabilize China's relations with Russia. It was signed in Nirchinsk in 1689 and followed by another at Kiakhta in 1729. The treaties prescribed that, in exchange for kow-tows in Beijing by Russia's emissaries, China's emissaries would kowtow at the czar's court in St. Petersburg. The trade missions, which crossed the bor-ders in increasing numbers, would simply exchange gifts without court appearances. In a great break from precedent, Russia was allowed to send a permanent emissary to reside in Beijing, but it was not allowed to trade by sea.

As the volume of outside trade began to expand rapidly during the eigh-teenth century, China's government found it necessary to create new ways of dealing with the outside world. In 1720 Guangzhou merchants formed the first of the trading organizations *(cohongs),* which became the official points of contact between China and European merchants. After 1757 Guangzhou (Canton) became the only port legally open for foreign trade. But no foreign-ers were allowed to live there; the employees of their firms had to reside in nearby Macao. Women were not to be allowed in the foreigners' Guangzhou warehouse-wharves and men could leave them, for an escorted walk in a park, only three times a month. By 1784 the United States began trade with Guangzhou.

The *cohongs* had to pay government officials large sums of money from their profits; they recovered this by demanding bribes and arbitrary fees from the foreigners. And the Chinese government kept creating new regulations to control the personal behavior of foreigners, restricting their movement outside Macao. In 1741 a disabled British ship had pulled into Hong Kong harbor and was refused assistance. Complaints about unfair trade practices had to be mediated by the very *cohongs* with which the foreigners were trading. In 1759 Britain's East India Company sent an emissary to the emperor to complain about these trade restrictions; he was imprisoned. With Britain now the largest seafaring trader in China, King George III sent an expedition to Beijing in 1793 to ask for the right to exchange ambassadors, let British live in Guangzhou and create warehouses to trade in other ports, allow missionaries to preach Christianity, and establish an outpost on an island near the mouth of the Yangtze River. Its leader, Lord Macartney, came laden with tribute consisting of Britain's latest manufactures. Qianlong, China's longest-serving emperor and one of its greatest, greeted him warmly (dispensing with a kowtow) and sent him home with many boxes of gifts and a long letter addressed to King George (Schurmann and Schell, 1967:104, 113; Cameron, 1975: 22–45), turning down all his requests. It explained the following:

• All foreigners living in China live in special neighborhoods that they cannot leave, wear Chinese garb, cannot open businesses or interact with Chinese subjects, and are never permitted to return home. Ambassadors could not function that way, and China does not need other religious doctrines. The letter adds, "The distinction between Chinese and barbarian is most strict" (Cameron, 1975:33).
• Europeans are permitted to reside in Macao and trade through Guangzhou *cohongs*. They can buy what they want there and are making large profits. Provisions have been made for settling disputes to the satisfaction of Europeans. Rules forbidding Europeans to set foot in Guangzhou and other parts of China cut down on the chance for disputes between Chinese and barbarians and give foreign trading organizations control over their own people.

■ From the Opium Wars to the People's Republic

These rules prevailed until the British fleet forced the Chinese to sign the Treaty of Nanjing in 1842, ending the first Opium War, which is discussed in Chapter 6 (Wally, 1958). During the subsequent half century, European powers invaded China on numerous occasions; after the peace negotiations that followed, China signed twenty more treaties reinforcing the new rules created by the Treaty of Nanjing and extending them to interaction with Japan, the United States, Peru, Brazil, Russia, and all the major European nations (Tung, 1970:19–31; Bau, 1921:93–180; Cameron, 1975:45–52). Though it was greatly weakened, none of these countries acquired China as a colony. But its sovereignty and interaction with foreign lands had been completely transformed. Suddenly foreigners were able to reside in special neighborhoods in a variety of "treaty ports" (Murphey, 1970; Johnson, 1995). They were able to learn Chinese, dress and behave as they pleased, open businesses, trade with anyone, travel in other parts of the cities where they lived, interact with Chinese subjects and propagate their religion, and travel to their homelands whenever they wished. They built industries and railroad lines and hired Chinese workers for jobs at home and overseas. Their boats plied inland waterways. Consuls appointed by foreign governments communicated directly with Chinese officials. Under new rules of "extraterritoriality," foreigners accused of crimes were tried under their own laws (Fishel, 1975).

The new rules required China, for the first time, to establish a national customs office and foreign affairs ministry (in 1861) and to open a school (soon transformed into a college) to train interpreters for Chinese officials dealing with foreigners. By the 1870s China was sending ambassadors abroad and no longer requiring ambassadors received by the emperor to kowtow (Hsu, 1980:81–82). Smarting from its military defeats and loss of sovereignty, the Qing government took steps at "self-strengthening" by acquiring a modern navy, establishing naval and military academies, and sending students abroad to learn about modern technical subjects (Liao, 1984:21–37; Wang, 1966:41, 99; Schurmann and Schell, 1967:206–248; Cameron, 1975:95–111).

Meanwhile (as Chapters 3, 4, 6, and 8 explain), China faced civil wars, disintegration of Beijing's control from the center, extensive migration by many able people, and social and economic problems caused by rapid population growth and economic change. Seeing its weakness, foreign powers took control of countries that had once been China's vassals and of territory within China.

- As discussed in Chapter 6, the Japanese took Formosa (Taiwan), the Ryukyu Islands (Okinawa), the Pescadores Islands, and the Liaodong peninsula in Manchuria.
- The French took control of Vietnam. They also demanded and received a lease for a port on Hainan Island (Map 2.2).
- The British took Burma. They also leased a port city on the north side of Shandong (Map 2.2) and Kowloon and the New Territories on the mainland opposite Hong Kong.

- Germany forced the Qing to lease it the port of Qingdao (now famous for its beer) and surrounding territory on the Shandong peninsula (Map 2.2).
- Nearby in Manchuria, the Russians received a lease for Port Arthur (Lushun, on the southern tip of Liaoning; Map 2.2).

In retaliation for some missionaries being killed during the Boxer Uprising (see Chapter 12), foreign troops actually occupied Beijing's Forbidden City from 1900 to 1901, forcing the emperor and empress dowager to flee. Supported by France and Germany, Russia used the chaos to occupy Manchuria (Heilongjiang, Jilin, and Liaoning; see Map 2.2), which prompted an alliance between Britain and Japan to protect their interests (Hsu, 1980:115–138; Tung, 1970:51–56; Liao, 1984:40–52; Cameron, 1975: 163–186).

In 1905 Japan defeated Russia in a war; the two signed a peace treaty in Portsmouth, New Hampshire, mediated by President Theodore Roosevelt (see Hunt, 1983). Roosevelt and the European powers were concerned about protecting the territorial integrity of China. The treaty acknowledged that Korea was under Japan's sphere of influence and agreed to the withdrawal of all foreign troops from Manchuria, except for some territory containing railway lines whose lease Russia was to transfer to Japan. Both Russia and Japan were to be allowed to station some troops in Manchuria to protect the railway. The Japanese received Port Arthur. This set the stage for forty-five years of conflict (Hsu, 1980:138–141; Schurmann and Schell, 1967:249–260; Cameron, 1975:201–231; Home, 1996) in which Japan would play a major role (see Table 7.1).

In 1910 Japan annexed Korea. For supporting Britain in World War I (and despite China's strong objection), the 1919 Treaty of Versailles gave Germany's land leases in China's Shandong peninsula to Japan, kicking off the May Fourth Movement of protest discussed in Chapter 13 (Tung, 1970:154–190; Wang, 1966:306–361; Bau, 1921:181–283). To counter the Soviet takeover of Russia, Japan occupied land bordering Manchuria. The Soviets kept claim to Russian railroad lines running through Manchuria, which angered Japan. In 1931 Japan occupied Manchuria and set it up as the puppet state of Manchukuo (Duara, 2003). In 1937, Japan attacked China and occupied large portions of it (as discussed in Chapter 4) until Japan's surrender to the Allied Forces in 1945.

■ Foreign Policy Under Mao

During the "united front" between the communists and Chiang Kai-shek's Nationalists, which lasted from 1936 until the end of World War II, the

Table 7.1 Important Dates in China's Foreign Policy

1842	Treaty of Nanjing ends first Opium War
1861	Founding of Customs Office and Foreign Affairs Ministry
1895	Treaty of Shimonoseki cedes Formosa to Japan
1900	British occupy Forbidden City after Boxer Uprising
1905	Treaty of Portsmouth allows Japanese troops in Manchuria
1919	Treaty of Versailles gives Japan Shandong land leases
1931	Japan occupies Manchuria
1945	End of World War II brings KMT-communist combat
1950	Start of Korean War and U.S. Seventh Fleet in Taiwan Strait
1953	Korean War armistice
1955	Bandung Conference of "nonaligned" states
1956	Tibetan rebellion
1960	Break in relations with USSR
1962	Sino-Indian border war
1964	China explodes atomic bomb
1965	United States enters Vietnam War
1970	China takes Taiwan's United Nations seat
1972	U.S. president Richard Nixon visits China
1975	End of Vietnam War
1979	United States and China establish diplomatic relations
1987	Tibetan rebellion
1989	USSR General Secretary Mikhail Gorbachev visits China
1997	Hong Kong joins China
1999	Macao joins China
2001	Beijing chosen as site of 2008 Olympics
2002	China and Taiwan join World Trade Organization

United States and the Soviet Union could deal with the communists and the Nationalists at the same time. Even when the united front broke down, both gave technical and military assistance to the Nationalists while maintaining friendly contact with the communists (Sheng, 1998). As the Japanese surrendered, the Nationalist and communist armies turned to fight one another for control of China. The United States assisted only the Nationalists (Westad, 1992; Tucker, 2001), while Joseph Stalin attempted to play both sides. He turned over control of enormous arms stockpiles and the city of Harbin to the communists and trained and supplied Mao Zedong's troops; he gave the Nationalists command of all the other Manchurian cities (after dismantling many industries and seizing many assets for shipment to the Soviet Union) and maintained good relations with Chiang Kai-shek. Thus, once he captured Beijing and Chiang's Kuomintang (KMT) government fled to Taiwan in 1949, Mao felt uneasy taking on Stalin as an ally, but he had nowhere else to turn because he found himself isolated diplomatically (for revealing insights into his foreign policy during this period, see Hunt and Niu, 1995). Britain quickly recognized the People's Republic of China (PRC) (Jain, 1976:24–47) but also continued to recognize the legitimacy of Chiang's regime in Taiwan. Though he made overtures to President Harry Truman, the United States did not respond (Garver, 1993:40). The spread of communism in Eastern Europe was making the United States hesitant to carry on further relations with communist regimes. Therefore, needing foreign assistance, Mao accepted aid from the Soviet Union; this uneasy relationship lasted until 1960. Two days after North Korea attacked South Korea in June 1950, the U.S. Seventh Fleet moved into the Taiwan Strait to protect the Nationalists from invasion by Mao's forces; the United States would not recognize the PRC until 1979. Before exploring these developments further, we should assess Mao's strategic considerations as he assumed power.

After 100 years of division and foreign intrusion, Mao sought to reestablish China's traditional borders and to reassert influence over all the regions that once paid tribute to China. That tribute had recognized China's moral and cultural superiority as well as its physical dominance. As a communist, Mao wanted to rid China and its neighbors of imperialist masters and to persuade its neighbors of the superiority of China's communist system. At the same time, he wanted to continue to attract capitalist investment so as to rebuild China's economy and to develop friendly trade relations with foreign nations. That combination of goals called for a delicate balancing act that involved several elements.

• The 11 million overseas Chinese, mostly residing in Southeast Asia, might provide technical skills and investment capital. But as their countries received independence from the colonial powers, they wished to incorporate their Chinese populace into their own citizenry. If the PRC were to continue treating these overseas Chinese as its own citizens, it risked alienating the governments of these new nations.

• Guerrilla movements were challenging the legitimate governments in many of these countries. As China's leader, Mao realized they could help him assert China's dominance over the region. As a communist, he was sympathetic to their revolutionary aspirations of returning power to the exploited lower classes, but he also wanted peace on his borders while he consolidated power and fought outside challengers. He did not want to force neighboring governments into treaties that would give the United States bases on China's borders or into retaliation against their Chinese communities. He wanted the support of the wealthy Chinese living in those countries, who hated the guerrillas and were also being wooed by Chiang Kai-shek to support the KMT in Taiwan. And the guerrillas also had loyalties to their own countries and might not ultimately side with China.

• The PRC wanted admission into the United Nations and other bodies that could provide it with access to world markets and participation in international decisionmaking. But it was determined to defeat Chiang Kai-shek's Nationalist forces, which had fled to the island of Taiwan while insisting (as explained in Chapter 6) that they were still the rightful government of all China. Only one could hold China's United Nations seat, and both had supporters there.

• Mao wanted to abrogate "unequal treaties" drawn up between imperial powers and former Chinese governments, but he also wanted trade, investment, and assistance from those imperial powers.

Overseas Chinese stood squarely at the center of all those concerns, so Mao's government could not walk away from them. More overseas Chinese had contact with the KMT and other parties in China than with the communists; both sides needed their money and support to continue fighting one another. Many overseas Chinese were facing political repression and finding it hard to get education or employment; some were joining guerrilla movements in their own countries. The new communist regime initially responded with a simple offer: come back home and help rebuild China. It offered them inexpensive education if they stayed to become residents of China, and higher salaries than locals. It created special banking arrangements, housing, shops, grain allotments, and travel privileges for overseas Chinese and for local relatives of overseas Chinese receiving monetary remittances from them. It urged them to create enterprises in China. Nearly half a million Chinese came back (Fitzgerald, 1972:33). In addition, the government encouraged Chinese families with relatives abroad to write them to solicit money. It still looked upon all these overseas Chinese as China's citizens; they could become citizens of other nations and still retain (dual) citizenship in China.

By 1957 the People's Republic had discovered the amount of technical talent and money and political support it could attract through these policies was limited, and many Chinese who had stayed home resented the special privileges accorded those who had left, so it reversed course, unleashing a rectification campaign (see Chapter 4) to limit the rights of these returnees and urge Chinese to cut off their contacts with overseas relatives. By then, it also was negotiating agreements with Burma and Indonesia, the only Southeast Asian countries with which it had diplomatic relations, allowing (for the first time in history) overseas Chinese who became citizens of those nations to break their affiliation with China, if they chose to do so. Those choosing this course would no longer receive favors or protection from China and would no longer be considered Chinese citizens. Furthermore, China now encouraged schools to be built for Chinese students by wealthy Chinese in Southeast Asian countries to teach local languages and history and skills that would prepare them for local employment.

Events in Korea and Vietnam made this normalization possible. North Korea invaded South Korea in June 1950. Until then, Mao's government had shown little interest in Korean affairs; the Soviet Union was North Korea's principal ally. China had been informed by those two countries shortly before the invasion took place and let North Korean troops stationed on its territory return home to participate. But the entry of United Nations forces on the side of South Korea and the U.S. Seventh Fleet into the Taiwan Strait as well as imposition of a trade blockade roused China's concern (Chen, 1994; Garson, 1995; Cumings, 1981, 1990; Chang, 1990; Zhang, 2001). In August, the United Nations proposed to China that it mediate a truce in exchange for a United Nations Security Council seat. However, in October, General Douglas MacArthur's troops crossed into North Korea and headed toward the Yalu River (the same river the Japanese had crossed when they invaded Manchuria). Beijing lies within 400 miles of that border. China immediately mobilized troops and sent them secretly into North Korea; they succeeded in pushing the United Nations forces back into South Korea (Hinton, 1972:40–49; Garver, 1993:285–286; Gittings, 1974:181–184; Jain, 1976:49–70). A truce was signed three years later, leaving Korea divided. The United States suffered 160,000 casualties and China over 700,000 (including one of Mao's sons), leaving deep antagonism and suspicion on both sides. The United States was now firmly committed to "containing" China, holding it within its boundaries and isolating it diplomatically. But China was also angry at the Soviet Union for starting a war on its borders in which China—not the USSR—suffered deep casualties (Nelson, 1989; Ross, 1993; Sheng, 1998). Hence China now made an all-out effort to improve relations with smaller neighboring Asian countries.

In Vietnam, Ho Chi Minh began guerrilla warfare against the French at the end of World War II. In 1949, Chinese Red Army troops moved to the Vietnamese border to chase remaining Kuomintang Nationalist troops from China (Chen, 1969:212–278; Whiting, 2001). In the next few years, China's government gave Ho's forces small amounts of technical assistance. After the Korean War armistice was signed in 1953, this aid grew dramatically. Ho was attacking governments supported first by the French and then by the Americans, who now were moving to encircle China. Though many leaders of newly independent nations had themselves begun by resisting colonial rulers and therefore might have sympathy for Ho's attempts, they also were wary of attempts by the Soviet Union, the United States, or China to involve them in the Cold War. And communist guerrillas threatened their regimes as well. So China was careful to restrict its support to the Viet Minh in Vietnam, declaring that communist forces in Laos (an area of interest to India) and in Cambodia, where China lent support to Prince Sihanouk, should seek separate settlements. Meanwhile, remnants of KMT troops remained in those areas, supported by the United States.

In 1955 China agreed to end support for communist guerrillas operating in Burma (which, in 1949, had been the first Asian government to recognize Mao's regime); China gave little support thereafter (Tung, 1970:357–362; Gurtov, 1971:89–118; North, 1974:93–96). During talks in 1960, Burma and China agreed to some concessions on territory they claimed. When a more radical socialist government gained power in Burma in 1963, defeating the Maoist guerrillas, it took a harder line against China.

In 1955, leaders of African and Asian nations held a conference in Bandung, Indonesia, to declare a neutral path toward "peaceful coexistence," avoiding alliance with either the Soviet Union or the United States. Zhou Enlai (Han, 1994; Wilson, 1984; Shao, 1996), representing China, was a major presence at this conference, declaring China's intent to sign agreements with these nonaligned nations to settle differences over dual citizenship by overseas Chinese, guerrilla warfare waged against independent nations, border disputes, and other contentious issues. As part of these efforts, China distributed hundreds of millions of dollars in aid to developing nations (Garver, 1993:221; Hinton, 1972:248–262; Jain, 1976:112–156; Ojha, 1969:174–209). Zhou Enlai was competing for allegiance of these nations with India, which also declared its neutrality while seeking aid from the Soviet Union.

Taiwan's continuing insistence that foreign governments allow Chinese residents to fly Nationalist flags and obey their policies strengthened the PRC's position on normalizing relations. Taiwan's legislature contained seats representing overseas Chinese. As late as 1970, the KMT kidnapped two Manila newspapermen of Han ancestry in the Philippines who did not consider themselves citizens of Taiwan and placed them on military trial for violating Taiwan's emergency regulations (Fitzgerald, 1972:76). Many Southeast Asians saw these assertions and actions as interference with the sovereignty of their own nations. By taking steps to break off ties with overseas Chinese, the PRC was attempting to distance itself from this approach (which had been habitual with Chinese governments during the past century) and thus gain more confidence among governments that feared subversion by overseas Chinese. In addition, few Chinese were now emigrating from the mainland into Southeast Asia.

Acts by surrounding countries made the PRC's attempts at normalization more difficult. Thailand had outlawed separate educational institutions for overseas Chinese (Gurtov, 1971:5–48). Many Southeast Asian countries suppressed Chinese newspapers. The 1955 nationality treaty with Indonesia allowed Chinese who had accepted Indonesian citizenship to regain Chinese citizenship by moving out of Indonesia, leaving many Indonesians wondering whether naturalized Chinese would remain loyal to their adopted country (Sukma, 1999). In 1956 South Vietnam forced all Chinese to declare Vietnamese citizenship and excluded them from Chinese education and most retail trade. In 1960, Indonesia also banned Chinese from retail trade, their principal source of livelihood, and closed many Chinese schools and newspapers. The heat over this controversy sparked riots; the Chinese government sent ships to carry 100,000 refugees to asylum in China. After 1963, China also extricated refugees when repression in India followed the Sino-Indian border skirmishes (discussed in the last section of Chapter 6).

To quell these fears about the loyalty of overseas Chinese, Zhou Enlai announced that Chinese everywhere were free to choose their own citizenship; he encouraged them to become citizens of and obey the laws of the lands where they resided and to marry local people. Overseas Chinese who chose to retain Chinese citizenship would be expected to obey the laws of the lands where they resided, but ultimately they were subject to the jurisdiction of the PRC and not of Taiwan. And no Chinese should be forced to accept citizenship against their will (Fitzgerald, 1972:112–114, 140–161).

In 1960, China and the Soviet Union broke off relations (Hinton, 1972:205–230; Ojha, 1969:111–145; Jones and Kevill, 1985:17–25; North, 1974:109–127). The Soviet Union, concerned about China's Great Leap Forward (see Chapter 4) and development of an atomic bomb, refused it further aid (Lewis and Xue, 1988; Lin, 1988; Ryan, 1989). Seeking to gain influence in South and Southeast Asia under its own policy of "peaceful coexistence," Khrushchev supported Indonesia and India—which was also developing atomic weaponry—in their disputes with China (see Chapter 6 on the dispute with India). Cut off now from all the great powers and arguing with its neighbors, China gave even higher priority to becoming a nuclear power (Lewis and Litai, 1988; Lin, 1988; Ryan, 1989). By 1963, the Soviet Union had moved troops to protect the Outer Mongolian border (see Mongolia on Map 2.1) from uncertainties in China; meanwhile, it was airlifting supplies to North Vietnam and Laos. An increasingly militant China was sending aid to forces fighting white colonialists in Rhodesia and Mozambique, to Albania, and to the neutral Sihanouk regime in Cambodia (Gurtov, 1971:49–82). In 1964, China exploded an atomic bomb. This helped it restore dignity and greatness in the eyes of smaller countries of the region but heightened the determination of the United States to halt its projection of power and caused some Americans to regret not invading China when they had the chance.

In the fall of 1964, Khrushchev was removed from office in Russia; his successors returned to a militant communism closer in spirit to that of Mao. The new leaders invited Zhou Enlai to see whether relations could now be improved and to enlist China's support in the Soviet Union's new resolve to substantially aid North Vietnam, but Mao remained suspicious. Soviet troops remained on the Mongolian border. In the summer of 1965, regular U.S. forces entered the Vietnam War for the first time. Once again, the United States was actively countering an invasion backed by the Soviet Union in a country on China's border. Hard lines were being drawn.

■ The Cultural Revolution

In 1966, Mao launched the Cultural Revolution (Hinton, 1972:127–162; Chapter 4). For a time in 1967, elements of the extreme left within the Red

Guards took over the Foreign Ministry. By the end of that year, Zhou Enlai reemerged as a conciliator to begin restoring order, but for much of the next decade, China's domestic and foreign policy had to accommodate the wishes of the extreme left (Barnouin and Yu, 1997). This brought mistrust even among nations that had begun to feel more comfortable with China's policies. The radical elements were holding rallies and pillorying officials throughout China, talking about extending permanent revolution to all the rest of the world. Pol Pot in Cambodia, Sendero Luminoso guerrillas in Peru, and the Naxalite rebels in India sent emissaries to Beijing.

Such militant behavior and rhetoric helped the United States amass more support in the region for fighting the Viet Minh in Vietnam. Ironically, China was trying hard to stay out of the Vietnam War. Having sustained enormous losses in Korea, fearing an attack by the Soviet Union on its western border, and facing disruption at home from the Cultural Revolution, Mao hoped to avoid sending in Chinese troops (Karnow, 1984:452–453). The main proponents of greater intervention were professional elements of the military displeased that their troops were bogged down at home carrying out public works and propaganda. They advocated spending more on weapons and equipment that could be used for armed conflict.

The radicals' desire for worldwide revolution caused problems for the Chinese in Indonesia. In the confusion surrounding a 1965 military coup in Indonesia, local inhabitants in many places slaughtered Chinese neighbors. Initially, refugees were welcome in China; China's policy was to repatriate Chinese rather than encourage them to revolt. After the 1967 seizure of the Foreign Ministry, however, this policy changed (Liao, 1984:169–188; Gurtov, 1971:113–124); the radicals now encouraged overseas Chinese to rebel. This only increased resistance abroad. By the end of 1967, Outer Mongolia was expelling overseas Chinese. Chinese in Burma, Cambodia, Penang, Macao, and Hong Kong clashed with authorities. Red Guards harassed overseas Chinese visiting China from abroad on trade missions and wrote to some of them, informing them that their houses and property in China were being seized. Letters and parcels from abroad were confiscated, and Chinese were discouraged from writing to relatives abroad. By 1969, suspicion of China in Indonesia grew so great that its government declared the 1955 nationality treaty null and void.

The radicalization of China's Foreign Ministry was short-lived, however. By late 1967 Mao was calling upon Zhou Enlai and the army to reestablish some order and restrain the Red Guards (Gurtov, 1971:125–158; Zhu, 1998). Overseas Chinese engaged in rebellion would not receive material support from China. A 1969 border incursion by radical Chinese troops was decisively trounced by Soviet troops (Jones and Kevill, 1985:92–96). Slowly, China sought to restore normal relations with the outside world. In 1970, Mao asked U.S. journalist Edgar Snow to stand with him on the reviewing stand for

National Day. The following year, Zhou Enlai met secretly with Henry Kissinger; in October, China took Taiwan's seat in the United Nations. Richard Nixon's visit to Beijing in 1972 dramatized the changing relationship (Hollridge, 1997; Tucker, 2001). Soon Japan and a host of other nations established diplomatic relations. Japan was especially well poised to take advantage of the new era. Ever since the end of World War II, it had quietly resumed trade and diplomatic contacts with China. Now those relations were legitimized, and Japanese businessmen had a head start on setting up new enterprises in China.

In 1975, North Vietnamese troops entered Saigon, and the last U.S. troops were airlifted out. The following year, both Zhou Enlai and Mao died. On January 1, 1979, the United States and China established full diplomatic relations. Weeks later, relations between Vietnam and China were in disarray. China crossed the border with troops; within a month, their poorly equipped and trained troops were beaten back by superior Vietnamese forces. This was the ultimate proof of how weak Mao's policies had made China. After three decades of hostility, China and the United States were renewing relations, both smarting from defeat by a nation that had long pitted them as adversaries (Ross, 1995). Ironically, the United States had fought North Vietnam as part of an effort to stop China from extending its political power into Southeast Asia; now Vietnam was holding back China's troops from entering Vietnam.

■ Joining the World Community

Chapters 4–6 discussed the enormous economic growth China has experienced since Deng Xiaoping took the reins of power by 1980. Deng brought an end to the Cultural Revolution, freeing China to try his economic reforms. China's new position in the international community also facilitated reform. It was now a member of the United Nations Security Council and had diplomatic relations with the United States. And the Cold War was coming to an end. China was free to assume a normal position in world affairs (Liao, 1984:211–233). It could press aggressively to establish trade ties for its reforming economy. With the Soviet Union disintegrating, large numbers of traders were crossing the borders of its former republics to buy goods for their depleted economies. China set out to ease trade across the borders with Nepal, Mongolia, Burma, Laos, and Thailand (bringing a flood of unwelcome opium along with other goods). In 1989 Soviet leader Mikhail Gorbachev visited Beijing, and in 1992 China settled part of a border dispute with Russia (which resulted in the signing of a formal border agreement in 1997) and started importing Russian technology. China helped Thailand fight Moscow-backed Vietnamese and Cambodian forces until a Cambodian peace settlement in 1991 allowed it to withdraw support from Khmer Rouge guerrilla forces there and cut all ties with Thai communists. No longer a military ally or adversary, Vietnam gradually emerged as a trading partner with China and the West; China opened trade across its border in 1990. In 1989 China ended support for Malaysian communist guerrillas, and in 1990 Singapore and Indonesia established diplomatic relations with China. Businesspeople from around the world began to explore the "China market."

The military intervention at Tiananmen Square in 1989 brought a chill to China's foreign relations for a time. But after Deng toured the Pearl River delta region early in 1992 and announced that in the new "socialist market economy" the reform efforts would be speeded and that China's people should explore capitalist techniques, investment began to pour in (see Chapter 5). Now China carries on trade (and diplomatic relations) with virtually every foreign nation. It belongs to the World Bank and signed the nuclear nonproliferation treaty in 1984 (though it has continued to sell nuclear materials abroad).

Only North Korea remains a hard-core communist nation. China treats it with respectful reserve, urging restraint when South Korea (which established diplomatic relations with China in 1992) or the United States has sought serious retaliation or sanctions against its nuclear program or military threats. Since 1997 it has worked closely with the United States and South Korea in negotiations to open North Korea to the outside world. It has also aided North Korea with grain, oil, and fertilizer, and is North Korea's biggest trading partner.

As we saw in Chapter 6, Hong Kong and Taiwan have become China's biggest partners in investment and trade. Japan, the United States, Western Europe, and Singapore joined in more slowly but have grown into sizable partners as well. However, a number of controversies still clouded this interaction.

■ Regional Conflicts

China maintains a traditional concern about the regions to its south (in Southeast Asia) and west (in Central Asia; see Map 2.1). Since the second century B.C.E., some of China's greatest emperors have extended its borders in those directions. Its main traditional enemies—the Annamese and Champas (from Vietnam), Turks, Mongols, Manchus, Zunghars, Tanguts, Tartars, Russians, and Tibetans (from Central Asia)—lived in or invaded territory there. Those areas remain of great strategic concern to China. As just indicated, China has recently accommodated some of its disputes in Southeast Asia, although its relations with Tibet remain tense (see Chapter 6). It also faces unrest among Muslims and other minorities in Xinjiang Autonomous Region, who are influenced by Islamic fundamentalists in regions to the west of China. China sold arms to Iran, Pakistan, and Iraq in hopes of cooperation on keeping border security. It outbid U.S. oil companies for rich oil fields in Kazakhstan, which will take on increasing strategic importance when its new oil pipelines become operative, and in Indonesia.

The attack on the World Trade Center on September 11, 2001, brought a new phase to those conflicts. China promptly offered aid to the United States to fight terrorism in those regions. Pakistan became an ally in the overthrow of the Taliban in Afghanistan and the war on terror. China renewed its program of seeking out rebel leaders in Xingjiang and giving them death sentences, often on meager evidence, now with acquiescence from the United States and European nations (Smith, 2001; Becker, 2001). And it voted in the Security Council to support the United States in its efforts to stop Iraq's weapons program. Though China expressed opposition to the subsequent U.S. attack on Iraq in March 2003, China and Russia were the first two nonparticipating nations that President Bush called to mend fences.

Chapter 6 discussed some of China's historical disputes with India. The relations between the two countries remain tentative and complex. India and China have competed over control of strategic passes on China's western borders, dominance over Tibet and Nepal, and leadership among third world nations. While India courted support from the Soviet Union, China supplied arms to India's adversaries in Pakistan, Saudi Arabia, Iran, and Iraq, helping Afghan forces fight the Soviet invasion there. When it became apparent in 1989 that China was selling Pakistan nuclear materials, India stepped up its arms race with China. Breaking a treaty obligation with India, China sold arms to Nepal; when India set up a blockade, it trucked them in. Then in 1990 pro-Indian forces overthrew Nepal's government. Ironically, India's open border with Nepal has let Maoist rebel groups seek asylum in India while carrying on guerrilla warfare against Nepal's government. Nepal's border with China, meanwhile, remains sealed with firm passport controls. China remains angry that the Dalai Lama, along with many Tibetan refugees, has political asylum in India. In 1997 China agreed to cut back arms sales to Pakistan, but continued to supply them. In 2001, during the war to overthrow the Taliban in Afghanistan, heavy fighting broke out in Kashmir, and Pakistan and India threatened to use nuclear weapons against each other. China resists taking India's side in the Kashmir dispute, but shares India's hatred of Islamic militants there. So the two sought accommodation. For the first time, direct flights between China and India commenced. A panel of experts was given authority to find a compromise over disputed Kashmir terrain held by China but claimed by India, and Arunachal Pradesh terrain held by India but claimed by China (see Chapter 6). In 1992, China helped create the Shanghai Cooperation to settle border disputes with Russia, Kazakhstan, Kyrgyzstan, Tajikistan, and Uzbekistan.

Another point of tension lies in the waters southeast of China. The South China Sea (see Map 2.4) is dotted with many islands, which are potential launching points for military assaults and control of the vast petroleum reserves on the ocean floor. The Portuguese began the eventual European domination of China by occupying islands there. Both China and Taiwan lay claim to the Spratly and Paracel Islands north of Borneo and to the South China Sea surrounding them (including seabed near the Natuna Islands, where Indonesia is developing a huge natural gas project), in violation of the United Nations Law of the Sea convention, to which China is a signatory (Valencia, 1996). For the first time since the Ming dynasty, during the 1990s China sent a navy into the open sea as part of its improved training and deployment of troops. Visits by those ships to the Spratly, Paracel, and Natuna Islands cause concern to the governments of Malaysia, the Philippines, Indonesia, and Taiwan (Catley, 1997). Meanwhile, China, Taiwan, and Japan all claim ownership over the Diaoyu Islands in the East China Sea (Map 2.4). After a radical nationalist Japanese group erected a lighthouse there in 1996, Japan (declaring the islands their "exclusive economic zone") set up a coast guard patrol nearby, which in 1998 sank a vessel carrying twenty-five Hong Kong protesters, who were rescued by accompanying Taiwanese protest ships. To ease some of these concerns, in 1998 the United States signed an accord with China designed to avoid naval and air conflicts at sea.

Incidents continued; the Philippine navy still arrested Chinese fishermen, and Vietnamese troops on the islands fired warning shots at Philippine planes. In 2002, China signed an agreement (not legally binding) with members of the Association of Southeast Asian Nations (ASEAN). All ten nations agreed to refrain from activities that would aggravate tensions in the area, including occupation of new islands. New structures on already-occupied islands, and the Paracel Islands, are not mentioned. In recent years China has installed communications equipment on disputed islands it occupies and staged large-scale military exercises there. That activity is likely to continue.

■ Broader Conflicts

The most difficult controversy obstructing China's efforts to join the world community is its puzzling relationship with Taiwan—the unresolved civil war. Their only point of agreement is that both are part of the same country. China insists that Taiwan is part of mainland China; Taiwan insists that it is the rightful ruler of China (or an independent nation). Countries establishing diplomatic relations with China are forced to end relations with Taiwan. Taiwan is the largest investor in China, and its trade volume with the United States nearly matches that of China. Chapter 6 discusses the diplomatic moves under way to try to bridge these radical differences.

The United States, ever since it brought the Seventh Fleet into the Taiwan Strait in 1950, has pledged to defend Taiwan against attack by China. It extended diplomatic recognition to China in 1979 with the stipulation that it

Robert Gamer

Troops touring the Great Wall
during a holiday excursion

Robert Gamer

would allow Taiwan and China to settle their differing interpretations of what "one China" meant, so long as neither party launched a military attack on the other, and that the United States would still continue to supply Taiwan with "defensive" weapons.

In 1999, while intervening in Yugoslavia, U.S. planes bombed the Chinese embassy in Belgrade, killing a number of staff members there. This provoked outrage on campuses and among citizens in China. That began a period of especially strained relations between China and the United States. Only months later, Chen Shui-bian came to power in Taiwan, and China threatened to invade if his new government sought to declare independence. Meanwhile, China is making a major push to add to its arsenal of cruise and land-based missiles, supersonic jets, helicopters, destroyers, submarines, tanks, satellites, and other advanced weaponry, together with radar and the most advanced software and electronics. Much of it comes from Russia, but Israeli, British, French, and even U.S. firms are vying to sell it advanced weapons and technology needed to design and operate them (Lague, 2002). China itself is building new aircraft and ships, many of which are the most advanced possessed by countries in the region. In response, the United States agreed to sell Taiwan new classes of weaponry. Members of Congress called for supplying Taiwan, in addition, with submarines, antisubmarine aircraft, a new class of Aegis destroyers, and a highly advanced "theater" missile system. When President George W. Bush took office in 2001, China feared he would let Taiwan purchase these additional weapons. It also rejected U.S. assertions that it was helping Iraq improve its air defenses. Then in April a U.S. spy plane was rammed by a Chinese plane and forced to land in China; China demanded a full apology from the United States before returning the crew. The United States issued a cautious apology, but meanwhile allowed Chen Shui-bian to visit the United States, over China's protests. And the United States agreed to sell Taiwan most of the proposed array of new weaponry. But with Taiwan's military leaders still closely allied to the KMT and not yet fully subordinate to civilian rule, Chen is reluctant to purchase many of these weapons.

After this high drama, a new phase began in relations between the United States and China. By the end of 2001 Beijing had been chosen as the site of the 2008 Olympics, China and Taiwan were admitted into the World Trade Organization, and China was cooperating with the United States in the war on terror. By the end of 2002 President Bush had visited China twice, Hu Jintao had visited the White House, and Jiang Zemin had visited Bush's ranch shortly before stepping down as general secretary of the Communist Party. A Beijing exhibition celebrated the thirtieth anniversary of Nixon's visit to China. A U.S. Navy ship visited a port in China, and top military commanders exchanged visits. And U.S. secretary of state Colin Powell reiterated U.S. support for "one China" and against independence for Taiwan. Meanwhile, the new top leadership of the People's Liberation Army (PLA) is likely to continue to push for high military spending and vigilance against Taiwan (Karmel, 2000), while the United States helps Taiwan add to its arms capacities. Both these entities continue to have a military capacity far below that of the United States (though China is fast catching up to Japan's military capacity), and their training and technical support lag behind the capacity of the new weaponry. But their relative capacities in relation to each other grow more even, and more lethal (Hickey, 2001). The great danger is that they could trigger warfare, and that casualties for all participants could be high if it breaks out. The rising trade, investment, travel, and communication between Taiwan and China, the entry of both into the World Trade Organization, and the increased cooperation between the United States and China reduce, but do not eradicate, that threat.

■ China's Role in the World

In 1997 the value of Thailand's currency collapsed, sparking the Asian economic crisis (see Chapter 5). Soon Malaysia, Indonesia, and other Southeast Asian countries had similar difficulties, and stock markets fell in Hong Kong, Japan, and other countries of the region. China immediately offered Thailand U.S.$1 billion in loans to help stabilize the value of its currency and promised aid to Indonesia as well; later the International Monetary Fund (IMF) stepped in with many billions of dollars in loans. These devalued currencies meant that products from Southeast Asia could sell for less in the United States and Europe. China was tempted to devalue its own currency to remain competitive, but chose not to. Knowing that this might further deflate all the region's currencies and standards of living, it chose instead to raise interest rates and take other uncomfortable measures to hold the value of their currencies firm. Unlike Japan, it cooperated closely with the IMF to bolster Asia's currencies. It has also invested heavily in Southeast Asia, buying oil and gas fields, timber, coal and copper mines, palm oil plantations, and other resources, and setting up manufacturing plants for its products. That helps surrounding countries, along with overseas Chinese who invest heavily in China, but also fuels old resentments against Chinese. China is also that region's second largest source of tourists (behind Japan).

In 2002, China and ASEAN nations signed an accord creating a free trade area. Some of its members envision this as the beginning of a common market that will eliminate all tariffs within the region. That will be difficult to achieve. But this agreement, together with the agreement on the disputed islands, contributes to stability in the area. China also gives foreign aid to Cambodia and its longtime ally Prince Sihanouk. It is criticized by countries along the Mekong River for its series of hydroelectric dams upstream (one second in size only to the largest of the Three Gorges dams—see Chapter 9).

It is working with those countries on a program to dynamite the rapids and shoals in the Mekong to improve navigation, over the objections of environmentalists and the Thai army.

China has many problems to overcome as it seeks to become a major player in the international economy and community of nations. Its abuses of human rights (Foot, 2001), infringements of copyright laws, official corruption, uncertain legal protections on contracts, crackdowns on political expression, treatment of children in orphanages, mislabeling of products to circumvent trade quotas, restrictions on foreign companies, and breaking of promises not to sell certain arms abroad or goods made in prisons all cause concern abroad. During the first year after entry into the World Trade Organization it passed 2,300 new laws and abolished 830 others to address these problems. However, Beijing does not always have control over the activities in the provinces where many of these abuses emanate. And its fear of disruption makes it hesitant to allow much extension of political freedoms.

Beijing's government wants to restore unity and power to China, and it wants to make its people prosperous. The two objectives are hard to accomplish simultaneously. It wants its own populace to feel—after the era of "unequal treaties" and Japanese occupation—that their nation is strong and able to resist outside pressure. Yet it does not want to frighten overseas Chinese and European investors and traders. After the Korean and Vietnam Wars, and decades of U.S. military aid to Taiwan, it remains wary of U.S. military and political intentions in the region. Yet it wants U.S. economic and political support, and it benefits from selling to the U.S. market, which absorbs about a fourth of its exports. It wants to attract investment both from Taiwan businesspeople and from overseas Chinese investors elsewhere; at the same time, it does not want those investors to feel that an independent Taiwan would be a safe place to site their factories and export their goods.

When it threatens to invade Taiwan, China's government appeases officers in its own military who believe in unification or want a greater role for the military, appeals to the nationalistic sentiments of its people, warns Taiwanese who are tempted to support party factions advocating independence that this could bring serious consequences, warns the United States that it will not tolerate any warming of relations with Taiwan or new expansion of its military presence in the region, and warns overseas Chinese that if they side with Taiwan they are dangerously involving themselves in China's internal politics and upsetting economic stability in the region.

However, threats to take over Taiwan also tempt U.S. political leaders to call for restrictions on trade and cultural relations with China and greater military assistance to Taiwan. They bring caution to U.S., European, Japanese, and overseas Chinese investors in China; they complicate China's efforts to join and work with international trade and financial organizations; and they raise doubts about whether China can be trusted as a partner in international affairs.

Ironically, the hostility, combined with offers of conciliation each side knows the other will not accept, helps bolster economic development and wards off political extremism in both countries. The leaders of both countries can use hostile actions by the other as a means to gain support from their own people and fight off internal rivals for power by arguing that they would disrupt investment and economic growth or trigger warfare. This shadowboxing helps keep the two regions economically interdependent, but the danger is that it also fosters continuing distrust that could blow up into civil war and economic chaos, should China, Taiwan, or the United States spark it through a rash move. The shadowboxing could turn to real boxing.

It is important for Americans to understand what is and is not shadowboxing, and the dynamics of this game (Blackman, 1997; Solomon, 1999; Ning, 2000; Lampton, 2001b). The powers that played the most dominant roles in opening China to international relations—Portugal, Spain, Britain, Japan, Russia, France, and Germany—have stopped exerting major military and political power in the region. Today the United States is the principal player. Unless Japan takes on a greater military and political role, the United States stands as the main power that can prevent China from dominating its own region, because the United States controls China's entry into international trade organizations, access to advanced technology, and acceptance as a part of the world community, as well as the most advanced weaponry.

The United States distrusted China's motives in the Korean and Vietnam Wars, fearing it wanted to dominate the region. China, in turn, feared that the United States might invade it. Many Chinese still fear that calls upon China to behave in conformity with world standards are thinly disguised demands that China give up its traditional moral codes and adopt U.S. standards instead. During the periods of greatest tension, Americans have feared that China wants to impose its system on the world, and Chinese have feared that the United States wants to impose its system on China. Whenever the U.S. government speaks or acts to counter what it considers to be China's provocations, nuclear buildup, arms sales, infractions of contract or international law, or violations of human rights, it reinforces those fears.

China's government often cannot control the actions of its citizens, or even its own members. The United States was threatening to retaliate against Beijing over breaches of international copyright laws; meanwhile a study found that two-thirds of Shenzhen's 35,000 companies lie to the government about their boards of directors and business activities. Beijing must persuade foreign powers that it is trying to abide by its own agreements while convincing its own provinces it is not caving in to foreign pressure to discontinue traditional practices when it asks local governments and businesses to abide by the law. Things get more complicated when local *guanxi* networks include members of prominent Beijing families. New Politburo member Jia Qinglin was party chief in Fujian during emergence of a large smuggling ring there, and did little to intervene; his wife had close dealings with some of the participants. Another Politburo member, Li Changchun, was party chief in Henan when thousands were being infected with HIV from contaminated blood; he tried to suppress news reports about this. Both were closely associated with Jiang Zemin. China is being asked to contravene an ancient standard in order to enforce a new and alien one; however much its leaders see the justification for this new behavior, they feel the pressure to continue in the old ways.

Confucian "rectification of names" calls for people to stay true to themselves by maintaining proper relationships. People do not maintain a proper relationship with someone to whom they owe deference if they challenge a direct order from them. In Western terminology, that would cause the person who issued the order to "lose face." This goes beyond machismo or personal hurt from being challenged; it puts the person issuing the order into an improper relationship with the person to whom the order was issued. They must reject the improper challenge to their authority in order to maintain a proper relationship with the person who is expected to obey them. A more proper way to redress grievances is to quietly send back word through third parties that you are unhappy; this gives your superior a chance to quietly issue new orders more acceptable to you. Those third-party messages are delivered formally through carefully coded language.

Open confrontation is generally reserved for top leaders fighting over who will control the nation—two men arm wrestling to show everyone who is boss. No top leader can allow ordinary members of society to openly challenge him because that would prove he was no longer capable of holding on to his rightful place in society. And there is no way to reach accommodation in such battles; either one individual wins, or the other.

But international diplomacy, which China has entered into such recent times, depends on nations, on a regular basis, issuing direct challenges to one another's policies before working things out behind the scenes. Much is accomplished through frank, quiet conversations among key participants. But first there is frank, open debate. Modern democracies work in this manner as well. China has the skills for negotiating behind the scenes, but it has little familiarity with negotiating amid a sea of criticism. As a result, a threat by a foreign nation to impose trade sanctions if human rights violations do not cease may be met by a threat by China (now in arm-wrestling mode) to explode an atomic bomb or send troops somewhere for an exercise; to the outside world, this seems irrational at best and threatening at worst. To break this impasse, both sides must learn to adapt to the other's techniques of negotiating (Irwin, 1997; Yu, 2002). For example, the Western nations wishing to impose trade sanctions in response to human rights violations are learning to deliver those threats more quietly and indirectly, and the Chinese are learning to ignore criticisms from Western media and public officials not directly involved in the negotiations. In an atmosphere inevitably breeding distrust, such adaptations in tactics by either side are hard to achieve. Both sides are making large strides in learning to communicate. As China's economy continues to grow, trade interdependence increases, tourism increases, and cell phones and Web connections proliferate, that communication grows easier.

The great Tang emperors presided over an empire that extended, for brief periods during their reigns, from Vietnam to the Aral Sea. Caravans and ships brought them offerings of the greatest cultures and trade items of their day. Today, China's "empire" can be even more dramatic. It presides over a landmass rich with fertile fields and natural resources. Its populace is the largest in the world, highly resourceful and organized to sustain its needs and produce for the marketplace. Its leading entrepreneurs have the deepest investment pockets on the planet. And its people have migrated to every corner of the globe. China is faced with a great irony. To maintain its unity, it must continue to accommodate the needs of the planet, enriching its economy through its compatriots at home and abroad. A bad economy at home means dissatisfaction and disintegration. The recent era of good economic growth has been accompanied by a weakened center at Beijing as provinces gain more economic power. Yet as cities grow more prosperous, the countryside falls further behind. Ultimately, Chinese leaders know that their prosperity and grasp on power depends on holding their regions and resources together for physical security and economic strength. In fact, China's greatest foreign policy challenge is holding them together, and it will require a combination of ancient and modern skills. The challenge is much greater than keeping the sea lanes or the Silk Roads open and marauders away from the capital city or inspiring awe and fear among subjects. And it is much greater than learning the fundamentals of European diplomacy. China must learn more about the rest of the world, and the rest of the world must learn more about China. Weiming Tu (2002) points out that the Enlightenment in the West used Confucian China as its primary reference society, a place that "got right without revelatory religion" (see Chapter 12) and that understood "fraternity," but by the nineteenth century Enlightenment thinkers were asserting that China was "feudal" and the rest of the world must adapt to Western liberalism. He suggests that China and the West will find that there is much to learn from one another. China must clear out the corruption and the worst excesses of the old order. The global community "must transcend the parochial dichotomy between 'the West and the rest'" (Tu, 2002:132). The two sides must become aware of how their actions impact one another's values and lives (Gamer, 2002:280). In the words of Vaclav Havel (2002:xxi):

> Authority, whether that of the father of a family or the leader of the state, is, for Confucius, a metaphysically anchored gift, which does not draw its force from the strength of its instruments of power but from its heightened responsibility. Although the two value systems of the East and the West are some-

times contrasted, they often share the same experience. They stray from their own deepest spiritual roots. If both were able to return to these roots, not only would they be better in themselves, but they would more easily understand each other.

President Theodore Roosevelt brokered the Treaty of Portsmouth because he felt it was not in the U.S. national interest for China to be divided up among Japan and the European powers. If that is the consensus within today's major foreign policy community, China's leaders in Beijing and Taipei (Taiwan's capital) can continue a working relationship; amid all the sound and fury, their actual policy demands on one another over investment, commerce, environmental pollution, international crime and drug trafficking, terrorism, travel, and other important matters often are compatible. If, however, other powers want China or its government to disintegrate or change faster than it is prepared to, or if both sides distrust each other's fundamental motives, those capitals are on a collision course. Even if all major players agree on goals, danger lurks. Traditional posturing among China's leaders has crossed over into bloodshed in the past. So has modern diplomacy. When those two traditions meet, a misstep or misreading of body language can have disastrous results. This is why it is important for each side to learn the rules of the other's game.

■ Bibliography

Ash, Robert (ed.). 2001. *China's Integration in Asia: Economic Security and Strategic Issues*. London: Curzon Press.

Austin, Greg, and Stuart Harris. 2001. *Japan and Greater China: Political Economy and Military Power in the Asian Century*. Honolulu: University of Hawaii Press.

Barnett, A. Doak. 1985. *The Making of Foreign Policy in China: Structure and Process*. Boulder: Westview Press.

Barnouin, Barbara, and Yu Changgen. 1997. *Chinese Foreign Policy During the Cultural Revolution*. New York: Columbia University Press.

Bau, Mingchien Joshua. 1921. *The Foreign Relations of China: A History and a Survey*. New York: Fleming H. Revell.

Becker, Jasper. 2001. "China's 'Home-Grown' Terror." *South China Morning Post*, November 21.

Blackman, Carolyn. 1997. *Negotiating China: Case Studies and Strategies*. London: Allen and Unwin.

Boardman, Robert. 1976. *Britain and the People's Republic of China, 1949–74*. London: Macmillan.

Brown, Michael E., Owen R. Cote Jr., Sean M. Lynn-Jones, and Steven E. Miller (eds.). *The Rise of China: An International Security Reader*. Cambridge: MIT Press.

Cameron, Nigel. 1975. *From Bondage to Liberation: East Asia 1860–1952*. Hong Kong: Oxford University Press.

Catley, Bob. 1997. *Spratlys: The Dispute in the South China Sea.* Brookfield, VT: Ashgate.
Chang, Gordon H. 1990. *Friends and Enemies: The United States, China, and the Soviet Union, 1948–1972.* Stanford: Stanford University Press.
Chen, Jian. 1994. *China's Road to the Korean War: The Making of the Sino-American Confrontation.* New York: Columbia University Press.
Chen, King C. 1969. *Vietnam and China, 1938–1954.* Princeton: Princeton University Press.
——— (ed.). 1972. *The Foreign Policy of China.* Roseland, NJ: East-West.
Clark, Gerald. 1966. *In Fear of China.* Melbourne: Lansdowne Press.
Clubb, Edmund O. 1971. *China and Russia: The Great Game.* New York: Columbia University Press.
Cohen, Warren I. 2000. *America's Response to China: A History of Sino-American Relations.* 4th ed. New York: Columbia University Press.
———. 2001. *East Asia at the Center: Four Thousand Years of Engagement with the World.* New York: Columbia University Press.
Conklin, Jeffrey Scott. 1995. *Forging an East Asian Foreign Policy.* Lanham, MD: University Press of America.
Cumings, Bruce. 1981, 1990. *The Origins of the Korean War.* 2 vols. Princeton: Princeton University Press.
Deane, Hugh. 1990. *Good Deeds and Gunboats: Two Centuries of American-Chinese Encounters.* San Francisco: China Books and Periodicals.
Deng, Yong, and Fei-Ling Wang (eds.). 1999. *In the Eyes of the Dragon: China Views the World.* Lanham, MD: Rowman and Littlefield.
Dosch, Jorn, and Manfred Mols. 2001. *International Relations in the Asia-Pacific.* New York: St. Martin's Press.
Duara, Prajenjit. 2003. *Sovereignty and Authenticity: Manchukuo and the East Asian Modern.* Lanham, MD: Rowman and Littlefield.
Elleman, Bruce. 2001. *Modern Chinese Warfare.* London: Routledge.
Fairbank, John K., and S. Y. Teng. 1941. "On the Ch'ing Tributary System." *Harvard Journal of Asiatic Studies* 6:135–148.
Faure, David, and Helen F. Siu (eds.). 1995. *Down to Earth: The Territorial Bond in South China.* Stanford: Stanford University Press.
Faust, John R., and Judith Kornberg. 1995. *China in World Politics.* Boulder: Lynne Rienner.
Fishel, Wesley R. 1975. *The End of Extraterritoriality in China.* Berkeley: University of California Press.
Fitzgerald, Stephen. 1972. *China and the Overseas Chinese: A Study of Peking's Changing Policy, 1949–1970.* Cambridge: Cambridge University Press.
Foot, Rosemary. 2001. *Rights Beyond Borders: The Global Community and the Struggle over Human Rights in China.* Oxford: Oxford University Press.
Gamer, Robert E. 2002. "Development Reflecting Human Values." Pp. 279–294 in Barbara Sundberg Baudot (ed.), *Candles in the Dark: A New Spirit for a Plural World.* Seattle: University of Washington Press.
Garson, Robert. 1995. *The U.S. and China Since 1949: A Troubled Affair.* New York: Associated University Presses.
Garver, John W. 1993. *Foreign Relations of the People's Republic of China.* Englewood Cliffs: Prentice-Hall.
———. 1997. *The Sino-American Alliance: Nationalist China and American Cold War Strategy in Asia.* Armonk, NY: M. E. Sharpe.
Gittings, John. 1974. *The World and China, 1922–1972.* London: Eyre Methuen.

Goh, Bee Chen. 1996. *Negotiating with the Chinese.* Brookfield, VT: Ashgate.

Goodman, David S. G., and Gerald Segal. 1997. *China Rising: Nationalism and Interdependence.* London: Routledge.

Graff, David A. 2001. *Medieval Chinese Warfare, 300–900.* London: Routledge.

Gurtov, Melvin. 1971. *China and Southeast Asia—The Politics of Survival: A Study of Foreign Policy Interaction.* Lexington, MA: Heath.

———. 2002. *Pacific Asia? Prospects for Security and Cooperation in East Asia.* Lanham, MD: Rowman and Littlefield.

Gurtov, Melvin, and Byong-Moo Hwang. 1998. *China's Security: The New Roles of the Military.* Boulder: Lynne Rienner.

Han, Suyin. 1994. *Eldest Son: Zhou Enlai and the Making of Modern China, 1898–1976.* New York: Farrar, Straus, and Giroux.

Harding, Harry (ed.). 1980. *China's Foreign Relations in the 1980's.* New Haven: Yale University Press.

———. 1992. *A Fragile Relationship: The United States and China Since 1972.* Washington, DC: Brookings Institution.

Harris, Stuart, and Gary Klintworth (eds.). 1995. *China as a Great Power: Myths, Realities, and Challenges in the Asia-Pacific Region.* New York: St. Martin's Press.

Havel, Vaclav. 2002. "Foreword." Pp. xix–xxii in Barbara Sundberg Baudot (ed.), *Candles in the Dark: A New Spirit for a Plural World.* Seattle: University of Washington Press.

Hibbert, Christopher. 1970. *The Dragon Wakes: China and the West, 1793–1911.* New York: Harper.

Hickey, Dennis van Vranken. 2001. *The Armies of East Asia: China, Taiwan, Japan, and the Koreas.* Boulder: Lynne Rienner.

Hinton, Harold C. 1972. *China's Turbulent Quest: An Analysis of China's Foreign Relations Since 1949.* New York: Macmillan.

Holdridge, John H. 1997. *Crossing the Divide: An Insider's Account of the Normalization of U.S.-China Relations.* Lanham, MD: Rowman and Littlefield.

Howe, Christopher (ed.). 1996. *China and Japan: History, Trends, and Prospects.* Oxford: Oxford University Press.

Hsiung, James C. 2001. *Twenty-First Century World Order and the Asia Pacific: Value Change, Exigencies, and Power Realignment.* New York: St. Martin's Press.

Hsiung, James C., and Steven I. Levine (eds.). 1992. *China's Bitter Victory: The War with Japan, 1937–1945.* Armonk, NY: M. E. Sharpe.

Hsu, Immanuel C. Y. 1980. "Late Ch'ing Foreign Relations, 1866–1905." Pp. 70–141 in John K. Fairbank and Kwang-Ching Liu (eds.), *The Cambridge History of China,* vol. 2, *Late Ch'ing, 1800–1911,* pt 2. Cambridge: Cambridge University Press.

Hu, Wiexing, Gerald Chan, and Daojiong Zha. 2001. *China's International Relations in the Twenty-First Century.* Lanham, MD: University Press of America.

Huang, J. H. 1993. *Sun-Tzu: The Art of War.* New York: Quill.

Hunt, Michael H. 1983. *The Making of a Special Relationship: The United States and China to 1914.* New York: Columbia University Press.

———. 1998. *The Genesis of Chinese Communist Foreign Policy.* New York: Columbia University Press.

Hunt, Michael, and Niu Jun. 1995. *Toward a History of Chinese Communist Foreign Relations, 1920s–1960s: Personalities and Interpretive Approaches.* Washington, DC: Woodrow Wilson International Center for Scholars.

Iriye, Akira. 1967. *Across the Pacific: An Inner History of American-East Asian Relations.* New York: Harcourt Brace and World.

Irwin, Harry. 1997. *Communicating with Asia: Understanding People and Customs.* London: Allen and Unwin.

Jain, J. P. 1976. *China in World Politics: A Study of Sino-British Relations, 1949–1975.* New Delhi: Radiant Press.

Jian, Sanqiang. 1996. *Foreign Policy Restructuring as Adaptive Behavior: China's Independent Foreign Policy, 1982–1989.* Lanham, MD: University Press of America.

Johnson, Linda Cooke. 1995. *Shanghai: From Market Town to Treaty Port, 1074–1858.* Stanford: Stanford University Press.

Johnston, Alastair Iain, and Robert S. Ross. 1999. *Engaging China: The Management of an Emerging Power.* London: Routledge.

Joint Economic Committee, U.S. Congress (ed.). 1997. *China's Economic Growth: Challenges to U.S. Policy.* Armonk, NY: M. E. Sharpe.

Jones, Peter, and Sian Kevill. 1985. *China and the Soviet Union, 1949–84.* Harlow, Essex: Longman.

Karmel, Solomon. 2000. *China and the People's Liberation Army: Great Power or Struggling Developing State?* New York: Palgrave.

Karnow, Stanley. 1984. *Vietnam: A History.* New York: Penguin.

Kau, Ying-mao, and Susan Marsh. 1993. *China in the Era of Deng Xiaoping: A Decade of Reform.* Armonk, NY: M. E. Sharpe.

Kennedy, Scott (ed.). 2003. *China Cross Talk: The American Debate over China Policy Since Normalization—A Reader.* Lanham, MD: Rowman and Littlefield.

Kim, Samuel S. (ed.). 1998. *China and the World: Chinese Foreign Policy Faces the New Millennium.* 4th ed. Boulder: Westview Press.

Kueh, Y. Y. (ed.). 1997. *The Political Economy of Sino-American Relations: A Greater China Perspective.* Hong Kong: Hong Kong University Press.

Lague, David. 2002. "Buying Some Major Muscle." *Far Eastern Economic Review* 65(3) (January 24): 30–34.

Lampton, David M. (ed.). 2001a. *The Making of Chinese Foreign and Security Policy in the Era of Reform, 1978–2000.* Stanford: Stanford University Press.

———. 2001b. *Same Bed, Different Dreams: Managing U.S.-China Relations, 1989–2000.* Berkeley: University of California Press.

Lewis, John Wilson. 1994. *China's Strategic Seapower: The Politics of Force Modernization in the Nuclear Age.* Stanford: Stanford University Press.

Lewis, John Wilson, and Xue Litai. 1988. *China Builds the Bomb.* Stanford: Stanford University Press.

Li, Hongshan. 1998. *Image, Perception, and the Making of U.S.-China Relations.* Lanham, MD: University Press of America.

Liao, Kuang-sheng. 1984. *Antiforeignism and Modernization in China, 1860–1980: Linkage Between Domestic Politics and Foreign Policy.* New York: St. Martin's Press.

Lilley, James, and David Shambaugh. 1999. *China's Military Faces the Future.* Armonk, NY: M. E. Sharpe.

Lin, Chongpin. 1988. *China's Nuclear Weapons Strategy.* Lexington, MA: D. C. Heath.

Liu, Ta Jen. 1996. *U.S.-China Relations, 1784–1992.* Lanham, MD: University Press of America.

Madsen, Richard. 1995. *China and the American Dream.* Berkeley: University of California Press.

Medvedev, Roy. 1986. *China and the Superpowers.* New York: Basil Blackwell.

Mitter, Rana. 2000. *The Manchurian Myth: Nationalism, Resistance, and Collaboration in Modern China.* Berkeley: University of California Press.

Murphey, Rhoads. 1970. *The Treaty Ports and China's Modernization: What Went Wrong?* Ann Arbor: University of Michigan Papers in Chinese Studies no. 7.

Murray, Geoffrey. 1998. *China: The Next Superpower.* New York: St. Martin's Press.

Mydans, Seth. 1998. "Indonesia Turns Its Chinese into Scapegoats." *New York Times,* February 2, p. A3.

Myers, Ramon H., Michel C. Oksenberg, and David Shambaugh (eds.). 2001. *Making China Policy: Lessons from the Bush and Clinton Administrations.* Lanham, MD: Rowman and Littlefield.

Nathan, Andrew J., and Robert S. Ross. 1997. *The Great Wall and the Empty Fortress.* New York: Norton.

Needham, Joseph W. 1971. *Science and Civilization in China,* vol. 4, pt. 3. Cambridge: Cambridge University Press.

Nelsen, Harvey. 1989. *Power and Insecurity: Beijing, Moscow, and Washington, 1949–1988.* Boulder: Lynne Rienner.

Ning, Li. 2000. *The Dynamics of Foreign-Policy Decisionmaking in China.* 2nd. ed. Boulder: Westview Press.

North, Robert C. 1974. *The Foreign Relations of China.* 2nd ed. Encino, CA: Dickenson.

Ojha, Ishwer C. 1969. *Chinese Foreign Policy in an Age of Transition: The Diplomacy of Cultural Despair.* Boston: Beacon.

Oksenberg, Michel, and Elizabeth Economy (eds.). 1998. *Involving China in World Affairs.* Washington, DC: Brookings Institution.

Robinson, Thomas W., and David Shambaugh (eds.). 1994. *Chinese Foreign Policy: Theory and Practice.* Oxford: Oxford University Press.

Ross, Robert S. (ed.). 1993. *China, the United States, and the Soviet Union.* Armonk, NY: M. E. Sharpe.

———. 1995. *Negotiating Cooperation: The United States and China, 1969–1989.* Stanford: Stanford University Press.

——— (ed.). 1998. *After the Cold War: Domestic Factors and U.S.-China Relations.* Armonk, NY: M. E. Sharpe.

Roy, Denny. 1998. *China's Foreign Relations.* Lanham, MD: Rowman and Littlefield.

Ryan, Mark. 1989. *Chinese Attitudes Toward Nuclear Weapons.* Armonk, NY: M. E. Sharpe.

Sanders, Sol W. (ed.). 2001. *Through Asian Eyes: U.S. Policy in the Asian Century.* Lanham, MD: University Press of America.

Sawyer, Ralph D. 1993. *The Seven Military Classics of Ancient China.* Boulder: Westview Press.

———. 1996. *The Complete Art of War: Sun Tzu/Sun Pin.* Boulder: Westview Press.

———. 1998. *One Hundred Unorthodox Strategies: Battle and Tactics in Chinese Warfare.* Boulder: Westview Press.

Schurmann, Franz, and Orville Schell (eds.). 1967. *Imperial China: The Decline of the Last Dynasty and the Origins of Modern China.* New York: Random House.

Scobell, Andrew. 2003. *China's Use of Military Force: Beyond the Great Wall and the Long March.* Cambridge: Cambridge University Press.

Segal, Gerald, and Richard Yang (eds.). 1996. *Chinese Economic Reform: The Impact on Security.* London: Routledge.

Shambaugh, David (ed.). 1995a. *Deng Xiaoping: Portrait of a Chinese Statesman.* Oxford: Oxford University Press.

———— (ed.). 1995b. *Greater China: The Next Superpower.* Oxford: Oxford University Press.

Shao, Kuo-Kang. 1996. *Zhou Enlai and the Foundations of Chinese Foreign Policy.* New York: St. Martin's Press.

Sheng, Michael M. 1998. *Battling Western Imperialism: Mao, Stalin, and the United States.* Princeton: Princeton University Press.

Shih, Chih-yu. 1993. *China's Just World: The Morality of Chinese Foreign Policy.* Boulder: Lynne Rienner.

Shinn, James (ed.). 1996. *Weaving the Net: Conditional Engagement with China.* Washington, DC: Brookings Institution.

Simon, Sheldon. 2001. *The Many Faces of Asian Security.* Lanham, MD: Rowman and Littlefield.

Smith, Craig S. 2001. "China, in Harsh Crackdown, Executes Muslim Separatists." *New York Times,* December 16.

Soderberg, Marie. 2002. *Chinese Japanese Relations in the Twenty-First Century.* London: Routledge.

Solomon, Richard H. 1999. *Chinese Negotiating Behavior: Pursuing Interests Through "Old Friends."* Herndon, VA: U.S. Institute of Peace Press.

Spanier, John W. 1959. *The Truman-McArthur Controversy and the Korean War.* Cambridge: Belknap Press of Harvard University Press.

Sukma, Rizal. 1999. *Indonesia and China: The Politics of a Troubled Relationship.* London: Routledge.

Sutter, Robert G. 1996. *Shaping China's Future in World Affairs: The Role of the United States.* Boulder: Westview Press.

————. 1998. *U.S. Policy Toward China: An Introduction to the Role of Interest Groups.* Lanham, MD: Rowman and Littlefield.

————. 1999. *Chinese Policy Priorities and Their Implications for the United States.* Lanham, MD: Rowman and Littlefield.

————. 2002. *The United States and East Asia: Dynamics and Implications.* Lanham, MD: Rowman and Littlefield.

Swaine, Michael D., and Ashley J. Tellis. 2000. *Interpreting China's Grand Strategy: Past, Present, and Future.* Santa Monica, CA: RAND.

Tan, Qingshan. 1992. *The Making of U.S. China Policy: From Normalization to the Post–Cold War Era.* Boulder: Lynne Rienner.

Tehranian, Majid (ed.). *Asian Peace: Security and Governance in the Asia Pacific Region.* New York: I. B. Tauris.

Teng, Su-yu, and John Fairbank. 1965. *China's Response to the West: A Documentary Survey, 1839–1923.* Cambridge: Harvard University Press.

Tu, Weiming. 2002. "Confucian Humanism and the Western Enlightenment." Pp. 123–135 in Barbara Sundberg Baudot (ed.), *Candles in the Dark: A New Spirit for a Plural World.* Seattle: University of Washington Press.

Tucker, Nancy Bernkopf. 2001. *China Confidential: American Diplomats and Sino-American Relations, 1945–1996.* New York: Columbia University Press.

Tung, William L. 1970. *China and the Foreign Powers: The Impact of and Reaction to Unequal Treaties.* Dobbs Ferry, NY: Oceana.

Unger, Jonathan. 1996. *Chinese Nationalism.* Armonk, NY: M. E. Sharpe.

Valencia, Mark J. 1996. *China and the South China Sea Disputes.* Oxford: Oxford University Press.

Van Ness, Peter. 1970. *Revolution and Chinese Foreign Policy.* Berkeley: University of California Press.

Vogel, Ezra. 1990. *One Step Ahead in China.* Cambridge: Harvard University Press.

Waley, Arthur. 1958. *The Opium War Through Chinese Eyes.* Stanford: Stanford University Press.

Wang, Gungwu. 1999. *China and Southeast Asia: Myths, Threats, and Culture.* Singapore: World Scientific.

Wang, Y. C. 1966. *Chinese Intellectuals and the West, 1872–1949.* Chapel Hill: University of North Carolina Press.

Wataru, Masuda. 2000. *Japan and China: Mutual Representations in the Modern Era.* Trans. Joshua Fogel. New York: Palgrave.

Westad, Odd Arne. 1992. *Cold War and Revolution: Soviet-American Rivalry and the Origins of the Chinese Civil War, 1944–1946.* New York: Columbia University Press.

Whiting, Allen S. 1960. *China Crosses the Yalu: The Decision to Enter the Korean War.* New York: Macmillan.

———. 2001. *The Chinese Calculus of Deterrence: India and Indochina.* Ann Arbor: Center for Chinese Studies, University of Michigan.

Wilson, Dick. 1984. *Zhou Enlai: A Biography.* New York: Viking.

Xiang, Lanxin. 1995. *Recasting the Imperial Far East: Britain and America in China, 1945–1950.* Armonk, NY: M. E. Sharpe.

Yang, Richard H., and Gerald Segal (eds.). 1996. *Chinese Economic Reform: The Impact of Security.* Boulder: Lynne Rienner.

Yu, Peter Kien-hong. 2002. *The Crab and Frog Motion Paradigm Shift: Decoding and Deciphering Taipei and Beijing's Dialectical Politics.* Lanham, MD: University Press of America.

Zagoria, Donald. 1962. *The Sino-Soviet Conflict, 1956–1961.* Princeton: Princeton University Press.

Zhang, Shu Guang. 2001. *Economic Cold War: America's Embargo Against China and the Sino-Soviet Alliance, 1949–1963.* Stanford: Stanford University Press.

Zhang, Yongjin, and Rouben Azizian. 1998. *Ethnic Challenges Beyond Borders: Chinese and Russian Perspectives of the Central Asian Conundrum.* New York: St. Martin's Press.

Zhao, Quansheng. 1996. *Interpreting Chinese Foreign Policy: The Micro-Macro Linkage Approach.* Oxford: Oxford University Press.

Zhao, Suisheng. 1998. *Power Competition in East Asia: From the Old Chinese World Order to the Post–Cold War Regional Multipolarity.* New York: St. Martin's Press.

Zhu, Fang. 1998. *Gun Barrel Politics: Party-Army Relations in Mao's China.* Boulder: Westview Press.

Population Growth
and Urbanization

Ma Rong

Each of the prior chapters has dealt with some common themes that, taken together, provide a basis for understanding the growth and dispersion of China's populace. China has long been divided between more prosperous and populous coastal regions and interior regions with fewer people, harsher conditions, and vast untapped natural resources. It has long had entrepreneurs in cities and the countryside producing an abundance of crops and goods, mostly in those coastal regions. And the market economy they supply has been at its liveliest when effective rulers unify great portions of the country; since those rulers usually have emerged from interior parts of the continent, this creates both a tie and a tension between the interior and the coast.

China's prosperity has hinged on three balancing acts: between city and country, between population and food, and between regions of hardship and regions of prosperity. Many Americans have heard of China's spectacular building boom in its cities, its controversial "one-child" birth control policy, and the contrast between life in modern areas like Shanghai and Hong Kong and the more traditional life in minority areas of the interior. China had extensive urbanization long before the rest of the world; but cities have always depended on the countryside for their prosperity, and the line between city and countryside has always been blurred. One cannot thrive without the other. China must grow or import enough food to feed its rising population and find ways to spread prosperity inland if its current boom is to continue. These are not new problems or new solutions, but the magnitude of both is far greater than ever in the past. Food production and population have long risen simultaneously, but ultimately they reach a point where they cannot sustain one another, bringing social crisis. And China has never been able to survive with two nations, one rich and one poor; it needs social service networks linking the capital and regional cities to keep that kind of polarization from occurring. China's future success depends on maintaining these fine balances, but it will not be easy.

■ City and Countryside in History

China has always been a country on the move. Its history brought a succession of droughts, floods, plagues, famines, rebellions, conquerors, and great public works projects. All of these involved movement of great numbers of people. Emperors and soldiers built cities, moving people by force for their construction and occupation; in times of rebellion, angry peasants burned those cities. People in leaner regions of the north moved south and west to seek greater prosperity, often creating new cities in the regions they entered or settling close to existing ones. Cities were generally built by soldiers and rulers, but they were sustained by commerce, which moved both people and goods.

In *The City in Late Imperial China* (1977), William G. Skinner makes the case that a principal role of cities in late imperial China was as commercial centers. In these cities, public officials and merchants interacted to tap and regulate markets and means of production, creating wealth both for citizens and for government. However, the cities were not the only place that generated wealth. Many villages, in fact, produced goods in cottage industries along with raising crops, and helped maintain canals, roads, and streams that served as transportation networks to move their goods to and from the cities. Nearly everyone in and around the urbanized areas helped supply, and purchased from, this trade.

Cities were often located along major canals or rivers. The short Miracle Canal (Ling Qu) linked the Xiang River, which flows into the Yangtze, with the Gui River, which flows toward Guangzhou; it was begun in the third century B.C.E. The Grand Canal (begun much later, in the sixth century C.E., using 2 to 3 million laborers) linked the Yangtze River valley with the Yellow River and later Beijing. Over the centuries, these and other canals were frequently rerouted to fit the needs of commerce and conquest, and their maintenance required extensive labor (Van Slyke, 1988:69–72). Huge quantities of grain moved along these waterways, along with troops, all manner of manufactured goods, small merchants, and thousands of boatmen and their families. Officials extracted taxes and tolls, and merchants extracted profits, from this trade. The roads and waterways helped rulers hold China together and conquer people along the periphery.

To keep their rule alive, officials also established towns in areas with less commerce to control the populace and maintain defense networks. In contrast to the commercial centers, many of these centers cost the government a good deal of money to maintain while generating little revenue. As one moved inland, the number of such cities tended to increase (see Skinner, 1977:221). It was not the case that these centers were associated with poverty and the commercial cities were associated with wealth. Many of the laborers who contributed to the prosperity of the commercial cities worked very hard for little income. Many of the clans living around the administrative towns engaged in little commerce beyond their villages but may have supported themselves adequately on their small farms. City inhabitants had to garner money either from the capital or from outside commerce to prosper. Threats of outside attack or social unrest could help attract such funds to cities that had little outside commerce; the capital might also send money if the town formed a useful link to control neighboring regions.

The role of cities as centers of trade and administration began very early in China's history. In Chapter 3, Rhoads Murphey discussed the rise of cities as early as the Shang dynasty (see Table 3.1); his mention of the battle for dominance between the commercial towns and cities of the state of Qu in the Yangtze River valley and the frontier feudal fiefdom of Qin, which finally unified China, highlights their dual role as political and commercial centers. Cities surrounded by tall walls and "defense-rivers" were the settlements for governmental offices and the army. Cities were built to protect both urban and rural residents during wartime. Towns with no significance in administration, whose main occupation was trade, did not have walls and large populations (Elvin and Skinner, 1974). Since the Qin unification of China in 221 B.C.E., the country has needed to establish a strong administration system to manage the large territory. Therefore, big cities developed in China much earlier than in Europe. In the Tang dynasty (C.E. 752), the population of the capital city, Chang'an (present-day Xi'an; see Map 3.1), was around 2 million (Chao and Xie, 1988:191); it was a center of both governance and commerce. In comparison, big cities developed in Europe much later, and their main expansion occurred after the industrial revolution in the eighteenth century.

As indicated in Chapters 3 and 4, the Song dynasty was a period of great commerce, with a fifth of the populace moving to towns and cities to engage in these pursuits (Chao, 1987:56). In the centuries following, urbanization increased as overall population began to rise rapidly (see Figure 8.1). At the beginning of the nineteenth century, China had 1,400 cities of over 3,000 people; more than half of the cities with a population above 10,000 were the seats of prefectures and provincial administrations (Rozman, 1982:209). China's population exceeded 300 million people by 1800 (Chao and Xie, 1988:378). In western and northern China, where the economy is less developed and population density is low, the main function of cities and towns is still administrative (Chang, 1981). Manufacturing and services are limited there, and a large proportion of the urban labor force works in governmental institutions.

Figure 8.1   Historical Changes in China's Population

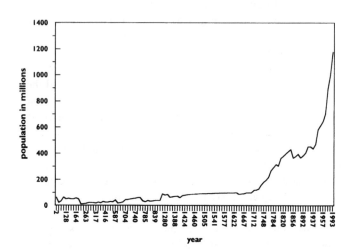

In contrast, many "market towns" in the coastal regions (especially in Jiangsu, Zhejiang, Fujian, and Guangdong provinces) have a more prosperous economy and high population densities. Trade, manufacture, handicraft, transportation, and services are important functions played by these towns. Some of them grew up rapidly and even became large cities. After the Opium Wars (1839–1842), the population of the treaty ports along the coast began to rise rapidly. Shanghai was only a country town with a few thousand people at the beginning of the eighteenth century, but it became the largest city in East Asia a century later since it served as the main trade center and transportation port between China and other countries. Today, although the general level of urbanization in China is lower than in most other countries, China has a number of big cities in its coastal regions. By 2000, the population of Beijing exceeded 10.8 million, and Shanghai's population reached 12.6 million. There were eighteen cities in China with a population over 2 million in 2000 (World Bank, *Development Indicators,* 2001).

■ Population and Food

It is well known that China is the most populous country of the world, with 1.26 billion people—about one-fifth of the total world's population, which stood at 6 billion in 2000. The population of China was greater in 2000 than the combined populations of the United States (280 million), Russia (146 million), Japan (127 million), Indonesia (207 million), and all of Europe and Central Asia (474 million) combined. The country with the world's second largest population is India, with 998 million in 2000. Because of India's higher annual birthrates (26 per 1,000 versus 16 per 1,000 in China), its population is expected to surpass China's during the twenty-first century.

By world standards, China's population has been high throughout recorded history; but its absolute numbers have been much lower than at present. Figure 8.1 shows that China's population exceeded 100 million in 1685, based on census and other records of population accounting during different dynasties for the purpose of tax collection and army recruitment, which are not entirely accurate but give some general sense of population sizes. From the first "census" (household accounting) in C.E. 2 to the one in C.E. 1400, China's population experienced a long process of instability. Sometimes the population increased at an annual rate of 4 to 5 percent under peaceful and prosperous social conditions, perhaps even exceeding 100 million during the twelfth century at the height of the Song dynasty; sometimes wars and famines decreased it by 30 to 40 percent. By the height of the Ming dynasty in the fifteenth century it had risen to 150 million, dipped again with the wars that brought it to office, and then moved into steady growth after those wars ended in 1681. It took seventy-nine years to exceed 200 million (in 1759), another twenty-eight years to exceed 300 million (in 1787), and another forty-three years to exceed 400 million by 1830—doubling in seventy-one years (Chao and Xie, 1988:378). Because of foreign invasion (such as the Opium Wars and the 1931–1945 Japanese occupation) and civil wars (the "Taiping Heavenly Kingdom," and the war between the Communist Party and Kuomintang; see

An old city street in Chengdu, Sichuan

Chapter 4), "the century between 1851 and 1949 was one of societal break-down . . . an annual average population growth rate of only 0.3 percent" (Banister, 1991). Then China entered into a period of spectacular rise in population.

Food was a major factor in determining population. As Rhoads Murphey pointed out in Chapter 3, China's civilization was able to sustain itself because of the cultivation of rice and wheat. Wars, epidemics, and floods killed people directly. Along with droughts, they also destroyed fields and crops, leading to starvation, lowered fertility rates, and infanticide (killing babies at birth) to avoid having to share food with newborn infants. For many centuries, China's population rose and fell on the basis of how much grain it could grow and store. Then in the eighteenth century, new plants arrived from the New World and Europe: sweet potatoes, maize (corn), Irish potatoes, and peanuts—all of which could grow abundantly on previously unused terrain—along with new, more productive strains of rice from Southeast Asia. Especially in southern China, more people could marry at earlier ages and have more children, who had an increased chance to live because of better nutrition for both mother and infant.

One tactic used by armies in the civil wars and foreign invasions from which China suffered from the mid–nineteenth to mid–twentieth centuries was to break dikes and cause flooding. Bad weather also brought periodic droughts. Granary storage systems were emptied and extended families and communities scattered. Combined with the disease, direct killings, and other hardships brought by war and social disorder, these losses of crops brought great loss of life. Chapter 4 gave some estimates of those losses. Yet despite all this hardship, China's population crept upward during this period, adding more people than all of China had supported before the seventeenth century. The new crops helped this to happen.

The arrival of the People's Republic of China (PRC) in 1949 brought peace, the economic stabilization measures discussed in Chapter 4 that ended the high inflation of food prices, the return of peasants to the land, and measures to provide basic medicine and hygiene. The first modern census, conducted in 1953, showed a population of 582 million. Twenty-nine years later, in 1982, it surpassed 1 billion.

From 1958 to 1961, there was a serious famine in China. Both natural disasters (drought) and policies of rural development (the "commune system" and the Greap Leap Forward) had impact on the famine and resulted in negative population growth rates in the early 1960s. The mortality rate was very high (Banister and Preston, 1981). The high birthrates in the late 1960s and 1970s are called "compensative births" by demographers, since many people who did not bear children during the famine wanted to have them right after (Tien, 1983:16). The total fertility rate (expected average number of children per woman at the end of her childbearing years) decreased to 3.3 in 1960 and jumped back to 5.8 in 1970.

Great regional variation in demographic dynamics exists among different areas of China. Table 8.1 shows the demographic indexes of several selected provinces and autonomous regions. For example, the birthrate was as high as 5.27 percent in Sichuan in 1970, but it was only 1.38 percent in Shanghai that same year. The death rate was very high in Sichuan in 1970 (1.26 percent), but it was as low as 0.5 percent in Shanghai. Variation also exists between urban and rural areas and between rich areas and poor areas within each province or autonomous region (Caldwell and Srinivasan, 1984). But the general trend is for the birthrate to exceed the death rate and for population to rise faster in rural areas than in urban.

There has always been a basic argument or debate within the government and among demographers in the PRC over whether family planning is necessary and what should be the "proper standard" or limitation in family planning programs. In other words, how many children should a couple have? The most famous debate was between the president of Beijing University (Ma Yinchu) and Chairman Mao Zedong in 1957.

Based on his study and population projections, Ma (an economist) called on China to control births and encourage family planning. At a meeting of the National People's Congress, he warned that China's population would reach 1.5–2.6 billion (at an annual growth rate of 2 to 3 percent) in fifty years, and that such a huge population would become an intolerable burden preventing China from becoming a prosperous industrialized nation. To solve the problem, he suggested setting up a goal of two children per family (Ma Yinchu, 1957). His suggestion was supported by some senior officials, including Zhou Enlai; a movement was organized, mainly to call people's attention to

Table 8.1   Regional Variation in Demographic Indicators

Region	Crude Birth Rate (% increase)				Crude Death Rate (% decrease)			
	1970	1980	1990	2000	1970	1980	1990	2000
Tibet	1.94	2.24	2.76	1.76	0.76	0.82	0.92	0.66
Xinjiang	3.67	2.18	2.47	1.88	0.82	0.77	0.64	0.70
Guangdong	2.96	2.07	2.40	1.53	0.60	0.54	0.53	0.54
Jiangsu	3.07	1.47	2.05	0.91	0.69	0.66	0.61	0.65
Inner Mongolia	2.89	1.85	2.01	0.99	0.58	0.55	0.58	0.55
Sichuan	5.27	1.19	1.78	1.21	1.26	0.68	0.71	0.70
Heilongjiang	3.48	2.36	1.75	1.06	0.58	0.72	0.53	0.55
Beijing	2.07	1.56	1.34	0.62	0.64	0.63	0.54	0.53
Shanghai	1.38	1.26	1.13	0.53	0.50	0.65	0.64	0.72
China as a whole	3.34	1.82	2.10	1.52	0.76	0.63	0.63	0.46

Sources: China Population and Information Research Center, 1985:848–850; China Population and Information Research Center, ed., 1991; National Bureau of Statistics of China, 2001:91; *Provincial Statistical Yearbook,* 2001.

population issues without policy enforcement. This was the first family planning campaign, from 1955 to 1957 (see Figure 8.2), just before the terrible famine.

At the time, Mao was worried about the possibility of war between China and the United States. The Korean War was not formally ended, and the situation on the Taiwan Strait was hostile and fragile, as explained in Chapters 6 and 7. He believed China needed to maintain a large population to survive a nuclear war, since it had no nuclear weapons to deter such an attack. Mao said that even if nuclear bombs killed half of the population, China would still have millions left to continue fighting. Mao rejected Ma's suggestion on the basis of this strategic thinking. Then Ma was criticized very seriously as "the new Malthus" and lost his position and influence. Malthus was an eighteenth-century thinker who gave a gloomy forecast that the world's population is destined to grow faster than food supplies.

But China was not involved in nuclear war with either the United States or the Soviet Union. As can be seen in Figure 8.2, the birth rate shot up after the period of famine during the Great Leap Forward (1958–1960) and the government called for a second family planning campaign. Fertility rates declined again during the Cultural Revolution (1966–1976). After those periods of chaos they rose once more, as Ma Yinchu had predicted. The government announced the third family planning campaign with a new slogan: *wan, xi, shao* (late marriage, long birth intervals, and fewer births) (Lyle, 1980).

As the population pressure on land, urban jobs, housing, and social spending became more serious, it was clear that a rapidly growing population would make the "four modernizations" (of agriculture, industry, the military, and society and technology) announced in 1978 an impossible dream. So in the 1980s, the Chinese government finally set up a more restrictive birth control policy,

Figure 8.2   Demographic Dynamics During China's Family Planning Campaigns

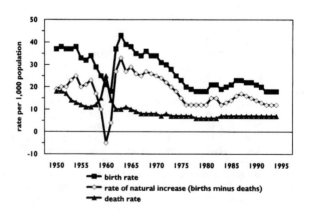

the one-child campaign (Tien, 1973, 1983; Milwertz, 1996). Under this policy, China's fertility rates and mortality rates both stabilized (as Figure 8.2 shows), resulting in a low natural rate of population increase. Unlike the experiences of industrialized countries, where social and economic development gradually lead to low fertility, government policy and enforcement have played a key role in this transition in China (Aird, 1978; Chen and Kols, 1982).

Some argue that low fertility will be spontaneously adopted by people after economic and societal development and that no policy enforcement is really needed (see Beaver, 1975). But in China's case, the huge population and a high birthrate obviously hinder social and economic development. In 1982, 80 percent of China's population were traditional farmers and over 32 percent of the populace over the age of twelve were illiterate. Such individuals are apt to have large families, straining food supplies and government support services at a time when resources need to be devoted to building an infrastructure for modernization that could bring societal and economic development.

Generally, urban residents accepted the one-child policy. First, equal education and work opportunities for women had already encouraged them to have fewer children. Second, the pension systems of governmental institutions and state-owned enterprises made people less worried about needing children to support them after retirement. Third, the expenses of kindergarten, schools, and other costs related to child raising increased very rapidly, and it became very difficult to raise more than one child if the parents wanted their offspring to enjoy satisfactory and competitive living and study conditions. In rural areas, however, especially poor ones where many farmers want more boys to carry on their family name, no pensions are available, and the expenses of raising children are still low, people want two or three children. Under the incentives of the household responsibility system, added offspring also provide field help to increase family income. So it is hard to enforce the family planning program in rural areas (Goodstadt, 1982), especially because local authorities in many rural regions are sometimes lax about doing so. This policy has been enforced at the local level. Many urban and rural localities have softened their enforcement; some (including Beijing) have stopped mandating that women seek approval before having a second child. In 2002 the first national legislation addressing this policy area, the National Law on Population and Family Planning, allows localities to permit certain couples the right to have a second child, with the stipulation that they must pay a "social support tax" for this privilege. A program begun in 1995 is bringing education on contraception and reproductive health to rural areas.

Since Han people, especially farmers, have a strong preference for boys, the sex ratio at birth increased from 108.5 boys in 1982 to 110.2 boys in 1990 for every 100 girls. One of the reasons is the higher possibility that couples will decide to have an abortion when they learn the new baby will be a girl.

But it is also very likely that many rural households did not report the births of girls, which may in turn make the ratio more even (Zhen Yi et al., 1993). In regions where local administrators are more zealous about enforcing birth control, people often fail to report births of both sexes, and it is difficult to estimate the total number who were not reported to administration and registered by censuses.

When the Chinese government recognized the difficulties in enforcing the one-child policy in rural areas, it made many local adjustments in birth regulations to allow farmers to have more than one child. For example, if the first child is a girl or has some disease or if the father is the only son of his family, a second child is allowed. By estimation, there are generally two children per family in most rural areas in China, whereas the one-child policy is generally followed in cities (Peng, 1991). In Chapter 11, Laurel Bossen discusses this topic further.

As can be seen in Tables 8.2 and 5.2, the Chinese population has two major characteristics: large size and low education. Among the total population above age fifteen in China in 2000, at least 9 percent of males and 25 percent of females were illiterate. Because many rural primary schools have very poor teaching conditions and many teachers only received primary school education themselves, the quality of education for a large proportion of graduates of rural primary schools is considered very low. With such a low qual-

Table 8.2   Selected Development and Demographic Trends in China

	1950	1960	1970	1980	1990	2000
Total population (in millions)	552.00	662.00	830.00	987.00	1,120.00	1,266.00
GNP per capita (U.S.$)	—	—	—	290.00	370.00	884.75
% urban[a]	11.20	19.70	17.40	19.40	26.00	36.33
Infant mortality per 100 births[b]	13.80	8.56	5.15	3.76	3.70	3.00
Crude birthrate (% increase)	3.70	2.09	3.34	1.82	2.10	1.52
Crude death rate (% decrease)	1.80	2.54	0.76	0.63	0.63	0.46
Rate of population growth (%)	1.90	−0.45	2.58	1.19	1.47	0.88
Total fertility rate per childbearer[c]	5.80	3.30	5.80	2.20	2.30	1.9
Life expectancy (female)[b]	49.20	58.00	63.20	69.20	71.10	72
Life expectancy (male)[b]	46.70	56.00	61.10	66.20	67.80	68

Source: World Bank, 1982–2001.
Notes: a. Wang, 1986:284; National Bureau of Statistics of China, 2001:91.
b. Lin, 1986:238; World Bank, 2001.
c. Yan and Cheng, 1993; Huang, 1993; World Bank, 2001.

ity in education, skill training, and social experiences, a huge population will have a more negative than positive impact on China's development.

The importance of family planning becomes even clearer if we carefully examine the connection between natural resources in China and population growth. Arable land in China covers less than 250 million acres (101.2 hectares) and has continually decreased because of urban expansion and construction of dams, roads, bridges, and new factories. The arable land per capita in 1998 was 0.26 acres (0.1 hectares) in China, one-seventh that of the United States, one-fifteenth that of Canada, and one-twenty-eighth that in Australia (Qu and Li, 1992:53). India, with 432 million acres (174.4 million hectares) of arable land, has fewer people than China. Therefore, the pressure of population on grain production is worse in China than in India. The Chinese government argues that, with 7 percent of the world's arable land and the need to feed 21 percent of the world's population, there was no other choice for China to maintain its social stability and proceed into modernization except practicing family planning.

The outlook for other natural resources in China is equally grim. Only 17.5 percent of China's territory has forest cover, compared to 25 percent for the United States, 64 percent for Japan, 72 percent for Finland, and 30 percent for the world as a whole (World Bank, *Development Indicators,* 2001). Water is one of the most important natural resources. The per capita surface water runoff—the amount of water that flows on the surface to use for drinking, agriculture, sanitation, and industry—is only one-fourth the world average and one-fifth that of the United States (Qu and Li, 1992:117). Furthermore, China's water resources are unequally distributed. Most of the cities in northern China experience serious water shortages, whereas southeastern China is often threatened by floods. (In Chapter 9, Richard Edmonds discusses all these problems in greater detail.) With such shortages and imbalanced geographic distribution between population and natural resources, birth control and family planning are necessary measures. The difficulties of increasing food production for a growing population are substantial.

Despite the one-child policy, China's population continues to grow and is predicted to become stable around 2033, after reaching 1.5 billion (Lu and Lin, 1994:104). Researchers in western China suggest that one of the most important reasons for the poverty problem there is the region's continuing high fertility (Zhou, 1994). China's population was 723 million in 1964; if the fertility rate, mortality rate, and natural growth rate had stayed the same as they were that year, China would have had a population of 2.075 billion by 1995. Now, with the fertility rate a third of what is was then, the expected population by 2015 is 1.4 billion. Even under the family planning program, the annual number of newborn babies in China (25 million) still exceeds the total population of Australia (19 million), which has a territory equal to 80 percent of China's territory.

■ **City and Countryside Today**

Given the necessity of feeding its people, China must have enough people in the countryside to maintain the food supply while managing the gravi-
tation to towns and cities that naturally accompanies modernization. Because
of the geographic characteristics and distribution of natural resources, China's
population is not equally distributed. The plateau and deserts in the western
part of China can support only a very small population. As can be quickly
grasped by looking at Maps 2.2 and 2.3 and drawing a diagonal line from
western Heilongjiang to western Yunnan, 94 percent of the total population
live in the southeastern part of China (about 36 percent of the total territory),
whereas 6 percent live in the northwestern part (about 64 percent of total territory). This pattern has not changed for centuries. Furthermore, the most populous cities lie to the southeast. Although China's average density is 125 persons per square kilometer, its coastal regions are considered among the most
crowded places in the world, with a population density of over 600–1,000 persons per square kilometer. Anyone who visits Beijing, Shanghai, or even rural
areas in the coastal regions will certainly have a very strong impression about
the high population density there. It is even difficult for urban people to move
on streets and in shops on weekends and holidays, and there are very short distances between villages in rural areas.

In 1949, the PRC established a centrally planned economic system on the
model of the Soviet Union. In order to manage food and housing supplies,

Shanghai's busiest shopping street, Nanjing Lu

employment, education, and other public facilities under the governmental plans, a residential registration system was created in 1953 to control the size of urban populations and the volume of rural-urban migration (Goldstein and Goldstein, 1985:9–12). Under this policy, the proportion of urban residents in the total population was kept around 20 percent for a long period of time, much lower than in other nations.

The Great Leap Forward, which began in 1958 (see Chapter 4), resulted in about 20 million rural people migrating into cities to participate in an urban industrial expansion. Since the factories were established in a hurry and there were many problems in management and the quality of the labor force, many new factories did not make profits and had to be closed. Then the government had to tell the 20 million new urban residents to move back to rural areas (Tien, 1983:28). After this crisis, the government set up a very restricted system of urban population control. Anyone who wanted to move from one place to another had to apply for an official transfer, and it was difficult to obtain approval for a move from the countryside into a town or city, especially into big cities. Kam Wing Chan (1996) argues that this system helped stabilize cities as they industrialized.

During the Cultural Revolution (1966–1976), the government arranged a special type of urban-rural migration for city middle school graduates. They were sent to rural areas in the periphery, army reclamation farms, and urban suburbs for "reeducation" (Banister, 1987:308). They were compelled to learn from farmers and herders and work as one of them. The total number of these students was around 1.2 million. After the Cultural Revolution, a large portion of these students returned to the cities of their origin, resulting in a rural-urban return migration.

Following the new economic reforms in the 1980s, migration control has loosened. The grain coupons (which could only be used in each province) and hotel clerks' requests for "travel approval" for checking into hotels were abandoned. Now people may travel anywhere in the country, though official local residential status is still needed when applying for a formal job in governmental institutions. Migration abroad has also become more convenient if the visa is approved by foreign countries. According to the 1990 national census, 237,024 persons were living abroad and had temporarily canceled their local residential registration (Population Census Bureau, 1993:7). That number is growing. Yet all this new freedom of movement comes with a price: the social guarantees and stability of neighborhoods and communities that the regulations helped establish are not as firm.

▧ Health Care

One guarantee under pressure is health care. Life expectancy at birth has increased significantly in China since 1950. At that time, it was only

49.2 years for women and 46.7 years for men; by 1990 it had risen to 71.1 years and 67.8 years (see Table 8.2). The improvements in income and housing have had a positive impact on people's nutrition and health. The general improvement of mass education has also had some indirect impact on reducing mortality. More children attend school; only 1.5 million children graduated from primary school in 1952, whereas 19 million did so in 1994 (State Statistical Bureau, *Statistical Yearbook,* 1995:588). Students learn about biology, nutrition, sanitation, infectious diseases, and simple medical treatments, which in turn help them to manage their life in a healthier way. One disease they have learned little about is AIDS, which is spreading rapidly among intravenous drug users and prostitutes, and from infected blood in transfusions; this taboo topic is gradually beginning to be addressed. The United Nations estimates that the present 1 million people infected will grow to 10 or 15 million by 2010.

The health care facilities managed by the government also play an important role in reducing mortality and increasing life expectancy. After 1949, university-educated doctors and nurses became available to urban workers. "Barefoot doctors," who received basic paramedical training and were supported by their local villages, proved very helpful in controlling infectious diseases and offering simple treatment of urgent cases in rural areas. But the gap between the quality of health care facilities in rural areas and cities remained wide. Before the reforms of the 1980s, there were two different health care systems in rural and urban China. In rural areas, a system called the "collective health care system" was in practice. At that time, all rural dwellers belonged to communes, which controlled management of the land; they were divided into brigades and finally into smaller production teams. Brigade members all contributed equal levies to a fund that supported their health care. When they became ill, the fund paid half their bill; they paid the rest. Urban workers had better coverage than that. The ministries, schools, and state-owned factories and shops, for which over 90 percent of urban employees worked, paid all medical expenses and provided employees with doctors and hospitals near their workplace. The work units also covered 70 to 80 percent of the health care expenses of employee dependents. So urban workers had better access than rural dwellers to hospitals and fully trained doctors and paid few of their own medical bills.

Since the system reform in the 1980s, the collective health care system has lost its financial base because all lands and properties were redistributed among peasants. Now the peasants pay health care expenses by themselves. The former "barefoot doctors" now either open their own private clinics and make money from their services or have switched into other activities. These clinics are under the regulation of county bureaus of public health care. In some poor areas, local doctors with medical degrees left their villages and moved to rich regions and even cities in order to earn a higher income.

Poorer regions are suffering from a serious shortage of doctors and health care services.

In urban areas, state-owned enterprises are now facing serious financial problems as they compete with private companies and joint ventures. Often they must cut back drastically on the health coverage they offer their employees. Fifty-eight cities have established health insurance programs, which they encourage all factories to join; their employees must pay monthly premiums in exchange for coverage. In rich regions along the eastern coast, where township enterprises prosper, local health insurance systems are successfully established at town and even village levels. In other regions of China, the urban and rural health care facilities have been largely maintained by subsidies from central or provincial governments, whose budgets are increasingly strained. Individuals working for small cooperative enterprises or large private firms, and farmers, have no medical coverage and must pay fees for medical care. They can buy private health insurance policies to cover major hazards, and the government has begun offering low-cost insurance to rural dwellers, but few are yet covered. Many new hospitals with advanced equipment are being built in cities. One reason for the appeal of Falun Gong, and of Dr. Hong Zhaoguang, whose self-help health books (emphasizing exercise, diet, and right thinking) have sold millions of copies and whose inspirational lectures are jammed with listeners, is their promise of simple and inexpensive ways to cure diseases and stay healthy.

▓ Housing

The housing system in rural China, like health care, differs from that in towns and cities. Under the PRC, with the exception of a few private houses that residents built or bought before 1949, all houses and apartment buildings in urban areas were managed by government institutions. These apartments were assigned to employees who needed to pay only a small amount for rent. In rural areas, the peasants built their houses themselves after obtaining official permission from village, town, and county authorities for land use.

When the economic reforms were first instituted after 1978, this worked to the advantage of rural dwellers. Under the household responsibility system, which let them lease land and sell crops in markets, many of them acquired savings that they used to build themselves houses; these are often quite large (especially in more sparsely populated areas like Yunnan). Sometimes this is done by families themselves, and sometimes by the village or township leaders. Meanwhile, urban dwellers remained confined to the apartments assigned them—often only one or two rooms for a family, with a tiny kitchen and toilet sometimes shared with another family. Since low rents cannot cover the expenses of maintenance, the buildings were often in poor repair. Sometimes young workers live in dormitories for several years, even after marriage, before being assigned an apartment. Hence reform of the urban housing system became one of the key issues in the 1980s. During the 1990s, urban governments rapidly accelerated the building of tall housing blocks with larger, more modern apartments. Since 1998, all workers moving to new apartments must purchase them, while rents are gradually rising for those in older apartments. The final goal of housing reform is to sell most apartments to the residents with subsidies from the institutions that employ them. Now the skylines of cities are filled with modern apartment buildings, and superstores sell the array of goods one might expect to find in a Home Depot, Wal-Mart, or Ikea in the United States.

Meanwhile, many villages located close to larger cities have created new factories and other cooperative enterprises under the reforms. They, too, are using the income to build blocks of apartment buildings, along with schools, retirement homes, hospitals, and other amenities. Hence these rural areas are coming to look more like cities, and their inhabitants are being assigned housing in a manner resembling cities. However, as one moves farther away from urban areas, less of this development is to be found.

■ Redefining the Distinction Between City and Countryside

The relaxation of restrictions on travel from the countryside into cities and towns has resulted in some 80 million temporary migrants moving from villages into cities; these people are not counted as "permanent urban residents" (Goldstein and Goldstein, 1991:1–4; Solinger, 1999; Zhang, 2001; Qian, 1996). It is estimated that about 3 million temporary residents or migrants live in Beijing; Shanghai has about that number as well. Some of them have lived and worked in cities for several years and have no intention of returning to villages. Referred to by city folk as "peasant workers," they are hired for construction teams, by city factories, and as domestic servants in residents' houses, or they set up small shops and businesses. A proportion of these temporary migrants should be considered urban, since they join the urban economy and urban life in many aspects.

With the exception of Shanghai and Zhejiang province, these workers are not entitled to housing, health care, or any other benefits in the cities where they have come to work and must often live in makeshift housing they construct themselves or in crude dormitories provided by their temporary employer. Having grown up in the countryside, they may find it difficult to adapt to urban life. City dwellers are inclined to shun them. They often leave their families at home initially; if they bring or acquire spouses and children, they will be without health care and schooling. Some of them may engage in crime or even become involved in criminal syndicates. Resentments against them by long-term city residents sometimes lead to confrontation. When they travel back to villages for spring festival and then return to the cities where they usually work, the trains and railway stations throughout China become congested.

These "peasant workers" are part of even bigger changes in urban life. Wrecking balls and the tall cranes (often jokingly referred to as the "national bird") rising from construction sites herald a complete transformation in the way urban people live and the way cities blend with surrounding towns and villages. Unlike in Europe or the United States, city planners in China need not contend with long legal battles to acquire property for development projects. Much of the land is not private and is available for conversion to public uses. So entire city streets and blocks are frequently torn down to make way for public development projects.

Many of China's ancient cities had walls, which were still in place in 1949. Most urban dwellers then lived in small, low-rise houses within those walls. To make way for new roads, public squares, government buildings, factories, and high-rise housing, many sections of those walls were torn down, and building extended outward from the center. Still, many of the older urban neighborhoods remained. Today, such old-style buildings and houses, and the original round of postwar construction, are being rapidly torn down and replaced with modern freeways, bridges, high-rise offices, shopping centers, hotels, and apartment buildings. Beijing, Shanghai, and other large cities have been nearly entirely rebuilt, with only small patches of old neighborhoods. This has provided residents with better housing and hygiene, but it has also

Jennifer Ashby

New freeways, mass transit overpass, and apartments in Shanghai

Beijing traffic, 2001

scattered the population and made it harder to maintain neighborhood activities. Often people are moved to an apartment miles from where they work, requiring them to use buses, bicycles, or subways to commute long distances.

With new cars rapidly being added to the mix, traffic jams grow in intensity; extensive new construction of elevated highways, subways, and large bridges is seldom adequate to keep up with the rising demand. China has become the world's fourth largest car market. In 1990 China had 5 million motor vehicles and 1 car per 1,000 people; by 2000 that had grown to 8 million vehicles and 3 cars per 1,000. In 2002, over 1 million cars were sold in China, 40 percent to individuals; Volkswagen sells more cars in China than in the United States. In Shanghai, the entire rural area to the east of the city has been converted into the Pudong Development Zone, transforming the farms that formerly occupied the land into industrial parks, apartment and office blocks, motorways, and port facilities; begun in 1990, this zone already covers an area as large as that occupied by Shanghai itself (Yeung and Sung, 1996; Gamer, 1998). The same phenomenon is occurring in all of the new special economic zones along the coast and inland and around all major cities (Davis et al., 1995). Workmen are constructing ring roads, which soon become clogged with traffic and surrounded by new high-rise buildings, airports, amusement parks, and other urban amenities. Shanghai boasts the world's first magnetic levitation train, which covers the 30 miles from downtown to the main airport in seven minutes.

Pudong, viewed from Shanghai. In the 1980s, this was all farmland

Within this maze of construction may lie the outlines of older towns and villages, caught up in a megalopolis; surrounding the construction are villages a few miles away that are carrying out similar construction to support new township enterprises. Much of the development is, in fact, directed by local authorities rather than the national government. This can result in considerable confusion about what is local and what is metropolitan. There has been a debate on the strategy of future urbanization in China for several years. The official strategy put forth by the government in 1980 is to "control the population size of large cities, properly develop middle-sized cities, and encourage the development of small cities and towns" (Ma Rong, 1992:141). Some experts emphasized the importance of small towns since they could absorb surplus rural laborers by developing township enterprises and could depend on their own revenues without much provincial or national governmental investment. Instead, much of the emphasis has been on developing the large cities.

Changes in the government's definition of what constitutes an urban area emphasize the difficulty of coming to grips with these problems. The definition may change to accommodate policy needs. For example, in 1963 when 20 million people were asked to return to rural areas after the failure of the Great Leap Forward, the criteria for setting up a "township" and a "city" became more restricted (to become a township, a village needed at least 2,100 non-agricultural residents, rather than the prior 750), so that villages could not declare themselves one of these to keep out migrants. Cities were required to have 100,000 inhabitants rather than the 20,000 needed previously, so that suddenly the portion of the populace officially living in towns and cities was radically reduced, showing "compliance" with the shift back to the countryside.

After 1980, however, the government wished to encourage the formation of townships so that they could set up township enterprises and take over responsibilities like education and health care, which were formerly handled by communes. Under the law implemented in 1984, any seat of county government could become a town, as could any former rural commune with a nonagricultural population over 2,000, and many border posts, mine settlements, tourist places, and villages in minority ethnic group regions. Under the new standards, the total number of towns increased from 2,781 in 1983 to 6,211 in 1984. And by 1986, towns with a permanent nonagricultural population over 60,000 and whose total value of annual domestic production exceeded 200 million yuan could apply for city status—down from 100,000 (Ma Rong, 1992:120, 128–129). Suddenly, many more people officially lived in towns and cities that could include them in plans for township and urban enterprises, health care, education, new housing blocks, and other initiatives.

In the 1980s, some provinces in China began practicing a new system called "city managing county." Then it became a trend to change prefectures (an administrative level between province and county) into "cities." Those new "cities" actually cover many rural areas and their population cannot be classified as urban residents. A parallel trend is to change *xiang* (former communes) into towns, and these towns also include a large number of rural peo-

New stadiums in Shanghai

ple. If these "city" and "town" residents are classified as "urban," China's "urban population" would exceed 50 percent of the total.

Under the 2000 national census, only people in areas directly managed by town or city governments or under urban districts or street committees can be designated as urban—about 36 percent of the total population, or 455 million people, which is closer to world standards for classifying urban population; 77 percent of the United States and 44 percent of the world populace live in urban areas. But it is clear that cities, towns, and villages in China are increasingly intertwined in their governance, economies, and social connections. As cities grow out from their former boundaries, towns build modern buildings and amenities, and factories in the countryside produce expanding quantities of goods for the world market, the populations and social support programs of villages, towns, and cities will increasingly need to coordinate their efforts. Furthermore, the rapid decline of employment in the state sector leaves many unemployed and without support programs. Some of the older industrial towns and cities are crumbling rather than developing. Finding a balance here, like finding a balance between a rising population and food supply, will not be easy.

China's Development Research Council estimates that 12 percent of the registered urban populace, over 50 million people, are unemployed, and 37 million can be classified as urban poor (Murphy, 2002b). In addition, as just indicated, tens of millions of migrants flock to the urban areas from the countryside seeking temporary work; some 200 million urban workers are unemployed or underemployed (Murphy, 2002a). Most of these have lost access to free health care. Those in the cities often live in government housing and their children have access to schools. None of these services are generally available to the migrants. Only 20 million people currently receive Minimum Living Standard Allowances, a program to assist those in poverty. And migrations to towns and cities can leave villages with fewer resources to offer such services for those who remain, especially when they are far from urban markets, where they can sell their produce, and when they have marginal dry or hilly land. Since much of this migration involves movement from poorer inland areas toward the coast and since those most in need of such public services are in those villages or have left them, failure to adequately address these problems can increasingly leave China polarized between rich and poor. The middle class is growing, but the poor are a larger group and growing even faster. Strikes and protests are on the rise. Yet the Asian Development Bank estimates that urban populations will double during the next decade (Lague, 2003).

■ Ethnic Minorities

Deeply entwined in these attempts to find balance between urban and rural is the need to keep the less urbanized inland provinces, largely inhabited by ethnic minorities, from falling behind the more urbanized and prosperous coastal provinces as modernization continues. China is a multiethnic country. There are fifty-five ethnic groups in China (93 percent are Han and the rest are minorities), according to criteria established by the PRC (for an excellent introduction to this topic, see Dreyer, 1976). The central government of China established many autonomous areas for the different ethnic minority groups: 5 autonomous provinces, 62 autonomous prefectures, and 659 autonomous cities and counties. These areas—mostly in inland areas away from the coastal plains—cover over 60 percent of China's total territory. Even in those autonomous areas, much of the population is from the Han majority group, who also tend to be among those in the most modernized sectors of the economy.

Ninety-one percent of China's total population in 1995 was Han; the non-Han portion of the populace grew from 6 percent in 1953 (35 million) to 9 percent in 1995 (108 million). In 2000 there were nine ethnic minority groups with populations over 4 million (see Table 8.3), while twenty-two groups contained fewer than 10,000 people. Table 8.3 makes it apparent that several groups had a very high growth rate between 1982 and 1990, though between 1990 and 2000 that slowed substantially. This stems largely from the fact that ethnic minorities are exempt from the new family planning program. Not only are they having more children than the rest of the populace, but investigations have found that during the 1980s many individuals who had been classified as Han, but had a blood relationship with a minority, registered themselves as a minority (Manchu, Tujia, Miao, Mongolian, etc.) so as to be exempt from family planning and to take advantage of other special privileges enjoyed by ethnic minorities. The central government allows ethnic minorities to enter colleges and universities with lower test scores, gives them priority for promotions in government institutions, and affords them other advantages to help

Table 8.3   **Ethnic Minorities with a Population of More than 4 Million (in millions)**

Ethnic Minorities	1982	1990	2000	Growth (%) 1982–1990	Growth (%) 1990–2000	Annual Growth Rate (%) 1982–1990	Annual Growth Rate (%) 1990–2000
Zhuang	13.38	15.49	16.18	15.7	4.5	1.8	0.4
Manchu	4.30	9.82	10.68	128.2	8.8	10.9	0.8
Hui	7.23	8.60	9.82	19.0	14.2	2.2	1.3
Miao	5.02	7.40	8.94	46.9	20.8	5.0	1.4
Uygur	5.96	7.21	8.40	21.0	16.5	2.4	1.5
Yi	5.45	6.57	7.76	20.4	18.1	2.4	1.7
Tujia	2.83	5.70	8.03	101.2	40.9	9.1	3.5
Mongolian	3.41	4.81	5.81	40.7	20.8	4.4	1.9
Tibetan	3.85	4.59	5.41	18.6	17.9	2.2	1.7

Sources: Population Census Bureau, 1985, 1993; *Provincial Statistical Yearbook,* 2001.

them rise economically. However, many of them are not familiar with Mandarin, the language in which higher education is conducted, and come from families too poor to send them to school or they attend crowded rural schools with low standards and high dropout rates.

The central government and the National People's Congress established a basic law for the autonomy of ethnic minorities, which pledges respect for the language, religion, and traditional clothing of ethnic minorities and guarantees them equal rights. Among the fifty-five ethnic minority groups, two (Manchu and Hui) use the Mandarin language of the Han majority; fifty-three groups speak their own languages. Before 1949, only eighteen had written languages. In 1956 the government helped twelve groups create a new written language and helped three others revise their written language. There is also diversity of religion among ethnic minority groups in China. Of the fifty-five minorities, four are largely Tibetan Buddhists, four are Hinayana Buddhists, and ten are Muslim; others adhere to primitive religions such as shamanism. The government has also instituted programs to provide financial subsidies and investment to autonomous regions and to give more favorable consideration in education, housing, employment, cadre selection, social welfare, and childbearing to individuals belonging to ethnic minority groups.

Urbanization in minority regions developed rapidly after 1949. The population of Hohhot (the capital city of Inner Mongolia Autonomous Region) and Urumqi (the capital city of Xinjiang Uygur Autonomous Region) more than doubled as they became newly industrialized cities. In Inner Mongolia Autonomous Region as a whole, urban population was 15.1 percent in 1953 and increased to 28.9 percent in 1982 and 36.3 percent in 1990. The urban area of Lhasa (the capital city of Tibetan Autonomous Region) has expanded at least twelve times since 1952, when the Agreement on Measures for the Peaceful Liberation of Tibet was signed.

The rapid growth of urban populations in ethnic minority regions is due partly to in-migration from Han majority regions, partly to natural increase of urban residents, and partly to rural-urban migration of local minorities. By moving into cities and living with Han urban residents—who have lived in cities and towns in many minority regions for centuries—these ethnic minorities gradually adapt to urban life and integrate with the Han (Mackerras, 1995). Their language, religion, culture, and customs are respected by others under the law, but when they adopt a modern urban lifestyle, some of their customs gradually disappear. Many of them now wear suits, use telephones and computers, listen to popular music, and believe that modernization is the only way for the future of their groups. Some elderly people have difficulties adapting to urban life, and the generation gap that exists among all Chinese people extends to China's ethnic minorities as well.

Although the basic situation in coastal areas and cities has greatly improved with regard to income, housing, and public health care facilities, about 70 million people in China still live below the poverty line (annual per capita income of less than 200 yuan, or U.S.$25), while millions more live close to the poverty line. These people usually have high birthrates, high mortality rates, and a low life expectancy. Many of them live in these autonomous regions, largely outside the monetary economy. Promoting the development of these "poverty regions" is a key issue in China today.

■ Challenges

At the beginning of the chapter, I referred to three "balancing acts" China must perform—between city and country, between population and food, and between regions of hardship and regions of prosperity. By now it must be evident that these three issues are themselves interrelated. The main challenges faced by China in the twenty-first century regarding population and urbanization are as follows:

1. China's population will continually increase even under the one-child policy designed to keep it down, reaching 1.5–1.6 billion in the 2030s. These people must have food, jobs, housing, and social services.

2. Because of family planning and the one-child policy, China is facing the problem of dealing with an aging population. It is expected that 6.72 percent of the total population of China (about 87 million) will be sixty-five or older by the year 2000 (Li, 1993:107); increasingly, a single child will be responsible for aging parents.

3. About 250–300 million laborers will switch from agriculture into the nonagricultural sector in the next ten to fifteen years, which will result in a huge volume of rural-urban migration.

4. Because of the rapid growth in the urban population due to both natural increase and migration, the pressure on housing and public services (including health care, schools, transportation, and the energy supply) will become very serious.

5. Since most human resources and capital move from the poor regions to prosperous regions under the market economy system, poverty in western China and ethnic minority regions will increase. Whether the national goal of modernization of China can be reached in the twenty-first century will largely depend on how successfully the Chinese government handles these challenges.

■ Bibliography

Aird, John S. 1978. "Fertility Decline and Birth Control in the People's Republic of China." *Population and Development Review* 4(2):225–253.

———. 1982. "Population Studies and Population Policy in China." *Population and Development Review* 8(2):267–297.

Banister, Judith. 1984. "An Analysis of Recent Data on the Population of China." *Population and Development Review* 10(2):241–271.

———. 1991. *China's Changing Population.* Stanford: Stanford University Press.

Banister, Judith, and Samuel H. Preston. 1981. "Mortality in China." *Population and Development Review* 7(1):98–110.

Beaver, Steven E. 1975. *Demographic Transition Theory Reinterpreted.* Lexington, MA: Lexington Press.

Birdsall, Nancy, and Dean T. Jamison. 1983. "Income and Other Factors Influencing Fertility in China." *Population and Development Review* 9(4):651–675.

Caldwell, John C., and K. Srinivasan. 1984. "New Data on Nuptiality and Fertility in China." *Population and Development Review* 10(1):71–79.

Chan, Kam Wing. 1996. *Cities with Invisible Walls: Reinterpreting Urbanization in Post-1949 China.* Oxford: Oxford University Press.

Chang, Sen-Dou. 1981. "Modernization and China's Urban Development." *Annals of the Association of American Geographers* 71(2):202–219.

Chao, Kang. 1987. *Man and Land in Chinese History: An Economic Analysis.* Stanford: Stanford University Press.

Chao, Wenlin, and Xie Shujun. 1988. *History of China's Population.* Beijing: People's Press (in Chinese).

Chen, Pi-chao, and Adrienne Kols. 1982. "Population and Birth Planning in the People's Republic of China." *Population Reports* J-25.

China Population and Information Research Center. 1985. *Almanac of China's Population.* Beijing: China Social Science Press.

——— (ed.). 1991. *China's Fourth National Population Census Data Sheet.* Beijing: China Population and Information Research Center.

Chung, Jae Ho (ed.). 1999. *Cities in China: Recipes for Economic Development in the Reform Era.* London: Routledge.

Clausen, Soren, and Stig Thogersen. 1995. *The Making of a Chinese City: History and Historiography in Harbin.* Armonk, NY: M. E. Sharpe.

Coale, Ansley J. 1981. "Population Trends, Population Policy, and Population Studies in China." *Population and Development Review* 7(1):85–97.

———. 1984. *Rapid Population Change in China, 1952–1982.* Report no. 27 of the Committee on Population and Demography. Washington, DC: National Academic Press.

Davis, Deborah S. 1999. *The Consumer Revolution in Urban China.* Berkeley: University of California Press.

Davis, Deborah S., Richard Kraus, Barry Naughton, and Elizabeth J. Perry. 1995. *Urban Spaces in Contemporary China: The Potential for Autonomy and Community in Post-Mao China.* Cambridge: Cambridge University Press.

Day, Lincoln H., and Ma Xia. 1994. *Migration and Urbanization in China.* Armonk, NY: M. E. Sharpe.

Dikotter, Frank. 1992. *The Discourse of Race in Modern China.* Stanford: Stanford University Press.

——— (ed.). 1997. *The Construction of Racial Identities in China and Japan.* Honolulu: University of Hawaii Press.

Dreyer, June Teufel. 1976. *China's Forty Millions.* Cambridge: Harvard University Press.

Elvin, Mark, and G. William Skinner (eds.). 1974. *The Chinese City Between Two Worlds.* Stanford: Stanford University Press.

Esterich, Joseph W. (ed.). 2000. *Remaking the Chinese City: Modernity and National Identity, 1900–1950.* Honolulu: University of Hawaii Press.

Fairbank, John K. 1979. *The United States and China.* 4th ed. Cambridge: Harvard University Press.

Gamer, Robert E. 1998. "The Continuing Transformation of the Welfare State: Planning and Funding Housing and Transportation in Shanghai, London, Paris, and Kansas City." *Political Crossroads* (Australia) 6(1):57–77.

Gates, Hill. 1996. *China's Motor: A Thousand Years of Petty Capitalism.* Ithaca: Cornell University Press.

Gaubatz, Piper Rae. 1996. *Beyond the Great Wall: Urban Form and Transformation on the Chinese Frontiers.* Stanford: Stanford University Press.

Goldstein, Melvyn C., and Cynthia M. Beall. 1991. "China's Birth Control Policy in the Tibet Autonomous Region: Myths and Realities." *Asian Survey,* March.

Goldstein, Sidney. 1985. *Urbanization in China: New Insights from the 1982 Census.* Papers of the East-West Population Institute no. 93. Honolulu: East-West Center.

Goldstein, Sidney, and Alice Goldstein. 1985. *Population Mobility in the People's Republic of China.* Papers of the East-West Population Institute no. 95. Honolulu: East-West Center.

———. 1991. *Permanent and Temporary Migration Differentials in China.* Papers of the East-West Population Institute no. 117. Honolulu: East-West Center.

Goodstadt, Leo F. 1982. "China's One-Child Family: Policy and Public Response." *Population and Development Review* 8(1):37–58.

Guldin, Gregory Eliyu (ed.). 1997. *Farewell to Peasant China: Rural Urbanization and Social Change in the Late Twentieth Century.* Armonk, NY: M. E. Sharpe.

Harris, Marvin, and Eric B. Ross. 1987. *Death, Sex, and Fertility: Population Regulation in Preindustrial and Developing Societies.* New York: Columbia University Press.

Henriot, Christian. 1993. *Shanghai, 1927–1937.* Berkeley: University of California Press.

Huang, Rongqing. 1993. "The Mortality of China in the 1980s." Pp. 137–143 in Chinese Association of Population Studies (ed.), *Selected Papers Presented at the Sixth National Conference on Population Science of China.* Beijing: Chinese Association of Population Studies (in Chinese).

Ikels, Charlotte. 1996. *The Return of the God of Wealth: The Transition to a Market Economy in Urban China.* Stanford: Stanford University Press.

Jefferson, Gary H., and Thomas G. Rawski. 1992. "Unemployment, Underemployment, and Employment Policy in China's Cities." *Modern China* 18 (January): 42–71.

Kaup, Katherine Palmer. 2000. *Creating the Zhuang: Ethnic Politics in China.* Boulder: Lynne Rienner.

Kiang, Heng Chye. 1999. *Cities of Aristocrats and Bureaucrats: The Development of Cityscapes in Medieval China.* Honolulu: University of Hawaii Press.

Kirby, Richard, Ian Bradbury, and Guanbao Shen. 2001. *Small Town China: Governance, Economy, Environment, and Lifestyle in Three Zhen.* Burlington, VT: Ashgate.

Lague, David. 2003. "The Human Tide Sweeps into Cities." *Far Eastern Economic Review* 166(1) (January 9): 24–28.

Li, Li. 1993. "The Present Situation, Characteristics of Aging in China and Countermeasures." Pp. 105–110 in Qu Geping (ed.), *Population and Environment in China.* Beijing: Chinese Press of Environmental Science (in Chinese).

Lin Fude. 1986. "An Analysis of China's Birth Rates." Pp. 237–246 in *Almanac of China's Population 1985.* Beijing: Chinese Social Sciences Publishing House (in Chinese).

Lu, Lei, and Lin Fude. 1994. "The Future of Population Growth with a Low Fertility Rate." Pp. 101–106 in Chinese Association of Population Studies (ed.), *Selected Papers Presented at the Sixth National Conference on Population Science of China.* Beijing: Chinese Association of Population Studies (in Chinese).

Lyle, Katherine Ch'iu. 1980. "Report from China: Planned Birth in Tianjin." *China Quarterly* 83:551–567.

Ma, L. J. C., and E. W. Hanten (eds.). 1981. *Urban Development in Modern China.* Boulder: Westview Press.

Ma Rong. 1992. "The Development of Small Towns and Their Role in the Modernization of China." Pp. 119–154 in Gregory E. Guldin (ed.), *Urbanizing China.* New York: Greenwood Press.

Ma Yinchu. 1957 and 1981. "New Essay on Population." Pp. 174–195 in *Collected Works of Ma Yinchu on Economics,* vol. 2. Beijing: Peking University Press (in Chinese).

Mackerras, Colin. 1995. *China's Minority Cultures: Identities and Integration Since 1912.* New York: St. Martin's Press.

Milwertz, Cecilia Nathansen. 1996. *Accepting Population Control: Urban Chinese Women and the One-Child Policy.* London: Curzon Press.

Murphy, David. 2002a. "Buried Deep Down on the Farm." *Far Eastern Economic Review* 165(17) (May 2): 24–26.

———. 2002b. "Nothing More to Lose." *Far Eastern Economic Review* 165(44) (November 7): 30–33.

Peng, Xizhe. 1991. *Demographic Transition in China.* Oxford: Clarendon Press.

Pieke, Frank N., and Hein Mallee (eds.). 2000. *Internal and International Migration.* London: Curzon Press.

Population Census Bureau. 1985. *Tabulation on the 1980 Population Census of the PRC.* Beijing: Chinese Statistical Publishing House.

———. 1993. *Tabulation on the 1990 Population Census of the PRC.* Beijing: Chinese Statistical Publishing House.

Poston, Dudley L., Jr., and David Yaukey (eds.). 1993. *The Population of Modern China.* New York: Plenum Press.

Qian, Wenbao. 1996. *Rural-Urban Migration and Its Impact on Economic Development in China.* Brookfield, VT: Ashgate.

Qu Geping, and Li Jichang. 1992. *Population and Environment in China.* Beijing: Chinese Press of Environmental Sciences (in Chinese).

Rozman, Gilbert (ed.). 1982. *The Modernization of China.* New York: Free Press.

Salaff, Janet W. 1973. "Mortality Decline in the People's Republic of China and the United States." *Population Studies* 27(3):551–576.

Sanderson, Warren C., and Jee-Peng Tan. 1996. *Population in Asia.* Brookfield, VT: Ashgate.

Skinner, William G. (ed.). 1977. *The City in Late Imperial China.* Cambridge: Harvard University Press.

———. 2001. *Marketing and Social Structure in Rural China.* New York: Association for Asian Studies.

Sneath, David. 2000. *Changing Inner Mongolia: Pastoral Mongolian Society and the Chinese State.* Oxford: Oxford University Press.

Solinger, Dorothy J. 1999. *Contesting Citizenship in Urban China: Peasant Migrants and the Logic of the Market.* Berkeley: University of California Press.

State Statistical Bureau. 1950–1995. *Statistical Yearbook of China.* Beijing: Chinese Statistical Publishing House.

———. 1995. *Urban Statistical Yearbook of China, 1993–1994.* Beijing: Chinese Statistical Publishing House.

Steinhardt, Nancy Shatzman. 1999. *Chinese Imperial City Planning.* Honolulu: University of Hawaii Press.

Tang, Wengfang, and William L. Parish. 2000. *Chinese Urban Life Under Reform: The Changing Social Contract.* Cambridge: Cambridge University Press.

Tien, H. Yuan. 1973. *China's Population Struggle: Demographic Decisions of the People's Republic, 1949–1969.* Columbus: Ohio State University Press.

———. 1983. "China: Demographic Billionaire." *Population Bulletin* 38:2.

———. 1984. "Induced Fertility Transition: Impact of Population Planning and Socio-Economic Change in the People's Republic of China." *Population Studies* 38:1–16.

Van Slyke, Lyman P. 1988. *Yangtze: Nature, History, and the River.* Reading, MA: Addison-Wesley.

Wang, Gabe T. 1999. *China's Population: Problems, Thoughts, and Policies.* Burlington, VT: Ashgate.

Wang Xiangming. 1986. "Urbanization of China's Population." Pp. 283–292 in *Almanac of China's Population 1985.* Beijing: Chinese Social Sciences Publishing House (in Chinese).

Wenlin, Zhao, and Xie Shujun. 1988. *History of China's Population.* Beijing: People's Press.

Wolf, Arthur P. 1984. "Fertility in Pre-Revolutionary Rural China." *Population and Development Review* 10(3):443–480.

World Bank (ed.). 1982–2002. *World Development Report.* New York: Oxford University Press.

——— (ed.). 1997–2002. *World Development Indicators.* Washington, DC: World Bank.

Xu, Yinong. 2000. *The Chinese City in Space and Time: The Development of Urban Form in Suzhou.* Honolulu: University of Hawaii Press.

Yan, Rui, and Cheng Shengqi. 1993. "Age-Specific Death Rates and Life Expectancy in the Past Forty Years." In Chinese Association of Population Studies (ed.), *Collected Papers Presented at International Conference on Fertility Sampling Surveys of China.* Beijing: Population Press of China (in Chinese).

Yeung, Yue-man. 2000. *Globalization and Networked Societies: Urban-Regional Change in Pacific Asia.* Honolulu: University of Hawaii Press.

Yeung, Yue-man, and Sung Wun-wing. 1996. *Shanghai: Transformation and Modernization Under China's Open Policy.* Hong Kong: Chinese University Press.

Yeung, Yue-man, and Xuiwei Hu (eds.). 1991. *China's Coastal Cities: Catalysts for Modernization.* Honolulu: University of Hawaii Press.

Zhang, Li. 2001. *Strangers in the City: Reconfigurations of Space, Power, and Social Networks Within China's Floating Population.* Stanford: Stanford University Press.

Zhao Wenlin and Xie Shujun. 1988. *History of China's Population.* Beijing: People's Press.

Zhen Yi, Tu Ping, Gu Baochang, Xu Yi, Li Bohua, and Li Yongping. 1993. "Causes and Implications of the Increase in China's Reported Sex Ratio at Birth." *Population and Development Review* 19(2):283–302.

Zhou Qing. 1994. "Ideas of People About Births in Poor Regions and Countermeasures to Change Their Ideas." Pp. 70–73 in Chinese Association of Population Studies (ed.), *Selected Papers Presented at the Sixth National Conference of Population Science of China.* Beijing: Chinese Association of Population Studies (in Chinese).

China's Environmental Problems

Richard Louis Edmonds

Chapter 8 discussed human problems; this one discusses the environment in which humans live and their interaction with it. The quality of China's environment has deteriorated considerably since the founding of the People's Republic of China (PRC) in 1949. Doubling the population since 1949 has hastened deforestation, desertification, soil erosion, water shortages, and pollution. Pessimistic observers say that the current population of 1.3 billion already may have exceeded the number that the country can hope to support at a good standard of living. Negative predictions suggest that the population could reach a point above which minimal living standards cannot be sustained during the first half of the twenty-first century. Even the most positive observers see the combination of population and economic growth placing serious strains on China's geography.

Modification of China's environment, however, goes back a long way in time, as Rhoads Murphey explained in Chapter 3. When humans first arrived on the Loess Plateau in north-central China (see Map 2.4), this area, generally considered to be the earliest home of Chinese civilization, was probably covered with a mixture of forests and grasslands. Intensive use of some of these lands led to a reduction in vegetation and serious erosion on the plateau centuries ago. Similar problems occurred elsewhere as the proto-Chinese people proliferated, spread out from the Loess Plateau and the North China Plain, and incorporated other groups over the past 2,000 years (Edmonds, 1994:28–35). Even though the Han Chinese did evolve some ecologically sound agricultural practices that improved the quality of the soil, they stripped the land of forests as they spread southward (Vermeer, 1998:247–259). As they spread to the north and west (at a much slower pace), they began to farm virgin land and substantially degraded many of these cool, dry, or fragile areas. Since the mid–eighteenth century, the pace of farming has intensified as the population grows. During the 1950s, the Chinese focused on reconstructing a war-torn country and devising means to promote rapid economic growth. Although these efforts led to better attempts at hygiene and health care, the communists generally viewed natural resources as a commodity to be exploited to create wealth for the state and, in theory, the Chinese people. After the creation of communes during the mid-1950s, many hillsides were cleared and wetlands filled to create new farmland. During the years of the so-called Great Leap Forward (1958–1961), huge numbers of trees were felled for fuel to produce low-quality steel in small, highly polluting home furnaces. From 1960 to 1962, China was hit with a drought that, combined with these policies, produced the so-called Three Bad Years (1960–1962) of widespread famine. In 1966, just as the country was devising policies designed to avoid recurrence of such a catastrophe, Chairman Mao Zedong proclaimed the Cultural Revolution. Close to a decade of political unrest and lawlessness followed and ecological degradation became commonplace (Shapiro, 2001).

Current efforts to deal with ecological problems began in a modest way around 1972 after the PRC sent a delegation to the First United Nations Conference on the Human Environment. In 1973 the government created the National Environmental Protection Agency, and environmental planning became included in national plans. Some Chinese academics and policymakers argued that economic development could not continue without considering its impact upon the environment; others argued that China must follow the "pollute first and clean up later" phase that the developed world had experienced before pollution control received high priority. In 1979 the government promulgated an Environmental Protection Law (for trial implementation). Under this law, the agency began to write environmental impact statements on proposed heavy industry, manufacturing, and infrastructure projects. However, the recommendations of these impact statements were often ignored.

From 1982, discussions began on a development strategy calling for low waste–high efficiency planning. The concept of harmonious development *(xietiao fazhan),* similar to the idea of sustainable development formulated by the Bruntland Commission, was adopted as official policy. It was supposed to increase efficiency by initiating recycling and pollution-abatement measures. However, the new, small entrepreneurs who have flourished after economic reform have not complied with the plan, and it has been difficult to implement.

Poverty and the lack of education also make it hard for China to overcome its environmental problems. Many of China's remote counties still do not have rural extension services. This fact, combined with high illiteracy rates, makes it hard to teach the rural populace how to preserve the environment. A full-fledged Environmental Protection Law was adopted in 1989, but environmental policy decisions have continued to be held back by priorities that accentuate economic growth and corruption.

■ Contemporary Environmental Problems

Pollution has grown rapidly in China. The most threatening environmental problems are the reductions in water supply, vegetation, soils, and other natural resources. China has much less land area, forest cover, and water resources per person than the average country. Cropland accounts for only 10 percent of China's total area, and both the per capita level and the total quantity of arable land are decreasing despite some recent attempts to reclaim wastelands.

■ Water Shortages

China's water shortage grew steadily throughout the reform period. The country currently supports 22 percent of the world's population with only 8 percent of the world's water. Many rivers, lakes, reservoirs, and aquifers are shrinking or have dried up during the last three decades, and China has stopped expanding its irrigated area since the beginning of the 1980s. Water shortage is at its worst north of the Huai River (roughly, in a line due west along the mouth of the Yangtze River; see Map 2.4), where 64 percent of China's cultivated land has access to only 19 percent of the country's water, and there is considerable annual variation in precipitation. The water table in northern China has fallen more than 200 feet (60 meters) since 1970. Some eastern and northern cities such as Shanghai and Tianjin (Map 2.2) are sinking as the earth settles to adjust to this loss of water and construction of large buildings. In southern China, this reportedly is happening in forty-five cities. The subsiding can lead to floods during storms and can destroy building foundations. Although rising sea levels, increased erosion, and geological movements of the earth's crust can be responsible for this condition, the lowering of the water table also is a key factor.

The water supply problem is most acute around big cities in northern China, where precipitation levels are lower than in the south. Major efforts to save water by recycling or to increase water through diversion projects began only in the 1980s. The Huang (Yellow) River has stopped flowing virtually every year since 1985, and dried up for seven months in 1998, resulting in the August 2002 announcement of a ten-year project to tackle environmental problems (Cheung, 2002). In addition, a project has begun to move water north via the Grand Canal and from the future Three Gorges (Sanxia) project, discussed later, by 2015. As northern China's water shortages continue to grow, conservation of existing water resources is of primary importance— even with the south-north water diversion project. Because irrigation water is often used in an inefficient manner, the government has modestly increased charges and advocated dry-land farming (Crook and Diao, 2000:28). Water quotas assigned to industries have resulted in some savings and water associations have helped improve water management in rural areas. Increased recycling of wastewater by industry should also help. So far, household water use has not been very wasteful. As incomes continue to increase, however, and more people move from older housing into homes with modern plumbing, domestic water consumption will increase.

▉ Forest Loss and Recovery

Official statistics indicate that in 2001 China had forest cover equal to 16.55 percent of the country's total area, which is roughly half the world average. Overall, vegetation cover decreased from 1949, with rises noticeable in official data only since the late 1980s. All major basins now experience annual floods and drought, in part due to forest loss. About two-thirds of China's forests are devoted to timber production, whereas one-eighth are devoted to "economic" trees (nuts and fruit) and to protection forests.

The Forestry Law was revised in 1998, and now has some clear implementation directives, but much of it reads more like a wish list than concrete legislation. Bans on logging were put into effect during 1998 in the northeast and in the Yellow and Yangtze River valleys. Despite this, in some remote areas, lack of state control rules out enforcement of laws. Illegal logging activities have been widespread, especially as the market economy makes it easy to sell timber. The state wood-supply system was excessively wasteful due to a lack of realistic pricing mechanisms. Recent moves toward higher, more appropriate timber prices appear to have reduced some of the waste, but add to the incentive to log. Fire and disease also continue to reduce vegetation cover.

Overall efforts since the 1950s to replant forests have not been very successful. Forest management has been corrupt and inefficient; the natural forests that remain today have been saved largely by inaccessibility. In the early 1980s, a complex forestry responsibility system was first established. In general, these contracts give a private entity (individual, household, or cooperative) rights to trees on leased land with the entity obliged to sell a quota of the trees to the collective at a fixed price or to pay a fee. Several large forestation projects are being implemented. The Three Norths Shelterbelt Project *(sanbei fanghulin)*, begun in 1978, is northern China's major reforesting project. By 1996 the project had already fulfilled 73.5 percent of its target for 2050. The Greening of the Plains Project, administered at the county *(xian)* level, was completed in 2000 and did similar planting on ten of China's major plains, river valleys, and deltas. The Greening of the Taihang Mountains Project, begun in 1986, is supposed to plant 4 million hectares by 2010 and had achieved close to two-thirds of its target by 1997. The 11,000-mile-long (18,000-kilometer) Coastal Protective Forest Project, begun in 1988, had met close to only 30 percent of its target by 1997. Plans were to create 13,750 square miles (36,000 square kilometers) of coastal forests by 2000. In 1998 a

National Forest Protection Program was initiated and the government announced its intention to revise the tax incentives to encourage private forestry ventures. To date most of the complex taxes on timber have not gone into reforestation efforts.

China covers 3.69 million square miles (9.56 million square kilometers). It remains to be seen whether these projects meet their goals and whether they add more trees than those being cut down in the interim. While projects have been helpful, the overall situation on the ground today is that trees are much younger and less diverse. Therefore, the available timber situation is worse than statistics of area planted suggest. China's Agenda 21 aims to have China's forests fully sustainable for production and ecosystem protection by the mid–twenty-first century. In terms of forest cover, the goal is to reach 26 percent by 2050.

The Obligatory Tree-Planting Program, adopted in 1981, requires all Chinese citizens above eleven years old to plant three to five trees each year or do other relevant forestry work. Most Chinese cities show the benefits of urban tree-planting programs, many of which have been obligatory. However, the total area of public greenery in Chinese cities continues to decrease as building construction receives priority.

A shelterbelt project of 77,000 square miles (200,000 square kilometers) began in 1990 along the middle and upper reaches of the Yangtze River. This soil erosion control program, known as the Chang (Yangtze) River Middle and Upper Reaches Protective Forest Construction Project, is not due to be completed until the year 2030. By 1997, enthusiastic reports suggested that the project had completed 61.6 percent of it target, was enjoying high tree survival rates, improving microclimates, and generating timber revenue.

The Continual Production Timber Forest Base Construction Project was set up in 1988 to create 77,000 square miles (200,000 square kilometers) of timber forests over a thirty-year period. Efforts up to 2000 concentrated on creating timber forests in the Lesser and Greater Hinggan Mountains of the northeast and in the hills of the southwest, as well as in the southeast, where possible. The government hopes that by 2010 these forests will be contributing enough timber to satisfy China's timber needs (National Environmental Protection Agency, 1994:70–73).

■ Soil Erosion and Nutrient Loss

China has one of the most serious soil erosion problems in the world. Conservative estimates suggest that one-sixth of the nation's arable land is affected. Between 5,000 and 10,000 million metric tons of soil are washed down rivers each year. The loss in fertility has been suggested to equal 40 million tons of chemical fertilizer (Wang et al., 1989:ii). Rapid soil erosion has contributed to China's overall environmental degradation in several ways.

Riverbeds, lakes, and reservoirs are silting up and have had their hydroelectric and flood control storage capacity reduced. The loss of good-quality topsoil has reduced arable land and threatens to cause serious food shortages in the near future.

Some of the most severe erosion occurs in northern portions of the semiarid Loess Plateau of north-central China (see Map 2.4). According to some reports, the plateau loses about a third of an inch (0.838 centimeters) of topsoil each year. The Chang (Yangtze) River valley in central China and Heilongjiang and eastern Inner Mongolia in the north are other badly affected areas. Even areas in the far south that once had little erosion—like Yunnan, Hainan, and Fujian—have had severe soil erosion in the last two decades.

China has made considerable effort to stem the flow of topsoil. Over half of the 210,000 square miles (544,000 square kilometers) of eroded land that has been improved since the mid-1950s has been planted with trees, and another fifth has been terraced. In addition, about 30,000 check dams have been built across small gullies to control erosion. In recent years, the focus shifted from individual plots to entire river basins and from central to local government. The problem is the massive scale of the effort required. As the erosion is being checked in one area, it may be increasing in another.

The increased erosion has largely resulted from policies implemented during the 1950s that opened steep slopes, formerly forested areas, and wetlands to farming. Now many of those areas must be returned to forests and herding, which affects the peasants using the land. The household responsibility system gives individual households control of land management. Enforcement of regulations to take steep slopes out of cultivation, replace crops with privately managed forests, and introduce new conservation techniques requires their cooperation. However, many of the areas in which the policy needs to be carried out are generally poor and hard to reach with grain shipments during the transition from agriculture to forestry or herding. Therefore it is hard to persuade peasants to change or to enforce policies.

Even where they are not yet degraded to a point that crops will not grow, China's soils are of poor nutrition. For example, the rich yields of southern China have been obtained only through heavy labor inputs and the widespread use of manure and composted matter. The natural organic content of China's soil averages less than 1.5 percent. The second national soil survey undertaken in the 1980s found overall soil fertility dropping, partly because farmers were leaving fewer fields fallow for shorter periods as they sought to maximize output and increase their incomes in the marketized rural economy. However, one must remember that there is great regional variety in China's soils. Today, particularly in eastern provinces, some peasants are beginning to practice "ecological agriculture," combining farming, animal husbandry, and forestry with local food processing and reuse of residual materials.

On Hainan Island (Map 2.2) and in nearby regions of the south, peasants have grown three rounds of crops a year in a field. When the only crop they grow is rice in flooded wet-paddy fields and drainage is poor, gleization (depletion of oxygen from iron compounds in the soil) can reduce the land's ability to grow rice or other crops. Approximately one-sixth of China's paddy lands suffer from this. In addition, many of the soils in the populous southeast are acidic, rendering crops susceptible to acid pollution, more commonly known as acid rain. This possibility is increased by large amounts of industrial pollutants in the atmosphere.

■ Desertification and Salinization-Alkalinization

Each year, the Chinese estimate that about 1,300 square miles (3,436 square kilometers) of arid to semiarid land becomes "desertified," degraded into a desertlike barren landscape; this is a faster pace than in prior years. Approximately 1.8 percent of China's total land area can be considered human-induced desertified land. An almost continuous belt of degraded land stretches for 3,400 miles (5,500 kilometers) from northwest to northeast China (see Map 2.4). Desertification already affects millions of people and vast areas of pasturage, cropland, and rangeland, as well as railway lines and roads. Sandstorms related to desertification caused about 4.5 billion yuan (about U.S.$750 million) of direct economic loss per annum in the early 1990s (Government of China, 1993:5), and these are growing worse.

Desertification over the past decade and a half has largely occurred on agricultural land that can be restored. However, the northwest arid region is also showing a modest increase in desertification that will be hard to rectify. In 1992 the former Ministry of Forestry began a National Sand Control Ten-Year Plan. In 1994 China signed the United Nations Convention on Combating Desertification, which the People's Congress ratified in 1996.

Although China has improved an estimated 15,000 square miles (39,000 square kilometers) of salinized-alkalinied land since 1949, problems of salinization and alkalinization are becoming more serious due to inefficient drainage and excessive irrigation, which have increased the levels of salts in the soil. Various estimates indicate that a fifth of China's irrigated cropland has become salinized. Crops sensitive to salt cannot grow on this land. It appears that the total area affected by salinization is continuing to grow. Overpumping in coastal areas has also allowed saltwater to seep into the groundwater supply. The major land reclamation projects carried out during the Great Leap Forward in the late 1950s destroyed many wetlands, which had helped dissipate excess water during flood periods. This led to increased flooding and salinization of flooded areas. Today, more wetland areas are being filled for industrial development and housing, making this problem worse.

■ Pollution

China's industries are major polluters. By 2001, over half of the total length of China's seven major river systems was categorized in the lowest two grades of water quality, with the Hai, Liao, and Huai Rivers having the worst quality (Government of China, 2002). Pollution of surface water in the cities is serious and continues to worsen. Some rivers are becoming warmer from all the wastewater dumping. In 1998, water pollution alone resulted in economic losses of 247.5 billion yuan or 3.1 percent of the annual GDP (Yao, 2002).

Water pollution is more serious in populous eastern China than in the west. In general, only lakes and reservoirs that provide drinking water have been protected, and even some of these, such as Guanting Reservoir near Beijing, have levels of ammonia nitrogen higher than the national standards. Pollution is especially severe in lakes near urban areas such as Jinan, Nanjing, Shanghai, and Wuhan.

Although surrounding ocean has not become too seriously polluted, there have been some alarming recent cases of pollution of the coastal seas and some estuaries and bays. The most poignant case was pollution of the Bo Sea off the northern China coast, which had become so serious that a fifteen-year cleaning program was launched in 2001. However, pollution off the China coast around Shanghai and Hangzhou cities and farther south around Guangzhou, Hong Kong, and Macao is probably the worst in China today.

Pollution from organic chemicals and heavy metals has been serious in places, although heavy metal pollution has been reduced in recent years. Inorganic nitrogen and phosphorus generally exceed the Chinese maximum limit in coastal waters. Oil concentrations above fishery standards have been found in coastal waters like the Pearl River delta area around Guangzhou, Dalian Bay, and Jiaozhou Bay. Red tides, which refer to seawater discolored by certain types of marine plankton that feed on pollution and are fatal to many forms of marine life, continue to increase along China's coastline.

The groundwater around some cities has been found to contain phenols, cyanides, chromium, chlorides, nitrates, sulfates, and an increasing degree of hardness. Wells have had to be shut down. In recent years, this pollution has improved in some cities and grown worse in others. Lowered water tables around some coastal cities have added to salinization of groundwater.

Water pollution problems are by no means confined to urban areas. In suburban and rural areas with relatively high densities of farm animals, an increase in nitrates can be detected in the soil and water. To get some idea of the problem, in 1999, farm animal wastes in China were estimated to be 2.4 times industrial solid wastes by volume. Many small rivers have become anoxic—no longer able to sustain aquatic life. Many lakes such as Tai Lake and Dianchi are suffering from eutrophication—overloads of organic pollution. During the 1980s and 1990s, many highly polluting small industries were created by township enterprises in rural areas. Because enterprises in the densely populated lower Chang (Yangtze) River valley and the Zhu (Pearl) River delta are often located in small towns and villages with rivers or canals connecting them, the water pollution from one town often affects the drinking and irrigation water supplies in nearby villages and the surrounding farmland. By 2000, use of wastewater to irrigate had increased to 7.3 percent of total irrigation water, or 1.6 times the amount used in 1980 (Zhang, 2001).

Although China has undertaken many efforts to improve soils in a wide range of environments, soil pollution has negated much of this initiative. It has been said that one-fifth of all cropland is suffering from heavy metal pollution, and the crop reduction from this is estimated to be 100,000 metric tons, with another 120,000 metric tons of polluted grain produced (Chen, 1998).

Increased and improper applications of chemical fertilizers, coupled with growing livestock production, have also led to degradation of soil quality in rural areas. China's fertilizer usage is higher than the world average and peasants often use nitrogen-rich human and animal wastes as fertilizer. Combining human and animal wastes with fertilizer made of plant and rock materials results in balanced enhancement of crop output, but when human and animal wastes are combined with nitrogen-rich chemical fertilizer, the soil receives too much nitrogen and crop yields drop (Liang, 1989:254).

Although the production of organochlorine pesticides was banned by the government in 1983 and the percentage of cereal grains with residues exceeding permissible limits went down by the second half of the 1980s, overall pesticide use is still heavy and excessive in some areas. In 2000, a survey undertaken on fruit and vegetable markets in sixteen provincial-level units found that 20 to 45 percent of the fruits and vegetables tested exceeded permitted levels of fourteen agricultural pesticides or seven heavy metals (Guo, 2001). The extensive use of pesticides in the past also means that pests have developed stronger resistance to chemicals.

During the period of communization, the Chinese had considerable success using various combinations of plants and animals as a method of integrated pest management instead of pesticides. Such integrated pest management can only be effectively practiced over a wide area; by 1979 they were using this method over a larger area than any country in the world. With the demise of communes and the return to family farming, however, individual farmers have reverted to using pesticides. Research into pest control is advanced in China, although practice in the field lags behind the model research stations.

When chemical fertilizers became more available around 1980, many peasants stopped using human waste as fertilizer, and "night soil" collection became a problem in cities used to disposing of waste by carrying it out to the fields. The use of manure and human wastes as fertilizer has increased again since the mid-1980s, but there are worries that now more industrial wastes from the increasing number of rural enterprises are mixed in. Moreover, the consumption of imported and domestic chemical fertilizers roughly doubled between 1980 and 1990.

A partial solution to both the solid waste and the energy shortage problems in rural China has been biogas. Biogas, also known as marsh gas or gobar gas, is methane produced by the decomposition of organic matter. The gas can be generated in reactors into which crop waste, animal and human excrement, and a fermenting agent are placed. The residual sludge from this process is organic and makes an excellent fertilizer.

In 1978 the Chinese said there were 7 million biogas reactors in use, mostly in southern China. These reactors, while important locally, produced less than 2 percent of China's total energy supply (Glaeser, 1990:262). The transformation to family farming generally has hurt the production of biogas, since the communes provided a larger scale operation for reactors, and the labor force needed to maintain them. Although biogas made a small comeback in the early 1990s, in 1992 the number of reactors in use was still below the totals for the late 1970s. In 1999 the United Nations Development Programme (UNDP) began to help Chinese livestock and poultry farms to commercialize biogas. Then in 2002, the government announced plans to have 50 million farm households (one-fifth of the national total) using biogas by 2010. Such calls, while welcome, seem overly optimistic.

As the economy expands, so does the amount of household rubbish. As of 2000, average refuse output per capita was 970 pounds (440 kilograms), higher than average grain output per capita. Total household rubbish was 100 million tons per day, increasing 8–10 percent each year (Qu, 2000). Trash in Shanghai and many other urban areas contains as much heavy metals and other inorganic matter as that found in any city in Europe or North America. Two-thirds of China's cities have garbage disposal crises. Around mining sites in rural areas, tailings of milled ore residues create reservoirs of polluted water. A considerable proportion of the waste released by industry is dumped directly into rivers and streams.

China's urban refuse also contains a large amount of coal ash. Although some of this is being put to use for paving roads, more is generated than can be used. Although urban China is shifting from solid fuels to gas, this is offset by the growth of city populations, such that the refuse problem remains.

Most urban refuse is removed by truck or boat to farms or rural dumping sites at ever-increasing distances from cities; very little of it is sorted or treated. Shanghai is one of the few cities building sorting facilities. Plastic containers and other nondegradable forms of refuse are increasing; one positive step has been the decision of the railways to start using biodegradable packaging for foods sold on trains. China has a serious shortage of incinerators and of systems for lining dump sites to prevent polluted water from the trash from seeping into the surrounding groundwater. Research into how to bury rubbish in lined landfills began only in 1986 and the first modern incineration plant was built in Shenzhen in 1987. Today, what incineration does occur often wastes the heat generated and produces air pollution.

About 2.5 percent of industrial solid waste in China is classified as "dangerous." China only recently began to set up toxic waste storage sites, the one in Shenyang being funded by the World Bank and another one in Tianjin. In 1998, a list with forty-seven major categories of dangerous wastes was promulgated and China hopes to have eight regional disposal centers controlling the toxic waste situation in 2005.

A nuclear power station became operational at Qinshan in Zhejiang province during 1991, stations at Daya Bay and Ling'ao in Guangdong are now running, and one was installed at Tianwan in Jiangsu in 2001 (Map 2.2). The proximity of the Daya Bay plant to Hong Kong was a sensitive issue in the special administrative region because the PRC lacked experience in nuclear power generation. So far the Chinese say that monitoring at power plants has indicated no perceivable impacts on the surrounding environment. Nuclear power as of 2002 accounted for only 1 percent of China's power supply compared to 22 percent in the United States, 33 percent in Japan, and 77 percent in France.

Air pollution plagues most urban areas, although the types of pollutant and their sources vary from region to region. It is estimated that industry accounts for over 80 percent of China's total waste gas emissions. In recent years, some state-controlled enterprises have improved their gas cleaning. However, since growth of the state sector has stagnated while venture enterprises expand rapidly (often using polluting technology), such improvements do not necessarily indicate reductions in air pollution.

Particle levels in Chinese cities are far worse than in most urban areas in industrialized countries. The push for industrial development caused China's coal consumption to rise steadily throughout the 1980s. As of the late 1980s, over 76 percent of China's energy was produced by burning coal. This ratio is not likely to go down much until at least 2025, when pipelines from newly acquired oil fields in Kazakhstan are completed and make petroleum more steadily available. In addition to the sheer quantity of coal burned, China's severe particle pollution problem is in part due to the fact that less than 20 percent of the coal undergoes washing to remove particle impurities, and most coal is burned in small to medium-sized furnaces, often with rather poor efficiency. Progress made in particle control has been largely offset by increased coal consumption.

The percentage of particles emitted from household chimneys that is recovered by pollution control devices is much lower than in industry. Many homes in Chinese cities use coal, and coal combustion is responsible for the majority of China's particle emissions. Lung cancer rates among housewives are higher than in any other occupation, with the small coal stoves found in most kitchens and the heavy use of hot oils for cooking the most likely causes. The low smokestacks on household stoves further intensify the street particle problem, with combustion efficiency in non-industrial uses running low.

Particle levels are particularly high in the cities of the north. In 1997 the average daily particle levels in northern Chinese cities were 381 micrograms per cubic meter ($\mu g/m^3$), with levels in southern cities around 200 $\mu g/m^3$. London normally has 48 $\mu g/m^3$, and the World Health Organization (WHO) recommends 90 $\mu g/m^3$ as the maximum particle level for safety. As China continues to industrialize, various elements have been added to the particle pollution.

China is the third largest emitter of sulfur dioxide (SO_2) in the world after the former Soviet republics and the United States. Sulfur dioxide, like particulate, is closely connected with coal smoke. As with particles, levels of sulfur dioxide are more severe during winter in the northern Chinese cities than in the south. Beijing, Xi'an, and Shenyang (all on Map 2.2) have been listed among the world's ten worst cities for sulfur dioxide concentrations. However, in the summer months, certain southern cities such as Chongqing, Guiyang, and Changsha (also on Map 2.2) can have higher SO_2 levels than northern cities. Northern China urban SO_2 daily average levels were 72 $\mu g/m^3$ and southern China levels were 60 $\mu g/m^3$ in 1997. The WHO's safe level for SO_2 is 60 $\mu g/m^3$.

Coal combustion is also responsible for two-thirds of the nitrogen oxides (NOx) emitted in China. Nitrogen oxide pollution is not yet serious when compared with particles and sulfur dioxide. In 1997 the urban daily average nitrogen oxide level for a sample of northern cities was 49 $\mu g/m^3$, and southern cities had 41 $\mu g/m^3$. Those levels are roughly the same as in recent years and in the early 1980s and are close to Chinese safety standards. Use of gasoline for cars and industry is increasing rapidly, so emissions of carbon monoxide, hydrocarbons, and nitrogen oxides should grow; catalytic converters on new vehicles became mandatory in 2000. Traffic congestion in cities has created levels of NOx at intersections that often exceed the safety level. Preparing for an increasing number of photochemical smog problems and ozone alerts, the National Environmental Protection Agency and the police put together regulations for managing the supervision of auto emissions in 1990.

China is one of the few areas in the developing world with a major acid pollution problem. Nearly 30 percent of the country's total area is subject to acid rain. Acid pollution in China is caused largely by high levels of domestic sulfur dioxide emissions from burning coal. The problem is most serious in the area east of the Qinghai-Tibetan Plateau, including the Sichuan Basin and south of the Chang (Yangtze) River (see Map 2.4). It is particularly serious in the far south because the high temperatures in the atmosphere there help sulfur dioxide convert to acid faster than in most northern industrial countries; indeed, the areas with the most severe acid pollution—Changsha, Nanchong, Ganzhou, Huaihua, and Wuzhou—are all in the south (National Environmental Protection Agency, 1995). More than half of the rainfall in southern China is now overly acidic. The situation became so serious in the Pearl River delta that the government decided to build no more thermal power plants there after 1995 (Ke, 1995). The good news is that the area affected seems to have stabilized since 1995. That said, only one of the seventeen coal-burning power plants in Guangdong with a capacity of over 120,000 kilowatts had installed desulfurization facilities as of 2002. Some new wind-powered electrical generating plants are also under construction.

Waste gases have been found to be seriously affecting vegetation. Serious corrosion of metal and damage to concrete also has been thought to be caused by acid pollution. The Chinese have been trying to combat the impact of air pollution on vegetation cover by testing various plant varieties for resistance to specific compounds.

Until recent years, noise has received low priority compared with other forms of pollution. Prior to 1975, China produced virtually no noise-testing equipment and had no factories producing noise control equipment. Before 1982, there were no standards set for construction materials. Many buildings were built with steel-reinforced concrete panels little more than an inch (3 or 4 centimeters) thick. When one walks on the stairs in these buildings, the noise produced sounds like drumbeats. Machine-sound levels in Chinese factories of the 1980s often exceeded 90 dBA (decibel amperes) (Fang, 1989:177). Noise in most Chinese cities exceeds the suggested Chinese standards, with the 2001 area weighted average for 176 cities between 47.2 and 65.8 dBA (Government of China, 2002). For reference, at constant exposure, the level considered damaging to the ear is 75 dBA; serious hearing impairment can occur after eight hours of exposure at 100 dBA (Jones, Forbes, and Hollier, 1990:107–108, 300). With the new millennium, the Beijing municipal government decided to invest 1 billion *renminbi* in controlling traffic noise pollution to within 69.5 dBA in 2002 and 68 dBA by 2007. Beijing will invest in sound insulation windows on frontage buildings, 100 kilometers of low-noise screen barriers along roads, a 15-kilometer low-noise road surface demonstrative project, and vehicle noise examinations.

The pollution problem is compounded by the favoritism that many industries receive from the government, which allows them to operate inefficient equipment without scrubbers or sewage treatment. Official statistics suggest that progress was made in the treatment of industrial wastes and that levels of air, water, and noise pollution in many major Chinese cities dropped between 1989 and 2002. The picture in rural China is less clear.

Many waste-producing industries have relocated from the urban areas to the countryside over the past two decades. There has been some moderate success in the control of rural pollution, particularly water pollution in eastern China. Many rural areas, particularly along the prosperous east coast, have employed complex and intensive waste-recycling systems to produce high-value products such as silk and freshwater fish. In some cases, pollution in rural areas has been reduced by consolidating small plants so their wastes can be treated and minerals recycled. However, the number of serious cases of untreated rural wastes being discharged is still growing. Statistics from 2001 suggest that rural township industries account for 53.1 percent of China's industrial wastewater, which represents a substantial proportional increase compared with previous statistics.

At the end of 1988 there were only 220 municipal-sewage-monitoring stations, and the local industrial waste monitoring network was not completed until 1990 (Vermeer, 1990:40–41). Monitoring has increased since then and China plans to expand its environmental monitoring network further between 2003 and 2006. By 2006, China hopes to have automatic air-monitoring facilities in 259 cities and automatic water-quality monitoring at 98 spots on major rivers. As of 2002, automatic air-monitoring systems had been set up in 179 cities, and 80 automatic water-monitoring stations had been set up on major rivers.

As we have seen, pollution problems continue to grow or at best stabilize in China despite significant efforts in recent years to address them. The costs of pollution have been tremendous in economic terms. The message that pollution control can be profitable as well as healthy got home to the Chinese leadership during the 1980s. The task for the future is to experiment with methods to regulate emissions effectively and to get the government to raise its investment in pollution control to a higher proportion of gross domestic product (GDP). Some of these measures are now coming into place.

■ Nature Conservation

China is known as a treasure house for many rare species of wildlife. The first nature reserve and laws directly dealing with nature conservation appeared in 1956; by 1965, several more reserves had been established. In the early 1980s, the government set up a wildlife protection bureau, an office to control import and export of endangered species, and the China Wildlife Conservation Association. By 1987 the State Council was alarmed enough about the hunting and smuggling of wildlife to issue a directive to local governments admonishing them to increase their surveillance and punishments. In 1988 the government devised China's first wildlife protection law, which stipulated details of administration and punishments. In 1992 the State Council promulgated Regulations on the Protection of Terrestrial Wild Fauna of the People's Republic of China, and the government published the first volume of

China's *Redbook on Flora: Rare and Endangered Flora.* Local governments have followed suit with similar laws and regulations, but many species continue to dwindle. At the end of 2001, there were 1,551 nature reserves in China covering about 12.9 percent of China's national territory. In addition, there is an expanding system of over 1,000 forest parks geared for tourism. In 2002, the State Bureau of Forestry established a Forest Parks Administration Office for their management. China also had established over forty national geological parks by 2002.

The administration of nature reserves in China is not uniform, however. Many of China's nature reserves are considered national nature preserves (171 in 2001), and others are classified as provincial or local. Different reserves are often administered by different organizations and at different government levels. On the whole, the forestry bureaus tend to dominate because nature conservation work began in the Ministry of Forestry (now called the State Forestry Administration).

Vertebrate species are protected in the PRC at first-class or second-class levels of protection. China also has three categories of protected plant species. Animals and plants receiving first-class protection are those that are endemic, rare, precious, or threatened. Those accorded second-class protection are species whose numbers are declining or whose geographical distribution is becoming more restricted. The third-class species are plants of economic importance, and thus harvesting is to be limited. In general, the method for preserving wildlife has been to establish nature reserves in the areas where they live and breed or to establish artificial breeding centers. Certain endangered species are recovering. However, some animal populations continue to remain low or decrease. For example, increased nutrient loading and industrial pollution in lakes along with the construction of dams and weirs have led to reductions in fish and crustacean yields and species. Often, in order to increase food production, crab and carp eggs have been stocked in lakes, leading to a reduction of indigenous species.

International wildlife organizations have been interested in working with China because of its varied environments as well as their concern that many aspects of nature conservation in China could be better managed. In 1979 China became a member of the Man and the Biosphere Program of the United Nations Educational, Scientific, and Cultural Organization (UNESCO). In 1981 China signed the Convention on International Trade in Endangered Species (CITES) of Wild Fauna and Flora. Of the plant and animal species protected under this treaty, over 640 are found in China. China also has sites on the UNESCO World Heritage Commission's list, and nature reserves included on the International Important Wetlands List. In 1992 the China Council for International Cooperation on Environment and Development was established, and in 1995 a nongovernmental organization, the International Association of Artificial Plant Life Community and Biodiversity in Tropical

Regions, set up its headquarters in Kunming, capital of Yunnan province (Map 2.2). Many of the larger reserves have research organizations attached, sometimes with international cooperation.

In 1981 an agreement was signed with the World Wildlife Fund to protect and study the giant panda, with an initial project completed in 1988. Although archaeological evidence indicates that pandas once were distributed widely over southern China, their range now has shrunk to small areas in southern Shaanxi, Gansu, and Sichuan. During 1975 and 1976, 138 giant pandas were found dead along the Sichuan-Gansu border (Map 2.2). The cause of their death was the deterioration of the arrow bamboo and square bamboo groves that provide their food (Enderton, 1985). This panda famine stimulated a series of attempts to preserve the animal's habitat. However, in 1983 about 965 square miles (2,500 square kilometers) of arrow bamboo groves (47 percent of the total arrow bamboo groves along the same mountainous border) again started to die out, and several dozen pandas died from starvation (Schaller, 1993). The total giant panda population of China is now estimated to be over 1,000, with another 110 bred in captivity.

As of 2002 there were twenty-six nature reserves that protect the giant panda in Sichuan province alone, nine of which are national-level reserves (Xu, 2002). Of these, the Wolong Nature Reserve is the oldest and most famous. Keeping track of this solitary animal is a difficult task, even though the panda's food range is limited. Pandas are difficult to capture, and identification of individual animals is not easy. The work is made more difficult by the farmers and lumberjacks who live within the nature reserve and sometimes deliberately harm pandas. In 1987 two groups of people were caught and punished, some with life imprisonment, for killing pandas and trying to sell the skins. The range of the animal has continued to decrease from about 7,500 square miles (20,000 square kilometers) in 1970 to half that in 1990, although the ban on cutting of natural forests in Sichuan in 1998 may help reverse this pattern.

In 2000 Volkswagen donated a considerable amount of money for the establishment of a panda research center at the Beijing Zoo, and the San Diego Zoo has helped the Wolong Nature Reserve improve the survival rate of pandas born in captivity. Cooperation between China and other countries as well as multinational corporations in conserving animals other than the giant panda also increased throughout the 1980s and 1990s. For example, in 1983 the Japanese joined efforts to protect birds; construction on a Sino-Japanese Friendship Center for Environmental Protection began in 1992. China, Nepal, and Pakistan have discussed establishing "international parks," and in 1994 China signed an agreement to establish joint nature reserves with Russia and Mongolia. However, as ecotourism grows, the desire to bring in tourist revenue could compromise the conservation aspects of such parks. Cases of national parks being turned into tourist spots are all too common (Dangerfield,

1995:10–11). The effects of tourism on China's nature preserves have rarely been positive. Wealthy Hong Kong, Macao, and Taiwan residents and overseas Chinese pay large amounts for tiger bones, elephant tusks, and parts of other endangered species, risking their survival all over Asia (Coggins, 2003).

Most environmentalists would argue that China's efforts at nature conservation are too little, too late. The total area for nature reserves is still not what it should be and the distribution of nature reserves is out of balance, although efforts to redress these issues have been significant in recent years.

The Chinese admit that administration of their nature reserves is uneven. The various units that administer the nature reserves have a tendency to look for short-term economic advantage or protect only those aspects of the environment beneficial to their bureau's interests. In addition, the scale of some of China's nature reserves is too small to be effective. Often, state forests or forest parks are located next to nature reserves; joint management of these could bring increased conservation benefits. Sometimes reserves are zoned for various revenue-generating or productive purposes, compromising their conservation role.

The lack of laws relating specifically to nature reserves prior to 1988 created confusion. Now that laws standardizing procedures for establishing nature reserves, management procedures, and penalties for violations have appeared, there is a need for clear enforcement of local versions pertinent to specific circumstances. Serious instances of killing and smuggling endangered species still occur.

For laws and their enforcement to be successful, the nature reserve managers must consider solving the economic and social problems of the local inhabitants. Attempts have been made in some of the nature reserves to compensate local dwellers. At Wolong, farmers have resisted relocation to nontraditional village housing. The government has been trying to solve employment problems for some local people by training them as forest rangers or nature reserve staff.

Enforcement problems are compounded by the low level of environmental education among the inhabitants of areas surrounding the reserves. Low levels of education also make it very difficult to find well-qualified staff to manage the reserves. Under such circumstances, some nature reserves are reserves in name only. In many cases, logging and hunting are still happening in areas where such activities are prohibited by law.

Most Chinese environmentalists point to the long-term economic value that improved management of nature conservation brings. This is the only argument that will attract the attention of a government intent upon rapid economic development. China's policymakers have come to understand that nature conservation is a necessity for the country's long-term survival. So far the overseas help and the dedication of Chinese researchers have moved the agenda forward.

■ The Three Gorges Dam

The most environmentally controversial project in China today is the construction of the Three Gorges (Sanxia) Dam on the Yangtze River in western Hubei province. The Sanxia area, which extends for 125 miles (200 kilometers) along the river, is rich in historical sites and evokes many ancient Chinese legends (see Hengduan Shan on Map 2.4). It contains six historic walled cities, ancient plank roads cut into cliffs, Stone Age archaeological village sites, many old temples and burial sites, and miles of spectacular caves. It is also home to a multitude of plants and animals. The sublime beauty and strategic significance of the Three Gorges have been celebrated for centuries in the works of China's poets and travelers. Today a boat trip through the gorges still offers one of the most breathtaking journeys in China. To build a dam in an area of such cultural and natural treasures is bound to cause irredeemable damage.

The proposal for building a dam at Sanxia dates to the 1920s, and arguments for and against the project have persisted among various ministries and provinces since the 1920s (Edmonds, 1992; Luk and Whitney, 1993; Qing, 1997). The climate of repression in the aftermath of the Tiananmen demonstrations in 1989 helped to stifle public opposition. The 1991 Yangtze and Huai River floods brought the issue to the fore; since a principal objective of the dam was flood control, the stance of proponents was strengthened. Defi-

Robert Gamer

Wu Gorge, the center of the Three Gorges,
before construction of the new dam

ant gestures in the National People's Congress during formal approval in the spring of 1992 over the dam issue included a record-breaking number of delegates voting against the project or abstaining and an unprecedented walkout by two delegates.

Construction began in December 1994. The contracts are awarded on a bidding system with foreign companies involved. The main course of the Yangtze River was successfully dammed in 1997, and the first generator installed in 2001. The reservoir started filling in April 2002, when the second channel was dammed. There was intensive pressure to remove 550,000 residents and demolish their homes by the end of 2002. By June 2003, the dam's first turbines are scheduled to begin generating electricity. By the opening of the 2008 Olympics, the water level will have risen 575 feet. When the reservoir is full in 2010, water will flow out northeastward into the Danjiangkou Reservoir on the Han River as part of the south-north water diversion project discussed earlier. The city of Chongqing, standing at the western end of the proposed reservoir, has been separated from Sichuan province and given the same national municipal status as Beijing, Tianjin, and Shanghai. The cities of Yichang (Hubei), Wan Xian, and Fuling (Sichuan) have been designated as "open cities." China hopes to use this opportunity to bring coastal prosperity inland. Arguments as to whether the dam should be constructed at all concentrated on several key questions: flood control, water supply, navigation, energy supply, safety, human dislocation, and ecological damage.

The dam at Sanxia will control about half of the Yangtze River valley's annual volume of flow. The 12 million people and 2,000 square miles (5,200 square kilometers) of good fields in the Jianghan Plain just below the dam site will receive the greatest flood protection. The dam supposedly will give the Jianghan Plain 100-year flood protection instead of the 40-year flood protection calculated to be the optimum obtainable from further investment in existing dikes. In addition, water will be diverted to water-deficient northern China.

With completion of the Sanxia Dam, 10,000 dead-weight metric ton (dwt) vessels will be able to get as far as Chongqing for more than half the year, reducing river freight costs from Wuhan (Map 2.2) to Chongqing by approximately 36 percent. Without the dam, no vessels larger than 2,000 dwt can make the voyage (Wang, 1990:95).

The Sanxia Dam is planned to have an 18,200-megawatt generating capacity, making it the world's largest hydroelectric generating plant (and the world's largest in terms of tons of concrete). When completed, it should supply an estimated one-eighth as much electricity as was generated in China during 1991. Proponents stress that building a large dam at Sanxia is more cost-effective than building a series of small dams on tributaries upstream or constructing coal-fired plants, and that the site is best for distributing electricity up and down the Yangtze River valley as well as north to Beijing and south to Guangzhou. Proponents estimate it will cost about U.S.$8.7 billion and the Chinese say that the project so far is on budget, although some specialists project the costs as being up to 50 percent higher. The dam supposedly should help pay for itself with fees from its electricity.

Proponents say that the dam will be safe from military attack, deny that it lies in an earthquake zone, and assert that it will not burst in case of an earthquake. They also argue that construction will not involve large-scale human dislocation. Resettlement costs should be low because more than half of those displaced come from small towns, and their incomes are skyrocketing through the sale of goods and services to construction workers.

Proponents also feel that ecological damage will be minimal. Because only 4 percent of the land to be flooded consists of plains, the loss of good agricultural land will not be serious. Moreover, paddy land for rice is irrigated during the summer, when nutrient-rich silt loads would be least affected by impounding water at the dam. Air and water pollution that would have been generated by coal-fired power plants will be avoided, and there is also little evidence to suggest that the reservoir will create breeding grounds for disease-carrying parasites. The reservoir shall have great fish-raising potential and a positive effect on local microclimates. Some historical artifacts currently sited below the new water level are to be moved to higher locations before the reservoir fills.

Opposition to the Sanxia Dam from within China has persisted, though with little airing in the press (for one rare airing by scientists, see Chen and Chen, 1993). Overseas opposition has been considerable. Opponents argue that flood control would only be relevant to the area directly below the dam. Major rainstorms upstream could flood areas there, and clear-water releases from the dam could lead to undercutting of dikes downstream. Some suggest that dikes already being raised in height on lower portions of the river combined with several dams on tributaries would be a far more effective and less expensive means of flood control, with less aesthetic and environmental harm. For the first time in the history of any hydraulic project, manila grass is being grown on Sanxia-project dike banks to stop erosion—a cheap and simple solution that opponents say should be used more widely before more drastic solutions as this dam are attempted. They also point out the mutually exclusive functions of a flood prevention dam and a power-generating dam: a dam used for hydropower generation should have its reservoir largely full of water, whereas one used largely for flood control should be kept almost empty.

Others argue that building a series of small dams along the Yangtze, using smaller ships, and extending hours of navigation would increase efficiency without as big a risk. Opponents also suggest that the buildup of silt upstream (accelerated by the loss of vegetation there in recent years) could lead to increased flooding above the dam or actually burst it. Considerable amounts of electricity will be lost in transmission over long distances, and there are questions about the efficiency of such large generators. Critics cite past big-dam construction experiences that do not inspire confidence. Gezhouba Dam, just downstream, took eighteen years to finish at a cost close to four times the original estimate. Its locks have been experiencing serious failures, which appear to be due to basic design flaws and lack of maintenance. In early August 1995 a passenger vessel nearly smashed through a lock gate. If this happened at the future Sanxia Dam, with water depths of over five times more on either side of its locks, such an incident could result in a great disaster.

Some 1.13 million to 1.6 million people living in the area that will be flooded will have to be relocated by the year 2009, costing up to a third of the total estimated budget; compensation costs will rise along with rural incomes and inflation (though a third of the people who have been relocated for dam construction in China since 1950 are still extremely poor and short of food, and another third are no better off than they were before). Opponents point out that there has been significant opposition to resettlement so far and there are cases of peasants refusing to move. Over 150 towns and a portion of Chongqing will be flooded. Furthermore, the land being submerged is more productive than the land being used to compensate peasants being moved; they are farming on steeper slopes with more potential for soil erosion.

It was suggested that construction of the Sanxia Dam means there will be little funding left to carry out any other water-management projects. So far this does not seem to have been the case, but it is something that must remain a speculation. Opponents point out that the official cost analysis does not include change in the future value of China's currency or certain social and environmental costs. Some also suggest that disruption of navigation during the construction period could have serious economic consequences.

Some postulate that the reservoir might cause the water table to rise and trigger landslides. Opponents also point out that there are geological fault belts near the reservoir area. Earthquakes greater than 4.75 on the Richter scale have been recorded, and increased pressure upon the bottom of the new reservoir could cause stronger earthquakes in the future.

Up to 800 historical sites will be inundated by the new reservoir. There are worries about the effect of the dam on climate, the creation of disease-fostering habitats, pollution from submerged mines, impacts on downstream ecosystems, and the future of some forms of wildlife. A slowed flow rate may reduce the ability of the river to flush out pollutants. It could also result in land being lost along the coast because the balance between silt being deposited from the river and wave erosion will be altered.

The political situation in the PRC is such that domestic public opinion cannot block a project so long as the leadership is in favor of it. This project seems to be yet another attempt by China to catch up to developed nations and solve problems with grand projects, as occurred during the Great Leap Forward, which was disastrous in terms of human suffering and ecological damage. Less spectacular measures such as preventing soil erosion by replanting forests, constructing reservoirs on tributaries, dredging the river and adjoining lakebeds, improving the central- and lower-course dikes, expanding flood-water-retention districts, improving flood-warning systems, and educating the local populace are included in the project. Although they might be more effective standing alone as elements of a sustainable river management program, their faithful implementation can help reduce the ecological, economic, and social costs of a superdam while improving flood control, rapidly generating hydroelectric power, and facilitating navigation.

■ Prospects for China's Environment

The Chinese government's traditional stand on international environmental cooperation was summed up by the Chinese delegate's speeches at the United Nations Conference on Environment and Development, held in Rio de Janeiro during June 1992. Poverty was the main cause of environmental degradation in developing countries, and thus it was not reasonable to expect these countries to maintain lower emission levels or install expensive equipment to control emissions on their own. Instead, the developed nations should transfer funds and technology to help poorer countries reduce emission levels, since in the case of China it is thought that by 2050 global warming may submerge all of its coastal areas, which are currently less than 13 feet (4 meters) above sea level, forcing relocation of about 67 million people. This viewpoint was part of a foreign policy initiative to assume leadership of developing countries' environmental bloc. At the same time, China has joined global environmental change programs and set up its own organizations. The State Council rapidly approved its own Agenda 21 (emulating the objectives issued at the Rio Conference) on March 25, 1994, making it one of the first developing countries to do so.

In the new millennium, China has modified this stand as it moves into the world order. For example, in August 2002, China ratified the Kyoto Protocol, which aims to cut greenhouse gas emissions. Stiffer regulations aimed at conservation and efficiency are appearing. Citizen-based environmental groups are becoming more tolerated, although they remain closely watched if their activities are deemed to be political. However, resources devoted to environmental work still are not sufficient to halt degradation.

As previously mentioned, the most threatening of China's environmental problems is the continuing destruction of resources, particularly in poor western and central areas. The fragile ecosystems of the western and border areas are under great strain. Since the 1950s, considerable numbers of Chinese have been relocated westward in order to develop poor areas and reduce population pressure in the east. The expansion of settled agriculture and industry in traditional herding pastures and oases of the west has led to serious degradation. These areas must no longer be seen as destinations for surplus population. Instead, population densities in parts of the west must be reduced and emphasis put on animal husbandry and forestry where possible. Thus the current "Go West" policy of the Chinese government could have very serious ecological implications for this region.

Although resource degradation also is serious in the east, the immediate problem facing the better-off population of eastern China is pollution. Pollution is widespread in rural areas. Most rural enterprises use outdated equipment, cannot afford to spend money on pollution abatement, and are inefficient energy users. In particular, rural industries have caused serious water-quality degradation. The central government can only guess at the seriousness of the total picture. Dealing with the rural industry pollution problem will require a tremendous investment by the Chinese government, as well as strict enforcement of regulations. On an optimistic note, progress is being made in some of the more wealthy eastern rural areas.

The best that can be hoped for China as a whole is that the pace of water depletion, deforestation, soil erosion, and desertification will slow in coming years. If efforts at reforesting and population control during the 1980s and 1990s prove successful, we can expect to see benefits sometime after 2010. Efficient management also would help reduce environmental problems. The Environmental Protection Law calls for environmental assessments as part of construction projects. However, such assessments are often not carried out for small-scale projects, and until the mid-1990s their results often were ignored in large-scale projects. Reaffirmation of the need for assessments announced during 2002 is a welcome sign. In addition to more funds and personnel, there is need for more public openness to assessment information.

Many analysts feel that raising prices of polluting fuels and industrial inputs will increase economic efficiency and improve China's environmental problems. Such pricing policies have helped to control some forms of degradation, such as pollution by the state-run industries, and have aided in the promotion of environmentally friendly products. Although an array of price reforms have been introduced during the past decade, pressure from government nonetheless remains the main force regulating investment in environmental control, since many inputs are still underpriced.

Ultimately, though, China's environmental problems cannot be solved solely through price reform or regulatory policies. If the country is to feed and clothe all its people and provide a good standard of living in the next century, China needs strict population control, extensive environmental education, increased wealth and infrastructure, political stability, and a more open society where information can be obtained and opinions freely expressed. The degree to which these goals are met in the coming years will have far-reaching implications not only for China's environment but for the whole earth.

■ Bibliography

Chen, Guojie, and Zhijian Chen. 1993. *Sanxia gongcheng dui shengtai yu huanjing yingxiang de zonghe pingjia yanjiu* [Research into comprehensive assessment of the ecological and the environmental influence of the Sanxia Project]. Beijing: Kexue Chubanshe [Science Publishers].

Chen Tongbin. 1998. "Woguo turang huanjing wuran wenti jidai yanzhong" [Great attention is needed to control soil pollution]. *Keji Ribao* [Science and Technology Daily], December 22. www.enviroinfo.org.cn/agriculture/pollution_and_pollution_control/c503_en.htm.

Cheung, Ray. 2002. "Yellow River Water Shortages to Worsen." *South China Morning Post,* December 21.

Coggins, Chris. 2003. *The Tiger and the Pangolin: Nature, Culture, and Conservation in China.* Honolulu: University of Hawaii Press.

Crook, Frederick W., and Xinshen Diao. 2000. "Water Pressure in China: Growth Strains Resources." *Agricultural Outlook* (January–February): 25–29. www.ers.usda.gov/publications/agoutlook/jan2000/ao268g.pdf.

Dangerfield, Lara. 1995. "Growing Treasures." *China Now* 153:11–12.

Edmonds, Richard Louis. 1992. "The Sanxia (Three Gorges) Project: The Environmental Argument Surrounding China's Super Dam." *Global Ecology and Biogeography Letters* 4(2):105–125.

———. 1994. *Patterns of China's Lost Harmony: A Survey of the Country's Environmental Degradation and Protection.* London: Routledge.

——— (ed.). 2000. *Managing the Chinese Environment.* Oxford: Oxford University Press.

Enderton, Catherine Shurr. 1985. "Nature Preserves and Protected Wildlife in the People's Republic of China." *China Geographer* 12:117–140.

Fang Danqun. 1989. "Woguo zaosheng kongzhi jinzhan" [Noise pollution control and prospects in our country]. Pp. 171–180 in Zhongguo Huanjing Kexue Xuehui [China Environmental Science Institute] (ed.), *Zhongguo huanjing kexue nianjian* [China Environmental Science Yearbook]. Beijing: Zhongguo Huanjing Chubanshe [China Environmental Publishers].

Glaeser, Bernhard. 1990. "The Environmental Impact of Economic Development: Problems and Policies." Pp. 249–265 in Terry Cannon and Alan Jenkins (eds.), *The Geography of Contemporary China: The Impact of Deng Xiaoping's Decade.* London: Routledge.

Government of China. 1993. "1992 Report on the Environment in China." *China Environment News* (Beijing), June, p. 5.

———. 2002. "2001 Huanjing gongbao" [2001 Report on the Environment in China]. www.zhb.gov.cn/index3.htm.

Guo Xiao. 2001. "'Cailanzi' wuran Qiaoxiang jingzhong" [Alarm bell is sounded for the pollution of vegetables on dinner tables]. *Jingji Ribao* [Economic Daily], October 20. www.enviroinfo.org.cn/agriculture/pollution_and_pollution_control/d102229_en.htm.

Jones, Alan Robertson, Jean Forbes, and Graham Hollier. 1990. *Collins Reference Dictionary: Environmental Science.* London: Collins.

Ke We-hong. 1995. "No More Thermal Plants for Delta." *China Environment News* (Beijing), June, p. 1.

Lee, Yok-shiu F., and Alvin Y. So. 1999. *Asia's Environmental Movements: Comparative Perspectives.* Armonk, NY: M. E. Sharpe.

Liang, Xiaoyan. 1989. "Analysis of the Stability of the NPK Effects on Rice in Guangdong Province." Pp. 249–254 in E. Maltby and T. Wollersen (eds.), *Soils and Their Management: A Sino-European Perspective.* London: Elsevier Applied Science.

Luk, Shiu-hung, and Joseph B. R. Whitney (eds.). 1993. *Megaproject: A Case Study of China's Three Gorges Project.* Armonk, NY: M. E. Sharpe.

Ma, Xiaoying, and Leonard Ortolano. 2000. *Environmental Regulation in China: Institutions, Enforcement, and Compliance.* Lanham, MD: Rowman and Littlefield.

National Environmental Protection Agency. 1995. *Report on the State of the Environment in China 1994.* Beijing: National Environmental Protection Agency.

———, National Long Range Planning Institute. 1994. *Zhongguo huanjing baohu xingdong jihua 1991–2000 nian* [China's Environmental Protection Activity Plan 1991–2000]. Beijing: Zhongguo Huanjing Kexue Chubanshe [China Environmental Science Publishers].

"Programme Makes Country Greener." 1996. *Beijing Review* (Beijing), March 25–31, p. 6.

Qing, Dai. 1997. *The River Dragon Has Come! The Three Gorges Dam and the Fate of China's Yangtze River and Its People.* Trans. Ming Yi. Armonk, NY: M. E. Sharpe.

Qu Xia, 2000. "Laji zhe daqian" [Waste is valuable]. *Zhongguo Huanjingbao* [China Environment News], January 6. www.enviroinfo.org.cn/waste_management/disposal_treatment/recycling/b012047_en.htm.

Ross, Lester. 1988. *Environmental Policy in China.* Bloomington: Indiana University Press.

Sanders, Richard. 2000. *Prospects for Sustainable Development in the Chinese Countryside: The Political Economy of Chinese Ecological Agriculture.* Burlington, VT: Ashgate.

Schaller, George. 1993. *The Last Panda.* Chicago: University of Chicago Press.

Shapiro, Judith. 2001. *Mao's War Against Nature: Politics and the Environment in Revolutionary China.* Cambridge: Cambridge University Press.

Smil, Vaclav. 1993. *China's Environmental Crisis: An Inquiry into the Limits of National Development.* Armonk, NY: M. E. Sharpe.

Tsai, Terence. 2001. *Corporate Environmentalism in China and Taiwan.* New York: Palgrave.

Vermeer, Eduard B. 1990. "Management of Environmental Pollution in China: Problems and Abatement Policies." *China Information* 5(1):34–65.

———. 1998. "Population and Ecology Along the Frontier in Qing China." Pp. 235–279 in M. Elvin and Liu T. (eds.), *Sediments of Time: Environment and Society in Chinese History.* Cambridge: Cambridge University Press.

Wang, Xianpu, Jianming Jin, Liqiang Wang, and Jisheng Yang. 1989. *Ziran baohuqu de lilun yu shijian* [Theory and practice of nature reserves]. Beijing: Zhongguo Huanjing Kexue Chubanshe [China Environmental Science Publishers].

Wang, Zuogao. 1990. "Navigation on Yangtze River and the Three Gorges Project." *Bulletin of the Permanent International Association of Navigation Congresses/ Bulletin de l'Association Internationale Permanente des Congres de Navigation* 70:86–96.

Xu, Lianbing. 2002. "Sichuan 26 ge ziranbaohuqu gaishan daxiongmao xixi huanjing" [Sichuan's 26 natural reserves improve the living environment for giant pandas]. *Sichuan Ribao* [Sichuan Daily], December 6. www.enviroinfo.org.cn/biodiversity/endangered_species/animals/e120617_en.htm.

Yao Weijie. 2002. "Shui wuran yaosuan jingji zhang" [Water pollution must have an economic cost]. *Kexue Ribao* [Science Times], December 5. www.enviroinfo.org.cn/water_pollution/e120516_en.htm.

Yuan, Guolin. 1995. "Sanxia gongcheng de xingjian dui Changjiang liuyu jingji fazhan de ladong zuoyong" [The push effect of construction of the Sanxia Project on regional economic development for the Chang River valley]. *Zhongguo Sanxia jianshe* [China Three Gorges Construction] 5:5–7.

Zhang Zichen. 2001. "Shengtai nongye: Gengdi mianji chao yimu zhongzhi yangzhi huanjing wuran xingshi yiran yanjun" [Ecological agriculture: The grim situation on environmental pollution through cultivation and breeding]. *Jingji ribao* [Economic Daily], June 5. www.enviroinfo.org.cn/agriculture/pollution_and_pollution_control/d060629_en.htm.

Family, Kinship, Marriage, and Sexuality

Zang Xiaowei

The family is a fundamental social unit in every society. In no aspect of culture are the diversities of human societies more striking than in the institutions of the family and marriage. Families meet basic human needs of mating, reproduction, the care and upbringing of children, care for the aged, and the like, but families in different societies meet these needs in differing ways (see, for example, Goldthorpe, 1987:163; Goode, 1963). Likewise, families across societies vary in their responses to new trends in employment, education, recreation, travel and relocation, contraception, housing, child care, and labor saving devices.

For example, a majority of Americans begin sexual activity before marriage—a radical change from the past. In a 1988 study, half of fifteen- to nineteen-year-old females reported having sexual intercourse (Brook-Gunn and Furstenberg, 1989:249–257; Day, 1992:746–749; Small and Kerns, 1993: 941–952). The number of unmarried couples living together has tripled in less than two decades (Giddens, 1992). The divorce rate in the United States is believed to be the highest in the world, with about half of recent marriages expected to end in divorce (Moore, 1989, 1992). New alternatives to traditional marriage, such as single parenthood, are becoming commonplace.

In China, too, premarital sex, divorce, and staying single are also on the increase—but at a much slower rate. Hollywood, rock music, and individual paychecks sing their siren songs there, too, but have been slower to disrupt family life. Loyalty to one's family takes precedence over all other obligations, perhaps more than in any other culture.[1] Even China's constitution contains detailed provisions about the family, discussing the care of the elderly and the upbringing of young children. In doing so, it echoes the emphasis of Confucius on the primary role of the family. That emphasis is weakening in

China's culture, but its roots are so deep that the changes are likely to remain gradual.

■ Family Structure

Sociologists usually divide families into four basic structural categories: the first category is single men and women living alone, including those who have not married and those who are widowed or divorced. The second category, the nuclear family, consists of a couple and their unmarried children. It also includes childless couples or one of the parents (the other either dead or divorced) living with one of their married or unmarried children. The third category is a stem structure of an extended family, containing an aged parent or parents, one married child and his or her spouse, and perhaps grandchildren as well. Finally, the extended family differs by having two or more married siblings living together with their children and a grandparent or two.

In traditional China, the ideal family was an extended family consisting of five generations living together under one roof, sharing one common purse and one common stove, under one family head. Confucianism expressed a preoccupation with familial relations and ethics. Families organized on the basis of "proper" relationships were considered by Confucian scholars to be fundamental to the maintenance of social harmony and political stability in China. The younger generation was ethically bound to support, love, and be obedient to their seniors.[2]

The Chinese imperial state, which relied on Confucianism as its ideological foundation, strongly supported the traditional family institution. A local magistrate, for example, might erect a large memorial arch testifying to a widow's virtue for her refusal to remarry, or give an extended family a placard of honor to promote the ideal of five generations living harmoniously under one roof. Dividing the extended family, especially when aging parents were still alive, was strongly discouraged because it went against Confucian ethics (Mann, 1987).

Parents arranged marriages for their offspring, sometimes before they were old enough to live together and consummate the marriage. When a boy married, he brought his bride to live with his parents. When the father died, he divided his estate equally among his sons. Thus marriage did not lead to the creation of a new household. Usually, new families were created through partition of the family estate after the death of the father. Each son might use his share as the economic foundation for a new, smaller family he now headed, moving out of the parent's house to establish a nuclear family. One son might stay with or take in the widowed mother to create a stem family. Because of this cyclical process, at any given time most families were small. Some included parents (or one surviving parent) living with one or more married sons and perhaps their children. Others were limited to parents and their unmarried children and were thus similar to many present-day Western families in size and composition.[3] Extended families with five generations living together were rare.

Family size was restricted not only because of divisions but also because of high infant mortality rates in imperial China and low life expectancy. However, rich families were more successful than the less well-to-do in raising their children to maturity. Rich families also tended to have higher birthrates than the less well-to-do because of better nutrition and the practice of polygamy (i.e., a man having two or more wives at the same time); the presence of additional women greatly increased the likelihood of more children. Although polygamy was generally acceptable in precommunist China, rich families were far better able to afford it. Consequently, rich families were larger than average in size; many of them were extended families including several generations and could be extremely large. For example, in 1948 two U.S. scholars claimed after their fieldwork in a Chinese village that "the Kwock and Cheung families are very nearly of equal size, having an estimated 500 to 750 members each, while the smallest unit is Choy, with about 200 to 300 members" (Baker, 1979:1).[4]

In the late nineteenth century, because of Western penetration into China, new bourgeois and working classes emerged in Chinese coastal cities along with a new intellectual elite. Since they obtained their incomes through employment outside the family, these individuals were freed from control by family elders. They were exposed and receptive to the new cultural and intellectual forces entering China from Japan and the West. Hence they agitated for legal and cultural reforms to promote the ideals of marriage based upon free and romantic attachments and equality of men and women with respect to marriage, property, and inheritance.[5] The reforms led to an increasing trend in urban China toward smaller nuclear family units and growing freedom of choice for men and women in choosing marriage partners. Since the 1930s, most urban Chinese have resided as nuclear families (Zang, 1993; Tsui, 1989; Whyte and Parish, 1984:chap. 6). Tables 10.1 and 10.2 show that by 1900, over half of urban Chinese families included in those surveys took the nuclear form.

Chapters 4 and 8 discussed the increasing urbanization and rapid industrialization that followed establishment of the People's Republic of China (PRC) in 1949. Those trends contributed further to the separation of nuclear families from control by their elders, especially in cities. There nuclear families tend to make decisions about and engage in reproduction, residence, food preparation, consumption and expenditure, and child rearing with little involvement by their elders (Parish and Whyte, 1978; Whyte, 1992:317–322; Whyte and Parish, 1984:chap. 6).

The stem family structure has not disappeared in urban China, however. Young couples may choose to live with their retired parents for free child care;

Table 10.1 Family Structure of Grooms' Families (percentage)

					Year of Marriage				
Family Structure	1900–1938	1939–1945	1946–1949	1950–1953	1954–1957	1958–1965	1966–1976	1977–1982
Single family	14.9	18.3	15.5	20.9	18.5	20.0	16.2	6.0
Nuclear family	50.8	49.3	50.5	50.3	48.3	51.5	59.3	66.6
Stem family	17.6	17.8	18.9	17.8	17.8	18.0	16.3	19.0
Joint family	8.9	7.2	8.8	4.0	6.1	2.7	3.5	2.4
Others	6.7	6.0	5.6	6.6	7.3	5.9	3.2	4.6
N.A.	1.1	1.1	0.6	0.4	2.0	1.9	1.5	1.5
Number of cases	563	612	465	473	493	629	869	879

Source: Zang, 1993:42.
Note: N.A. = no answer; respondents did not answer question.

Table 10.2 Family Structure of Brides' Families (percentage)

Family Structure	Year of Marriage							
	1900–1938	1939–1945	1946–1949	1950–1953	1954–1957	1958–1965	1966–1976	1977–1982
Single family	5.7	6.9	7.7	8.6	7.8	7.0	4.3	1.7
Nuclear family	54.7	55.5	53.0	48.6	51.2	56.2	65.9	67.5
Stem family	25.3	21.1	23.5	27.8	22.1	21.8	19.6	20.5
Joint family	8.4	6.9	8.5	6.7	9.4	7.2	4.2	3.7
Others	4.2	7.9	5.8	7.6	7.4	4.8	4.1	4.1
N.A.	1.6	1.8	1.5	0.6	2.0	3.0	1.8	2.6
Number of cases	570	622	468	475	498	641	877	889

Source: Zang, 1993:41.
Note: N.A. = no answer; respondents did not answer question.

Early morning dancing and mahjong in the park

housing shortages may force young couples to live, at least for a few years, with their parents who have housing units. These considerations may stabilize or even increase the number of stem households temporarily (Riley, 1994: 798–801; Tsui, 1989).

In rural areas, families continued to be organized along traditional lines until 1949. This is not surprising, given that the rural Chinese economy before 1949 was overwhelmingly based on traditional technologies and organizations. Traditional family forms were changed after 1949 (Fei, 1962; Stacey, 1983; Wolf, 1985). An important factor causing the change in rural areas was the long period of collectivization (1955–1980). Prior to it, the father's indisputable authority in the family had been based on his control over and management of family property, farmwork, and dealings with the outside world. Collectivization abolished the private ownership of the means of production and transformed peasants into wage earners in collectives organized by the Communist Party. The farming family was no longer a production enterprise. With the family's well-being based mainly on the earnings of individual family members working for their collective unit or in other ways outside the family context, the father's authority was reduced significantly. There were no large family landholdings that would encourage brothers to stay together under their father's authority. Brothers tended to move out of their parent's house shortly after marriage, being constrained only by the cost and availability of new housing. However, the stem family structure survived the collectivization campaign as some parents continued to live with one of their married sons for old-age support and security.

Parental authority did not disappear totally during the collectivization period. Sons generally stayed in their father's village. Many peasant parents remained deeply involved in the marriages of their children, even if the young couple had become acquainted on their own. Parental power over their children's marriages derived from the fact that a groom usually required his parents to give his bride's family a large cash gift before marriage, which could be worth several years of his family's earnings. Parental power was also based on the parents' responsibility for preparing the wedding ceremony and housing for their son and would-be daughter-in-law.

In a truly dramatic policy shift, in the late 1970s a process of decollectivization was carried out by the government to stimulate China's rural economy. As Chapters 3 and 4 explained, by the early 1980s agriculture in China once again became the undertaking of individual families, who now lease land on a long-term basis (fifteen-year or twenty-five-year contracts are common) from the collectives they worked for previously. Recent fieldwork and reports reveal that this policy shift has had unintended implications for family organization. Although most families are still nuclear and stem in form, rich families are reappearing in the countryside, with some larger than average and similar to the typical extended family since they contain married brothers.[6]

Finally, Table 10.3 indicates that most urban married couples surveyed either live by themselves (neolocal) or close to the groom's family (patrilocal). William Lavely and Xinhua Ren (1992:378–391) point to similar trends in rural China. Only a small minority of Chinese couples choose to stay with the bride's family (matrilocal residence). However, in Yunnan province in southwestern China, matrilocal residence has been the norm among some minorities. In these matrilineal societies, a groom moves into his bride's house and has no control over the household estates and other assets. In sum, although nuclear families are the norm, many stay in close contact with parents and grandparents. And few Chinese live alone.

■ Marriage

In imperial China, marriage was not based on love and romance. Young people had very little say in marriage, either about timing or about partners. Many marriages were arranged by parents and thus were "blind," with the bride and the groom not even meeting each other until the wedding day. Frequently, two sets of parents contracted marriages between young children, who did not begin to cohabit until they were older. All this gave parents effective control over the marriages of their offspring.[7] Arranged marriage was a crucial part of a family's strategy for success. Through marriage, old alliances

Table 10.3 Postmarital Residence (percentage)

Postmarital Residence	Year of Marriage							
	1900–1938	1939–1945	1946–1949	1950–1953	1954–1957	1958–1965	1966–1976	1977–1982
Neolocal residence	30.5	39.5	41.7	52.2	57.2	55.1	47.3	32.1
Patrilocal residence	59.1	49.5	47.7	37.1	31.9	27.5	34.7	46.7
Matrilocal residence	8.6	8.5	7.9	7.8	8.4	12.2	14.0	18.1
Others	0.5	0.6	1.5	2.1	1.6	3.1	3.2	2.5
N.A.	1.2	1.8	1.1	0.8	0.8	2.2	0.8	0.7
Number of cases	570	622	468	475	498	641	877	889

Source: Zang, 1993:40.
Note: N.A. = no answer; respondents did not answer question.

between families could be strengthened and new ones formed. Parents secured support in their old age. Resources were transferred from one family to another.[8]

Parental influence in the marriage institution was gradually eroded after the turn of the twentieth century as reformers and revolutionaries denounced the personal misery and suicides that had resulted from arranged marriages. Especially in cities, young people struggled to change traditional practices like the Confucian ideals of filial piety, arranged marriage, and the subordinate role of women in the family. These struggles led to significant changes in the marriage institution, one of which was the age at which youths married.[9] Tables 10.4 and 10.5 show that during the 1930s about 10 percent of urban brides surveyed were under fifteen years of age; by 1950 that practice was reduced significantly. Early marriages of males decreased during the same period. According to the latest official statistics, in 1994 the average marriage age for women at first marriage was twenty-three years (Zang, 1993; Whyte, 1990; Whyte and Parish, 1984:chap. 5). Early marriage has not been eliminated under the communist regime, however. In 1990 China still had over 8 million marriages of girls under fifteen in rural areas; this figure was halved by 1994. Over 90 percent of early marriages are found in rural areas. By 1994, 71 percent of Chinese above the age of fifteen were married, while 6 percent were widows or widowers, and fewer than 1 percent were divorced. Twenty-two percent were still single ("China's Current Marriage Patterns," 1995).

Table 10.6 shows how freedom of choice in choosing one's mate has increased in urban China since 1900. Proceedings dominated by parents arranged more than half of all marriages between 1900 and 1938; by 1982, such practices almost disappeared. By then, four in every five couples married of their own volition. Chinese women today enjoy much more freedom in selecting mates than their counterparts who married before 1949 (Diamant, 2000).

Parents and older associates still play a major role in this process, however. First, as Table 10.6 shows, introductions by friends and coworkers are important for young people to find prospects. Studies indicate that workplace officials do their best to serve the needs of young people, including their marital concerns, in exchange for their political loyalty and obedience. Single young people are subjected (or treated) to frequent informal matchmaking activities by friends or colleagues. At times such matchmaking can become almost a project of a workplace, with the responsibility usually falling on the shoulder of official organizations such as the Communist Youth League, the trade union, and the Federation of Women (Whyte, 1990; Whyte and Parish, 1984:chap. 5).

Second, casual dating was rare prior to the 1990s; dating was viewed by the public as an ad hoc agreement to marry, rather than as a mechanism for selecting an eventual partner, as in the United States (Hsu, 1981). A recent sur-

Table 10.4   Groom Age at First Marriage (percentage)

Age at First Marriage	Year of Marriage							
	1900–1938	1939–1945	1946–1949	1950–1953	1954–1957	1958–1965	1966–1976	1977–1982
15 and under	5.5	2.6	2.4	0.2	0.2	0.0	0.0	0.0
16–17	8.0	5.6	5.2	3.2	0.4	0.2	0.0	0.0
18–20	21.0	21.6	16.3	21.8	9.3	2.4	0.8	0.0
21–24	30.9	29.4	30.3	30.7	36.9	24.5	8.9	2.8
25–29	22.0	24.0	29.2	27.7	35.2	47.1	58.2	59.2
30–35	8.9	10.8	11.8	11.4	23.4	19.6	27.3	33.5
36–40	2.0	2.6	2.4	2.7	2.6	3.5	2.8	2.5
41 and over	1.1	2.9	1.7	1.9	2.0	2.9	2.1	2.1
N.A.	0.7	0.5	0.7	0.4	—	—	—	—
Number of cases	563	612	465	473	493	629	869	879

Source: Zang, 1993:39.
Note: N.A. = no answer; respondents did not answer question.

Table 10.5 Bride Age at First Marriage (percentage)

Age at First Marriage	Year of Marriage							
	1900–1938	1939–1945	1946–1949	1950–1953	1954–1957	1958–1965	1966–1976	1977–1982
15 and under	9.5	4.3	3.0	1.7	0.2	0.5	0.0	0.0
16–17	26.3	19.3	18.6	15.2	4.6	2.4	0.0	0.0
18–20	40.9	37.9	37.2	40.0	36.6	19.3	3.8	0.2
21–24	17.9	26.5	26.3	26.5	36.6	40.9	35.0	14.2
25–29	4.7	7.9	11.1	11.6	15.9	29.0	53.9	72.4
30–35	0.4	3.2	2.6	3.8	4.8	4.8	4.9	10.9
36–40	0.0	0.8	1.3	1.3	1.4	2.1	0.5	0.3
41 and over	0.05	0.0	0.05	0.0	0.0	1.1	1.9	1.9
N.A.	0.25	0.1	2.80	—	0.8	—	—	—
Number of cases	570	622	468	475	498	641	877	889

Source: Zang, 1993:38.
Note: N.A. = no answer; respondents did not answer question.

Table 10.6 Changes in Aspects of Freedom of Mate Choice (percentage)

Mate-Choice Patterns	Year of Marriage								
	1900–1938	1939–1945	1946–1949	1950–1953	1954–1957	1958–1965	1966–1976	1977–1982
Parental arrangement	53.9	36.3	30.6	19.8	11.2	3.1	0.8	0.9
Introduction								
by relatives	24.0	27.2	25.9	25.7	24.1	21.2	17.8	15.2
Introduction by friends	15.1	23.3	24.4	29.9	34.3	42.3	44.2	48.3
Own effort	5.0	9.8	14.5	18.5	25.7	26.4	33.5	31.7
Others	0.5	1.0	0.4	1.9	0.6	1.4	0.6	0.1
N.A.	1.6	2.4	4.5	4.2	4.0	5.6	3.1	3.8
Number of cases	570	622	468	475	498	641	877	889

Source: Zang, 1993:39.
Note: N.A. = no answer; respondents did not answer question.

vey found that nine out of ten Chinese women never had another person they considered marrying beside their eventual husbands. Less than 30 percent had other boyfriends. Many women said they rarely or never dated their future husbands; even for those who did, the dates almost always came after the decision to marry, rather than prior to it (Xu and Whyte, 1990).

Thus, many Chinese young people have to make a vital decision about their lives without being able to gain experience first via casual dating. Sometimes parents are able to exert considerable influence. U.S. anthropologist William Jankowiak did fieldwork in a city in Inner Mongolia in the 1980s and reports that Chinese mothers are often a deciding force in their children's choices of marital partners (Jankowiak, 1993:chap. 8). Other studies indicate that urban mothers are often involved in many aspects of their daughters' lives; this involvement includes choosing and introducing their friends. Young women may prefer to find a husband without parental help, but it is often difficult in the social context of the Chinese city, where places to date like dance halls, karaoke clubs, and fast food restaurants were rare and beyond most budgets before the 1990s. Instead they have to rely on the introductions of all those around them—parents, classmates, friends, and relatives (Riley, 1994:794–798).

Further, children usually live with their parents until they marry. This pattern is both expected by cultural norms and reinforced by the shortage of housing and the government's rules that do not allow unmarried people to acquire public housing easily. Young people live in close physical proximity to their parents during the time when they choose a spouse, thus giving their parents ample opportunity to meet, judge, and comment on their boyfriends or girlfriends. Young Chinese would not want their parents to arrange their marriages, and almost all parents agree. However, they show little obvious resistance to, and seem to genuinely accept, a certain amount of parental influence and involvement. A 1996 Hong Kong survey found that even there—dressed in the most current Western fashions and grunge clothing, and surrounded by Planet Hollywood, the latest Hollywood releases, and giant dance halls blaring the latest rock music—75 percent of young respondents say they should obey their parents in their choice of friends, 91 percent say they should study hard, and 87 percent say their parents should determine how they get on with other family members (Elegant and Cohen, 1996; Leung, 1997).

Similar changes in mate choice also occurred in rural China.[10] Working in a collective gave young peasants opportunities for daily contact unavailable to them in the past, which increased their freedom to marry someone of their own choosing. Recent decollectivization has not changed this situation; young peasants still have greater freedom of choice. A marriage may be arranged by the parents, but the son and daughter will be given the opportunity to meet and agree to the match, or a young couple may become acquainted on their own and ask their parents to prepare the wedding. Ongoing economic reforms have allowed young peasants to migrate into urban areas (Zang, 1995), thus increasing their contact with urban culture and reinforcing the trend toward greater freedom of mate choice in the countryside.

Since the late 1980s, young people have less need for introductions by parents and friends because ongoing economic reform has changed China's landscape significantly. New housing, dance halls, movie theaters, fast food joints, and discretionary income enabling young people to frequent them, combined with long distances traveled to work, help young men and women meet one another on their own. As explained in Chapter 13, movies, novels, and magazines are introducing Western ideas of love and marriage. It can be reasonably predicted that more and more young people will get married of their own volition in the future, without introductions by friends and family.

■ Marital Breakdown

Divorce is another trend that mirrors the experiences of other countries. Causes of marital breakdown in China include the failure to deliver emotional support or a gratifying sexual relationship, family violence, the fading of romantic love after marriage, and extramarital affairs. In addition, political changes have had great impact on divorce in China. In 1953, China experienced a surge in divorces. Scholars interpret it as a consequence of the promulgation of the Marriage Law in 1950, which for the first time allowed women to ask for divorce. Many married women regarded divorce as a way out of intolerable arranged marriages. In rural areas, enforcement of the law was short-lived, as explained in Chapter 11. After the mid-1950s, divorce tended to be an urban phenomenon and, even there, remained rare (Conroy, 1987:54–55; Stacey, 1983).

Many China experts claim that a large number of divorces occurred during the Cultural Revolution (1966–1976). The impact of the Cultural Revolution on divorce is difficult to assess with accuracy because of the lack of data. The extraordinary social upheavals and fear of persecution often led one partner to sue for divorce when the other got into political trouble. The implications for the whole family of one member's political wrongdoing were potentially disastrous. Divorce proceedings were initiated not because of a lofty sense of ideological outrage against the offending spouses but for the purpose of social survival and protection of the children's future (Conroy, 1987:55–56; Liang and Shapiro, 1983; Thurston, 1987).

Divorce has been on the upswing in China since the 1978 economic reforms (Conroy, 1987:58; Li, 2002). Extramarital affairs have increased. At the same time, contemporary Western ideas on marriage have gradually entered China. All these are said to have contributed to a rising divorce rate

Table 10.7   Divorce Rates in Cities, Towns, and Countryside

	Divorce Rate in 1994 (per thousand)	Increase over 1990 (per thousand points)
City	9.8	2.1
Town	7.9	1.5
Countryside	6.2	0.8

Source: "China's Current Marriage Patterns," 1995.

(see Table 10.7). From 1987 to 1990, divorces increased fourfold. Married people in their thirties exhibit the highest divorce rate. According to a report by *South China Morning Post* in April 2002, the divorce rate in China "jumped from three percent in the 1970s to 13 percent in 2000. And in some cities such as Shanghai it has climbed above 25 percent." In 1994, there were 6.19 million divorced people, living mostly in cities. There have been 2 million divorces a year since 2000, and the number of broken marriages "is on the rise and is set to rise further still partly due to a rise in people's expectations of relationships." The rising number of extramarital affairs has also contributed to divorces. In Shanghai, about 40 percent of divorces were filed because of extramarital affairs, 38 percent because of personality conflicts, and only 3 percent because of an unhappy sex life (Li, 2002:6). Nevertheless, the divorce rate is growing in China at a much slower pace than in the United States or Europe. In 2002 the National People's Congress amended the Marriage Law to deal with marriage violence, and a drama series on national television dealt with the topic.

The Chinese are becoming less negative toward marital breakdowns. A survey conducted in Beijing at the end of 1994 reports that over 85 percent of the respondents agreed that divorce should proceed if there were sufficient reasons. The findings contrast with the previous dictum that divorce meant a loss of face (Zhao and Geng, 1992).

■ Family Relations

The traditional Chinese family was most emphatically male-centered with respect to the distribution of authority, patterns of employment, residence, inheritance, a pronounced preference for male offspring, and oppression of women. In imperial China even illiterate farmers knew about the Confucian Three Obediences, by which women were to be governed: as an unmarried woman she must obey her father, as a married woman she must obey her husband, and as a widow she must obey her adult sons (Stacey, 1983:chap. 1; Mann, 1987; Saso, 1999). As Laurel Bossen points out in Chapter 11, in some regions and households women found ways to assert some independence, but these opportunities were limited.

Female infanticide—the killing of female babies at birth—was practiced among some poor families before 1949. Poor parents might sell their daughters into slavery at three or four years of age or as prostitutes or concubines at twelve or fourteen years (Buck, 1930; Johnson, 1993:61–87; Wolf, 1980). Even marriage did not bring women a higher status in the family. If a wife displeased her husband or her mother-in-law, she could be returned to her parents, and in times of economic stress, she might be rented, leased, or sold outright to a more prosperous man. She would obtain a degree of authority in her own right only after the passage of many years. Her position was weakest when she was still childless (sonless); it improved when she bore a son, and it grew even stronger when a daughter-in-law came under her direction. And by the time she entered into advanced age, her authority began to approximate that of her husband; if his was the earlier death, full power within the family might sometimes then be in her hands.[11]

China experts attribute women's oppression to Confucian patriarchal ideology and women's economic dependence on men.[12] The roots of women's subordination were undermined by the communist revolution of 1949 and subsequent economic and social changes. However, incidents of wife abuse and sex discrimination in the workplace still exist.[13] Although the practice of poor peasant parents selling their daughters into marriage and prostitution has almost been eliminated since 1949, there has been traffic in women and children since reforms started in 1978. In particular, traffickers target young peasant women seeking jobs in cities. Several female university students were tricked and sold into marriage; their stories shocked the nation.

Female infanticide was largely discontinued under Mao Zedong's regime as the rural economy improved. However, this practice has shown signs of revival since the Chinese government started the one-child per household family planning policy in the late 1970s. Persons not in compliance with the family planning policy face heavy fines or demotions or, on rare occasions, forced abortions. However, in most of rural China, where there is virtually no social security, peasants rely on their sons for old-age support. Some couples continue having children until a baby boy is born, regardless of the consequences. Others avoid breaking the family planning policy by practicing female infanticide and aborting female fetuses until they bear a son. Sex-selective abortions occur in urban China on a much less frequent basis because of the existence of social security systems there (discussed in Chapter 8). A few parents abandon their baby daughters in front of orphanages so they will be able to give birth to another child without violating the family planning policy (Johnson, 1993). The Western media are bombarded with graphic stories about the mistreatment of orphans, most of whom are females, in some Chinese orphanages.

Despite these unfortunate instances, blatant discrimination against Chinese women has been reduced significantly under the communist regime. In particular, since 1949 urban Chinese women have achieved a degree of economic independence as they work with men in state or collectively run organizations. In urban China, it is unusual for a woman not to work outside the home (Entwisle et al., 1994; Whyte and Parish, 1984:chap. 7). In rural areas, the collectivization campaign moved many production decisions from the household to production teams, thus facilitating rural women's participation in agricultural work.

Although the political campaigns that the Chinese Communist Party carried out between 1949 and 1976 inflicted tremendous pain on Chinese society, one of their by-products was the weakening of Confucian patriarchal ideology—a tradition that was one of the major targets of these political movements. As a result, the inequality between the sexes is diminishing. A good example of this movement toward gender equality is the gradual expansion of women's influence within the home. Chinese men are more ambivalent and less secure today than in the past about their position within the family; they believe that female domestic power is authentic, and even if they do not approve, they are powerless to change the situation. Emily Honig and Gail Hershatter (1988:311) report on conversations about this. U.S. anthropologist William Jankowiak (1993) notes that urban Chinese men are keenly aware that the style with which women present themselves shifts depending on the social context; although a woman may prefer to speak softly on a date, once married she may begin shouting commands at her husband and children even in front of the neighbors (not unlike Laurel Bossen's recounting of the wife's revenge against the husband addicted to opium in Chapter 11). Many urban women believe that relations with their husbands should be on the basis of equality. Jankowiak observes that urban Chinese women were able to initiate divorce, organize the Sunday visiting schedule to favor their own natal families over their husband's, and effectively ignore an overbearing mother-in-law or husband.

The growing domestic power of women also stems from the affection and love they command from their children. In China, the mother has been typically characterized as being affectionate, kind, lenient, protective, and even indulgent. The father, in contrast, is a stern disciplinarian, more concerned with the demands of propriety and necessity than with feelings, and is feared by his children. Mother-child relations tend to be close and affectionate, in contrast to father-child relations, which are more formal and perhaps even marked by tension and antagonism (Ho, 1986, 1987, 1989; Bellah, 1970; Hsu, 1981; Jing, 2000). Furthermore, young people in China today mainly rely on

A boy imitates the sculptures in the ultramodern
Wangfujing shopping street near Tiananmen Square

social institutions outside the family for employment and education (Stacey, 1983). Fathers, unless they are powerful officials, have little to offer their children and have experienced a decline in influence over their children. It is difficult for fathers to attract attention and affection from their children.

This is not so with mothers. In his research, Jankowiak (1993:242–244) noticed that mothers exercise tremendous psychological control over their offspring and are the center of the family's communication network; they are the glue that binds families together. Chinese youth adore and confide in their mothers. It is culturally understood and acceptable that sons or daughters will at some point exchange harsh words with their father, but it is considered bad and regrettable if this happens with their mother. Once Jankowiak asked his informants to imagine walking across a bridge with their mother and father. Suddenly the bridge collapsed and everyone was thrown into the water. Jankowiak asked them, if you could save only one person, who would it be? Of his twenty-nine informants (nineteen males and ten females), twenty chose to save their mother, and the remaining nine refused to answer.

My own research indicates that most urban Chinese respect their fathers. Children usually do not challenge orders from their fathers, who seldom issue direct orders to their children. Both parties carefully seek to avoid direct confrontation. A mother usually functions as the intermediary between her husband and their children. As the status of mothers evolves, the traditional hierarchical family authority structure is gradually disappearing in China.

■ Sexuality

The sexual bond between husband and wife is part of the basis of marriage, which in turn is the basis of the family. Every society carefully regulates the sexual behavior of its members, channeling their biological potential into legitimate outlets that are socially regarded as natural and moral. In China before the 1980s, an extremely high premium was placed on premarital virginity and conjugal fidelity. If an individual was caught in premarital sex or adultery, he or she would face serious punishments: mass criticisms, forced confessions, demotions, or dismissal. Occasionally, an adulterer would be brought to court and sentenced to imprisonment on a verdict of hooliganism or rape (Cui, 1995:15–18).

Generally speaking, sex was a taboo topic in China before the 1980s. Any materials relating to sex, even nude works of art, were strictly forbidden. Even marital sex was not discussed. Today many people still avoid talking about sex either privately or publicly. A 1990 survey reported that over half of respondents never discussed sex with others (Zhao and Geng, 1992:1–4).

Public discourse on sexuality has occurred in the Chinese media since the 1980s (Cui, 1995:15–18; Honig and Hershatter, 1988:51–59). The focus of the discussion is on chastity and self-restraint, emphasizing that sexual feelings, if not properly managed, can lead to physical harm and social ruin. Young women are told to channel and control the sexual desires of young men as well as their own and to defer acting on those desires until they reach the socially appropriate age for courtship and marriage. Parents are advised to arrange extracurricular activities for their children so that the youngsters will not lie in bed letting their imagination run wild with love scenes from television, movies, books, and magazines. The official press suggests that young people of both sexes should get plenty of exercise, refrain from sleeping in tight clothes or under heavy covers, and get out of bed to study or wash their faces in cold water if they become sexually aroused (Honig and Hershatter, 1988:59–67).

In the 1980s, many medical specialists advised that individuals who frequently masturbated should try hard to resist, lest they suffer from physical and mental disorders. Many people agreed. In a 1990 survey, more than half the respondents of both sexes insisted that masturbation was morally degenerate and harmful to health (Zhao and Geng, 1992:5–6). In comparison, only 4 out of 100 Americans in surveys conducted during the early 1970s agreed with such views (Eysenck, 1976:80).

At present, premarital sex is still looked on with disfavor in China. In a survey done in the 1980s among factory workers, four of every five young women did not consider it proper to have sex before marriage (Tsui, 1989). A 1995 survey reported the same disapproval rate. Many people consider a woman's virginity extremely important for a love relationship. In a recent survey, seven out of ten males said they would have felt great distress if their own brides had not been virgins (Zhao and Geng, 1992:9–10).

The high value placed on female virginity is also illustrated by wedding costs. In most parts of China, the groom's family assumes responsibility for wedding expenses and for furnishing the new house. Zhou Xiao (1989:280–281) reports that the amount of money spent by the groom's family depends very much upon whether the bride is a virgin. Wedding costs can be very high, and it is much more expensive to marry a virgin. In cities, if a woman has had sexual intercourse with her boyfriend, the wedding cost and other expenses are then not assumed solely by the male's family but are shared by the couple. In rural areas, where premarital sex is still rare, the price of lost virginity is even more apparent. Once a couple is engaged, if the bride is a virgin, the prospective groom sends betrothal gifts to the girl's family at frequent intervals, usually five to six times a year. The frequency drops to two or three times a year if she is no longer a virgin, and the value of the gifts also declines. Young women who have premarital sex become targets of gossip.

Zhou Xiao (1989:283–285) argues that Chinese women have much to lose from premarital sex, and Chinese men have much to gain. The most important source of social support for premarital sexual intercourse comes from the parents of young men. Premarital sex not only reduces the financial burden of wedding costs but also ensures the marriage. In some parts of China, a mother might encourage her son to have sex with his girlfriend by locking the young couple inside the bedroom. However, the "mother's lock" alone is not enough to bring about sexual intercourse. Some men use indirect and emotional strategies, playing on helplessness, empathy, and dependency to persuade women to have sex with them. A man may tell a woman that if she resists sexual intercourse his erect penis will break off and he will become sexually disabled forever, or that he will become very sick if no sexual intercourse follows or will experience terrible physical pain. Because of the lack of sex education, innocent women often give up their resistance out of love and concern for their boyfriends and fall prey to such tactics.

Thus, despite the heavy stress on virginity, premarital sex has occurred for a long time. A 1987 survey reported that more than half the abortions in a Chinese city were performed on unmarried women (Tsui, 1989). In a recent survey, one in every five respondents reported that they had engaged in premarital intercourse. Since the 1980s, people have developed a more liberal attitude toward premarital intercourse. Zhao Bo and Geng Wenxiu (1992: 10–11) maintain that when an engaged couple engages in premarital intercourse, few think it immoral or unchaste.

After marriage, wives are required to play a traditional role in sexual activities, passively waiting to have sex when the husband wants it; their task in marital intercourse is to satisfy their husbands' sexual needs (Honig and Hershatter, 1988:182; Jankowiak, 1993:233; Zhao and Geng, 1992:15). Although many urban Chinese do not think that husbands should insist on sexual intercourse when their wives are very reluctant, in reality many wives are inclined to satisfy their husbands' needs whenever they want intercourse. Jankowiak (1993:230–234) reports that when a wife does not like her husband, she may show more inclination to resist his advances and spend more time with the child and friends. When a man realizes his wife is pregnant, he is likely to seek sex less often. Some men go so far as to believe that if they continue to have sex with a pregnant woman, their sperm would enter the already-fertilized egg and create a deformed baby.

Among the young, sexual attitudes are changing. Reforms have reduced government control over the publishing industry, and "sex sells" has become one of its most important business principles. Publishers market their products with beautiful women and sensational stories such as "A Story of a Man and His Three Wives," and television films and shows deal with sex openly. (The government passed a law in 2001 prohibiting a man from taking a second wife; offenders will be sentenced to jail.) The enhanced knowledge about sex among the population is accompanied by a more tolerant attitude toward premarital sex and cohabitation. Some university students move out of student dormitories and rent flats outside the campus to live with their sweethearts, without any commitment to marriage. Such unions dissolve, without any bitterness, as soon as they graduate. Looser sexual restrictions, along with drug usage, are contributing to a growing AIDS problem in China (see Chapter 8). Still, there is little formal education about sex. Few use condoms. The government has instituted an advertising campaign to advocate their use.

Attitudes toward homosexuality are also changing. Such behavior remains unpopular. But some factors are changing. In 2001 the Chinese Psychiatric Association ceased to define homosexuality as a mental disorder. Gay bars and social clubs have sprung up in the major cities, with a lively subculture. Though no laws outlaw homosexuality, these establishments are subject to periodic police raids. Over 150 websites are available to China's gay community. Very few gays or lesbians are open about their sexuality. In 2001 a Hunan television station ran an episode of a popular talk show devoted to the topic, but it neither promoted nor rebroadcast the show for fear of retaliation from the authorities.

■ Ethnic Minorities

In 2001, I conducted urban fieldwork comparing patterns in marriage and household structure between the majority Han, and the Hui, the third largest minority group. In my sample (comparing couples in one city) I found that few Han or Hui couples (27.2 percent versus 29.4 percent) used friends or relatives for introductions before their marriage. However, the Hui were much more likely than the Han to use parental arrangements or matchmakers to find a prospective mate (23.5 percent versus 8.5 percent, and 7.6 percent versus 3.7 percent respectively). In comparison, the Han were more likely than the Hui to find a mate through co-workers (6.8 percent versus 2.6 percent). Also, 48.5 percent of the Han met their spouses on their own, compared with 32.8 percent of the Hui. It seems that the Hui rely more on "traditional" approaches in finding a mate than the Han. That helped shorten the average courtship time of the Hui couples—sixty-one weeks in comparison to eighty-three weeks.

The Hui insist on marrying Muslims or persons who promise to convert to Islam after marriage. This requirement reduces the odds for a Hui to meet a sweetheart from his or her workmates (8.6 percent of the couples in the sample were workmates, versus 17.6 percent of the Han), since there may not be many workers of the Hui ethnicity in his or her workplace. And there are no incentives for Han women to convert to Islam and marry Hui men, since the level of educational and economic attainment among the Han tends to be higher than that among the Hui.

Finally, I found rather similar patterns of living arrangements between the Han and Hui families. Nearly 70 percent of the Han live with their spouses and unmarried children, as compared with 65.5 percent of the Hui. Only 5.2 percent of the Han and 4.2 percent of the Hui were childless couples. Also, more than 11 percent of the Han and 12 percent of the Hui shared the same roof with spouses, married children, and parents; more than 25 percent of the Hui families and 13.3 percent of the Han families contain five to six persons.

■ Conclusion

As is true everywhere, radical changes in politics, the economy, and society brought on by modern life are affecting China's families and marriages. In rural China, the collectivization campaign changed peasants into wage earners who derived incomes from production teams, leading to the simplification of family structure and reduction in family size. The Marriage Law of 1950 and the Cultural Revolution during the 1960s made it acceptable for rural women to divorce. Since the 1980s, the government has decollectivized production teams, so that many economic functions have once again devolved to the family level and facilitated the reemergence of extended families in rural China. Yet rural youth have greater freedom than before to choose their own mates and make decisions about whether to stay or move to the city.

The family revolution occurred first in urban China (see Levy, 1949; Whyte and Parish, 1984:chaps. 5–6; Zang, 1993) as it experienced the penetration of Western influence and rapid industrialization. The lack of technological development in rural China kept out many of the forces of change that challenge traditional concepts of family life. This is still true today. In cities, families are changing more quickly. Urban youth can often move out of their parent's housing soon after they enter the workplace, they can meet prospective marriage partners without help from their parents and even engage in premarital sex, and they can set up households and nuclear families that give them some distance from parental influence. Yet they are still strongly inclined to heed advice from their parents and to keep in close contact with them. And women, who are freed by this from economic dependence on their fathers and husbands, remain deferential to the advice of parents and husbands. The heavy emphasis of the Chinese on obedience to fathers and loyalty to family is a strong leash holding back the pull toward individualism.

■ Notes

1. See Davis-Friedmann, 1991; Fei, 1992; Goode, 1963; Hsu, 1981:chaps. 3, 9; Jankowiak, 1993; and Madge, 1974:164.
2. For good introductions to traditional family life and Confucian prescriptions for it, see Baker, 1968, 1977, 1979; Freedman, 1958, 1966, 1968; Watson, 1982; Watson and Ebrey, 1991; Whyte and Parish, 1984; and Yang, 1946.
3. For descriptions of this process, see Baker, 1979:chap. 1; Cohen, 1976, 1992b; Fei, 1962; Hsu, 1943; Lang, 1946:chap. 2; and Sung, 1981.
4. For descriptions of life in such wealthy families, see Cohen, 1992b; Ebrey, 1978; Fei, 1962; Grafflin, 1981; Lang, 1946; Johnson, 1977; Pasternak, 1972; Tsui, 1989; Watson and Ebrey, 1991; and Yang, 1946.
5. See Chesneaux, 1965; Chow, 1960; Lang, 1946:chap. 5; Levy, 1949; and Ono, 1989.
6. For discussions of this, see Cohen, 1992a:370–373, 1992b; Huang, 1992; Judd, 1992:353–356; Nee and Young, 1991; Potter and Potter, 1990; Watson, 1987; and Whyte, 1992:317–322.
7. See Ono, 1989; Parish and Whyte, 1978; Salaff, 1973; Wolf, 1985; and Xu and Whyte, 1990:714.
8. See Croll, 1984; Ebrey, 1991:5; Potter and Potter, 1990:202; and Riley, 1994:792.
9. See Lang, 1946:chap. 4; Levy, 1949; Pa, 1972; and Witke, 1973.
10. See Harrell, 1992:331–336; Lavely and Ren, 1992; Parish and Whyte, 1978; Stacey, 1983; and Wolf, 1985.
11. See Wolf, 1985:chap. 1; Cohen, 1992b; and Johnson, 1983.
12. See Andors, 1983; Johnson, 1983; Stacey, 1983; and Wolf, 1985.
13. See Conroy, 1987:67; Entwisle et al., 1994; Gilmartin, 1990; and Honig and Hershatter, 1988.

■ Bibliography

Andors, Phyllis. 1983. *The Unfinished Liberation of Chinese Women, 1969–1980.* Bloomington: Indiana University Press.
Baker, Hugh. 1968. *A Chinese Lineage Village.* Stanford: Stanford University Press.

———. 1977. "Extended Kinship in the Traditional City." In William G. Skinner (ed.), *The City in Late Imperial China.* Stanford: Stanford University Press.

———. 1979. *Chinese Family and Kinship.* New York: Columbia University Press.

Bakken, Borge. 2000. *The Exemplary Society: Human Improvement, Social Control, and the Dangers of Modernity in China.* Oxford: Oxford University Press.

Bellah, Robert. 1970. "Father and Son in Christianity and Confucianism." Pp. 76–99 in Robert Bellah (ed.), *Beyond Belief.* New York: Harper and Row.

Blum, Susan D., and Lionel M. Jensen (eds.). 2002. *China Off Center: Mapping the Margins of the Middle Kingdom.* Honolulu: University of Hawaii Press.

Blumstein, Philip, and Pepper Schwartz. 1983. *The American Couples.* New York: Morrow.

Brook-Gunn, J., and F. Furstenberg. 1989. "Adolescent Sexual Behavior." *American Psychologist* 44:249–257.

Buck, John L. 1930. *Chinese Farm Economy.* Nanking: University of Nanking.

Chen, Nancy N., Constance D. Clark, Suzanne Z. Gottschang, and Lyn Jeffery (eds.). 2001. *China Urban: Ethnographies of Contemporary Culture.* Durham, NC: Duke University Press.

Chesneaux, Jean. 1965. *The Chinese Labor Movement.* Stanford: Stanford University Press.

"China's Current Marriage Patterns." 1995. *Beijing Review,* August 14–20, p. 11.

Chow, Tse-tsung. 1960. *The May Fourth Movement.* Cambridge: Harvard University Press.

Cohen, Myron. 1976. *House United, House Divided.* New York: Columbia University Press.

———. 1992a. "Family Management and Family Division in Contemporary Rural China." *China Quarterly* 130:357–377.

———. 1992b. "Family Organization in China." Pp. 3–16 in Myron Cohen (ed.), *Case Studies in the Social Sciences.* Armonk, NY: M. E. Sharpe.

Conroy, Richard. 1987. "Patterns of Divorce in China." *Australian Journal of Chinese Affairs* 17:53–75.

Croll, Elizabeth. 1981. *The Politics of Marriage in Contemporary China.* Cambridge: Cambridge University Press.

———. 1984. "The Exchange of Women and Property: Marriage in Post-Revolutionary China." In Renée Hirschon (ed.), *Women and Property: Women as Property.* London: Croom Helm.

Cui, Lili. 1995. "Sex Education No Longer Taboo." *Beijing Review,* April 3–16, pp. 15–18.

Davis, Deborah, and Stevan Harrell (eds.). 1993. *Chinese Families in the Post-Mao Era.* Berkeley: University of California Press.

Davis-Friedmann, Deborah. 1991. *Long Lives.* Stanford: Stanford University Press.

Day, R. D. 1992. "The Transition to First Intercourse Among Racially and Culturally Diverse Youth." *Journal of Marriage and the Family* 54:746–762.

Diamant, Neil J. 2000. *Revolutionizing the Family: Politics, Love, and Divorce in Urban and Rural China, 1949–1968.* Berkeley: University of California Press.

Dikotter, Frank. 1995. *Sex, Culture, and Modernity in China.* Honolulu: University of Hawaii Press.

Ebrey, Patricia B. 1978. *The Aristocratic Families of Early Imperial China.* Cambridge: Cambridge University Press.

———. 1991. "Introduction." Pp. 1–24 in Ruby Watson and Patricia Ebrey (eds.), *Marriage and Inequality in Chinese Society.* Berkeley: University of California Press.

Elegant, Simon, and Margot Cohen. 1996. "Asia's New Generation: Just Like Their Parents." *Far Eastern Economic Review* 159(49) (December 5): 52.

Entwisle, Barbara, Gail Henderson, Susan Short, Jill Bouma, and Zhai Fengying. 1994. "Gender and Family Businesses in Rural China." *American Sociological Review* 60(1):36–57.

Eysenck, Hans. 1976. *Sex and Personality.* Austin: University of Texas Press.

Fei, Hsiao-tung. 1962. *Peasant Life in China.* London: Routledge and Kegan Paul.

Fei, Xiaotong. 1992. *From the Soil.* Berkeley: University of California Press.

Freedman, Maurice. 1958. *Lineage Organization in Southeastern China.* London: Athlone Press.

———. 1966. *Chinese Lineage and Society.* London: Athlone Press.

———. 1968. *Family and Kinship in Chinese Society.* Stanford: Stanford University Press.

Gao, Mobo C. F. 1999. *Gao Village: Rural Life in Modern China.* Honolulu: University of Hawaii Press.

Giddens, Anthony. 1992. *The Transformation of Intimacy: Sexuality, Love, and Eroticism in Modern Societies.* Stanford: Stanford University Press.

Gilmartin, Christina K. 1990. "Violence Against Women in Contemporary China." Pp. 203–225 in Jonathan Lipman and Steven Harrell (eds.), *Violence in China: Essays in Culture and Counterculture.* Albany: State University of New York Press.

Glick, Paul C. 1984. "How American Families Are Changing." *American Demographics* 6:21–25.

Goldthorpe, John Ernest. 1987. *The Sociology of the Third World.* Cambridge: Cambridge University Press.

Goode, William. 1963. *World Revolution and Family Patterns.* New York: Free Press.

Grafflin, D. 1981. "The Great Family in Medieval South China." *Harvard Journal of Asiatic Studies* 9:31–64.

Harrell, Stevan. 1992. "Aspects of Marriage in Three Southwestern Villages." *China Quarterly* 130:323–327.

Ho, David. 1986. "Chinese Patterns of Socialization." Pp. 1–37 in Michael Harris Bond (ed.), *The Psychology of the Chinese People.* Hong Kong: Oxford University Press.

———. 1987. "Fatherhood in Chinese Culture." Pp. 227–245 in Michael E. Lamb (ed.), *The Father's Role: Cross-Cultural Perspectives.* Hillsdale: Lawrence Erlbaum.

———. 1989. "Continuity and Variation in Chinese Patterns of Socialization." *Journal of Marriage and the Family* 51:149–163.

Holmgren, Jennifer. 1995. *Marriage, Kinship, and Power in Northern China.* Brookfield, VT: Ashgate.

Honig, Emily, and Gail Hershatter. 1988. *Personal Voices: Chinese Women in the 80s.* Stanford: Stanford University Press.

Hsu, Francis. 1943. "The Myth of Chinese Family Size." *American Journal of Sociology* 48:555–562.

———. 1981. *Americans and Chinese.* Honolulu: University of Hawaii Press.

Huang Shu-min. 1992. "Re-examining the Extended Family in Chinese Peasant Society." *Australian Journal of Chinese Affairs* 27:25–38.

Jankowiak, William. 1993. *Sex, Death, and Hierarchy in a Chinese City.* New York: Columbia University Press.

Jing, Jun (ed.). 2000. *Feeding China's Little Emperors: Food, Children, and Social Change.* Stanford: Stanford University Press.

Johnson, D. 1977. "The Last Year of a Great Clan." *Harvard Journal of Asiatic Studies* 37:5–102.

Johnson, Kay Ann. 1983. *Women, the Family, and Peasant Revolution in China.* Chicago: University of Chicago Press.

———. 1993. "Chinese Orphanages: Saving China's Abandoned Girls." *Australia Journal of Chinese Affairs* 30 (July): 61–87.

Judd, Ellen. 1992. "Land Divided, Land United." *China Quarterly* 130:338–356.

Kinney, Anne Behnke (ed.). 1996. *Chinese Views of Childhood.* Honolulu: University of Hawaii Press.

Lang, Olga. 1946. *Chinese Family and Society.* New Haven: Yale University Press.

Lasch, Christopher. 1977. *Haven in a Heartless World: The Family Besieged.* New York: Basic Books.

Lavely, William, and Xinhua Ren. 1992. "Patrilocality and Early Marital Co-Residence in Rural China, 1955–1985." *China Quarterly* 130:378–391.

Leung, Lai Ching. 1998. *Lone Mothers, Social Security, and the Family in Hong Kong.* Burlington, VT: Ashgate.

Leung, Sai-Wing. 1997. *The Making of an Alienated Generation: The Political Socialization of Secondary School Students in Transitional Hong Kong.* Burlington, VT: Ashgate.

Levy, Marion. 1949 [1968]. *The Family Revolution in Modern China.* New York: Atheneum.

Li, Fei-kan Pa. 1988. *Family.* New York: Waveland.

Li, Raymond. 2002. "'Till Death Us Do Part' Forgotten as Revolution Shakes Society." *South China Morning Post,* April 20, p. 6.

Liang, Heng, and Judith Shapiro. 1983. *Son of the Revolution.* New York: Knopf/Random House.

Madge, Charles. 1974. "The Relevance of Family Patterns to the Process of Modernization in East Asia." In Robert J. Smith (ed.), *Social Organization and the Application of Anthropology.* Ithaca: Cornell University Press.

Mann, S. 1987. "Widows in the Kinship, Class, and Community Structures of Qing Dynasty China." *Journal of Asian Studies* 46(1):37–56.

Moore, K. 1989. *Facts at a Glance.* Washington, DC: Child Trends.

———. 1992. *Facts at a Glance.* Washington, DC: Child Trends.

Nee, Victor, and Frank Young. 1991. "Peasant Entrepreneurs in China's 'Second Economy.'" *Economic Development and Cultural Change* 39:293–310.

Ono, Kazuko. 1989. *Chinese Women in a Century of Revolution, 1850–1950.* Stanford: Stanford University Press.

Parish, William, and Martin Whyte. 1978. *Village and Family in Contemporary China.* Chicago: University of Chicago Press.

Pasternak, Burton. 1972. *Kinship and Community in Two Chinese Villages.* Stanford: Stanford University Press.

Popenos, David. 1993. "American Family Decline, 1960–1990: A Review and Appraisal." *Journal of Marriage and the Family* 55:527–541.

Potter, Salamith H., and Jack M. Potter. 1990. *China's Peasants: The Anthropology of a Revolution.* Cambridge: Cambridge University Press.

Riley, Nancy. 1994. "Interwoven Lives: Parents, Marriage, and Guanxi in China." *Journal of Marriage and the Family* 56:791–803.

Robertson, Ian. 1987. *Sociology.* New York: Worth.

Salaff, Judith. 1973. "The Emerging Conjugal Relationship in the People's Republic of China." *Journal of Marriage and the Family* 35:704–717.

Saso, Michael. 1999. *Velvet Bonds: The Chinese Family.* Honolulu: University of Hawaii Press.

Small, Stephen A., and D. Kerns. 1993. "Unwanted Sexual Activity Among Peers During Early and Middle Adolescence." *Journal of Marriage and the Family* 55:941–952.

Small, Stephen A., and Tom Luster. 1994. "Adolescent Sexual Activity: An Ecological, Risk-Factor Approach." *Journal of Marriage and the Family* 56:181–192.

Stacey, Judith. 1983. *Patriarchy and Socialist Revolution in China.* Berkeley: University of California Press.

Stack, Steven. 1994. "The Effect of Geographic Mobility on Premarital Sex." *Journal of Marriage and the Family* 56(1):204–208.

Sung, Lung-sheng. 1981. "Property and Family Division." Pp. 361–378 in Emily M. Ahern and H. Gates (eds.), *The Anthropology of Taiwanese Society.* Stanford: Stanford University Press.

Thurston, Ann. 1987. *Enemies of the People.* New York: Knopf.

Tsui, Ming. 1989. "Changes in Chinese Urban Family Structure." *Journal of Marriage and the Family* 51:737–747.

Udry, J. R., and J. O. G. Billy. 1987. "Initiation of Coitus in Early Adolescence." *American Sociological Review* 52:841–855.

Watson, Andrew. 1987. "The Family Farm: Land Use and Accumulation in Agriculture." *Australian Journal of Chinese Affairs* 17:1–27.

Watson, James. 1982. "Anthropological Perspectives on Historical Research." *China Quarterly* 92:589–622.

Watson, Ruby, and Patricia Ebrey (eds.). 1991. *Marriage and Inequality in Chinese Society.* Berkeley: University of California Press.

Whyte, Martin. 1990. "Changes in Mate Choice in Chengdu." Pp. 181–213 in Deborah Davis and Ezra Vogel (eds.), *Chinese Society on the Eve of Tiananmen.* Cambridge: Council on East Asian Studies, Harvard University.

———. 1992. "Introduction: Rural Economic Reforms and Chinese Family Patterns." *China Quarterly* 130:317–322.

Whyte, Martin, and William Parish. 1984. *Urban Life in Contemporary China.* Chicago: University of Chicago Press.

Witke, Roxane. 1973. "Mao Tse-tung, Women, and Suicide." Pp. 7–31 in Marilyn Young (ed.), *Women in China.* Ann Arbor: Center for Chinese Studies, University of Michigan.

Wolf, Arthur P. 1980. *Marriage and Adoption in China, 1845–1945.* Stanford: Stanford University Press.

Wolf, Margery. 1985. *Revolution Postponed.* Stanford: Stanford University Press.

Xin, Liu. 2000. *In One's Own Shadow: An Ethnographic Account of the Condition of Post-Reform Rural China.* Berkeley: University of California Press.

Xu, Xiaohe, and Martin Whyte. 1990. "Love Matches and Arranged Marriages: A Chinese Replication." *Journal of Marriage and the Family* 52: 709–722.

Yang, Martin. 1946. *A Chinese Village.* New York: Columbia University Press.

Zang, Xiaowei. 1993. "Household Structure and Marriage in Urban China: 1900–1982." *Journal of Comparative Family Studies* 24(1):35–43.

———. 1995. "Labor Market and Rural Migrants in Post-Mao China." *American Asian Review,* June.

Zhao, Bo, and Geng Wenxiu. 1992. "Sexuality in Urban China." *Australian Journal of Chinese Affairs* 28:1–20.

Zhou, Xiao. 1989. "Virginity and Premarital Sex in Contemporary China." *Feminist Studies* 15:279–288.

Zuo, Jiping, and Yanjie Bian. 2001. "Gendered Resources, Division of Housework, and Perceived Fairness: A Case in Urban China." *Journal of Marriage and the Family* 63(4):1122–1133.

11

Women and Development

Laurel Bossen

In Chapter 10, Zang Xiaowei introduced you to family and kinship in China and discussed the central role they play. He explained that, except in some regions like western Yunnan, China's families have been patriarchal, with property generally passing through the male line and the bride coming to live with the groom's family, which in turn defers to the authority of his father. As he indicated, that system still gave the mother-in-law some control over family affairs but made younger women vulnerable to abuses. Gradually, urbanization and economic development are giving women increased clout; to a greater extent than is true in most nations, politics has played a role as well. In this chapter we shall focus more closely on how life is changing for women as economic reform progresses.

The study of women and development in China during the twentieth century must be viewed in the context of China's political movements and the challenge of transforming China from a disintegrating imperial power into a modern nation. The most ambitious political transformations were introduced by the Communist Party when it took power in 1949. Unlike many other developing nations that have placed little or no priority on integrating women into development, China, under the leadership of the Communist Party, made explicit commitments to improving the status of women as part of its socialist agenda of promoting social and economic equality. China's self-proclaimed effort to "liberate" women has long generated a great deal of interest as a possible model for other nations. Those who favor government intervention to raise women's status while promoting economic development initially looked to China for inspiration and signs of success. Skeptics and critics of China's central planning and state control over information scrutinized China's claims and looked for independent evidence of achievement or failure. Since 1980, China's greater openness has led to better assessments of women's gains.

China's long historical tradition of male dominance and patriarchal authority is deeply embedded in its culture and institutions and not easily overturned. For two and a half decades of heavy state planning and promotion of revolutionary egalitarian goals, there was much talk about equality between the sexes. Since Mao Zedong's death in 1976, the emphasis on gender equality has subsided, and liberalizing reforms have permitted a return of market forces and revival of earlier cultural practices. The reforms have provoked concerns that old patriarchal patterns and abuses of women would resurface, and indeed, a more open society has allowed gender inequalities to become more visible. At the close of the twentieth century, critics in China and abroad strongly lament China's persisting structural inequalities and the unequal treatment of women both in the family system and in the state sector (Andors, 1983; Croll, 1983; Honig and Hershatter, 1988; Johnson, 1983; Stacey, 1983; Wolf, 1985). Moreover, China's strict family planning policies, discussed in Chapter 8, target women for control and place heightened pressure on women to give birth to sons (Greenhalgh, Zhu, and Li, 1994; Greenhalgh and Li, 1995). As a result of strict family planning quotas, the sex ratio of reported births in the 1990s shows an increasing problem of "missing girls"—a clear sign that males and females are not treated equally (Bossen, 2002; Croll, 2001). At the same time, as explained in Chapter 10, increasing levels of female literacy, education, and urbanism, along with smaller families and greater economic autonomy, bring new benefits to women and may undermine patriarchal traditions even where earlier policies failed. When reviewing the twentieth century as a whole, there are many reasons to consider it to have been a century of significant, if not always revolutionary, change for women as well as men. These changes, toward modernity and greater equality and opportunity for women, continue to be contested by entrenched interests. From the perspective of a single lifetime, they may appear to be slow and to fall short of the revolutionary claims of the Maoist period, but from the perspective of several centuries the achievements of the twentieth may indeed be revolutionary.

■ The "Traditional" Portrait of Chinese Women

Any assessment of women's participation and of the benefits they have gained in China's development must choose a starting point for comparison. In China, historical sources emphasize the stability and tenacity of patriarchal authority, tracing it back to Confucian times. There is relatively little information, however, about the local forms of gender inequality and family organization among China's nonliterate populations. Not until the twentieth century have social scientists systematically begun to investigate the condition of women of different classes and subcultures within Chinese society. Thus the "traditional" portrait of Chinese women is usually a generalized and timeless abstraction that ignores processes of historical change and regional variation in the ways gender was experienced.

In this traditional portrait, most women held positions in society that were greatly devalued and relatively powerless compared to those of men. Women's low status derived from the classical Chinese family and kinship system, with its emphasis on the centrality of males within an enduring framework of patriarchal households based on patrilineal descent (inheritance through the male line) and patrilocal residence (in the household of the groom's father) after marriage. The model Chinese family denied power and individual agency to women and youth; women as individuals lacked legal rights to own property such as land and were themselves liable to be transacted as property. Their parents arranged their marriages without their consent and transferred them as girls or young women to the homes of husbands who were strangers, there to live in a community dominated by their husband's patrilineal kin group. Parents also bound their daughters' feet, stunting their growth and hampering their mobility, to conform to an oppressive standard of female beauty and improve their daughters' chances in marriage. Women entered marriage with few resources and were required to submit to the authority of their husband's household, earning their keep by working obediently, preserving respect through marital fidelity, and gaining stature through the production of sons. Sons were generally considered far more valuable than daughters. When poverty threatened, infanticide, abandonment, the sale of children into servitude, or early marriage befell girls with much greater frequency than boys. The state did little to protect the rights of women and girls as such; rather it vested men with considerable powers as heads of households and patrilineal kin groups to manage the affairs of subordinate household members. Women had to look to fathers, brothers, husbands, or sons for whatever protection these men might offer.

This portrait depicts women's experience in Chinese history as one of universal, unremitting oppression and victimization. However, recent writings uncover considerable historical and regional variation in women's activities and rights and explore the degrees of flexibility within patriarchal structures (Jaschok and Miers, 1994; Ko, 1994; Watson, 1994; Hinsch, 2002; Tung, 2000). Rather than a single, unchanging system of patriarchy, contemporary studies reveal that earlier centuries witnessed significant shifts in women's economic activities, dowry and property rights, forms of marriage, legal rights, and even suicide patterns as well as differences in women's condition according to class (Bernhardt, 1996; Ebrey, 1993; Gates, 1989, 1996; Huang, 1990; Mann, 1991, 1994, 1997; T'ien, 1988). These studies illustrate the difficulty of determining precisely whether women in general gained or lost ground during previous historical periods. For instance, during the Song dynasty (960–1269), women gained the advantages of increased transmission of dowry property to daughters, of sustained ties to women's kin after marriage, of opportunities for elite daughters to learn to read and write, and of growing opportunities for women to earn money producing textiles. How does this progress weigh against the evidence of diminishing autonomy as indicated by the spread of foot binding and a growing market in women sold into various forms of servitude during that period (Ebrey, 1993:268)?

Although historians can trace some of the ways that women's rights became more limited in the subsequent Ming and the Qing dynasties (Bernhardt, 1996; Watson and Ebrey, 1991), it is risky to apply descriptions written by and for privileged elites (usually from a male perspective) to the population as a whole. Indeed, the standard notion that rural Chinese women made minimal contributions to the agrarian economy is now challenged by recognition of their significant roles in commercial textile production over the cen-

Elderly farm woman with bound feet, Yunnan, 1989

Laurel Bossen

turies (Huang, 1990; Shih, 1992). The stereotype of women as domestic subordinates, politically powerless and economically burdensome, is increasingly modified by evidence that Chinese women were not easily restrained; they were productive and expressive, and they found ways to pursue their own interests (Cass, 1999). Although historical studies do reveal recurrent patterns of patrilineal, patrilocal, and patriarchal institutions, they are also shown to change over time. Because the evidence on the ways different classes of women behaved and responded to these institutions is so incomplete, the direction of change over long periods of Chinese history remains elusive (Ebrey, 1993; Chaffee, 1991; Mann, 1991).

■ Women in the Late Nineteenth and Early Twentieth Centuries

In the mid–nineteenth century, gender relations varied according to regional conditions. For example, northern China developed an economic system in which women had more limited roles in dry-land farming and other work outside the home than women in the rice-farming south (Buck, 1937; Davin, 1975; Johnson, 1983:15; Potter and Potter, 1990). Female foot binding was more pervasive in northern China than in southern China, making it hard for women in the north to help in the fields (Davin, 1975; Johnson, 1983). Recent research links the regional distribution and intensity of female foot binding to economic changes that influenced parental decisions to prepare their daughters for spinning and weaving indoors or for manual labor in the fields (Bossen, 2002; Gates, 1997, 2001). Variations on the stereotypical patriarchal family and marriage system have also been reported in different regions. In particular, peripheral areas with ethnic minorities have often favored atypical marriage patterns. Well-known regional variations include villages with high rates of uxorilocal marriage, in which a man joined his wife's household, or minor marriage, in which parents adopted a small girl and raised her to become the future bride of their son (Fei, 1949; Pasternak, 1985; Wolf and Huang, 1980; Gates, 1996; Ono, 1989). A recent discovery that women in villages of southern Hunan embroidered poetic messages in their own unique "women's script" on fans and handkerchiefs for gift exchange between households contrasts with the prevailing image of universal illiteracy among rural women (Silbur, 1994).

Women from different classes had sharply contrasting lifestyles. Urban women from elite families had access to education and wealth, but respectability demanded that they not move beyond their doorways or interact with strange men. Meanwhile, women in rural rebel movements took an active part in public life. Women were active in rebel organizations in the Taiping Rebellion, the Red Spears movement, and the Boxer Rebellion of 1900 (Ono,

1989:10, 49; Perry, 1980:67, 204). The Taiping Rebellion (1851–1864), which is discussed further in Chapter 12, was a vast revitalization movement commingling Western Christianity with Chinese rebel traditions. The Taiping swept northward across China from the south, incorporating women as generals and soldiers under an ideology that stressed sexual equality. The Taiping rebels required followers to reject traditional patriarchal family structures, private property, polygamy, and foot binding and to live according to a radical system of sexual equality and segregation that prefigured communist experiments in social planning a century later. Women's participation in these movements suggests that even in the mid–nineteenth century patriarchal constraints on women were not completely accepted. As Maria Jaschok and Suzanne Miers observe, "The once ubiquitous stereotype of the long-suffering, meek, submissive Chinese woman as simply a victim of family interests, a vision of compliance and self sacrifice, stands thus revealed for what it is—a stereotype in need of reappraisal and an empirical context" (1994:9).

Although the state occasionally attempted to protect women (with decrees forbidding foot binding and infanticide), state policies generally offered women little protection. As Rubie Watson notes:

> They could be divorced, although it was nearly impossible for them to divorce; they had no rights to family property, yet they could be pawned or sold. They could not take the imperial exams and were barred from holding office. Their legal status was rather like that of a jural minor; even as adults they remained under the authority of a husband, or if he was dead, a son. If a woman remarried or was divorced, she was likely to lose control of, and even access to, her children. (1994:27)

The legal limitations on women prior to 1949 indicated that the state supported the system of male authority.

Through the nineteenth and early twentieth centuries, China experienced growing external pressures for change. Increasing foreign trade, political intervention, urbanization, and cultural contact pried open some parts of China's inward-looking social system and shifted the balance of power in different directions. Europeans, and particularly European missionaries, encountering Chinese culture were convinced that one factor contributing to China's backwardness was the low status of women, as symbolized by their bound feet and lack of education. This perception was shared by Chinese reformers, who also began to argue that China's development required an end to foot binding and the elevation of women's status so that they could perform their role as mothers of a modern nation more effectively (Ono, 1989:23–47; Zhang and Wu, 1995).

Behind female foot binding and lack of education lay the patriarchal family system that deprived women and young people of individual rights and power. China still permitted family heads to buy and sell lesser members: concubines, bondservants, and slaves (Jaschok, 1988; Jaschok and Miers, 1994; Watson, 1994; Gates, 1997, 2001). Women were duty-bound to produce a male heir; if all they could produce were daughters, a concubine might be brought in to perform this duty. Although children of both sexes could be sold by their parents, the preference for sons in a patrilineal kinship system meant that girls were more likely than boys to be wrenched from their natal homes at a tender age. And at marriage age, the daughters were required to move out to join their husband's household and to take orders from their husband and mother-in-law. Widely repeated proverbs regarding the worthlessness and powerlessness of women reinforced women's subordination in the family. Thus daughters were described as "goods you lost money on," and advice for wives was that "if you marry a dog, follow the dog; if you marry a chicken, follow the chicken."

Accounts of captive women and sayings such as these illustrate the worst possibilities—warning of what could and did happen in extreme cases and of what was legally allowed to happen. But they do not enable us to envision the lives of ordinary women in ordinary times and do not help us to assess the rate and direction of change. Much as modern newspapers headline the most attention-grabbing crimes, many writings on China repeat the most disturbing images and sayings as evidence of Chinese women's general oppression and victimization. These negative images have provided grist for the mill of foreign and Chinese nationalist reformers. One can be forgiven for suspecting that the more extreme images that could give exotic appeal to a travel writer or moral justification to the missionary did not accurately describe the situation of the majority of women. Along with those who were its obvious victims, many women lent their support to the patriarchal system. Scholars are beginning to assemble systematic and reliable accounts of the range of economic and social roles that women in China played, including the ways that they defended themselves from abuse and sought to better their lives.

One example is a biography showing that when faced with an evil husband, a woman might not submit to his decisions and sometimes had outside recourse, as Ning Lao did when her opium-addict husband sold her three-year-old daughter in 1889:

> "I have sold her."
> I jumped out of bed. . . . I seized him by the queue [the long hair braid mandated by the Qing as the proper hairstyle for men]. I wrapped it three times around my arm. I fought him for my child. We rolled fighting on the ground.
> The neighbors came and talked to pacify us.
> "If the child has not left the city and we can keep hold of this one, we will find her," they said.
> So we searched. The night through we searched. . . . We walked a great circle inside the city, and always I walked with my hands on his queue. He could not get away. (Pruitt, 1967:68)

Ning Lao recovered her child with the help of neighbors, not the law, though the buyers of her child threatened to sell her along with her daughter to recover her husband's debt. This account suggests that a woman's lack of legal means to contest a husband's authority was only one dimension. Local social support could shore up a mother's determination to oppose a husband's action.

In evaluating the impact of development and commercialization, it is hard to estimate the changing proportions of girls and women who were sold by their families on a commercial basis rather than married with well-defined rights and dowries (Gates, 1996:132–133; Watson, 1994; Jaschok and Miers, 1994; Honig and Hershatter, 1988). Although many authors described the nastier sides of life for Chinese women at the turn of the century—female infanticide, sales of women and girls, servitude, abduction, prostitution, and concubinage—it is difficult to know if these problems were constant, getting worse, or just getting more publicity. In addition, the harsh conditions faced by women need to be assessed against the harsh conditions that men faced, particularly among China's vast peasantry.

From the mid–eighteenth century, China's population grew rapidly from around 275 million in 1779 to 549 million by 1949 (Smith, 1990). Overpopulation, land shortage, soil exhaustion, and economic dislocation compounded the problems of China's peasants, who continued to farm with preindustrial technology. Although a few prospered, large numbers did not. From the nineteenth to the mid–twentieth century, agricultural crises affected China's political and economic instability, contributing to famines, banditry, rebellions, and warfare. From 1932 to 1949, the Japanese occupation and China's war against Japan, followed by the civil war between the communists and Nationalists, led to further dislocation.

Rural impoverishment and turmoil spelled misery for rural families. Infant girls were often abandoned, and young girls and women were frequently abducted, raped, and sold into various forms of servitude. Boys could also be sold as adopted sons or servants, and many men were dispossessed, impoverished, unable to form families, and condemned to wander in search of a livelihood. In addition, men could be conscripted and obliged to kill each other on behalf of China's competing armies (Mao, 1990; Fei, 1949; Stacey, 1983:198; Watson, 1976; Watson, 1994). Thus population growth and political instability in combination with overcrowded farms and declining incomes from traditional handicrafts meant that not only women were deprived of family support; large populations of surplus men, unmarried and unwanted, became beggars, bandits, soldiers, laborers, and lifelong bachelor-migrants and emigrants. In fact, exploring work and culture in the Pearl River delta, Rubie Watson (1994:41) observes that "it is not altogether surprising to find that the boundaries that separated servile men from free men were more rigidly drawn than those that delineated servile women from free women."

However, she adds: "Whether we can argue therefore that male servitude was harsher than female servitude requires further analysis."

Because the forms of dislocation were different for males and females, it is very difficult to determine whether women were singled out for bad treatment. There is simply insufficient information to show whether Chinese men or women experienced forced labor, poverty, malnutrition, and physical brutality in different proportions. Detailed demographic research comparing male and female life expectancies (such as Ts'ui-jung Liu's study of two Zhejiang clans from 1550 to 1850, in Hanley and Wolf, 1985:58, which shows male life expectancies were lower) could provide some insights. The frequent references to female infanticide and abandonment, child marriage, and the abduction and sale of women found in nineteenth- and early-twentieth-century reports indicate that many women suffered dehumanizing experiences (Jaschok, 1988; Spence, 1999). Describing China in the 1930s, Jonathan Spence (1999:384) writes: "In the absence of accurate data, all one can do is acknowledge that the variations of suffering were endless, and that as impoverished families died out, others emerged to take over their land and struggle for survival in their turn."

Traditional Chinese gender inequality has often been illustrated by comparing the most distressed groups of young women with the most advantaged groups of senior men. This procedure exaggerates gender inequality by confounding it with age and class inequalities. Juxtaposition of such sharply contrasting images of women and men makes it relatively easy to proclaim improvements for women and to "measure" change by showing that most women are now better off than the appalling traditional image. This method of viewing Chinese women stacks the deck toward finding that modernism (whether begun during the Republican first or communist second half of the twentieth century) improves women's status and also fosters the appearance that government policies promoting gender equality have been highly effective. One needs to keep this common source of distortion in mind when evaluating the communist revolution as a watershed.

Numerous women were experiencing very positive changes in the prerevolutionary period. By the early twentieth century, the demise of female foot binding had begun in parts of China in response to broad economic changes and industrialization, spurred on by government and missionary efforts to eradicate it (Bossen, 2002; Gates, 1997, 2001; Gamble, 1968). Among the urban elite, following the demonstrations of May 4, 1919, protesting China's treatment at the Versailles Peace Conference, a growing revolutionary movement (discussed at length in Chapter 13) saw women's equality as important for national development. Opportunities for women to achieve formal education were expanding, along with exposure to Western concepts of modernization and sexual equality. Western missionaries encouraged Chinese women to abandon the practice of foot binding, to pursue higher education, and to reject arranged marriages. By 1922, the number of Chinese women receiving university education had climbed to 887 out of a total 34,880 students, with women accounting for almost 9 percent of the students in Christian and foreign colleges. Western female missionaries also became role models and teachers for Chinese women, providing exposure to new concepts of public service and careers for women (Spence, 1999). Although government and missionary efforts to prohibit foot binding had some effect, early-twentieth-century processes of economic change and industrial employment probably had the more significant impact (Bossen, 2002; Gates, 2001; Gamble, 1968). By the 1920s, some of the coastal areas where foot binding once was prevalent had abandoned the practice. Eradication of the custom in remote areas, however, would wait until the communists achieved power.

One of the major changes experienced by rural women in the early twentieth century was the decline in their ability to contribute to the household through cottage industries (Ono, 1989:7; Fei, 1949; Honig, 1986:62–64). As traditional handicrafts were displaced by industrial products, households had to shed surplus labor. Underemployed men typically migrated to cities seeking work. They might return with wealth or remain away for years. For underemployed women, risks of childbearing and child rearing and other considerations made migration a less viable option. Young, unmarried women risked abduction and illegitimate pregnancy if they worked outside the home, and young married mothers also risked the health of their children if they brought them along or risked losing their ties to the children if they entrusted them to others (Pruitt, 1967). But a daughter or wife kept virtuously at home had declining value. Thus the early twentieth century witnessed significant movements of women out of the rural family setting. Sometimes they were traded as commodities for their sexuality or labor, and sometimes they acted as independent agents seeking work in urban industries or services, begging, peddling, working as fortune-tellers, or migrating overseas. Young girls, in particular, could be sold by their parents as domestic slaves, entertainers, or prostitutes (Jaschok and Miers, 1994); the girls were obliged to pay back the money given to their parents and so transferred their dependency to their purchasers.

Young women who managed to migrate to find industrial work in cities or overseas to plantations often formed sisterhoods of various types that provided mutual support outside the protective umbrella of the patriarchal family (Jaschok and Miers, 1994:14; Honig, 1986:210). In the silk-producing areas of southern China, industrial employment provided young women with opportunities to delay or evade marriage by earning their own incomes (Topley, 1975; Sankar, 1984; Stockard, 1989). Jaschok and Miers (1994:23, 40) refer to these women as "marriage resisters." Growing numbers of women found employment in the textile factories that had displaced their cottage industries. However, the depression of the 1930s brought falling world demand for silk, so rural and urban women again found themselves unemployed (Fei, 1949; Hershatter, 1991; Watson, 1994:33). Under such circumstances, girls and women could be compelled to join the ranks of young women providing domestic and sexual services in cities, where even greater numbers of displaced men also congregated seeking employment (Hershatter, 1991). To thrive and compete in this economy, literacy, mobility, steady work performance, new skills, and connections were required. Most rural women, newly arrived in the cities, were poorly prepared to compete.

■ Women's Status After the Communist Revolution

The communist revolution set out to transform China by creating an egalitarian society and promoting rapid development. Shortly after taking power, China's leaders began to transform the system of property rights, marriage rights, and labor relations. In retrospect it is clear that many of these changes were economically ill-advised and based on an oversimplified conception of rural life. For instance, the move from private to collective forms of agricultural production was expected to increase economic efficiency and productivity, yet for much of the revolutionary period, agricultural output only kept pace with population growth. The measures to produce social equality and to place women on a par with men were not thoroughly implemented; they left sufficient power concentrated in male hands to vitiate the reforms designed to benefit women.

The land reform program was intended to give peasants equal ownership of land. In 1950, the new Marriage Law gave "unmarried, divorced or widowed women the right to hold land in their own names" (Spence, 1999), which would enable them to become independent farmers. However, revolutionary theory soon gave way to pragmatism: rural men did not want to surrender control of family property. Enforcement of the law would have been very costly, requiring many educated officials as well as time and resources to register and protect titles for every rural adult as an individual. The party backed off and settled for a system in which women were counted as members of households to whom the land was distributed. Then the land and households were combined into collectives. The decision of how household income was to be distributed within the family remained in traditional male hands.

The Marriage Law of 1950 aimed to abolish the legal standing of arranged marriage, child marriage, and polygamy and to establish marriage as a voluntary contract between two equal adults, as well as to permit them to divorce. This measure, too, met with opposition, as peasant men labeled it "the divorce law" or the "women's law" (Ladany, 1992). Women who had been previously married by parental arrangements were thereby entitled to divorce their husbands. Combined with the newly acquired rights to land, women thought the law offered them a chance to break away from patriarchal control. However, women who sought to divorce faced strong opposition from their husband's family and the cadres. This led to considerable turmoil and violence against women—variously reported as violence by men who refused to accept divorce by their wives (Stacey, 1983:181), or by men who wanted to divorce and turned reluctant wives over to village militia for opposing the revolution (Ladany, 1992:60):

> Women had to fight their battles all alone, even under the threat of possible bloodshed. Many women were killed by their husbands or mothers-in-law, and many women chose to struggle to their deaths. During the year following the promulgation of the Marriage Law, more than 10,000 women were killed in South-Central China; in East China in 1950–52 the figure reached 11,500. During the two or three years following the Law's enactment some 70,000–80,000 people per year were killed over marriage-related issues throughout the country. (Ono, 1989:181)

Stacey similarly comments that "in a shocking number of cases women were murdered or driven to suicide when they attempted to gain their freedom" (1983:178).

The combined effect of the land and marriage reforms was perceived by married peasant men as a threat to their control over both land and labor. In 1953 the state gave orders to halt the violence, and campaigns to implement the Marriage Law were curtailed (Ladany, 1992:60; Stacey, 1983:181). The Marriage Law was intended to establish a more equitable basis for future marriages and to place the interests of the marriage partners above those of their parents. Older women, wanting control over the labor of their daughters-in-law, often objected to the increased freedom it offered younger women.

Following Marxist theory, the Chinese Communist Party held that women must work in the public sphere in order to achieve equality and contribute to socialist construction. Thus it became important symbolically to bring women out of the isolation of the household, where they worked for their husbands and families, and into production for society. Throughout the 1950s, women were increasingly pulled into nondomestic forms of labor that in theory would make them more productive. They joined agricultural work teams, and during the Great Leap Forward they participated in massive construction projects. In this respect, the Communist Party achieved a reversal of the direction of development seen in many Western countries where women are excluded from agricultural development (Momsen, 1991:66). In China, women were deliberately targeted and required to participate in farming in order to obtain income for their households.

In many parts of southern China where rural women already participated in the public sphere in both agricultural and nonagricultural activities, the policy would have had no effect on women's economic equality—although some women claimed collective labor organization promoted equality by getting men to do their share of the farmwork (Bossen, 1994a). In areas where men were unaccustomed to seeing women do agricultural work, the fact that women were able to earn work points from the collective probably softened their opposition.

Communist theory took little account of the labor-intensive nature of housework in houses that lacked running water and modern stoves. In addition to hauling water, tending wood fires, and doing laundry by hand, rural women often engaged in a variety of home-based semicommercial activities like food processing, textile production, gardening, and raising courtyard livestock. All this was on top of the hours women spent working on the collective farm. The policies to bring women into agricultural work with status equal to men did not require men to take care of an equal share of the domestic work.

Countless reports from villages across China indicated that the local systems of allocating work points for collective work discriminated against women. Women were awarded only a fraction of the work points that men were awarded for similar types and quantities of work. The work point rate, like a wage rate, was in almost all cases an attribute of gender. When the maximum work point rate for men was ten points, the maximum for women would be seven or eight. Where men got twenty, women would get fifteen, and so forth, in village after village. Furthermore, the work points of members of a household were tallied together by village leaders, and their value was then paid to the household head. This system was blatantly discriminatory and did not establish women as independent actors in the labor force. Women were unable to exercise any direct control over the income they earned.

The unchallenged custom of patrilocal residence also kept patriarchal authority intact in the vast majority of rural marriages (Diamond, 1975). Daughters still had to marry out of their natal villages, leaving only their brothers to inherit housing and family savings. Men remained in the village where they were born and retained effective power over collective village land and politics, making decisions about work points, and allocating other village resources (Bossen, 1994a, 1994b, 1994c, 2002; Croll, 1995; Davin, 1975; Stacey, 1983; Johnson, 1983; Judd, 1994b; Potter and Potter, 1990). Patrilocal residence has helped to preserve male predominance in the definition of justice and retarded the extension of civil rights to women.

Of all the measures taken by China to improve the status of women, one that seems the least controversial will probably prove to have the largest impact over the long run: the policy of promoting equal education for girls and extending primary school education to the rural areas. In view of the extremely low levels of literacy and the large disparities between the sexes before the revolution, China's early and consistent commitment to mass education has greatly benefited women of all regions. In 1951 the proportion of girls among primary school students was 28 percent. By 1958 it had reached

38 percent, and by the end of the Maoist period, in 1976, girls made up 45 percent of the elementary school population—a ratio that continues to the present. In secondary school, female participation climbed from 26 percent in 1951 to about 40 percent by 1998. In university the rise has been less spectacular; the proportion of women in university rose from 21 percent in 1951 and thereafter has fluctuated between 23 and 34 percent (All China Women's Federation, 1991:124, 136). Women still form a disproportionate number of China's illiterates, but this proportion continues to decline over time as larger proportions of the population attend school. The percentage of China's total population age twelve and over who were illiterate or semiliterate dropped from 32 to 27 percent between 1982 and 1987, while that of the female population dropped from 45 to 38 percent. Although gaps between the sexes remain at all levels, in comparison to other large agrarian nations, China is doing well (UNDP, 2002).

Continuing a process that had begun in the early twentieth century, women became an increasingly important part of the urban industrial work force during the revolutionary period. The participation of women in urban industrial work did not bring sexual equality, however. Under Communist Party planning, women largely remained in segregated industries with lower salaries. Women were also less likely to be assigned to large state-run factories where health, pension, and housing benefits were provided. Rather, their jobs were concentrated in the lower-paying, less prestigious community- and neighborhood-run industries that offered fewer benefits (Whyte and Parish, 1984; Wolf, 1985). They sometimes had access to day care facilities, but this benefit was never very widespread. Most urban women worked outside industry; their total package of wages and benefits remained significantly lower and less secure. Men continued to control the greater incomes and monopolize managerial positions. Unlike rural women, however, urban working women did collect their own wages.

Urban women faced another task that began to consume a great deal of time: standing in line at government stores for rationed products or locating scarce supplies on the black market. They also had to produce at home the goods they could not purchase. The predominantly male bureaucratic planners in communist China did not place a high priority on inventing or producing labor-saving products to reduce housework. Women in revolutionary China did not have access to washing machines or even to laundromats and commercial hand-laundry services. Rather, they faced traditional chores such as hand washing clothes for their family in a basin. Only in the reform period did appliances such as washing machines, electric rice cookers, in-home plumbing, refrigerators, stoves, fans, and vacuum cleaners begin to reduce the heavy drudgery of housework, daily shopping, and cooking that had fallen on women along with their obligation to perform "productive labor" for the state.

■ Women and Economic Reform

Since Mao's death, China has implemented reforms, gradually liberalizing the economy and permitting the revival of markets and private-sector activities. In the rural sector, the most significant reform has been the dismantling of collective farm management. Individual households can now contract collective lands and farm them under household management, taking responsibility for meeting state quotas or taxes in grain production. The household can then keep surpluses for its own benefit. This incentive system has increased output while reducing labor committed to agricultural production. Households increasingly allocate some of their members to profitable sideline activities or cottage industries and others to trade, transport, construction, and commercial and service activities located off-farm and often outside the village.

Village governments no longer require women to work in the fields in order to earn work points and contribute to household income. That does not mean women have stopped working in the fields, but they now have greater flexibility in the disposal of their time and more opportunities to earn individual income through commercial activities. The reforms unleashed a mass exodus of men from farming to more lucrative occupations. Young men in particular set out for cities and towns, unencumbered, as women were, by

Two elderly Han farm women and a middle-aged
teacher-farmer, holding her grandson, rest at midday

social concerns for their sexual conduct and reputations, to look for work where they could find it (Zhou, 1996:137). This revived the pattern of seasonal male labor migration that was well established before the revolution (see Chapter 8). Eventually, young unmarried women also joined this stream, although in lesser numbers, and with greater risk. Generally, young women migrated in search of urban employment through relatives or personal contacts, helping in family businesses or providing domestic service and child care. Some set off simply to take their chances on finding work in informal urban labor markets, clustering on city streets, waiting for employers to arrive seeking young women to work, usually as domestic servants. These young women, often unsophisticated and illiterate, are easy prey for those ready to recruit them as brides for rural bachelors or as prostitutes, often through deception (Wong, 1996; Zhou, 1996:221).

Married rural women have had much less freedom to migrate due to their responsibility for child care and the lack of housing for rural families (who have no urban household registration) in the cities. Married women have stayed on the farms, working and managing the land allocated to their households. Farming has become feminized in the sense that women in most regions of China supply the bulk of agricultural labor (Bossen, 1991, 1994c; Wolf, 1985; Judd, 1994a, 1994b), yet they have had little control over the land they farm. Village land is controlled by the village government. Through the 1990s village leaders allocated land on a per capita basis (so women are counted along with men) to individual households formed by married sons of the village, but individuals and households could not buy or sell their shares. Thus, successful women farmers cannot purchase land to increase production, and women who are poor farmers or who hate farming cannot sell their shares and use the capital to finance other activities. The land they work remains firmly under the control of the patrilocal households they joined at marriage; it is not an asset they can own as individuals.

The more open economy does give some rural women more occupational choice and control over money, however. Ellen Judd (1994a:204) outlines two strategies pursued by rural women in response to China's new policies toward economic development: household commodity production and employment in village industry. Those who live in rural communities with good commercial locations (near towns and cities or good transportation) can grow and sell crops above and beyond those required by state quotas. In addition, many villages and townships have established rural industries that employ women from their own and outside villages. Generally, they hire women at low wages and offer few benefits. In addition, younger women increasingly migrate long distances to reach urban and township enterprise zones that produce for export and pay higher wages. There, they work in sweatshops and on assembly lines producing items such as clothing or electronic products in a more competitive, capitalist fashion. These industries often pay their casual women workers higher wages than money-losing state industries, but the women have few protections in terms of safe working conditions or job security. Unlike the former collective system that paid women's work points to the household head, the market economy allows women to receive individual wages (Bossen, 1994a; Woon, 1990:153, 159). This often lets them accumulate their own personal savings and gain more economic independence—especially when they migrate or when male migration leaves them with greater control over household income. Yet in Beijing, Li Zhang reports that many young migrant girls work for urban migrant bosses in family-run cottage industries for very low pay, living in their employer's house under strict control with little freedom to go out (2001:126–129). In other areas, such as the Pearl River delta, where a large proportion of males have migrated overseas, wives who collect remittances from abroad have enjoyed prosperity by withdrawing from agriculture and other local production and investing in higher education for their sons and daughters (Woon, 1990:163).

A Han village factory worker brings her child to work

The reform period has brought liberalizing policies to the rural economy, but it has also tightened government controls on reproduction. The controversial family planning policy, discussed in Chapter 8, has meant that rural families have less choice over the number of children they raise than in the past. This policy limits urban families to one child but is more permissive in rural areas, favoring what Kay Ann Johnson calls a "one-son-or-two-child policy" (1996:81). Whether local governments enforce the limit as a two-child policy or let rural families have children until they produce a son, the policy has a profound effect on women. First, it is largely implemented through direct bodily controls on women, including intrauterine devices (IUDs), abortion, and sterilization, with X rays and ultrasound tests for pregnancy (Greenhalgh, Zhu, and Li, 1994). Second, the policy accentuates the importance of sons by forcing families to confront the risk of having no son at all if their first and second children are girls. This is believed to have increased China's unbalanced sex ratio by provoking families to get rid of daughters, whether through infanticide, abandonment, or sale, in order to try again for a son. In the past, such desperate measures were associated with extreme poverty, but under the growing prosperity of the post-Mao era they seem to result from both the excesses and the failures of government policy (Croll, 2001; Greenhalgh and Li, 1995; Johnson, 1996; Sen, 1994). The increasingly imbalanced sex ratios shown by China's census data in the 1990s are a sign that government has not established the foundations for gender equality.

The birth control procedures employed by the state are highly invasive of women's privacy, yet women do not perceive them as entirely bad. Withdrawal of state control of births would not leave women with the right to make their own decisions about reproduction. Rather, the patriarchal family, the traditional institution vested with social control over women's sexuality, could force women to bear more children than they wanted. Most rural women in China clearly do wish to bear children until, as required by custom, they produce a son, who secures their position within their husband's family and who legally owes them economic support in old age. But women may also welcome the power of the state against a family that wants them to produce an expanding labor force. Research on women's attitudes toward birth control suggests that they do not want to return to high fertility levels.

While the reforms of the economy and of family planning head in opposite directions toward lesser and greater state intervention, respectively, legal reform has stagnated. Beyond family planning, women's legal rights in rural areas are still largely unprotected by effective mechanisms of law enforcement. Outside personnel do not have the capacity or motivation to challenge the control of villages by local men linked by patrilineal descent. Village cadres entrusted with law enforcement ignore laws that, in theory, should protect women. Women who are abducted or coerced into marriages with village men get little support from village cadres. Newspaper accounts of efforts by women's families or the All-China Women's Federation to retrieve women who have been abducted to serve as wives in distant villages generally report a wall of silence, concealment, and noncooperation from villages where the women are held (Wong, 1996:293, 326–329).

The increased prosperity associated with the economic reforms, the greater access to market commodities, and the relaxation of communist moral doctrines surrounding marriage have permitted the revival of marriage transactions involving both bridewealth (usually in the form of funds given by the groom's family to the bride's family) and dowry (usually in the form of goods provided by the bride's family)—both of which were common prior to the revolution. Such marriage transactions were suppressed during the collective period but have escalated dramatically in the past decade (Yan, 1996). Although the payment of bridewealth does not mean that a bride has been purchased, the escalating demands for bridewealth make it difficult for men from poor villages to attract wives. These men are then tempted to resort to marriage brokers who use deceit or abduction to supply brides (Yan, 1996).

In urban China, the effects of the economic reforms on women have been mixed. The relatively small proportion of women workers who were once privileged to have access to state jobs found that in the more competitive reform economy, state industries were more likely to discharge their female employees and to demand male employees when hiring new workers or university graduates. Although the constitution of 1982 and a Women's Rights Protection Law of 1992 pledge to protect women, some observers argue that protective regulations requiring women to retire five years earlier than men and clauses prohibiting them from doing certain kinds of work (such as night shifts, work in harsh conditions, work that results in exposure to industrial poisons, or work that is physically strenuous) during menstruation, pregnancy, the postpartum period, and while nursing have the effect of fostering biologically based discrimination. Margaret Woo observes that "when faced with providing protective benefits, some factory managers simply chose not to hire women workers, or to dismiss them. Thus, in the city of Nantong, women constituted 70 percent of the total number of workers fired from their jobs in 1988" (1994:281–282). However, she argues that "the conclusion that women's interests have been subordinated to the state's goal of economic development is best supported by the conditions in the 'special economic zones,' which the government has set up to promote economic development. In these special economic zones, where female labor is needed, the 'return home' policy is not promoted, and protective regulations are non-existent" (1994:287). In these areas, women form a high proportion of the work force but are primarily temporary workers lacking the benefits and guarantees of state-sector workers.

The expansion of commercial activities in urban centers has offered women alternatives to state and private factory employment. Many of the new businesses in the informal sector have been established by women independ-

A university research scientist

ently or as family enterprises (Bruun, 1993; Von Eschen, 2000). Often these businesses sell labor-saving products and services that were unavailable in the days of revolutionary austerity, when manual labor was considered noble.

Improvements in household appliances came first to the urban sector, but the revival of free markets responding to supply and demand has rapidly brought industrial commodities even to farm families. They, too, have begun to invest in electric washing machines, rice cookers, microwave ovens, and other items that allow women to spend less time in drudgery. Increased disposable income in women's hands has also led to an explosion in the fashion industry that stimulates and caters to women's desires to be attractive, selling a profusion of beauty products and services. Purveyors of hair treatments, skin creams, shampoos, perfumes, jewelry, plastic surgery, and designer fashions in clothes and shoes increasingly beckon the daughters of a post-Mao generation, whose mothers uniformly grew up wearing drab blues and grays that were mandated by the Maoist unisex, antifashion ideology. Especially for urban women enjoying disposable income for the first time, these commodities bring excitement and a feeling of participation in the modern world. For rural migrants, they bring possibilities for purchasing some of the symbols of sophisticated urban lifestyles formerly denied them. After years of material sacrifice for the revolution and politically mandated denial of gender difference, Chinese women are now seeking different routes to social and economic success. Indeed, the frenzied consumer choices Chinese women are now making have caused Western feminists to gasp at the way they mirror Western women's insecurities as they join the never-ending quest for beauty and the latest designer labels (Honig and Hershatter, 1988; Wong, 1996).

■ Women and Politics

The Communist Party, as part of its commitment to sexual equality, initiated policies designed to bring women into the political process. It did so in part through affirmative action programs, setting quotas or targets for the minimum participation of women in political bodies, and by establishing the All-China Women's Federation, a national body to oversee women's interests. Critics have argued that the political bodies to which women were appointed are largely powerless. They also point out that the Women's Federation is not an organization arising in response to women's own initiatives; rather it is a government bureaucracy controlled by the party to transmit and implement party policies directed at women (Barlow, 1994:341–344).

What have Chinese women gained in the political sphere? Is their position in the formal political structure simply a pitch for "symbolic capital"—a way to enhance China's reputation among nations? Have communist policies generally improved women's possibilities for formal political influence? Have state policies imposing quotas and requiring female participation been effective?

At the highest national level, China is governed by the Communist Party and the National People's Congress. The highest body within the party is the Politburo, which consists of a core group, the Standing Committee; a larger group of full members (ranging from fourteen to twenty-six in different years); and another group of alternate members. As Stanley Rosen points out, since the Communist Party was founded, only three women (all wives of powerful men) have served as full members, but none of them were Standing Committee members. Only two women have served as alternate members (1995:317). Female membership in the party's Central Committee, the body from which the Politburo derives, with a membership ranging from 97 to 210 between 1956 and 1992, has averaged about 12 percent. Rosen observes that women's participation in these bodies peaked during the Cultural Revolution and since the reforms has been sliding back down toward the earlier levels.

The National People's Congress (the national legislature) is similarly divided between its Standing Committee, which has greater decisionmaking power, and the whole congress, which meets for policy discussion. Women's participation rate on the Standing Committee, a group ranging from 55 to 80 members between 1954 and 1993, averaged only 5 or 6 percent in the 1950s, increased to over 20 percent in the 1970s, and dropped back down to 12 or 13 percent in the late 1980s and 1990s (Rosen, 1995:320). The proportion of female representatives to the National People's Congress, a body of nearly 3,000 members, is higher and has increased from 12 percent in the 1950s to just over 20 percent in the 1970s, where it has remained fairly constant to the present (Rosen, 1995:320). In 1995, the United Nations *Human Development Report* based its evaluation of China's position in its gender empowerment index on the proportion of women in the National People's Congress, which many consider to be a body too large for actual decisionmaking. National People's Congress meetings discuss and ratify decisions already made in other bodies (Ogden, 1995:256). *New York Times* journalist Fox Butterfield recalls Chinese friends joking that "delegates to the National People's Congress had only two rights: to raise their hands to vote yes and to applaud the speeches of Communist leaders" (1982:421).

When moving down the hierarchy to lower, regional levels of the political structure, government reports on female participation tend to combine "head and deputy head" and "chief and deputy chief" positions. In this way, the proportions of females represented hover around 4 to 6 percent for city mayors, township heads, county chiefs, and prefectural and provincial governors. However, the vast majority of women are at the "deputy" or "vice mayor" level, with no women holding the highest position in party or government at provincial, autonomous region, or administered cities levels. This suggests strong reluctance to place women in positions of authority over men. At the lower levels of city, county, township, and small town, women hold only 1 to 2 percent of the top positions (Rosen, 1995:325). Most of the small proportion of women who reach higher office at these levels of government hold "vice" or "deputy" positions where they are usually one of several, and not to be promoted. Another consideration is that women in Chinese politics are often confined to the less influential spheres of responsibility, concentrating on issues concerning women, children, health, and education. In sum, although state quotas and priorities brought women into political bodies where they might otherwise be completely absent, the proportions tend to be so low and their positions so secondary and marginal that the state commitment to equality loses credibility.

In rural China, women rarely hold positions of political leadership. Apart from the sole position of director of women's affairs, local village councils are in almost all cases composed only of men. The director of women's affairs is typically designated the local representative of the national Women's Federation and has responsibility for women's work or family planning (Rosen, 1995:325–327; Bossen, 1994b, 2002; Croll, 1995; Huang Shu-min, 1989; Judd, 1994b, 2002; Potter and Potter, 1990). During the Cultural Revolution, Stanley Rosen (1995) and the Chinese sources he cites claim that women broke out of the mold and went beyond the typical women's slots. One reason for this may have been the policy of sending educated youths, including young women, to the countryside, where their literacy and knowledge of bureaucracy could be useful to village governments negotiating with outside officials. Urban, educated young women sent to rural areas had a chance to assume political positions at the lower levels of the political hierarchy. In the reform period this ended; educated urban youth were no longer being sent to the countryside, and those who had gone returned to the cities. Now that the pool of leadership is once again confined to native villagers, few women are selected. The common pattern today is similar to that found by Norma Diamond (1975) early in the revolutionary period. The few women active in village leadership usually come from among a small, atypical group of women who did not marry outside the village into which they were born.

In urban China, the increasing exposure to international standards not only in material goods but also in education and culture has stimulated efforts to revive an autonomous feminist movement within China. New forms of women's writing have begun to explore new ways of looking at women's experiences in China (Zhu Hong, 1994), and women intellectuals have begun to establish women's studies programs in universities (Du Fangqin, 2001). A growing number of young Chinese women have received university educations abroad and have returned with new views on feminism and human rights. The Marxist conception of women's liberation is gradually being displaced by debates about the nature and future of an autonomous women's movement and of more diverse ways of organizing women (Li, 1995; Hsiung et al., 2001). The tension between state control and autonomous women's groups was evident at the 1995 United Nations World Conference on Women, where the Chinese government did its best to restrain such groups, both among Chinese women and among their international counterparts.

■ Conclusion

China's revolutionary leaders sought to include women in development by emphasizing education, labor force participation, and marriage reform. Compared to the constraints women faced in the nineteenth and early twentieth centuries, when neither the state nor the family was obliged to treat them as individual citizens, Chinese women from all walks of life have benefited. More women than ever are working outside the home and receiving an education. These are very positive signs. On the negative side, persisting patriarchal institutions allow men to retain control of village politics and resources. One of the greatest weaknesses in China's legal system is that it still has neither granted women effective individual rights to land (whether as daughters, wives, or widows) nor permitted land to escape from the traditional control of patrilineal corporations in which women's influence is virtually nil.

In comparing the recent reform period to the earlier revolutionary period, it is clear that the state has abandoned most of its earlier efforts to command

greater female participation in the labor force, politics, and education. This
has resulted in stagnation in some areas but also some gains. Few women hold
meaningful political posts. The percentages of women receiving education
have stabilized at levels that have improved when compared to the nineteenth
and early twentieth centuries but are still unacceptable by the standards of
developed nations. Most women still work outside the home, but gender differences in remuneration remain significant. Women are still culturally constrained by traditional obligations to perform child care and housework
(Entwisle and Henderson, 2000).

Despite the weakened state support for equality, women in the reform
period have undeniably benefited, as have men, from greater opportunities for
occupational and residential choice. The marketplace has opened up new
opportunities for women to engage in commercial activities on their own
account and to earn cash incomes that are paid directly to women employees
rather than to household heads. Although women are now disproportionately
responsible for unskilled farmwork, young women are increasingly drawing
on their education and greater exposure to the outside world to take risks in
seeking urban and nonfarm employment. These trends tend to undermine
China's resistant patriarchal family institutions. However, women who
attempt to act independently in the labor market and in the marriage and sexual market, where there is growing demand for their services, need effective
legal protection against the resurgence of coercive practices. Particularly in
rural areas, women need better protection against violence, abduction, forced
marriage, and forced labor. Improved systems of communication and the
increasing levels of female education that enable them to use public communication (letters, the Internet, newspapers, the broadcast media, and telephones) to inform others when their rights are violated may help women to
obtain greater legal protection.

The government's family planning program uses heavy-handed methods
of enforcement aimed primarily at women that deprive them of choice, but it
also acts as a buffer against patriarchal demands for large families. Withdrawal of the state program would not necessarily empower women to make
their own reproductive choices or to limit childbearing. The state policies
bring about results that, for the majority of rural women fortunate enough to
bear a son, are probably close to what they would choose for themselves. For
the minority who fail to bear a son, there is a desperate desire to break the
rules—with direct consequences for baby girls who are unregistered, abandoned, or killed. The evidence of China's skewed sex ratios—which rose to
110 boys for every 100 girls under age four in the 1990s—points to systematic discrimination against girls (*Zhongguo renkou tongji nianjian,* 1995:6).
Given the biologically expected ratio of 106 boys for every 100 girls, the
missing girls are a reminder of significant institutionalized inequality, particularly in rural areas. In the short run, the social instability that can result from

a surplus of socially unattached males might become a concern to China's leaders. Over the long run, urbanization seems to reduce preference for having boy babies.

Finally, if one evaluates the role of women in China's development from a global perspective, there is reason for optimism. The efforts of the state to extend education and health care to its female population have improved women's life expectancies and given them more skills with which to participate in society than they had in the past. China is performing significantly better than India, its most obvious Asian analogy in terms of its size, agrarian population, and patriarchal traditions. India's maternal mortality rate is more than four times higher, and its mortality rate among children under age five is more than three times higher than China's. In China, women have longer life expectancy, later age at marriage, and higher literacy and educational levels than women in India (UNDP, 1994:144–156). Chinese women still have major battles to fight if they are to achieve equality, but now that the majority of women are educated and less encumbered by reproduction, they are better positioned to organize themselves and make their own demands in the future. In this respect, Chinese women have an interest in the development of more democratic institutions and an effective legal system that respects civil and human rights for all its citizens.

■ Bibliography

All China Women's Federation Research Institute. 1991. *Zhongguo funu tongji ziliao (1949–1989)* [Statistics on Chinese Women]. Beijing: Zhongguo Tongji Chubanshe [China Statistical Publishing House].

Andors, Phyllis. 1983. *The Unfinished Liberation of Chinese Women, 1969–1980.* Bloomington: Indiana University Press.

Barlow, Tani. 1994. "Politics and Protocols of Funu." Pp. 339–359 in Christina Gilmartin, Gail Hershatter, Lisa Rofel, and Tyrene White (eds.), *Engendering China: Women, Culture, and the State.* Cambridge: Harvard University Press.

Bernhardt, Kathryn. 1996. "Chinese Women's History." Pp. 42–58 in Gail Hershatter, Emily Honig, Jonathan Lipman, and Randal Stross (eds.), *Remapping China: Fissures in Historical Terrain.* Stanford: Stanford University Press.

Bossen, Laurel. 1991. "Changing Land Tenure Systems in China: Common Problem, Uncommon Solution." *Sociological Bulletin: Journal of the Indian Sociological Society* 40(1–2):47–67.

———. 1994a. "Gender and Economic Reform in Southwest China." Pp. 223–240 in Huguette Dagenais and Denise Piché (eds.), *Femmes, feminisme, et developpement* [Women, feminism, and development]. Montreal: McGill-Queens University Press.

———. 1994b. "The Household Economy in Rural China: Is the Involution Over?" Pp. 167–191 in James Acheson (ed.), *Anthropology and Institutional Economics.* Monographs in Economic Anthropology no. 12. Lanham, MD: University Press of America.

———. 1994c. "Zhongguo nongcun funu: shenma yuanyin shi tamen liu zai nong tian li?" [Chinese rural women: What keeps them down on the farm?]. Pp. 128–154 in Li Xiaojiang, Zhu Hong, and Dong Xiuyu (eds.), *Xingbie yu Zhongguo* [Gender and China]. Beijing: Shenghuo-Dushu-Xinhe Sanlian Shudian [SDX Joint Publishing Company].

———. 2002. *Chinese Women and Rural Development: Sixty Years of Change in Lu Village, Yunnan.* Lanham, MD: Rowman and Littlefield.

Bruun, Ole. 1993. *Business and Bureaucracy in a Chinese City: An Ethnography of Private Business Households in Contemporary China.* Berkeley: University of California, Institute for East Asian Studies.

Buck, John L. 1937. *Land Utilization in China.* Nanking: University of Nanking Press.

Butterfield, Fox. 1982. *China: Alive in the Bitter Sea.* Toronto: Bantam.

Cass, Victoria B. 1999. *Dangerous Women: Warriors, Grannies, and Geishas of the Ming.* Lanham, MD: Rowman and Littlefield.

Chaffee, John W. 1991. "The Marriage of Sung Imperial Clanswomen." Pp. 133–169 in Rubie Watson and Patricia B. Ebrey (eds.), *Marriage and Inequality in Chinese Society.* Berkeley: University of California Press.

Croll, Elizabeth. 1983. *Chinese Women Since Mao.* London: Zed Books.

———. 1995. *Changing Identities of Chinese Women.* Hong Kong: Hong Kong University Press.

———. 2001. *Endangered Daughters: Discrimination and Development in Asia.* London: Routledge.

Davin, Delia. 1975. "Women in the Countryside of China." Pp. 243–273 in Margery Wolf and Roxane Witke (eds.), *Women in Chinese Society.* Stanford: Stanford University Press.

Diamond, Norma. 1975. "Collectivization, Kinship, and the Status of Women in Rural China." Pp. 372–395 in Rayna Reiter (ed.), *Toward an Anthropology of Women.* New York: Monthly Review Press.

Du Fangqin. 2001. "'Manoeuvering Fate' and 'Following the Call': Development and Prospects of Women's Studies." Pp. 237–249 in Ping-Chun Hsiung, Maria Jaschok, and Cecilia Milwertz, with Red Chan (eds.), *Chinese Women Organizing: Cadres, Feminists, Muslims, Queers.* Oxford: Berg.

Ebrey, Patricia Buckley. 1993. *The Inner Quarters: Marriage and the Lives of Chinese Women in the Sung Period.* Berkeley: University of California Press.

Entwisle, Barbara, and Gail E. Henderson (eds.). 2000. *Re-Drawing Boundaries: Work, Households, and Gender in China.* Berkeley: University of California Press.

Fei, Hsiao-Tung. 1949 [1939]. *Peasant Life in China: A Field Study of Country Life.* London: Kegan Paul, Trench, and Trubner.

Fei, Hsiao-Tung, and C. I. Chang. 1948. *Earthbound China: A Study of Rural Economy in Yunnan.* London: Routledge and Kegan Paul.

Gamble, Sidney. 1968 [1954]. *Ting Hsien: A North China Rural Community.* Stanford: Stanford University Press.

Gates, Hill. 1989. "The Commoditization of Chinese Women." *Signs* 14(4):799–832.

———. 1996. *China's Motor: A Thousand Years of Petty Capitalism.* Ithaca: Cornell University Press.

———. 1997. "Footbinding and Handspinning in Sichuan: Capitalism's Ambiguous Gifts to Petty Capitalism." Pp. 177–194 in Kenneth G. Lieberthal, Shuen-fu Lin, and Ernest P. Young (eds.), *Constructing China: The Interaction of Culture and Economics.* Ann Arbor: University of Michigan Press.

————. 2001. "Footloose in Fujian: Economic Correlates of Footbinding." *Comparative Studies in Society and History* 43(1):130–148.

Gilmartin, Christina, Gail Hershatter, Lisa Rofel, and Tyrene White (eds.). 1994. *Engendering China: Women, Culture, and the State.* Cambridge: Harvard University Press.

Greenhalgh, Susan, and Jaili Li. 1995. "Engendering Reproductive Policy and Practice in Peasant China: For a Feminist Demography of Reproduction." *Signs* 20(3):601–641.

Greenhalgh, Susan, Zhu Chuzhu, and Nan Li. 1994. "Restraining Population Growth in Three Chinese Villages." *Population and Development Review* 20(2):365–395.

Hanley, Susan, and Arthur Wolf (eds.). 1985. *History and Population in East Asia.* Stanford: Stanford University Press.

Hershatter, Gail. 1986. *The Workers of Tianjin, 1900–1949.* Stanford: Stanford University Press.

————. 1991. "Prostitution and the Market in Women in Early Twentieth-Century Shanghai." Pp. 256–285 in Rubie Watson and Patricia B. Ebrey (eds.), *Marriage and Inequality in Chinese Society.* Berkeley: University of California Press.

Hinsch, Bret. 2002. *Women in Early Imperial China.* Lanham, MD: Rowman and Littlefield.

Honig, Emily. 1986. *Sisters and Strangers: Women in the Shanghai Cotton Mills, 1919–1949.* Stanford: Stanford University Press.

Honig, Emily, and Gail Hershatter (eds.). 1988. *Personal Voices: Chinese Women in the 1980s.* Stanford: Stanford University Press.

Hsiung, Ping-Chun, Maria Jaschok, and Cecilia Milwertz, with Red Chan (eds.). 2001. *Chinese Women Organizing: Cadres, Feminists, Muslims, Queers.* Oxford: Berg.

Huang, Philip. 1990. *The Peasant Family and Rural Development in the Yangzi Delta, 1350–1980.* Stanford: Stanford University Press.

Huang Shu-min. 1989. *The Spiral Road: Change in a Chinese Village Through the Eyes of a Communist Party Leader.* Boulder: Westview Press.

Jacka, Tamara. 1997. *Women's Work in Rural China: Change and Continuity in an Era of Reform.* Cambridge: Cambridge University Press.

Jaschok, Maria. 1988. *Concubines and Bondservants: A Social History.* London: Zed Books.

Jaschok, Maria, and Suzanne Miers (eds.). 1994. *Women and Chinese Patriarchy: Submission, Servitude, and Escape.* London: Zed Books.

Johnson, Kay Ann. 1983. *Women, the Family, and Peasant Revolution in China.* Chicago: University of Chicago Press.

————. 1996. "The Politics of the Revival of Infant Abandonment in China, with Special Reference to Hunan." *Population and Development Review* 22(1):77–98.

Judd, Ellen. 1994a. "Alternative Development Strategies for Women in Rural China." Pp. 204–222 in Huguette Dagenais and Denise Piché (eds.), *Femmes, feminisme, et developpement* [Women, feminism, and development]. Montreal: McGill-Queens University Press.

————. 1994b. *Gender and Power in Rural North China.* Cambridge: Cambridge University Press.

————. 2002. *The Chinese Women's Movement: Between State and Market.* Stanford: Stanford University Press.

Kantor, Rosabeth Moss. 1977. *Men and Women of the Corporation.* New York: Basic Books.

Ko, Dorothy. 1994. *Teachers of the Inner Chambers: Women and Culture in Seventeenth-Century China.* Stanford: Stanford University Press.

Ladany, Laszlo. 1992. *Law and Legality in China: The Testament of a China-Watcher.* London: Hurst.

Li, Xiaojiang. 1995. "Economic Reform and the Awakening of Chinese Women's Collective Consciousness." Pp. 360–382 in Christina Gilmartin, Gail Hershatter, Lisa Rofel, and Tyrene White (eds.), *Engendering China: Women, Culture, and the State.* Cambridge: Harvard University Press.

Mann, Susan. 1991. "Grooming a Daughter for Marriage: Brides and Wives in the Mid-Ch'ing Period." Pp. 204–230 in Rubie Watson and Patricia Buckley Ebrey (eds.), *Marriage and Inequality in Chinese Society.* Berkeley: University of California Press.

———. 1994. "Learned Women in the Eighteenth Century." Pp. 27–46 in Christina Gilmartin, Gail Hershatter, Lisa Rofel, and Tyrene White (eds.), *Engendering China: Women, Culture, and the State.* Cambridge: Harvard University Press.

———. 1997. *Precious Records: Women in China's Long Eighteenth Century.* Stanford: Stanford University Press.

Mao Zedong. 1990. *Report from Xunwu.* Translation and introduction by Roger Thompson. Stanford: Stanford University Press.

Momsen, Janet Henshall. 1991. *Women and Development in the Third World.* London and New York: Routledge.

Ogden, Susan. 1995. *China's Unresolved Issues: Politics, Development, and Culture.* 3rd ed. Englewood Cliffs: Prentice-Hall.

Ono, Kazuko. 1989. *Chinese Women in a Century of Revolution, 1850–1950.* Stanford: Stanford University Press.

Pasternak, Burton. 1985. "On the Causes and Demographic Consequences of Uxorilocal Marriage in China." Pp. 309–334 in Susan Hanley and Arthur Wolf (eds.), *History and Population in East Asia.* Stanford: Stanford University Press.

Perry, Elizabeth J. 1980. *Rebels and Revolutionaries in North China, 1845–1945.* Stanford: Stanford University Press.

Potter, Sulamith, and Jack Potter. 1990. *China's Peasants: The Anthropology of a Revolution.* Cambridge: Cambridge University Press.

Pruitt, Ida. 1967 [1945]. *A Daughter of Han: The Autobiography of a Chinese Working Woman.* Stanford: Stanford University Press.

Rosen, Stanley. 1995. "Women and Political Participation in China." *Pacific Affairs* 63(3):315–341.

Sankar, Andrea. 1984. "Spinster Sisterhoods." Pp. 52–70 in Mary Sheridan and Janet Salaff (eds.), *Lives: Chinese Working Women.* Bloomington: University of Indiana Press.

Sen, Amartya. 1994. "Population, Delusion, and Reality." *New York Review of Books,* September 22, pp. 62–71.

Shih, James. 1992. *Chinese Rural Society in Transition: A Case Study of the Lake Tai Area, 1368–1800.* Berkeley: Institute of East Asian Studies.

Silbur, Cathy. 1994. "From Daughter to Daughter-in-Law in the Women's Script of Southern Hunan." Pp. 47–68 in Christine Gilmartin, Gail Hershatter, Lisa Rofel, and Tyrene White (eds.), *Engendering China: Women, Culture, and the State.* Cambridge: Harvard University Press.

Smith, Christopher. 1990. *China: People and Places in the Land of One Billion.* Boulder: Westview Press.

Spence, Jonathan. 1999. *The Search for Modern China.* New York: W. W. Norton.

Stacey, Judith. 1983. *Patriarchy and Socialist Revolution in China.* Berkeley: University of California Press.

Stockard, Janice. 1989. *Daughters of the Canton Delta: Marriage Patterns and Economic Strategies in South China, 1860–1930.* Stanford: Stanford University Press.

T'ien, Ju-kang. 1988. *Male Anxiety and Female Chastity: A Comparative Study of Chinese Ethical Values in Ming-Ch'ing Times.* Leiden: E. J. Brill.

Topley, Marjorie. 1975. "Marriage Resistance in Rural Kwangtung." Pp. 247–268 in Margery Wolf and Roxanne Witke (eds.), *Women in Chinese Society.* Stanford: Stanford University Press.

Tung, Jowen R. 2000. *Fables of the Patriarchs: Gender Politics in Tang Discourse.* Lanham, MD: Rowman and Littlefield.

UNDP (United Nations Development Programme). 1994. *Human Development Report 1994.* New York: Oxford University Press.

Von Eschen, Kristin. 2000. "A Green Light for the Geti: The Divergent Experiences of Reform-Era China's Male and Female Private Entrepreneurs." M.A. thesis, Department of Anthropology, McGill University.

Wang, Zheng. 1993. "Three Interviews: Wang Anyi, Zhu Lin, Dai Qing." Pp. 159–208 in Tani Barlow (ed.), *Gender Politics in Modern China.* Durham, NC: Duke University Press.

Watson, James. 1976. "Chattel Slavery in Chinese Peasant Society: A Comparative Analysis." *Ethnology* 15:361–375.

Watson, Rubie. 1994. "Girls' Houses and Working Women: Expressive Culture in the Pearl River Delta, 1900–41." Pp. 25–44 in Maria Jaschok and Suzanne Miers (eds.), *Women and Chinese Patriarchy: Submission, Servitude, and Escape.* London: Zed Books.

Watson, Rubie, and Patricia B. Ebrey (eds.). 1991. *Marriage and Inequality in Chinese Society.* Berkeley: University of California Press.

Whyte, Martin King, and William L. Parish. 1984. *Urban Life in Contemporary China.* Chicago: University of Chicago Press.

Wolf, Arthur, and Huang Chieh-shan. 1980. *Marriage and Adoption in China, 1845–1945.* Stanford: Stanford University Press.

Wolf, Margery. 1985. *Revolution Postponed: Women in Contemporary China.* Stanford: Stanford University Press.

Wong, Jan. 1996. *Red China Blues: My Long March from Mao to Now.* Toronto: Doubleday.

Woo, Margaret Y. 1994. "Chinese Women Workers: The Delicate Balance Between Protection and Equality." Pp. 279–295 in Cristina Gilmartin, Gail Hershatter, Lisa Rofel, and Tyrene White (eds.), *Engendering China: Women, Culture, and State.* Cambridge: Harvard University Press.

Woon, Yuen-fong. 1990. "From Mao to Deng: Life Satisfaction Among Rural Women in an Emigrant Community in South China." *Australian Journal of Chinese Affairs* 25:139–169.

Yan, Yunxiang. 1996. *The Flow of Gifts: Reciprocity and Social Networks in a Chinese Village.* Stanford: Stanford University Press.

Zhang, Li. 2001. *Strangers in the City: Reconfigurations of Space, Power, and Social Networks Within China's Floating Population.* Stanford: Stanford University Press.

Zhang, Naihua, with Xu Wu. 1995. "Discovering the Positive Within the Negative: The Women's Movement in a Changing China." Pp. 25–57 in Amrita Basu (ed.), *The Challenge of Local Feminisms: Women's Movements in Global Perspective.* Boulder: Westview Press.

Zhongguo renkou tongji nianjian [China population statistics yearbook]. 1995. Comp.
Guojia Tongjiju [National Statistics Bureau] and Renkou Yu Jiuye Tongjiju [Population and Employment Statistics Bureau]. Beijing: Zhongguo Tongji Chubanshe [China Statistical Publishing House].

Zhou, Kate Xiao. 1996. *How the Farmers Changed China: Power of the People.* Boulder: Westview Press.

Zhu, Hong. 1994. "Women, Illness, and Hospitalization: Images of Women in Contemporary Chinese Fiction." Pp. 318–338 in Christina Gilmartin, Gail Hershatter, Lisa Rofel, and Tyrene White (eds.), *Engendering China: Women, Culture, and the State.* Cambridge: Harvard University Press.

Religion

Chan Hoiman and Ambrose Y. C. King

hinese religion is not a subject that can be approached in any straightfor-ward or uncontroversial manner. Chinese society and culture were rarely if at all dominated by any state religion or an associated order of church and priesthood worshiping a supreme godhead; yet its religious orders have generally been dominated by the state, and the state has been operated in accordance with religious precepts. The social order of the Chinese people has long been permeated by ritual practices with clear supernatural overtones, giving propitiatory ritual offerings to ancestors or idols; yet Chinese have seldom belonged to organized religious bodies. Scholars can therefore alternatively maintain that the Chinese are not a very religious people at all and that they are permeated with superstition of a magical, "prereligious" kind. Chinese scholars of a "New Confucian" bent retort that Chinese culture is verily "beyond belief," with spiritual reaches and depths that cannot be contained within the usual institutional or intellectual frameworks of religions. Even at the end of the nineteenth century, the missionary scholar Arthur Smith would still characterize the religious life of the Chinese people as simultaneously "pantheistic, polytheistic, and atheistic" (1894:chap. 26).

Scholars have taken many approaches to the study of China's religions. In the late nineteenth century, the great German sociologist Max Weber (1864–1920), undertook his famous study of China's religion (1964 [1922]) as part of his much broader examination of capitalism and comparative civilizations, approaching Chinese civilization from the perspective of two major "homegrown" religions, Confucianism and Daoism. He sought to demonstrate that the social structure of China contained components that can contribute to the growth of capitalism. But Confucian orthodoxy emphasized above all a "rational adaptation" to secular life, generating in the people a traditionalist and conservative propensity that became the decisive obstacle to the growth of aggressive modern capitalism. Daoism gave people some outlet from this conformity by promoting personal values, which also did not support capitalism. The so-called Weber thesis on Confucianism and the underdevelopment of capitalism in China has since become the subject of heated scholarly debates.

The Dutch sinologist Jan de Groot (1854–1921) conceived the ambitious vision of a comprehensive and detailed study of Chinese religion, which was published three decades earlier (1972 [1892]) than Weber's work. He was interested in Chinese religion as laid out in textual canons and as actually practiced in the religious life of the people. He richly detailed such topics as "the burial of the dead," "ancestor worship," and other ritual practices and advocated China's religion as a field of scientific study (Freedman, 1979).

Coming to the field a generation later than either Weber or de Groot and following Emile Durkheim's quest to unravel the "collective consciousness," Marcel Granet's seminal work (1975 [1922]) suggested that in China "peasant religion" was the foundation of the religion of the literary class—a point Charles Laughlin makes about China's whole literary tradition in Chapter 13. Granet (1884–1940) looked to archaic history for the "essence" of Chinese religion. Later an urban populace would develop a "feudal religion," and kings created an "official religion" to support their sovereignty. All this subsequently diversified into specific religious currents or doctrines.

More recently, a U.S. sociologist of Chinese descent, C. K. Yang, noted the contrast between "institutional" and "diffused" religions: "Institutional religion functions independently as a separate system, while diffused religion functions as a part of the secular social institutions" (1991:295). This basic distinction may be employed in addressing some of the alternative explanations we mentioned in the opening paragraph. Confucianism, by and large a diffused religion, functions through such secular institutions as the state, the family, and the education system. Only in the cases of Buddhism (imported from India) and, to a lesser extent, Daoism, can one speak of proper institutional religion with its monastic order and specialized priesthood. Diffused religion is inevitably a less powerful form of religiosity, merely providing spiritual rationale to secular institutions. Yang concluded that though Chinese religions were rich and dynamic on the surface, they were at heart restricted.

In this chapter, we want to give you an overview of how China's religions evolved and how they cover both the spiritual and the secular realms of life. We shall examine the development of China's religions in terms of the interplay between diversity and syncretism—how religious streams alternatively diversified and converged in China's history. At each stage in the unfolding of the Chinese religious universe, new impetus and horizons were opened up and then reconciled with existing beliefs. From this perspective, the development of Chinese religion remains an ongoing story, an ebb and flow between diversity and syncretism. We are suggesting that China has experienced three great historical periods or configurations of divergence and syncretism, when competing rites and doctrines (some "institutional" and some "diffused," in Yang's terminology) were juxtaposed and reconciled. The resulting syncretism, in time, would be broken up by the introduction of yet other beliefs. Those three historical configurations are summarized in Table 12.1. As you can see, the table leaves us with a question. The first coming together of diverse religious streams began to take place in the twelfth century B.C.E. The second began in the third century B.C.E., and the third in the tenth century C.E. As we approach the twenty-first century C.E., is a fourth syncretism emerging?

■ First Configuration: The Rise of Humanistic Religion

We begin with the legendary, Neolithic origins of Chinese religion. Marcel Granet would readily point out that much that is unique about the orientation of China's religion can be traced to that era. And Hans Kung and Julia Ching (1989) maintain that elements of those ancient beliefs and cults persist even to this date, still retaining their archaic, primitive mode.

As Table 12.1 indicates, ancient Chinese religious beliefs go back at least to the Neolithic and Bronze Ages and were widely practiced during the first, archaic dynasties in classical China (Eliade, 1982:3–6; Wang, 2000). During the Zhou dynasty, between 1122 and 256 B.C.E., they merged with some new ideas in a syncretic reconciliation of beliefs. The archaic gestation period of Chinese religion shared traits of primitive religions elsewhere. People became aware of and curious about nature and made crude, halting attempts to justify human social life on the basis of larger-than-life forces and ideas; especially relevant for the case of China were aspects of totemism, animism, and occultism.

Table 12.1 Development of Chinese Religions

First configuration (to 256 B.C.E.)	Ancient cults (2000–1123 B.C.E.): totemism, animism, occultism.
	Zhou syncretism (1122–256 B.C.E.): The rise of humanistic religion.
Second configuration (to C.E. 220)	Axial diversification (772–481 B.C.E.): Confucianism, Daoism, the Yin-Yang school.
	Han syncretism (206 B.C.E.–C.E. 220): The canonization of Confucianism.
Third configuration (to C.E. 1279)	Foreign impetus (1): Indian Buddhism, Near Eastern Nestorianism, Manichaeanism.
	Song syncretism (C.E. 906–1279): The rise of neo-Confucianism.
Fourth configuration (to C.E. 2003)	Foreign impetus (2): Christianity.
	Marxism-Maoism as antireligion.
	Toward a new syncretism?

▪ Totemism

Totemism is a familiar elementary form of religious belief, identifying human groups with species of animals, birds, or even plants from which they presumably descended. A group sharing the same totemic ancestor bonded together for community and warfare against groups sharing other totems. Scholars like Emile Durkheim and Claude Lévi-Strauss point out that this classificatory system based on common descent of a group from the same mythic animal, bird, or imaginary monster helped set people apart in their own minds from other groups sharing a different totem, providing them with a rich sense of prehistoric genesis based on legend. The proliferation of totemic groups generated dynamics of war and alliance. The first step toward a unified Chinese culture was allegedly achieved when the mythical Huang Di (the Yellow Emperor) fostered a federation of totemic groups powerful enough to sustain control over what became the heartland of China (Chang, Yu, and Ch'un, 1998). Down to the times of the Xia, Shang, and Zhou (see Table 3.1), the ruling dynasties and the kings were mainly the great chiefs who held the totemic alliances together. The passage into history took place at the point when totemic alliances were formalized into government and totemic groups became clans. Even today, Chinese often designate themselves "descendants of dragons," if not because they actually believe in it, at least because they still want to.

▪ Animism

Animism forms the other major strand of ancient Chinese beliefs. Again, it is a mentality widely shared among peoples of the ancient world. Animism is belief in the omnipresence of spirits, that other living creatures and even inanimate objects or phenomena also possess spiritual essences that can impact the lives of humans. It is usually regarded by anthropologists as the most basic form of religious belief, based on the inability to distinguish between objective reality and the fantasy world of spirits. Yet as the case of China demonstrates, animism can far outlive its ancient origins. Animism is well documented in the archaeological finds of the Shang dynasty, mainly in sacrificial inscriptions on tortoise shells and animal bones (Keightley, 1978). These inscriptions indicate that people believed in and made offerings to spirits of natural phenomena like thunder and rain, of natural objects like mountains and river, of beasts and birds, and especially of deceased humans. Many of these practices were to continue in the folk religions of China in later times.

▪ Occultism

Occultism is closely connected with animism and concerns how the supernatural influence of spirits can be detected or even changed for human purposes. In the mind of believers, spirits were usually given form and character closely resembling human beings and shared our temperaments as well. It is therefore logical to assume that human beings can communicate with these spirits and in the process perhaps take advantage of their power. This may be achieved by specialized religious personnel obtaining blessings from these spirits and foretelling the future through their power. And in archaic China, these religious personnel often held political roles as well, serving as the foundation of kingship (Ching, 1997). The Shang dynasty indulged extensively in occultist practice and also embraced the notion of the supreme lord *(di)*, the personified supernatural overlord of all beings, toward whom acts of offerings and divination were ultimately directed (Eliade, 1985:7–9). The worship of *di* can be interpreted in a polytheistic mode, where the all-powerful *di* presided over the spiritual pantheon of the animistic world and answered to the pleadings and inquiries of the people.

The three themes of totemism, animism, and occultism formed the religious scaffolding of remote, archaic China. In the passage from the Xia and Shang dynasties into the Zhou dynasty—and from prehistory into documented history—two important strands of prehistoric beliefs would be assimilated into and continued in the religion of Zhou. These beliefs were the worship of heaven *(tian)* on the one hand and ancestral worship on the other. Both of these motifs were to exert heavy influences on the religious life of China to come. The worship of *tian* is essentially the depersonalized version of the former worship of *di.* In the transition from Shang into Zhou, the personified supreme deity of *di* was to be gradually metamorphosed into an impersonal, transcendental force. Although this ultimate force was no longer cast in a humanized mode, it nonetheless had purpose and direction. Comprehending and abiding by the will and mandate of heaven *(tianming)* would be among the key religious principles in Chinese culture, as discussed in Chapters 3 and 4 (Loewe, 1986; Shahar and Weller, 1996). And the worship of *tian* would in later days converge with the imperatives of the *dao* (the way), whether defined in Confucian, Daoist, or Yin-Yang terms. As for ancestral worship, this is a heritage from totemism for which China has become particularly famous. It makes little difference that the early totemic ancestors were mainly legendary animals or even hybrids; they kindled a religious sentiment that constantly beckoned to the ancestral fountainhead, which would continue to oversee the conduct and welfare of the latter-day descendants. The impersonal, immutable *tian* and the highly personal, affectionate ancestors *(zu)* would form the two essential axes of supernatural beliefs, handed down as they were from the prehistoric past first to the Zhou civilization and in turn to Chinese culture as a whole.

■ Zhou Syncretism and Humanistic Religion

During the Zhou dynasty, these beliefs were assimilated and consolidated, especially in the Western Zhou. The individual traditions did not disappear; but society and scholars drew together important elements from all of them to bolster secular institutions along with religious ideas and practices (Eliade, 1982:9–13; Gotshalk, 1999b). Divination and other animistic, magical practices continued (also discussed in Chapter 13); but at the same time, thinkers and religious practitioners combined them with other religious traditions, picking what seemed best from each to form a new body of doctrines and rituals. It was truly a syncretism—a generally contrived, strained sense of integration that would last for a few centuries and finally begin to fall apart under that strain. Then new diverse religious strands would unravel, to be brought back together in a second syncretism, discussed below. This is how China's religious traditions have evolved amid the diversity and immensity of the Chinese religious universe—an interplay of unity and difference.

The Zhou syncretism emerged because, after a long prehistoric childhood, Chinese society had reached a stocktaking threshold requiring a more stable and "rational" framework of social life. As explained in Chapter 3, the Zhou people of the west toppled the Shang dynasty, which had grown corrupt and obsolete. They sought to create the underpinnings of a new social order. Although construction of the Zhou order was generally accredited to the Duke of Zhou, the younger brother of the founding emperor, it must also be seen as a product of its time (cf. Creel, 1970).

The Duke of Zhou presided over construction of a strong program of humanism, centering primarily around humanistic interests and ideals, that was to permeate all subsequent evolution of the Chinese religious world. The personified godhead of *di*—the closest that China ever came to professing a supreme, monotheistic deity—became the abstract, ramified force of *tian* and of nature, no longer intervening directly in the mundane details of social life. *Tian* was a "hidden god." Although *tian* and nature had purpose and will, they were part of bigger cosmic dynamics that had no use for divine design or intervention. And if human affairs must nonetheless abide by heavenly principles, they do so mainly for the sake of harmony and felicity in social life. In this way then, the rise of Zhou humanism signified an essential new twist in the religious consciousness of the Chinese, in which both the sacred and the profane derived their defining meanings from within the concrete operation of the secular, human world (Nakamura, 1964:chap. 15). This would be the all-important leitmotiv that both Confucianism and Daoism took up in later times.

Starting with this basic propensity toward a humanistic religion, Zhou syncretism placed dual emphases on rites and ethics that (in the absence of divine decrees) together set the standard of proper behavior. The notion of, and the word for, "rite" *(li)* had its origin in the archaic ritual of making offerings to the gods. People were instructed to participate in rites with sincerity and care, just as their ancestors had done when worshiping their pantheon of animistic spirits and *di,* the mandate of gods and heaven. In addition, practice of rite evolved into social institutions and ideological doctrines. Rite as social institution defined proper behavior in different social occasions—celebrations, initiations, mourning, interaction, and so on. Rites would shape the elementary social structure of the community, visually demonstrating the sovereignty and power of the rulers and the rights and responsibilities of different social roles. Philosophical and ideological frameworks justified and codified the practice of rites, ensuring their continuity even beyond the reign of Zhou. That codification was partly recorded in the canonical *Book of Rites,* the compilations of ancient documents broadly related to this movement.

In lieu of divine decrees, the intellectual foundation of *li*—and of Zhou humanism in general—was primarily ethical in character. At the heart of this ethic was the use of blood ties and kinship dynamics as the foundation of values and standards of social relationship. In the absence of divine ordinance, blood ties were to become the most sacred organizing principle of society. The Zhou dynasty presided over a feudal social order, with peasants bonded to the estates of noblemen. Feudalism was founded upon the lineage rule *(zhongfa)* system, which determined rights and duties on the basis of blood ties. This *zhongfa* system also prescribed the distribution and inheritance of family resources from one generation to another. It raised familial and filial values into "social absolutes," serving as the ethical cum sacred foundation of Zhou humanism.

Instead of following a more familiar pattern of religious movement from animism into polytheism and then into monotheistic religion, Zhou syncretism generally sought to break with theistic religion altogether. Henceforth, the "great tradition" of Chinese religion would be characterized above all by what Max Weber called "this-worldly religion"—religious beliefs having little to do with transcendental order and divine godheads (Weber, 1964:1–3). Already in the time of Zhou, an "enlightened" outlook had developed, affirming the primacy and autonomy of humanity as the sole source of both existential enigma and fulfillment and asserting that humanity remains truly autonomous only when ritually bonded to the community and its rulers. Thus the rise of Zhou syncretism set the distinct temperament of Chinese religious beliefs, marking the master trend that later stages continued to deepen and enrich but never did abandon or supersede.

■ Second Configuration: The Axial Age and the Rise of Confucianism

During later centuries, the Zhou syncretism broke down and contending schools of thought emerged. This lively stage of development, when such prominent schools as Confucianism and Daoism came into existence, is by far the most celebrated among observers. Beginning around 1000 B.C.E., India,

Greece, Mesopotamia, and China all experienced major advances in their civ-ilizations, independently of one another; scholars think of these civilizations as occupying several parallel lines or planes, each serving as axis to subse-quent progress of their civilizations, and call this period the "axial" age (see Chang, 1990; Roetz, 1993). In China these advances occurred during the so-called Spring and Autumn Period and Warring States Period and extended into the short-lived Qin dynasty (see Table 3.1). The Han dynasty would then seek a synthesis among these contending schools (Loewe, 1994). This second syn-cretism, building upon but moving beyond the first syncretism created earlier in the Zhou dynasty, stands unmistakably at the heart of cultural China. Even to this day, Chinese culture is identified as Han.

First we will focus on three schools among the many contending during the axial age: Confucianism, Daoism, and Yin-Yang. Then we will examine how the Yin-Yang cosmological framework was deployed as the scaffolding upon which Confucianism and Daoism acquired tenuous syncretic unity dur-ing the Han dynasty.

■ Confucianism

Confucius lived from 551 to 479 B.C.E. (see Table 3.1). He sought a return to the humanist emphasis on rites and ethics found in the earlier Zhou syn-cretism (Strathern, 1999; Yao, 2000). His, too, is essentially a "secular reli-gion," founded upon beliefs about proprieties of human conduct: social val-ues, social practice, and the image of the ideal person. In society and the individual, the ultimate ends of life coincide with the worldliness of the mun-dane here and now (see Fingarette, 1972; Strathern, 1999; Yao, 2000).

The social values associated with Confucianism center around the cardi-nal notion of *ren,* rendered variously by sinologists as "benevolence," "humaneness," and "compassion." In the *Analects*—the record of Confucius's teachings—*ren* is made the foundation of social life (Brooks and Brooks, 1998; Confucius, 1998). Divine authority should be respected but is generally irrelevant. *Ren* literally means "two persons"; it is not just a set of ethical rules but an inalienable inner necessity, a moral imperative for human personal and social existence. It cannot be approached as an individualistic ethic because human nature itself is inherently social; social interaction and relations between men will take priority over personal interest and experience. We have an innate moral mandate to show affection, sympathy, compassion, and benevolence toward our fellow humans by conforming to specific conven-tions of social behavior. Instinctive consciousness of that mandate sets humanity apart from other living beings. The value and goodness of *ren* is not something that should be validated by reason or logic. *Ren* is both higher and deeper than the mere exercise of intellect. In the end, mutual affection and sympathy—emotional bonds—best validate and vindicate its primacy. The individuals who exemplify these ideals by properly performing rites and social conventions are literally defining who they are, demonstrating their humanity.

The celebrated Confucian obsession with *li* (ritual and propriety) can be properly appreciated against this backdrop (Eliade, 1982:22–25). The elaborate and meticulous rituals governing social interaction are the practical articulation of the cherished ideal of *ren*—personal actors defining their own worth by the collective sentiment they show toward social solidarity (cf. Eno, 1990). Art, literature, and moral discourse must help individuals cultivate these social proprieties.

The Confucian distinction between gentleman *(junzi)* and commoner *(xiaoren)* also becomes clear in this context. Although achieving the remote ideal of becoming a Confucian sage is beyond the reach of most mortals, true followers of Confucianism can hope to become *junzi*—someone who desires and is far advanced in the attainment and practical pursuit of *ren*. A gentleman is not merely someone generally righteous, honest, and knowledgeable. These well-accepted virtues must be assessed and related in terms of the core value of *ren;* a true Confucian gentleman is not motivated to attain individual success or precious assets but rather shows his benevolence to others by practicing the social rituals with propriety. In contrast, the *xiaoren* (literally, "small-minded men") are imperfect in attaining *ren,* or humanity. The *xiaoren* is the direct opposite of the *junzi* not because he is perhaps evil-minded or dishonest, but mainly because he is only concerned with his own interest and private desire. At their worst, such individuals ignore the cardinal value of *ren* by expressing frustration and social discontent; at their best, they show their respect for it by giving special deference to *junzi*. (See Chapter 4 for more on the concrete interplay of these principles.) Confucianism intertwines ethics and religion to regulate social behavior. But it lacks a religious hierarchy to mandate its authority and is not inspired by divine authority from above, but rather by the inner benevolence of human nature itself (cf. Hall and Ames, 1987). Mo Tzu and Mencius, who lived shortly after Confucius, touch upon these ideas (Richards, 1996; Shun, 1997).

▩ Daoism

The other major indigenous religious tradition in China is Daoism, which (as indicated in Chapter 3) originated during the same period of axial diversification. The relation between Confucianism and Daoism is a contrast between orthodoxy and heterodoxy—a distinction made famous by Weber in his study of Chinese religion. Although Confucianism pertains overwhelmingly to the social aspects of human life, Daoism pertains more to nature and the individual (Rickett, 1998). Although Confucianism gives primacy to asserting and striving for social values, Daoism gives primacy to tactically avoiding these allegedly superficial pursuits. Daoism rose as a contrasting parameter to assert the values that Confucianism neglected. It was permissible and common for people to take on both Confucian and Daoist outlooks, letting each fill the void left by the other. The two together broadly demarcate the field of diversification in the axial age.

Standing at the heart of Daoism is the concept of *dao,* which can variously be understood as "the principle," "the way," and "the word" (Waley, 1988; Ames, Hall, and Bernstein, 2003). Thus, *dao* can be regarded as a mode of behavioral tactics, specifying the principles that are most closely compatible with the dynamics of human and natural affairs (Clarke, 2000; Roth, 1999). Or *dao* is perceived in more philosophical rubrics as "the way," postulating the presence of a universal pattern or law that underlies the conduct of social and natural phenomena. And if *dao* is seen as "the word," it denotes the need for doctrines and codes to be formulated and espoused in words or utterances, for the articulation of the *dao.* These three aspects of the *dao* all revolve around the concept of virtue *(de),* suggesting that *dao* is by nature virtuous (Eliade, 1985:25–33). These multiple meanings explain why *dao* remains so much an enigma in Chinese thought, readily associated both with the crudest kind of magical practices and with philosophical enlightenment of a lofty order. As a metaphor or concept of truth, *dao* was commonly evoked even in doctrines outside Daoism. For example, the Confucian classics were replete with the use of the concept when discussing truth and its method, albeit with specific Confucian reference.

Whether according to Laozi (Lao Tzu, 2001) or Zhuangzi (Chuang Tzu, 1994, 1996; Mair, 1998), the two legendary founders of Daoism, the gist of *dao* lies not in human endeavor but rather in evading the futility of human endeavor. The universe is the totality of all being, generated from an unimaginable cosmic void, the omnipresent *dao. Dao* is emptiness, mystical and all-pervasive. The world derives from that emptiness. Humans can achieve a linkage with that emptiness by refraining from individual ambition and social activity and seeking oneness with *dao.*

The belief in *dao* naturally reinforces a passive attitude of retreat. Extreme Daoists preached a social doctrine calling for small social units, with minimal government structure and as little social interaction as possible. They saw the numerous moral values and ethical codes cherished by the Confucians as unwanted baggage; if social ties and interaction were avoided or minimized to begin with, most problems the Confucians set out to confront would not even exist. Resigning to the *dao* can create a very different kind of individual and social order.

Other Daoist schools believe that moving in accordance with the propensity and force of the *dao* would make the individual much more compatible and effective in the world, rather than in retreat from it. Correctly perceiving and abiding by the movement of *dao* actually strengthens one's potential and power. By this ironic twist, the passivity of Daoist tenets is transformed into tactical endeavor. This tempts one to channel the force of *dao*—by magical or physical means—to become a source of religious fulfillment. The tremendous hidden power of the *dao* can be manipulated to fulfill other personal needs as well. Practices such as macrobiotic diets and divination can be used to achieve such utilitarian ends. This utilitarian dimension receives prominence in the later development of Daoism. Its canonical doctrines emphasize a detached, spontaneous life attitude commensurate with the natural unfolding of the *dao,* even as one carries out social responsibilities. The institutional religion that came to surround these doctrines could point to utilitarian personal benefits to be gained from adhering to the religion—an effective way of persuading worldly believers.

▨ The Yin-Yang School

The axial age in China boasted the blossoming of "nine currents and ten schools" *(jiuliu sijia).* Among them, the Yin-Yang school is another current standing at the heart of religious formation in China, with important practical implications for both Confucianism and Daoism. The Yin-Yang school systematized some of the magical practices from earlier primitive religion. It is generally deemed less important than Confucianism and Daoism because it is less sophisticated, but it helped reconcile these more elaborate doctrines and became responsible for many of the more speculative, magical tenets of both Confucianism and Daoism (Schwartz, 1985).

Yin-Yang is represented graphically as the opposition and complementarity of light and darkness—expressing their inherent difference while suggesting that the essence of each is somehow related to that of the other. The polarity of Yin-Yang also underlined part of Confucianism and Daoism. In addition, this polarity may be viewed as an ancient articulation of what later came to be

Yin and Yang in harmony

known as binary thinking. The Yin-Yang dichotomy is the primordial impulse of classification—the very first act of intellectual classification that preceded all subsequent acts of intellectual operation. Other contrasts such as weak-strong, low-high, feminine-masculine, cold-hot, absorbing-penetrating, passive-active, darkness-light, earth-heaven, and so on, can be defined by their juxtaposition as opposites—the master framework of Yin-Yang—irrespective of their actual substance or referents.

Yet the Yin-Yang school took this to much greater extremes. The manifestation and transformation in any phenomenon can be charted and even foretold in accordance with the interplay of Yin-Yang dynamics. The entire universe can become unified and understood under sets of Yin-Yang-related principles or pseudo-theories. There are, for instance, the five elements *(wuxin)*, which referred to the constitutive elements of the material world—fire, water, wood, metal, and earth. Each of these elements has different associations along the spectrum of the Yin-Yang principle, forming a unique system of checks and balances, harmony and conflict, diversity and unity. In addition, the four directions, four seasons, stellar configurations, aspects of human virtues, and so forth, all attain similar cosmological and magical attributes that resonate above and beyond their natural and human forms (Schwartz, 1985:chap. 9). By weaving together a closed cosmology that attributes order to the world and a teleology that shows its design and ultimate ends, the Yin-Yang school developed its immense appeal. The Yin-Yang dynamics became, in effect, the articulation, perhaps even actualization, of both the elusive *tian* and *dao*—of heaven on high and the way of life on earth.

▓ Han Syncretism: The Canonization of Confucianism

The Spring and Autumn Period (771–476 B.C.E.), when Confucius, Laozi, and Zhuangzi lived, was the last phase of axial diversification before the breakdown of the Zhou dynasty. The nine currents and ten schools of thought flourishing during that era shared some common traits with roots in the earlier Zhou syncretism (Smith and Kwok, 1993). Such continuities led to the famous hypothesis that the diverse schools of the axial age all originated from the former imperial officials of the Zhou government. Like the preceding Zhou syncretism, none of these schools looked to a single divine being as the ultimate source of religious spirit. Magic, spirit, hybrids, and a metaphorical heaven were still regarded as normal parts of the world where humans live. And the cornerstone of Zhou humanism stayed in place, whether in the Confucian values of *ren* and *li,* the Daoist postulate of the all-pervasive *dao,* or the Yin-Yang resonance *(ganyin)* among humans, world, and cosmos.

In this light, the founding of the Han dynasty in 206 B.C.E. following the Qin unification of China acquired different levels of meaning. In terms of intellectual and religious development, the Han period became the second major movement of syncretism in Chinese religious thought. Unlike the epochal breakthrough in Zhou humanism, however, Han syncretism can boast of no similar fundamental innovation, at least not in intellectual terms. Han syncretism is significant mainly in its practical consequence for Chinese religion. It was during the consolidation of Han syncretism that Confucianism was first favored above all other competing doctrines, that the writings of classical Confucianism were canonized as the supreme source of authority. But this process brought into Confucianism important strands from those competing doctrines and provided ways for other religions to coexist with it (Kramers, 1986; Loewe, 1994).

Han syncretism elected an orthodoxy only subsequent to the consolidation of a variety of thought currents. The dynasty opened on a Daoist note when the second emperor of Han, Wendi, chose to adopt a more withdrawn, noninterventionist approach to state administration, so that the country could recover from the protracted war of unification under the first Han emperor, Gaozu. Yet he did not attempt to privilege Daoism above other doctrines. It was the great Wudi (reigning from 140 to 87 B.C.E.) who instituted the Five Confucian Classics as the official syllabus of education. Dong Zhongshu (179–104 B.C.E.), the intellectual architect of this movement, advocated "dismissing the hundred other schools in respect of Confucianism alone." Dong was simultaneously the great advocate of Confucianism and its formidable revisionist, drawing into it Daoist and Yin-Yang themes and traditions of folk religion and magical practices.

Dong sought to reconcile heaven *(tian)* and humanity *(ren)*. His formulation for this is *tianren ganyin*—resonance between heaven and humans. From this perspective, human and transcendental realities are intrinsically linked. A primarily humanistic approach like classical Confucianism, which focuses solely on humanity, is too simplistic. The Yin-Yang school saw *tian* as essentially unchangeable, overpowering forces. Dong sought to revise that passive view by reintroducing the notion of supernatural forces that would oversee the conduct of men. This element, while not entirely absent in classical Confucianism, was greatly amplified by the hand of Dong. Confucius's humanism was too abstract and impalpable for common individuals. By making *tian* once again a supreme will accessible to human supplications through the intervention of supernatural forces, Dong gave Confucianism greater popular appeal. Heaven does not intervene directly into human affairs, yet heaven is responsive to human conduct. Misdemeanors and crime, beyond a certain threshold of seriousness and scale, would trigger signs from heaven, usually in the form of natural disasters and mystical omens. So humanity can decipher the way of heaven and build a moral social order on its basis. The purpose of life is not just harmony and well-being but ultimately to attain a state of unity with heaven *(tianren heyi);* this ideal would make orthodox Confucianism more explicitly religious (Loewe, 1986; 1994:chap. 6).

The emperor Wudi accepted not only Dong's version of Confucianism but also the proposal that Confucianism should be honored above all other schools of thought and beliefs. In subsequent ages, the Han syncretism came to be known as *Hanxue* (Han learning). *Hanxue* represented the first major reworking of Confucianism, not only by Dong but also through extensive exegetical works on the Confucian canon by other Han scholars. The Han syncretism, however, proved problematic for later Confucians; it was revisionist in spirit yet meticulously preserved the classical heritage. The Han dynasty collapsed at the end of the second century C.E., but it left behind an established Confucian tradition.

■ Third Configuration: Foreign Impetus and Neo-Confucianism

The two syncretic stages configuring Chinese religion up to this point involved ideas and doctrines that may seem somewhat removed from the modern conception of religion. There was little by way of established religious institutions, worship of a specific deity, or the use of sacred texts for transcendental communication. Even magical practice and beliefs were found only among marginalized Daoist and Yin-Yang cults. Orthodox Confucianism never set up a priesthood or houses of worship. In contrast to other major world religions, Chinese religion did not seek immortality, inner ecstasy, or salvation for its adherents. Chinese religious development was to remain heavily intellectual, secular, and humanistic. The purest form of belief was ultimately in humanity as such, for all its virtues, follies, and possibilities. But the adherents of this belief could attain the same fervor, commitment, and faith common to all religious traditions.

The next two configurations of religious development in China would be more complicated and colorful. Though the humanism persisted, it was subjected to searching challenges, the latest episode of which is still happening today. These challenges came largely from outside, in the form of foreign religious traditions that either sought to take root in China on their own or sought to trigger transformations of the Chinese religions from within (Demieville, 1986). The religions involved are Buddhism from India, the three religions of Abraham from Europe and the Near East, and finally Marxism-Maoism, which figured as yet another thought system of heavy humanistic-religious bent.

▩ Indian Buddhism

The great religious event dominating China's cultural landscape while Europe was experiencing its "Dark Ages" and medieval period was the introduction and expansion of Buddhism (de Bary, 1988:chap. 2; Chen, 1964). From that time forward, the tripartite epithet of Confucianism-Buddhism-Daoism *(ru-xi-dao)* would become the standard litany describing Chinese religion. In other words, Buddhism was the only foreign religion that has successfully taken root in China and exerted sweeping cultural and intellectual influence on mainstream religious belief. Buddhism is a highly institutionalized religion, with its own elaborate miscellany of sects and monastic orders, specialized personnel, institutional discipline, and theological doctrines. In contrast, Confucianism maintained a much more secular, moralistic outlook, precisely in its attempt not to separate social and sacred lives. And Daoism was largely split between its intellectual and institutional facade, with the Daoist institutions catering above all to the more magical, witchcraft-inclined aspects of religious life, whereas the loftier side of Daoist philosophy remained in the domain of intellectuals. Buddhism was the only "all-round" religion in traditional China, encompassing the full range of religious sentiment, forms, and levels of thought (Wright, 1977).

Buddhism seeks to "take flight" from the world, which allegedly only brings human suffering. It adopts a passive posture not unlike that of Daoism but seeks to extend this to its logical extreme, renouncing individual consciousness and cravings so as to better perceive the ontological abyss of nothingness *(sunya* in Sanskrit, *kung* in Chinese). Buddhism added new dimensions to indigenous Chinese religions.

Historically, Buddhism is another product of the world axial breakthrough, established in India around 600 B.C.E. by Siddhartha Gautama of the Sakya clan, who became Sakyamuni ("the sage of the sakyas," 1993). Modern scholarship has come to the broad consensus that the earliest documented arrival in China of Buddhists and their canon was during the early Han dynasty (see Table 3.1). Although Buddhism had practically no role to play in Han syncretism, it was during the Han dynasty that institutional support for Buddhism was first secured—royal sponsorship, monasteries in the capital city, the beginning of scriptural translation, and so forth (Tsai, 1994). And into the late Han and the subsequent era of political instability, Buddhism would greatly expand its influence, taking on first Daoism and then Confucianism to become a major religio-cultural force by the time of the Song dynasty (C.E. 960–1279), the other great era of syncretism in traditional China (Chen, 1964; Gernet, 1998 [1956]; Tsai, 1994; Weinstein, 1987). Buddhism became assimilated as an indigenous part of Chinese religious traditions via a twofold process: the translation of concepts and the search for original texts and developments of sects.

The initial assimilation of Buddhism was greatly facilitated by emphasizing facile similarity and overlap between Buddhism and the indigenous Daoist doctrine. This strategy was formally known as "matching of meanings" *(keyi)*. The broad application of *keyi* served two purposes. On the one

One of the seated
Buddhas carved into
Feilai Teng, "the Peak
which flew over from
India," a hill outside
Hangzhou, Zhejiang

Robert Gamer

hand, it secured acceptance and even popularity for Buddhism without significant resistance from the Chinese populace. On the other hand, and more important, the method also ensured that Buddhism would soon shed its Indian outlook and become assimilated into the Chinese religious world—truly achieving *keyi* as a method of cross-cultural communication.

Keyi refers to the practice of translating Indian Buddhist concepts into Daoist categories, a method pioneered by Faya, a fourth-century Chinese monk. *Keyi* could range from translating particular concepts, like the Sanskrit *sunya* (emptiness) into the Daoist *wu* (nothingness) or Buddha into the Daoist *shensen* (deities), all the way to systematically rendering entire sutras (Buddhist classics) into Daoist idiom and analogy, even annotating sutras with Daoist classics. The worth of Buddhism was measured by its ability to hold its own in debates on Chinese culture and scholarship. During the four divisive centuries of post-Han China, many of the well-known Buddhist monks and masters earned their celebrity by demonstrating unexpected depths and insights in Daoist learning. In outsmarting the Daoist-leaning Confucian scholar-officials of the time—during sessions of idle talk *(qingtan)*—famous monks like Daoan and Huiyuan gained respect and footing for Buddhism. *Keyi* would go a long way in transforming the foreign outlook of Buddhism into what would soon be regarded as properly Chinese.

The height of Buddhist influence came during the influential, unified Tang dynasty (C.E. 618–907). An imperial census of Buddhist communities counted 260,000 monks and nuns, 4,600 temples, and some 40,000 shrines altogether. Each temple and shrine owned land and other properties donated by believers, giving them great social and economic prominence. Clashes with local authorities and indigenous beliefs resulted in repression. This census, in fact, was compiled as a database for the short-lived official suppression of Buddhism in C.E. 845. During episodes of official repression, most temples and shrines were destroyed, their land confiscated, and their monks secularized (Chen, 1964:chap. 8).

During the Tang, Chinese Buddhism developed along two fronts—the accelerated assimilation of Indian Buddhism and the growth of native Buddhist sects (Weinstein, 1987). Famous Buddhist pilgrims went to India to systematically study Buddhist sutras and treatises *(lun)*. Moving beyond *keyi,* they felt compelled to explore these works at their source, taking on Indian Buddhism in its own terms. The most famous pilgrims were Yijing, Faxian, and especially the towering figure of Xuan Zang, who has become a rich source of inspiration and contribution not only to Buddhism but to Chinese culture in general (Wriggins, 1996). Xuan Zang left China for India in C.E. 629 and did not return until C.E. 645. During that time, he also visited Sri Lanka. He brought back a great number of original Sanskrit texts and spent the rest of his life rendering them into Chinese, a task continued by his disciples after his death. His is the best-known example of a Chinese pilgrimage seeking a more authentic understanding of religion in the world outside; Chapter 13 discusses Xuan Zang further. This enterprise of scriptural translation would be among the most significant, catalytic events in the growth of Chinese Buddhism (Tung, 2001).

Formation of Chinese Buddhism in the Tang divided into two streams: "the three sects under the creed" *(jiaoxia sanzong)* and the "alternative teaching outside the creed" *(jiaowai biequan).* The three sects were the more mainstream Tiantai, Huayen, and Faxian (Cleary, 1983; Gimello and Gregory, 1983). The alternative teaching refers to the highly unique and controversial development of Zen Buddhism (Lin-chi, 1999; Broughton, 1999; Faure, 1995). Both streams sought to reconcile Indian Buddhism with Chinese sociocultural conditions and in that process contributed significant progress to Buddhism at large. The three sects focused especially on doctrines that implored people to treat their fellow humans properly and embark on various stages of enlightenment, by way of compassionate deeds to help others lead a better earthly life and to start their own paths toward enlightenment (Bocking, 1995). Zen Buddhism, both in its moderate *(jian)* or radical *(dun)* version, sought spiritual liberation and enlightenment *(wu)* not through understanding doctrines and carrying out deeds, but by uncovering and acknowledging one's innate self *(jue)*, one's Buddhist nature *(foxing)*, trying to remove all thoughts and desires and connect with the universal mind during meditation. In thus breaking free from the constraints of culture or even of Buddhist doctrines themselves, this endeavor was the more extreme attempt to abandon the Indian roots of Buddhism altogether. This alternative stream of Buddhism and popular beliefs like the pure land *(jingtu)* sect, which proposed down-to-earth doctrines and ritual practices for different social occasions, would survive the suppression of Buddhism in the ninth century to become a part of Chinese culture. There was no perceived fundamental schism between such forms of Buddhism and Confucianism or Daoism. It was not unusual, in fact, for intellectuals or the lay public to adhere to parts of all these creeds (Li, 1999). In essence and fundamental philosophy, all defied the notions of any ruling supreme deity or heavenly salvation for individual souls.

◼ Near Eastern Manichaeanism and Nestorianism

During the Tang dynasty, Manichaeanism *(molijiao)* and Nestorianism *(jingjiao)* came to China from the Near East (Gernet, 1982:281–289). Manichaeanism was associated with the Zoroastrianism of ancient Persia, whereas Nestorianism was a heretical sect of early Christianity. The Tang dynasty maintained close contact with many of the adjacent regions and cultures, and the imperial capital, Ch'angan (Xi'an), housed a sizable community of foreigners, known generally as *hu*. This general milieu greatly facilitated the introduction of these religions, and their initial spread was somewhat sheltered by the success of Buddhism. Yet being much smaller in scale, they suffered heavily during the occasional crackdowns on Buddhism and other foreign religions during the Tang dynasty and after. The Nestorians were heavily subdued whenever nativism surged in China; they were also persecuted and denounced as heretical by the Christian Church in the West. The Manichaeans went underground to associate with Chinese popular cults seeking "millennial" uprisings against the state, inducing further suppressions in subsequent dynasties. These intensely theistic and otherworldly religions never commanded the same respect and attention as Buddhism. And yet they completed the spectrum of foreign religious impetus that entered China during the medieval time and may be seen as preparatory moments for the next major stage of Chinese religious development, when Christianity and the Christian civilization would clash against the Chinese world in the most ruthless manner possible.

▨ Song Syncretism

By the time of Tang, Confucianism, whether as state belief or moral philosophy, was by and large already part of the invisible, taken-for-granted ground rules of everyday life (Chiu-Dike, 2000). Daoism was somewhat in the middle, straddling the gap between superstition and high philosophy (Katz, 2000). Buddhism, too, catered to more down-to-earth religious needs while standing its ground in intellectual terms. Like Daoism, the schism between its role as folk religion and as moral pillar for society rendered its reception among both literati and commoner often eclectic and superficial. Once again, there was a need to draw together strains of thought and belief.

The dynamic of this development set the backdrop for the new syncretism of the Song (Hymes, 2002). This would be a syncretism operating at two levels of sophisticated religious ideas, and of folk beliefs and practice. Song syncretism reconciled both contending thought systems and the eclectic mosaic of folk beliefs and superstition. The Song dynasty saw the maturation of Chinese religious consciousness and its split into contrasting levels and aspirations (de Bary, 1988:chap. 3).

At the heart of the new syncretism was neo-Confucianism. This is often referred to as the "second phase" in the development of Confucianism, the

A diagram of the Supreme Ultimate, depicting the neo-Confucian image of the division and unity of the yin-yang poles

"first phase" being Confucianism in the time of Confucius himself (de Barg, 1975; Kasoff, 1984). Neo-Confucianism accommodated the doctrinal challenge from Daoism and Buddhism in Confucian terms, but not without cost. By focusing more on inner religious experience and less on human relations, it may even have weakened the Song dynasty's defense against encroaching nomadic invaders and hence hastened its demise (cf. Liu, 1988).

There were, broadly, four celebrated schools of neo-Confucianism, the Lian, Lo, Guan, and Min, named after the home territories of their respective founders (Kramer, 1986). These schools were not so much different "sects" of neo-Confucianism as different steps of development. They developed in nearly the chronological order given above, and their founders were often intellectual (and actual) kinsmen. The neo-Confucian schools all sought to strengthen, if not actually rebuild, the foundation that underlined the Confucian faith in morality, benevolence, and humanity (Wyatt, 1996). The rise of Buddhism (Gregory and Getz, 1999) and increasing popularity of Daoism rendered the emphasis on compassion or moral goodness no longer the prerogative of Confucianism alone. The same urge for virtuous conduct and mutual compassion figured prominently in Buddhism and even populist Daoism. The point was then both to reinforce and to rebuild the foundation of the Confucian faith, so that the Confucian way could be demonstrated to be distinctive from and superior to other alleged champions of virtue and humanity. For this purpose, two general agendas emerged.

The first agenda, undertaken mainly by the Guan school, sought to reaffirm the necessity of morality and benevolence by a familial analogy binding humanity with the universe. This position was pronounced with great persuasiveness and clarity in the manifesto of the Guan school—the Western Inscription *(ximing)* by Zhang Zhai (Kasoff, 1984). As presented in the *ximing,* heaven *(tian)* and earth *(kun)* were but the benevolent universal parents of humans. Within this ultimate parenthood, every relationship—social, material, and natural—must accord with prescribed ethical (filial) standards. The recognition of universal parenthood would render an ethical, benevolent worldview necessary and inviolable.

The second and eventually the more influential agenda was represented by Chu Hsi and the Min school. Instead of developing yet another set of beliefs like universal parenthood, Chu Hsi sought to create a more systematic metaphysical foundation for Confucianism (Chan, 1986, 1989; Tillman, 1992). His elaborate intellectual construction explored the dichotomy between *li* (principle) and *qi* (expression) in order to demonstrate the unity and universality of principle as opposed to the multifariousness of expression. He deepened the rationale and assumptions behind the Confucian world of belief. Influenced by Buddhist and Daoist practices, he sought to relate human needs and feelings to doctrine and ritual behavior, sidestepping Confucian ethics in favor of seeking "higher" and ultimate metaphysical reality by incessant probing of inner experience. Chu's approach brought a convergence in form and spirit (if not in doctrines) of the three religions but risked the danger of retreating into speculative musing and self-diagnosis. The subsequent development of neo-Confucianism into the Ming dynasty would be heavily tainted by the transcendental mood of a "Confucian Zen" (de Bary, 1975:141–217).

At the other end of Song syncretism was the growing popularity of folk beliefs and magical practices borrowing indiscriminately from the systematic religions, whose insight and fine points often eluded the ability and concern of the general public. These folk beliefs were characterized by an abundance of gods, worshiped either as local deities or as more universal idols. The figures popular among folk worship included historical figures, deceased local celebrities, and even Confucian sages, all of whom were turned into idols that, after proper sacrificial offerings, might bestow blessings and grant requests. They might simultaneously worship other deities like the Amitabe Buddha *(milafo)*, Kanon *(guanyin,* a Buddhist bodhisattva), the Jade Emperor *(yuhuang dadi),* Gods of the Five Mountains *(wu yue dijun),* and the Immaculate Lady of the Ninth Heaven *(jiutian xuannu).* Confucianism, Buddhism, Daoism, and popular legends all contributed to this pantheon (Gregory and Getz, 1999). These deities and idols could be worshiped selectively or collectively, depending on the needs of the worshipers (Yu, 2000). They were also worshiped regardless of their religious origins. This is syncretism in the strong sense of the term, with an easy sense of unity gained by simply ignoring gaps and incoherence.

Syncretic folk creeds formed as well. Manichaeanism *(molijiao)* dressed itself as a kind of higher-order Buddhism. Its spread within the population was

A traditional representation
of a Daoist deity

among the main contributing factors to millennial revolts against the dynasty. The well-known White Lotus sect *(bailianjiao)* also preached a form of simplified, eclectic doctrine advocating social reform. The White Lotus would lead a sustained underground existence into the early twentieth century.

After the Han dynasty, the development of Chinese religion became more complex. Daoism and Confucianism deepened their grasp on Chinese culture and society. At the same time, the outside world began to sink in. By the end of the Song dynasty, Chinese religious systems were generally confident of their own value and truthfulness. However, assaults were about to emerge that would call for even more profound and encompassing standards. After the Mongol kingdom overthrew the Song dynasty at the end of the thirteenth century, outside encroachment became broader and deeper; other exotic modes of faith, of religious sentiment and aspiration, asserted powerful new universalist claims.

■ Fourth Configuration: The Foreign Impetus of Christianity and Communism

The next major movement in the development of Chinese religion was the head-on clash with outside religious precepts, especially Christianity and Marxism-Leninism. Ironically, the Christian faith would take on a strong and relentless political overtone, whereas the political ideology of Marxism-Leninism would be intensified into religiosity of the most fanatical kind. The resulting nexus of cataclysm and innovation looms over Chinese civilization even to this day.

Christianity

As noted above, Christianity was first introduced into China during the Tang dynasty, in the form of Nestorianism (Bays, 1997). At that time however, both Nestorianism and Manichaeanism were broadly lumped together with Buddhism, regarded as variations among exotic Buddhist currents. It was not until the sixteenth century, during the Ming dynasty, that the Roman Catholic Church began the full-fledged process of eastward expansion, first into Japan and then China. Many of the first missionaries were Jesuit priests, like the famous Matteo Ricci (Li Madou), who came to China in 1583, and Niccolo Longobardi (Long Huamin), who arrived in the late sixteenth century. From the beginning, both the missionaries and the Roman Catholic hierarchy made numerous blunders; the Christian faith had nowhere near the success of Buddhism in converting the Chinese population. But the broader impact of the Christian civilization on China has been immeasurable. China would be forced literally at gunpoint to accept not only the operation of the missionaries in its territory but also many of the values and principles central to Christian civilization. In his chronicle of these momentous developments, Jacques Gernet (1985) characterizes the situation not so much in terms of religious differences but as whole civilizations clashing. We shall approach these dynamics in terms of doctrines, politics, and native reaction.

The question of doctrine was a thorny one right from the beginning. Confucians were simply playing out the religious consequences that follow from their particular conception and understanding of the world. In contrast, Christianity was based on a transcendental leap of faith different from any China had confronted before—the unconditional belief in the reality of the biblical God, the Holy Trinity, and eternal life for individual souls. This voluntary surrender of the autonomy of humans to an abstract and unknowable deity could well be seen by Chinese as a phase of simplistic religious impulse that the Chinese civilization had long since superseded. Although the worship of one god or another was fully permissible, this was usually regarded in China as the less enlightened attitude of the masses. And in any case, none of these deities can claim monopolistic authority. Thus, although Christianity was at first accepted as perhaps one more addition to the pantheon of the people, much as Nestorianism and Manichaeanism were, the idea that this particular god must replace all others would be difficult to accommodate (Kung and Ching, 1989). At risk of oversimplification, one can say that according to the higher humanistic aspiration of the Chinese literati, all deities were equally suspicious, whereas for the Chinese followers of folk religion, all deities were equally real. The Chinese people would be ill-prepared for the kind of "unreasonable" leap of faith adhered to in the West.

Two strategies were adopted by the missionaries to break this bottleneck, both with little effect. One strategy was to camouflage or soften the tough fabric of Christian doctrines, embracing local tenets and precepts and explaining away doctrinal differences by pointing out common grounds—assimilating with local mentality as Buddhism had done with the use of *keyi*. This was the strategy of Ricci and his Jesuit colleagues and represented a first effort toward indigenization of Christianity in China. Ricci himself appeared openly to embrace doctrines of Confucianism. He wore Confucian garb, took on a Chinese name (Li Madou), and rendered Christian tenets into Confucian rubrics. He stressed his knowledge of science and astronomy in order to gain respect and admiration. This was a strategy to avoid conflict with local beliefs on grounds of doctrinal differences, but it was at best facile. The fundamental opposition in doctrines was put in the background but was far from resolved: true converts, once baptized, must adhere to the core tenets of Christianity in their entirety. The second strategy, adopted largely as the official position of the Roman Catholic Church, was to insist on the hegemonic truth of Christianity right from the start. The church regarded the position of Ricci and other Jesuits as far too liberal. During the Qing dynasty in the eighteenth century, the Vatican officially denounced the Chinese worship of Confucian sages, ancestors, or local deities. This intolerant and impatient stance effectively made the first Chinese Christians into enemies in the eyes of other Chinese. The Qing government answered by expelling Christian missionaries.

From the nineteenth century onward, Christianity would be promoted on more than religious grounds. Together with a wide assortment of other values and institutions of Christian civilization as a whole, it would be forced upon China by military conflict and unequal treaties. The involvement of Christianity in the process provided a more high-minded alibi for what was clearly colonial exploitation. Backed by the full military strength of Christian nations like Britain, Germany, France, and to a lesser extent the United States, the increasing importance of Christianity was assured. The missionaries were aware of the human cost of colonial-style exploitation. The infamous Opium War of 1839 (discussed in Chapters 6 and 7), for example, had no better excuse than stark imperialist and commercial interests. The reaction of Christian churches and missionaries to the situation was two-pronged. On the one hand, if political sponsorship could ensure the expansion of Christianity in China, so much the better; in fact many of the Christian missionaries and their colleagues back home were not immune to ideologies of colonialism and racial superiority. Convinced of the prerogative of Christian faith, many missionaries were willing accomplices of politics. On the other hand, whatever the causes—or instigators—of China's social deterioration might be, this was a good opportunity for Christian churches to lend help. In the late nineteenth and early twentieth centuries, Christian churches in China set up welfare organizations of various kinds, running schools, hospitals, and even universities. Ironically, the Christian missionaries were determined to demonstrate their goodwill to a society devastated in its encounter with Christian civilization (Rubinstein, 1996; Sweeten, 2001). The intertwining of Christianity with colonial politics reached its high point at the turn of the twentieth century, when the alleged protection of Christian churches served as pretext for a number of military interventions into China, most notably the *Tianjin jiaoan,* the religious crime of the Boxers in Tianjin, discussed shortly.

As a result, the Chinese people often accepted or rejected the Christian faith for nonreligious reasons: to receive welfare or an education or to achieve the same earthly power as the imperialist invaders. The native response to Christianity was hence widely divergent and erratic. Two examples can serve to illustrate: the Taiping and Boxer Rebellions. The Taiping Rebellion (also discussed in Chapter 11) took place during the late nineteenth century; it lasted some fifteen years and laid waste to many of the southern provinces. Although it had all the trappings of Chinese peasant "millennial" movements of the past, it was also distinguished by its espoused allegiance to Christianity. The founder of the movement, Hong Xiuquan, actually claimed that he was yet another son of God and that Jesus Christ was his elder brother. Hong, as well as other leaders of the rebellion, also claimed to conduct direct communion with God (Spence, 1996; Shih, 1967). The movement, however, had little connection with or support from Western Christian churches, and the idea that Jesus could have a Chinese brother was not to be taken seriously by Jesus' Western followers. One can marvel at the extreme significance accorded Christianity, to become the ideological foundation of the *Taiping Tianguo* (Heavenly Kingdom of Eternal Peace). A different perspective is that perhaps Christianity had no special claim to supremacy—it was deployed as an expedient vehicle and pretext for articulating pent-up grievances, much as Manichaeanism and folk cults had been used in past rebellions (Shih, 1967). This mode of Christian fanaticism was clearly not what the Western Christian churches had in mind.

At the other extreme stood what might be seen as anti-Christian fanaticism, represented above all by the Boxer Rebellion *(yihetuan)* of 1900 (Esherick, 1987; Sweeten, 2001). The Boxer Rebellion was characterized by its all-out xenophobia. It was a state-sponsored populist cult, in the same folk-religious order as the White Lotus sect, the Mila sect, and other sects that stood behind historical millennial uprisings (Lutz and Lutz, 1998). Strengthened by support of the empress dowager and her imperial officials, the *yihetuan* appeared ready to confront the Christian religion and civilization head on. Confident that through magical incantation, spells, and other rituals, the true believers could withstand firearms and other forms of attack, the Boxer sect set out to destroy Christian churches and Western embassies, mostly in Beijing. Although the movement was short-lived, at its height it won widespread admiration from common people. The Boxers' destruction was disastrous for China. Eight Western countries formed a military alliance to protect their churches and other interests in China, and the Boxers' magic proved no match against bullets. The Forbidden City soon came under Western control. More unequal treaties (discussed in Chapter 7) would have to be signed before the fiasco of the Boxer Rebellion could be settled. The incident was representative of the nativistic paranoia against Christianity and Christian civilization. The naiveté of the uprising should not hide from view its deep-seated and widely shared objection against the imposition of a foreign faith and the world order that this implied.

The drama of Christian impact continues unabated even now, and the fortune of Chinese Christianity fluctuates with the political climate. It has suffered whenever anti-Western sentiments surge in China. Even under the best of circumstances, Christianity still has a hard time resolving its theological position with the Chinese religious tradition. This major obstacle may have receded somewhat by the late twentieth century, when the Chinese religious traditions themselves were on the wane, after the intrusion of yet another foreign system of thought, Marxism-Leninism.

■ Marxism-Maoism

In many respects, Marxism and Confucianism are comparable in the positions they occupied in Chinese religious life. Both are doctrines that concern the human order rather than transcendental reality. Both figure as the hegemonic thought system for China as a whole, yet neither can claim to be a religion as such. And both encompass the wide horizon between genuine humanistic sentiment and totalistic authoritarian propensities. These reasons help explain why, although the Christian challenge to Chinese culture was always looked upon with reservation, Marxism was more readily accepted as a viable alternative for China. Their assumptions and tenets may differ, yet at least Confucianism and Marxism operate on the same plane and address the same cluster of concerns. Of course, there are profound differences as well.

In contrast to the tangible humanism of Confucianism, Marxism as introduced to China by Mao Zedong is sweepingly utopian (Kolakowski, 1982:494–523). Confucianism emphasized the here and now, the "rational adaptation" to the world as the route of self-actualization and fulfillment. Utopian thinking was usually associated with folk cults or peasant movements. Marxism-Maoism is, however, forthright in postulating an ideal and inevitable future society, the realization of which is worth present material and human sacrifice. Based on this outlook, since 1949 the development of China has been conducted through a series of social experiments, designed to arrive at the ideal social form. Imitating the Soviet experience during the 1950s proved futile, leaving China to grope for its own way into socialism and thereby the communist utopia. The tremendous havoc and destruction brought on by the Great Leap Forward and the Cultural Revolution were understandable only in relation to their fundamental utopianism, which is very out of character with Confucianism but generally in keeping with the Taiping Rebellion and other millennial movements outside the mainstream of traditional Chinese culture. As in those movements, cultural and literary elites were marginalized. Instead, the society of socialist China would be founded upon the great alliance of the workers-peasants-soldiers *(gongnongbing)*.

The Marxian image of society also differs markedly from the Confucian in its emphasis on conflict and contradiction as forces of history. This is totally incompatible with the Confucian vision of a harmonious, benevolent society. The Marxian conception of social structure is one of change, of differentiation, and of the scramble for social resources. In playing out this dynamic process, individuals join with others of the same social position and interest in a systematic conflict against other social classes. Traditional Chinese culture would have little of this. Conflict and tension were always exceptions to the norm and could be readily redeemed by invoking ethical dogmas. Human nature is, after all, formed of the same benevolent, virtuous essence. To claim as Maoism did that revolution is the highest vehicle for individual and societal purification is to be fundamentally wrongheaded. The Confucian ideal of harmony *(he),* whether between two persons, person and society, or even person and cosmos, instead postulates a society that is intrinsically virtuous and benevolent, that minimizes the occasions of conflict and comes to resolution should these happen. And Daoism and Buddhism are by and large passive and withdrawn and certainly have not espoused conflict and destruction. One can see the extreme turnabout that took place in China with the holistic embrace of Marxism-Leninism-Maoism.

Should there still be any doubt regarding the religious—or antireligious—character of Marxism-Maoism, one need only consider that, whatever their substance and tenets, they were articulated above all as fanaticism and cult. The national malaise of the Cultural Revolution and the personality cult of Mao are cases in point. The religious overtone enters because the utopian promises of Maoism can never be sustained or validated by reason and evidence alone; they must be heightened by a state of mass elation.

▪ Toward a New Syncretism?

After Mao's death in 1976, China entered a phase of fundamental reconstruction in all major arenas of society. Socialism is still official ideology, but other competitors are rapidly on the rise—capitalism, nationalism, even the newest fad of postmodernism. All these are but symptoms of the basic disorientation of China in the aftermath of disenchantment with Marxism-Leninism-Maoism. A new mode of faith and belief is being sought to once again provide society with a viable image of social order and with moral and behavioral codes for the social actors. The post-Mao transformation cannot be resolved simply on pragmatic grounds, as Deng Xiaoping suggested. China's leaders have always articulated its ethical standards; after a period during which all prior beliefs were stridently attacked, it needs new guidelines. If the elementary belief system in social reconstruction remains vacuous, much of society would be in limbo and nihilistic or disintegrate into groups with differing belief systems.

The present Chinese government is recognizing the right to religious belief, both traditional and Western, but such freedom has limits. Specific constitutional articles prohibit and even deem treasonous religious beliefs or activities that run counter to national interest. Religion must stay within the bounds of politics. Churches and temples—in keeping with long tradition—may function only with the approval of the state; they must be registered. Or more metaphorically, the City of God is subordinated to the City of Man. This is the flip side of the separation between church and state. Based on this principle, the Chinese government is deemed justified in its tightened regulation of, for example, Tibetan Buddhism (see Chapter 6) and unregistered Christian worship. About half of China's 12 million Catholics remain unregistered, and despite intense negotiations the Vatican has been unable to break this impasse. Many Protestants refuse to register as well, not wanting to dilute their individual denominational identity within the "Three Self Patriotic Association" (Madsen, 1998; Lazado, 2001; Murphy, 2002). In this approach to religious policy, religions are not recognized as vehicles for any higher form of truth. They are rather tolerated as perhaps harmless pastimes for a worn-out nation. The fundamental enigma of society remains unanswered. As yet no belief system can serve as a source of meaning, direction, and identity for the already crises-laden society, let alone answer ultimate questions and needs of human existence (cf. MacInnis, 1989).

At present, a rough estimate is that one-tenth of the Chinese population (120 million) embrace religious beliefs of some form (Stockwell, 1993: 31–55), that is, religions with formal institutions operating within allowed political confines. In this light, China is currently a country with few true believers; religions are allowed only a trivialized existence. Both believers and nonbelievers are equally paralyzed amid the fundamental void of meaning and value. Only crude money motive, at present, seems to have given some momentum and purpose for those eager to upgrade their material life. One can hope that as material conditions improve, perhaps more attention will be given to elevating spiritual life as well.

The extent to which this projection will come true is hard to tell at this point. Yet advocates for various belief systems are at least preparing for this possibility. Foremost among them are the New Confucians, who seek to revive Confucianism as once again the belief system most appropriate for China. Of course, this cannot mean merely the reiteration of outdated tenets. Instead, New Confucianism would incorporate other ideological currents that played a part in the shaping of modern China and try to weave these different strands into the new syncretism of a Confucian "Cultural China" (Tu, 1991). The prospect of this drama is still being played out.

■ Religion and Chinese Society

Standing out in the sets of syncretism charted above is the secular, this-worldly character of Chinese religion. Each of the three great syncretisms in China's history—during the Zhou, Han, and Song dynasties—elevated a humanistic and collectivistic outlook above other competing theistic or pantheistic currents. It is in the final analysis this strongly practical, societal, and moral commitment to the here and now that distinguishes the spirit of Chinese religion. The answers to ultimate questions of existence and meaning are neither unknowable nor hiding in the transcendental beyond. They can be answered only by imputing the secular here and now with sacred authority and authenticity—by the clear-minded sacralization of the secular and mundane. The secret of Chinese religion does not lie in the quest for immortality, salvation, or ecstatic liberation. Rather, it is only in renouncing all these perhaps mystical ideals that the worldly reality would emerge as the only reality there is and hence the only source of meaning and value to questions both profane and sacred. In brief, the Chinese religious tradition renders the human order *(renlun)* itself sacred. If the social world is all that there is, then striving for social order and harmony would be the highest ideal that can be hoped for and the most sacred quest that human beings can conduct. Religious sentiment and commitment are defined above all by their focus upon the primacy of social relations, as the actual dynamics of the human order. Hence the celebrated Chinese emphasis on *guanxi* (relation) as the stuff that human order is made of (King, 1991). In the present context, this relationship may be taking on added importance.

There are two fundamental categories of *guanxi,* ascribed and achieved. In Confucian terms, ascribed relationships are the cornerstone of human order and more often than not have primacy over achieved relations. Ascribed relationships are part of the *wulun* (five orders), denoting the fundamental ties based on a priori principles like Mandate of Heaven and blood ties that the individual has no choice but to honor. These five orders include relations between emperor and ministers, father and son, husband and wife, one brother and another, and also between kin and friends. One is born or placed into the first four of these relationships, which are therefore ascribed. They help ensure that one's family and the country's leaders will command supreme loyalty. As to the fifth relationship, which is achieved, the relation between kin and between friends must also be conducted according to predetermined, proper principles and codes. These five relationships are the stable building blocks of human society and are the main obligations of every individual. In upholding these relationships, definite values and principles apply. The medium being exchanged in these relations must rise above the mundane concerns of economic or material benefit. It is essentially an exchange of goodwill, of human compassion *(renqing).* In thus exchanging acts of goodwill—in the form of gifts, help, favor, understanding, kind words, and so forth—mutual compassion among individuals and toward society as a whole can be better consolidated. In this way, Confucian ideals such as loyalty, filial piety, honesty, and agnatic ties are articulated into concrete social dynamics.

In addition to ascribed relationships, into which one enters without choice, one can also achieve *guanxi* with people of one's own choosing. These are usually classmates, fellow villagers, associates at work, or other people close enough to decide they will exchange *renqing* favors. In addition to a genuine sense of compassion, strategic calculation can come into play in the give-and-take of these achieved relationships. For example, one might use these exchanges to help get oneself out of debt or to incur debt from others. Such subtle strategies evolved into elaborate power games in Chinese social life. Many of the techniques invoked are Daoist in origin, as clever adoption of cherished moral values or propensities of the situation to favor oneself.

The emphasis on *guanxi* and *renqing* is by no means a thing of the past, as Chapters 4, 5, and 13 also attest (Kipnis, 1997; Gold, Guthrie, and Wank, 2002). Belief systems may displace one another, yet the same stress on human order persists. During the modern socialist era, the ascribed ethical ties have become weakened. Yet conversely, the obsession with achieved social relationships is on the rise as new market opportunities appear. It is well known that, nowadays in China, nothing much can be accomplished—regardless of the sphere of activities concerned—without getting in touch with the right person and setting up the right kind of ties. This network of social ties has in many respects replaced the open, institutional channels of social organization. That private network is an adaptation of Confucian ethics that has remained alive in spirit and practice today. Once again, the Chinese religious tradition gives shape to a society that focuses overwhelmingly on the personal affective side of social and cultural dynamics.

Chinese religion is essentially of this world, and it has withstood many of the forces that pull in other directions. Its emphasis on maintaining social order helps restore stability after periods of turmoil but also generally resists social change. Its emphasis on personal social relations also encourages people to tend to their own social circle at the expense of others to whom they do not owe direct obligations. This streak of conservatism can be both a blessing and a curse for China's enigmatic transition into the modern world and for its search for a new spiritual syncretism.

Standing at the turn of the new millennium, China is still searching for this new spiritual direction. While these quests are as yet unfulfilled, they bring Chinese religious dynamics into new terrain of a more problematic character. At heart is the persistent effort in drawing the fine line between state and religion, part of this focus on the primacy of social relations when approaching religious belief and practice. Toward this end, the Chinese government is vigilant against any social movement that might be viewed as a threat to state power in the name of (quasi-)religious faiths. At one side of the picture, this applies to separatist movements of Tibet and Xinjiang; both nativistic movements are founded to a large extent upon their respective religious traditions, namely Tibetan Buddhism and Islam (Dillon, 1999; Murata, 2000). The dramatic intertwining of religion and politics in these two regions is a much-publicized development that challenges the sovereignty and integration of the Chinese state. At the other side of the picture, even more dramatic is the confrontation between the government and the populist *qigong* movement. *Qigong* is a form of yoga that emphasizes a variety of breathing exercises, bodily postures, and even meditation. Much of the *qigong* movement is suppressed in the new era, after it overstepped the simple pursuit of health and stamina to become a stand-in for spiritual guidance and an active opponent of Chinese government policies. The term *xie jiao* (evil cult) is in particular invoked by the Chinese government against Falun Gong (Ownby, 2003), the must influential among the *qigong* currents, after 10,000 members of that organization—including a number of high-level members of the party and government—successfully staged a peaceful demonstration outside the Communist Party headquarters at Tiananmen Square in 1999. The intriguing trajectory whereby the quest for personal health can become transformed into a vehicle of "evil," goes a long way in underscoring the spiritual void of the majority of the Chinese population as the new millennium begins.

■ Bibliography

Ames, Roger T., David L. Hall, and Tracy Bernstein. 2003. *Dao de Jing: A Philosophical Translation.* New York: Ballantine.

Anthony, Carol K. 1998. *The Philosophy of the I Ching.* 2nd ed. New York: Anthony Publishing Company.

Armstrong, David E. 1998. *Alcohol and Altered States in Ancestor Veneration Rituals of Zhou Dynasty China and Iron Age Palestine.* Lewiston, NY: Edwin Mellen Press.

Balkin, Jack M. 2002. *The Laws of Change: I Ching and the Philosophy of Life.* New York: Pantheon.

Bays, Daniel H. (ed.). 1997. *Christianity in China: From the Eighteenth Century to the Present.* Stanford: Stanford University Press.

Blofeld, John Eaton Calthorpe. 1991. *I Ching: The Book of Change.* New York: Arkana.

Bocking, Brian. 1995. *Nagarjuna in China: A Translation of the Middle Treatise.* Lewiston, NY: Edwin Mellen Press.

Bodde, Derk. 1991. *Chinese Thought, Society, and Science.* Honolulu: University of Hawaii Press.

Bokenkamp, Stephen R. 1997. *Early Daoist Scriptures.* Berkeley: University of California Press.

Brooks, E. Bruce, and A. Taeko Brooks. 1998. *The Original Analects: Sayings of Confucius and His Successors.* New York: Columbia University Press.

Broughton, Jeffrey L. 1999. *The Bodhidharma Anthology: The Earliest Records of Zen.* Berkeley: University of California Press.

Buswell, Robert E., Jr. (ed.). 1990. *Chinese Buddhist Apocrypha.* Honolulu: University of Hawaii Press.

Chan, Wing-tsit. 1953. *Religious Trends in Modern China.* New York: Columbia University Press.

———. 1986. *Chu Hsi and Neo-Confucianism.* Honolulu: University of Hawaii Press.

———. 1989. *Chu Hsi.* Honolulu: University of Hawaii Press.

Chang, H. 1990. "Some Reflections on the Problems of the Axial Age Breakthrough in Relation to Classical Confucianism." In Paul A. Cohen and Merle Goldman (eds.), *Ideas Across Cultures: Essays on Chinese Thought in Honor of Benjamin I. Schwartz.* Cambridge: Harvard University Press.

Chang, Kwan-chih. 1963. *The Archaeology of Ancient China.* New Haven: Yale University Press.

Chang, Leo S., Yu Feng, and Ch'un Chang. 1998. *The Four Political Treatises of the Yellow Emperor: Original Mawangdui Texts with Complete English Translations and an Introduction.* Honolulu: University of Hawaii Press.

Chang, Po-tuan. 1987. *Understanding Reality: A Taoist Alchemical Classic.* Honolulu: University of Hawaii Press.

Chen, Kenneth Kwang Sheng. 1964. *Buddhism in China: A Historical Survey.* Princeton: Princeton University Press.

China Quarterly. 2003. Special issue on religion in China. Vol. 173 (March).

Ching, Julia. 1997. *Mysticism and Kingship in China: The Heart of Chinese Wisdom.* Cambridge: Cambridge University Press.

Chiu-Duke, Josephine. 2000. *To Rebuild the Empire: Lu Chih's Confucian Pragmatist Approach to the Mid-T'ang Predicament.* Ithaca: State University of New York Press.

Chuang Tzu. 1994. *Wandering on the Way: Early Taoist Tales and Parables of Chuang Tzu.* Trans. Victor H. Mair. New York: Bantam.

———. 1996. *Basic Writings.* Trans. Burton Watson. New York: Columbia University Press.

Chung, Chang-Soo. 2001. *I Ching on Man and Society: An Exploration into Its Theoretical Implications in Social Sciences.* Lanham, MD: University Press of America.

Clarke, J. J. 2000. *The Tao of the West: Western Transformations of Taoist Thought.* London: Routledge.

Cleary, Thomas. 1983. *Entry into the Inconceivable: An Introduction to Hua-yen Buddhism.* Honolulu: University of Hawaii Press.

———. 1993. *The Essential Tao: An Initiation into the Heart of Taoism Through the Authentic Tao te Ching and the Inner Teachings of Chuang Tzu.* San Francisco: HarperSanFrancisco.

Confucius. 1992. *The Analects.* 2nd. ed. Trans. D. C. Lau. Hong Kong: Chinese University Press.

———. 1993. *The Essential Confucius: The Heart of Confucius' Teachings in Authentic I Ching Order.* San Francisco: HarperSanFrancisco.

———. 1998. *The Analects of Confucius: A Philosophical Translation.* Trans. Henry Rosemont. New York: Ballantine.

Creel, Herrlee Glessner. 1970. *The Origins of Statecraft in China: The Western Chou Empire.* Vol. 1. Chicago: University of Chicago Press.

de Bary, William Theodore. 1975. *The Unfolding of Neo-Confucianism.* New York: Columbia University Press.

———. 1988. *The Message in the Mind in Neo-Confucianism.* New York: Columbia University Press.

———. 1991a. *East Asian Civilizations.* Cambridge: Cambridge University Press.

———. 1991b. *Learning for One's Self: Essays on the Individual in Neoconfucian Thought.* New York: Columbia University Press.

de Bary, William Theodore, and Irene Bloom. 1979. *Principle and Practicality.* New York: Columbia University Press.

de Bary, William Theodore, and Tu Weiming. 1998. *Confucianism and Human Rights.* New York: Columbia University Press.

de Bary, William Theodore, Wing-Tsit Chan, and Burton Watson (eds.). 1960. *Sources of Chinese Tradition.* 2 vols. New York: Columbia University Press.

de Groot, Jan Jakob Maria. 1972 [1892]. *The Religious Systems of China: The Ancient Forms, Evolution, History, and Present.* 6 vols. Leyden: E. J. Brill.

Dean, Kenneth. 1998. *Lord of the Three in One: The Spread of a Cult in Southeast China*. Princeton: Princeton University Press.

Demieville, P. 1986. "Philosophy and Religion from Han to Sui." In Denis Twitchett and John K. Fairbank (eds.), *The Cambridge History of China*, vol. 1. Cambridge: Cambridge University Press.

Dillon, Michael. 1999. *China's Muslim Hui Community: Migration, Settlement, and Sects*. London: Curzon Press.

Ebry, Patricia Buckley, and Peter N. Gregory (eds.). 1993. *Religion and Society in T'ang and Sung China*. Honolulu: University of Hawaii Press.

Eliade, Mircea. 1985. *A History of Religious Ideas: From Gautama Buddhas to the Triumph of Christianity*. Vol. 2. Chicago: University of Chicago Press.

Eno, Robert. 1990. *The Confucian Creation of Heaven: Philosophy and the Defense of Ritual Mastery*. Albany: State University of New York Press.

Esherick, Joseph W. 1987. *The Origins of the Boxer Uprising*. Berkeley: University of California Press.

Faure, Bernard. 1995. *The Rhetoric of Immediacy: A Cultural Critique of Chan/Zen Buddhism*. Princeton: Princeton University Press.

———. 1997. *Chan Insights and Oversights: An Epistemological Critique of the Chan Tradition*. Princeton: Princeton University Press.

Fingarette, Herbert. 1972. *Confucius: The Secular as Sacred*. New York: Harper and Row.

Foltz, Richard C. 2000. *Religions of the Silk Road*. New York: Palgrave.

Freedman, Maurice. 1979. "On the Sociological Study of Chinese Religion." In Maurice Freedman, *The Study of Chinese Society*. Stanford: Stanford University Press.

Fung, Yu-lan. 1952 [1937]. *A History of Chinese Philosophy*. Trans. Derk Bodde. Princeton: Princeton University Press.

Gernet, Jacques. 1982. *A History of Chinese Civilization*. Cambridge: Cambridge University Press.

———. 1985. *China and the Christian Impact*. Cambridge: Cambridge University Press.

———. 1998 [1956]. *Buddhism in Chinese Society: An Economic History from the Fifth to the Tenth Centuries*. Trans. Franciscus Verellen. New York: Columbia University Press.

Gimello, Robert M., and Peter N. Gregory (eds.). 1983. *Studies in Ch'an and Hua-Yen*. Honolulu: University of Hawaii Press.

Gold, Thomas, Doug Guthrie, and David Wank (eds.). 2002. *Social Connections in China: Institutions, Culture, and the Changing Nature of Guanxi*. Cambridge: Cambridge University Press.

Goldstein, Jonathan (ed.). 1998. *The Jews of China: Historical and Comparative Perspectives*. Vol. 1. Armonk, NY: M. E. Sharpe.

Gotshalk, Richard. 1999a. *The Beginnings of Philosophy in China*. Lanham, MD: University Press of America.

———. 1999b. *Divination, Order, and the Zhouyi*. Lanham, MD: University Press of America.

Graham, Angus C. 1989. *Disputers of the Tao*. La Salle, IL: Open Court.

Granet, Marcel. 1975 [1922]. *The Religion of the Chinese People*. Trans. Maurice Freedman. New York: Harper and Row.

Gregory, Peter N. (ed.). 1987. *Traditions of Meditation in Chinese Buddhism*. Honolulu: University of Hawaii Press.

——— (ed.). 1988. *Sudden and Gradual: Approaches to Enlightenment in Chinese Thought*. Honolulu: University of Hawaii Press.

Gregory, Peter N., and Daniel A. Getz (eds.). 1999. *Buddhism in the Sung.* Honolulu: University of Hawaii Press.

Hall, David L., and Roger T. Ames. 1987. *Thinking Through Confucius.* Albany: State University of New York Press.

———. 1995. *Anticipating China: Thinking Through the Narratives of Chinese and Western Culture.* Albany: State University of New York Press.

———. 1998. *Thinking from the Han: Self, Truth, and Transcendence in Chinese and Western Culture.* Albany: State University of New York Press.

———. 1999. *The Democracy of the Dead: Dewey, Confucius, and the Hope for Democracy in China.* New York: Open Court.

Han, Fei Tzu. 1996. *Basic Writings.* Trans. Burton Watson. New York: Columbia University Press.

Henricks, Robert G. 2000. *Lao Tzu's Tao de Ching: A Translation of the Startling New Documents Found at Guodian.* Columbia: Columbia University Press.

Ho, Ping-ti. 1975. *The Cradle of the East: An Inquiry into the Indigenous Origins of Techniques and Ideas of Neolithic and Early Historic China, 5000–1000 B.C.* Hong Kong: Chinese University of Hong Kong Press.

Hsu, Francis Lan Kwang. 1971 [1948]. *Under the Ancestor's Shadow.* Stanford: Stanford University Press.

Hsu, Immanuel Chung-yueh. 1995. *The Rise of Modern China.* 5th ed. New York: Oxford University Press.

Huang, Alfred. 1998. *The Complete I Ching: The Definitive Translation of the Taoist Master.* London: Inner Traditions International.

Huang, Tsung-hsi, and Julia Ching (eds.). 1987. *The Records of Ming Scholars.* Honolulu: University of Hawaii Press.

Hymes, Robert. 2002. *Way and Byway: Taoism, Local Religion, and Models of Divinity in Sung and Modern China.* Berkeley: University of California Press.

Ivanhoe, Philip J., and Bryan W. van Norden (eds.). 2001. *Readings in Classical Chinese Philosophy.* New York: Seven Bridges Press.

Jones, Charles Brewer (ed.). 1999. *Buddhism in Taiwan: Religion and the State, 1660–1990.* Honolulu: University of Hawaii Press.

Kasoff, Ira E. 1984. *The Thought of Chang Tsai (1020–1077).* Cambridge: Cambridge University Press.

Katz, Paul R. 2000. *Images of the Immortal: The Cult of Lu Dongbin at the Palace of Eternal Joy.* Honolulu: University of Hawaii Press.

Keightley, David N. 1978. *Sources of Shang History: The Oracle-Bone Inscriptions of Bronze Age China.* Berkeley: University of California Press.

Kieschnick, John. 1997. *The Eminent Monk: Buddhist Ideals in Medieval Chinese Hagiography.* Honolulu: University of Hawaii Press.

King, Ambrose. 1991. "Kuan Hsi and Network Building: A Sociological Interpretation." *Daedalus* 120 (spring): 2.

Kipnis, Andrew B. 1997. *Producing Guanxi: Sentiment, Self, and Subculture in a North China Village.* Chapel Hill, NC: Duke University Press.

Kleeman, Terry F. 1998. *Great Perfection: Religion and Ethnicity in a Chinese Millennial Kingdom.* Honolulu: University of Hawaii Press.

Kolakowski, Leszek. 1978. *Main Currents of Marxism: Its Rise, Growth, and Dissolution.* Vol. 3. Trans. P. S. Falla. Oxford: Clarendon Press.

———. 1982. *Religion.* New York: Oxford University Press.

Kramers, R. 1986. "The Development of the Confucian Schools." In Denis Twitchett and John K. Fairbank (eds.), *The Cambridge History of China,* vol. 1. Cambridge: Cambridge University Press.

Kung, Hans, and Julia Ching. 1989. *Christianity and Chinese Religions.* New York: Doubleday.

Lao Tzu. 1989. *Tao te Ching: A Bilingual Edition.* Trans. D. C. Lau. Hong Kong: Chinese University Press.

———. 1990. *Tao te Ching.* Trans. Victor H. Mair. New York: Bantam.

———. 1992. *Tao te Ching.* Trans. Stephen A. Mitchell. New York: HarperPerennial.

———. 2001. *Dao de Jing: The Book of the Way.* Trans. Moss Roberts. Berkeley: University of California Press.

Lazado, Eriberto P., Jr. 2001. *God Aboveground: Catholic Church, Postsocialist State, and Transnational Processes in a Chinese Village.* Stanford: Stanford University Press.

Li, Chenyang. 1999. *The Tao Encounters the West: Explorations in Comparative Philosophy.* Albany: State University of New York Press.

Lin-chi. 1999. *The Zen Teachings of Master Lin-chi: A Translation of the Lin-chi-lu.* Trans. Burton Watson. New York: Columbia University Press.

Lipman, Jonathan N. 1998. *Familiar Strangers: A History of Muslims in Northwest China.* Seattle: University of Washington Press.

Liu, James T. C. 1988. *China Turning Inward: Intellectual-Political Changes in the Early Twelfth Century.* Cambridge: Council on East Asian Studies, Harvard University.

Loewe, Michael. 1986. "The Concept of Sovereignty." In Denis Twitchett and John K. Fairbank (eds.), *The Cambridge History of China,* vol. 1. Cambridge: Cambridge University Press.

———. 1994. *Divination, Mythology, and Monarchy in Han China.* New York: Cambridge University Press.

Lopez, Donald S., Jr. (ed.). 1996. *Religions of China in Practice.* Princeton: Princeton University Press.

Lowe, Scott. 1992. *Mo Tzu's Religious Blueprint for a Chinese Utopia: The Will and the Way.* Lewiston, NY: Edwin Mellen Press.

Lutz, Jessie G., and Rolland Ray Lutz. 1998. *Hakka Chinese Confront Protestant Christianity, 1850–1900, with the Autobiographies of Eight Hakka Christians and Commentary.* Armonk, NY: M. E. Sharpe.

Lynn, Richard John. 1999. *The Classic of the Way and Virtue: A New Translation of the Tao-te Ching of Laozi as Interpreted by Wang Bi.* New York: Columbia University Press.

MacInnis, Donald E. 1989. *Religion in China Today: Policy and Practice.* New York: Orbis Books.

Madsen, Richard. 1998. *China's Catholics: Tragedy and Hope in Emerging Civil Society.* Berkeley: University of California Press.

Mair, Victor H. 1983. *Experimental Essays on Chuang-tzu.* Honolulu: University of Hawaii Press.

———. 1998. *Wandering in the Way: Early Taoist Tales and Parables of Chuang Tzu.* Honolulu: University of Hawaii Press.

Marshall, S. J. 2001. *The New Mandate of Heaven: Hidden History of the I Ching.* New York: Columbia University Press.

Mencius. 1984. *Works.* Trans. D. C. Lau. Hong Kong: Chinese University Press.

Mo Tzu. 1963. *Basic Writings.* Trans. Burton Watson. New York: Columbia University Press.

Moore, Charles A. (ed.). 1967. *The Chinese Mind: Essentials of Chinese Philosophy and Culture.* Honolulu: University of Hawaii Press.

Mungello, D. E. 1994. *The Forgotten Christians of Hangzhou.* Honolulu: University of Hawaii Press.

Munro, Donald J. 2001. *The Concept of Man in Early China.* Ann Arbor: Center for Chinese Studies, University of Michigan.

Murata, Sachiko. 2000. *Chinese Gleams of Sufi Light: Wang Tai-yu's Great Learning of the Pure and Real and Liu Chih's Displaying the Concealment of the Real Realm.* Ithaca: State University of New York Press.

Murphy, David. 2002. "Mass Appeal." *Far Eastern Economic Review* 164(51)(January 3): 32–35.

Nakamura, H. 1964. *Ways of Thinking of Eastern Peoples.* Honolulu: University of Hawaii Press.

Ng, On-Cho. 2001. *Cheng-Zhu Confucianism in the Early Qing: Li Guangdi (1642–1718) and Qing Learning.* Ithaca: State University of New York Press.

Ownby, David. 2003. *Falungong and China's Future.* Lanham, MD: Rowman and Littlefield.

Pas, Julian F. 1998. *Historical Dictionary of Taoism.* Lanham, MD: Scarecrow Press.

Penny, Benjamin. 2000. *Religion and Biography in China and Tibet.* London: Curzon Press.

Puett, Michael J. 2001. *The Ambivalence of Creation: Debates Concerning Innovation and Artifice in Early China.* Stanford: Stanford University Press.

Richards, Ivor A. 1996. *Mencius on the Mind: Experiments in Multiple Definition.* London: Curzon Press.

Rickett, W. Allyn. 1998. *Guanzi: Political, Economic, and Philosophical Essays from Early China, a Study and Translation.* Vol. 2. Princeton: Princeton University Press.

Robinet, Isabel. 1997. *Taoism: Growth of a Religion.* Trans. Phyllis Brooks. Stanford: Stanford University Press.

Roetz, Heiner. 1993. *Confucian Ethics of the Axial Age: A Reconstruction Under the Aspect of the Breakthrough Toward Postconventional Thinking.* Albany: State University of New York Press.

Roth, Harold. 1999. *Original Tao: Inward Training (Nei-yeh) and the Foundations of Taoist Mysticism.* New York: Columbia University Press.

Rubinstein, Murray A. 1996. *The Origins of the Anglo-American Missionary Enterprise in China, 1807–1840.* Lanham, MD: Scarecrow Press.

Sakyamuni. 1993. *The Lotus Sutra.* Trans. Burton Watson. New York: Columbia University Press.

Schipper, Kristofer. 1993. *The Taoist Body.* Trans. Karen C. Duval. Berkeley: University of California Press.

Schluchter, Wolfgang. 1981. *The Rise of Western Rationalism.* Berkeley: University of California Press.

Schwartz, Benjamin Isadore. 1985. *The World of Thought in Ancient China.* Cambridge: Belknap Press of Harvard University Press.

Shahar, Meir, and Robert P. Weller (eds.). 1996. *Unruly Gods: Divinity and Society in China.* Honolulu: University of Hawaii Press.

Shankman, Steven, and Stephen W. Durrant (eds.). 2002. *Early China/Ancient Greece: Thinking Through Comparisons.* Binghamton: State University of New York Press.

Shih, Vincent. 1967. *The Tai Ping Ideology.* Seattle: University of Washington Press.

Shun, Kwong-Loi. 1997. *Mencius and Early Chinese Thought.* Stanford: Stanford University Press.

Smith, Arthur Henderson. 1894. *Chinese Characters.* New York: Revell.

Smith, Richard J., and D. W. Y. Kwok (eds.). 1993. *Cosmology, Ontology, and Human Efficacy: Essays in Chinese Thought.* Honolulu: University of Hawaii Press.

Spence, Jonathan. 1996. *God's Chinese Son.* London: HarperCollins.

Stockwell, Foster. 1993. *Religion in China Today.* Beijing: New World Press.

Strathern, Paul. 1999. *Confucius in Ninety Minutes.* Chicago: Ivan R. Dee.

Sweeten, Alan R. 2001. *Christianity in Rural China: Conflict and Accommodation in Jiangxi Province, 1860–1900.* Ann Arbor: Center for Chinese Studies, University of Michigan.

ter Haar, B. J. 1999. *The White Lotus: Teachings in Chinese Religious History.* Honolulu: University of Hawaii Press.

Tillman, Hoyt Cleveland. 1992. *Confucian Discourse and Chu His's Ascendancy.* Honolulu: University of Hawaii Press.

Tsai, Kathryn Ann. 1994. *Lives of the Nuns: Biographies of Chinese Buddhist Nuns from the Fourth to Sixth Centuries.* Honolulu: University of Hawaii Press.

Tu, Wei-ming. 1991. "The Living Tree." *Daedalus* 120 (spring): 2.

———. 1993. *Way, Learning, and Politics: Essays on the Confucian Intellectual.* Ithaca: State University of New York Press.

Tung Yueh. 2000. *The Tower of Myriad Mirrors: A Supplement to Journey to the West.* Trans. Shuen-fu Lin and Larry J. Schulz. Ann Arbor: Center for Chinese Studies, University of Michigan.

Uhalley, Stephen, Jr. 2000. *China and Christianity: Burdened Past, Hopeful Future.* Armonk, NY: M. E. Sharpe.

Waley, Arthur. 1988. *The Way and Its Power: A Study of the Tao te Ching and Its Place in Chinese Thought.* New York: Grove Press.

Wang, Aihe. 2000. *Cosmology and Political Culture in Early China.* Cambridge: Cambridge University Press.

Wang, Bi. 1994. *The Classic of Changes: A New Translation of the I Ching.* Trans. Richard John Lynn. New York: Columbia University Press.

———. 1999. *The Classic of the Way and Virtue: A New Translation of the Tao-ti Ching of Laozi.* Trans. Richard John Lynn. New York: Columbia University Press.

Watson, Burton. 1967. *Basic Writings of Mo Tzu, Hsun Tzu, and Han Fei Tzu.* New York: Columbia University Press.

Weber, Max. 1964 [1922]. *The Religions of China: Confucianism and Taoism.* Trans. Hans H. Gerth. New York: Free Press.

Weinstein, Stanley. 1987. *Buddhism Under the T'ang.* Cambridge: Cambridge University Press.

Wilhelm, Helmut. 1977. *Heaven, Earth, and Man in the Book of Changes.* Seattle: University of Washington Press.

Wilhelm, Helmut, and Richard Wilhelm. 1995. *Understanding the I Ching: The Wilhelm Lectures on the Book of Changes.* Princeton: Princeton University Press.

Wilhelm, Richard (ed.). 1967. *The I Ching, or Book of Changes.* Trans. Cary F. Baynes. Princeton: Princeton University Press.

Wolf, Arthur P. (ed.). 1974. *Religion and Ritual in Chinese Society.* Stanford: Stanford University Press.

Wriggins, Sally Hovey. 1996. *Xuanzang: A Buddhist Pilgrim on the Silk Road.* Boulder: Westview Press.

Wright, Arthur F. 1977. *Buddhism in Chinese History.* Stanford: Stanford University Press.

Wyatt, Don J. 1996. *The Recluse of Loyang: Shao Yung and the Moral Evolution of Early Sung Thought.* Honolulu: University of Hawaii Press.

Yan, Yunxiang. 1996. *The Flow of Gifts: Reciprocity and Social Networks in a Chinese Village.* Stanford: Stanford University Press.

Yang, C. K. 1991. *Religion in Chinese Society: A Study of Contemporary Social Functions of Religion and Some of Their Historical Factors.* Prospect Heights, IL: Waveland Press.

Yang, Mayfair Mei-hui. 1994. *Gifts, Favors, and Banquets: The Art of Social Relations in China.* Ithaca: Cornell University Press.

Yao, Xinzhong. 2000. *An Introduction to Confucianism.* Cambridge: Cambridge University Press.

Yu, Chun-fang. 2000. *Kuan-yin: The Chinese Transformation of Avalokitesvara.* New York: Columbia University Press.

Yu, David C. 2000. *History of Chinese Daoism.* Vol. 1. Lanham, MD: University Press of America.

13

Literature and Popular Culture

Charles A. Laughlin

As we approach the end of this book, I want to encourage you to include China in the poetry, short stories, and novels you read, the movies you see, and other aspects of your entertainment and sports. If you've read this far, you have enough knowledge about people, places, events, and traditions to enjoy both current and classic literature and popular forms of entertainment from China. The themes are universal—love, bravery, murder and intrigue, drunken revelry, jealousy, adultery, war, heroic men and women, moral uprightness, physical prowess. They also provide a lively and entertaining way to learn more about China, now that you have begun. Today we have evidence that Chinese classics derived from popular culture; contemporary Chinese thinkers and writers often challenge an age-old distinction between elite and popular culture, between the civilized and the "vulgar." Some of China's most exciting new writers, like the Beijing novelist and screenwriter Wang Shuo, or Lillian Lee, the Hong Kong writer who wrote the novel behind the Academy Award–winning film *Farewell My Concubine,* attract attention precisely because they blur or even demolish this distinction, mixing the sublime with the ridiculous until they become almost impossible to distinguish. This challenge to stuffy elitism is not a modern invention.

Today we associate popular culture with mass media, advertising, and high technology. To bring Chinese popular culture into focus, though, we must highlight the ways tradition lives and breathes in the contemporary imagination. Popular culture has always been the driving force, stimulus for change, and source of variety for Chinese literature. Fathoming just how much writing has been produced in China over the past 3,000 years is somewhat like imagining the distance to the nearest galaxy. That literature embodies seething, wrangling cultural diversity. Confucianism dominated, but as

377

discussed in Chapter 12, many other traditions came into play as well. Over the long course of Chinese cultural history, writers and artists distilled into writing, visual arts, and drama a vast multiplicity of recreational, religious, and everyday social practices.

I recommend Chen Shou-yi's *Chinese Literature: A Historical Introduction* (1961) and Liu Wu-chi's *An Introduction to Chinese Literature* (1966) as standard histories of Chinese literature. But the story is told from the point of view of the "literati"—the elite class of intellectuals who mastered the difficult Chinese written language. It is true that almost all we know about popular culture in ancient and early modern China comes through the prism of the writings and art of the literate elite, who capture only part of the richness of creative popular expression in their times. Nevertheless, looking through this prism, we can reconstruct the rich and diverse cultural panorama lying behind it.

■ Writing: The Human Pattern

It is often thought that the Chinese language is totally different from other languages because of its tonality (often misunderstood as "musicality") and its pictorial elements. Such notions, though inaccurate, were an important inspiration for modernism (particularly Imagism) in English and French poetry. The Chinese writing system lends itself to such theories because its characters look a bit like pictures, but by the time the earliest Chinese texts were written, the pictures in Chinese characters had long since ceased to be the primary means through which meaning was conveyed.

Still, the fact that written Chinese did not develop into a phonetic system like the Greek and Roman alphabets had far-reaching implications for literacy and literary expression. Because written Chinese involved learning tens of thousands of distinct characters, it was very hard to learn to read and write even in the earliest times—so hard, in fact, that the few who were able to manage it remained a small and closely knit group throughout the centuries. Indeed, the "literati" can almost be equated with the ruling class insofar as literacy was the sole avenue to power and responsibility. The written language was their stock-in-trade, and it made them socially indispensable.

The practice of divination, or fortune-telling, in the Shang and Zhou dynasty (see Table 3.1) royal courts was the foundation for the use of images in the Chinese language. As an official ritual with great political significance (see Chapter 12), divination was one of the activities that first required developing and preserving common symbols. By putting interpretation (and thus symbolic ambiguity) at the center of reading, divination, in a sense, produced some of China's earliest literary texts. In Shang times, divination often involved applying a heated metal pin to a predrilled hole in a tortoise shell or the shoulder blade of a sheep, and the cracking pattern determined the cosmic response to the question. The diviner's task, then, in addition to ensuring the correct technique, was to interpret the cracks. The earliest examples of Chinese writing available to us today are the inscriptions on these "oracle bones" indicating the question asked and the significance of the response. The later (Zhou dynasty) technique of fortune-telling with milfoil or yarrow stalks relied on a standard manual of interpretation; responses fell into categories, each associated with a representative image that provided a context in which to interpret the situation of the questioner. The *Classic of Change (Yijing)* is the most famous such manual. In it, language provides indirect access to truth and cosmic forces through the ambiguity of literary images.

To the literate class of officials and diviners, language lay at the heart of relations between humanity and the natural world, the universe as a whole. In an early commentary on the *Classic of Change,* for example, the origin of human culture is associated with observation of natural patterns:

> When in ancient times Lord Bao Xi ruled the world as sovereign, he looked upward and observed the images in heaven and looked downward and observed the models that the earth provided. He observed the patterns on birds and beasts and what things were suitable for the land. . . . Nearby, adopting them from his own person, and afar, adopting them from other things, he thereupon made the eight trigrams in order to become thoroughly conversant with the virtues inherent in the numinous and the bright and to classify the myriad things in terms of their true, innate natures. (Lynn, 1994:77–80)

Later, the literary theorist Liu Xie expanded on this by conceiving of *wen* as "human markings," or the "pattern of humanity" in an organic world where everything has its own pattern:

> Dragon and phoenix show auspicious events in the brilliance of their design; the tiger by his brightness, the leopard by the tended lushness of his spots ever indicate a magnificence of manner. . . . If such things, unaware, possess the radiance of many colors swelling within, how can this human vessel of mind lack its own aesthetic pattern *[wen]*? (Owen, 1985:19)

Explanations like these show important assumptions that underlie use of language in early China. Writing preserves a symbolic connection between humanity and the universe, perceivable within specific concrete literary images that bring us closer to particular events and situations. Among ancient Chinese philosophers, the Daoists exploit literary techniques and images the most, but early Daoists were both imaginative and skeptical about the role of language. Daoist classics like Laozi's *Dao de jing* and *Zhuangzi* question the ability of human language to transmit truths. The seemingly paradoxical opening line of *Tao de jing* (Laozi, 1963:57), for instance, states that "the way that can be spoken of is not the constant Way." *Zhuangzi,* one of the earliest repositories of narrative literature in Chinese, compares language to a "fish trap": once you have caught the fish (meaning), the trap can be disposed of. The narrator, Zhuangzi, yearns for a companion who, like him, has transcended the limitations of language to discuss the undiscussable (Zhuangzi, 1981:140).

Confucius and his followers, though they had a very different worldview, shared with the Daoists a fondness for using analogy and metaphor. In contrast with Daoists, however, the Confucians' faith in language (and anxiety to apply it properly) made them careful editors, compilers, and interpreters of texts, with huge consequences for subsequent development of literature. They used writing to connect humanity with universal truths. Their compilation of the *Classic of Poetry (Shi jing),* the earliest existing collection of Chinese poetry, gave political and moral interpretations of even the most ordinary-sounding folk songs, whether or not such interpretation was justifiable, creating a tradition of reading and writing that took such interpretive leaps for granted. Similarly, the earliest historical records and descriptions of archaic rituals and court music became centerpieces of Confucian classical tradition; Confucius declared that their value lay in embodying the morally superior ways of ancient kings. In the Confucian tradition, reading and commenting on these texts centered on identifying and abstracting these moral principles and, through teaching and governing, putting them into practice in the contemporary world. The symbolic and interpretive functions of language come through also in Chinese philosophy of Confucius' time and the centuries immediately following. In the next section, we can see how Confucian attitudes toward literature and writing helped set the pattern for the relationship between elite and popular cultures.

■ Singers and Poets

Singing has been the most widespread and lasting medium for expressing personal and collective emotions: love, social grievance, the joys and suffering of labor. These experiences, activities, and emotions are the constant subjects of song, from ancient millet fields and orchards to royal palaces, aristocratic residences, urban taverns, merchants' pleasure gardens, and even today's dance halls and karaoke clubs, and are the source from which all forms of Chinese poetry emerges. Confucians' obsessive interest in the moral powers of literature conditioned the selection, interpretation, and survival of historical, literary, and philosophical texts from the earliest times. For the moral edification of future literate generations, they preserved texts embodying the virtues and moral principles they held most sacred: humanity, decorum, righteousness, and respect for superiors. Poetry was no exception. The literati observed truth and feeling in the songs of the common people and committed some of these songs to writing. But the Confucian filter could never hide the fact that singing, chanting, and telling stories is not always motivated by Confucian virtues. It is said that Confucius compiled the 305 poems of the *Classic of Poetry* from a pool of over 3,000 folk songs chosen to assess the morale of each state, yet even those 305 rarely extol Confucian virtues explicitly. The first of the collection's four sections, the "Airs of the States" *(Guo feng),* makes up about half of the entire collection yet consists largely of love songs, harvest chants, and complaints about government harshness and corruption.

Literati poetry, though, largely moved away from popular themes, immersing itself in the exquisite extravagance of palace life or indulging in obscure metaphysical speculation, using complicated formal techniques of rhyme, assonance, alliteration, meter, and tone. After centuries of evolution, poetry was brought to its highest level of artistry in the Tang dynasty by vastly expanding subject matter and themes. Tang poetry was fresh in that it expressed profound insights and powerful emotions from an engaging, familiar perspective. The poetry of Wang Wei (699–759), for instance, embodies the Buddhist transcendence of the individual self through an impersonal immersion into peaceful natural landscapes; the poet literally loses himself in the environment:

> Empty hills, no one in sight,
> only the sound of someone talking;
> late sunlight enters the deep wood,
> shining over the green moss again.
> (Watson, 1984:200)

In this quatrain, the senses of vision and hearing indicate consciousness, but there is no self, no "I." There is also no sermonizing about the spiritual dangers of attachment to the self and the world.

Li Bai (701–762), whose extravagant, romantic poetic personality has made him a favorite among Western readers, blends the expansive imagination of the *Songs of the South (Chu ci),* a Han dynasty work rich with botanical images and cosmic journeys derived from liturgical shaman chants (Qu Yuan, 1985), the paradoxical Daoist wit of *Zhuangzi,* and the reclusive, wine-soaked nature love of Tao Yuanming (a fourth-century poet whose rediscovery was a major catalyst for the Tang dynasty poetic renaissance), with an almost effortless command of existing poetic forms and techniques. In "A Night with a Friend," Li exploits the comfortable roominess of the ancient style to subtly bring together the classic themes of friendship, moonlight, landscape, and wine:

> Dousing clean a thousand cares,
> sticking it out through a hundred pots of wine,
> a good night needing the best of conversation,

a brilliant moon that will not let us sleep—
drunk we lie down in empty hills,
heaven and earth our quilt and pillow.
(Watson, 1984:212)

Li Bai's major competitor in the popular imagination for the title of
"China's greatest poet" is the slightly younger Du Fu (712–770), who has
quite a different poetic voice. People generally first notice Du Fu's gloomy,
severe themes and subject matter. But he is also one of the boldest technical
innovators, accompanying this progressiveness with a highly traditional (Confucian) attitude about the mission of poetry. From sad narratives of abandoned
women to critiques of official neglect of the people's suffering to expression
of his personal woes, Du Fu's poetic vision was deeply committed to social
aims. Du's "Dreaming of Li Bai" provides an alternative image of the latter
poet, down to earth and entangled in the tribulations of society and politics:

Parting from the dead, I've stifled my sobs,
but this parting from the living brings me constant pain.
South of the Yangtze is a land of plague and fever;
no word comes from the exile.
Yet my old friend has entered my dreams,
proof of how long I've pined for him.
He didn't look the way he used to,
the road so far—farther than I can guess.
His spirit came from where the maple groves are green,
then went back, leaving me in borderland blackness.
Now you're caught in the meshes of the law—
how could you have wings to fly with?
The sinking moon floods the rafters of my room
and still I seem to see it lighting your face.
Where you go, waters are deep, the waves so wide—
don't let the dragons, the horned dragons harm you!
(Watson, 1984:231)

Though their approaches differ considerably, the greatest Tang dynasty
poets expanded the thematic scope of poetry, making it more emotional and
personal. There are no Chinese, whether literate or not, who do not at least
know who Li Bai and Du Fu are and few who have never heard of Wang Wei.
Though these poets were basically refining a difficult, elite cultural form, their
resulting renown also made them almost heroic figures, even in the eyes of
ordinary people.

In Tang poetry and fiction, it is hard to confidently draw a distinction
between popular and elite culture. Some poems of famous Tang poets circu-

lated on all levels of society, even (orally) among illiterates. Especially popular was Bai Juyi (772–846), another teller of sad stories but with less of the sense of moral burden in Du Fu's work; Bai was interested in emotional effects brought about by a tragic story, particularly of a woman. The simplicity of his language, the ease of its rhythms, and his cultivated sensitivity to emotional suffering made him a medieval prototype of the modern singer-songwriter. By his own observation as well as that of his admirers (and detractors), Bai Juyi's poetry had penetrated the breadth of China at all social levels. In Bai Juyi's own words:

> In my travels from Changan to Jiangxi, over a distance of three to four thousand *li,* I have seen my poems written on the walls of village schools, Buddhist monasteries, and wayside inns as well as on the boards of passenger boats. And I have heard my songs sung by students, monks, widows, maidens and men in the streets. (Ch'en, 1961:314)

More interesting evidence of the popular attitude toward elite literature is provided by the huge collection of books and scrolls that were sealed up in the famous Dunhuang grottoes around the tenth century. Rediscovered in 1908, the Dunhuang manuscripts are a repository of Tang Buddhist and secular literature, much of it copied by common people not of the elite literati class. The manuscripts provide an alternative perspective on official literary history. There are texts in many non-Chinese languages and foreign narrative materials and forms even in the Chinese texts, and the collection gives physical evidence of a thriving, nonelite culture of writing and performance. Alongside copies of works by famous writers were found popularized tales from the Buddha's life or the lives of Buddhist saints that incorporate Chinese folklore and history and oral storytelling, as well as semiliterate attempts to imitate or parody elite forms. This is the beginning of a little-recognized trend of Chinese cultural history. From the Tang dynasty on, as the ability to read and write slowly seeped out of the literati's exclusive control, popular, folk, and foreign forms played a larger role in the elite culture itself. The line dividing "elite" from "common" was blurring.

By now it should be evident that I am using the term "popular culture" to refer to the full range of culturally oriented social activities from folk singing to religious ritual to secular performing arts, involving performers and spectators from all social classes. From the late Tang dynasty on, different forms of entertainment for city dwellers (including merchants, laborers, and artisans) as well as for literati began to influence elite writing. Storytelling in the marketplace and at temple fairs, with its roots in Buddhist popular evangelism, influenced the emergence of written vernacular tales about ordinary people. And the literate class (including semiliterate merchants with highly cultivated tastes) began to develop its own distinctive forms of "popular culture."

Much of this leisure culture of the literate centered on collecting and appreciating exquisite objects (vases, tea bowls, ancient bronzes), fashioning carefully landscaped gardens within private estates, and enjoying various entertainments provided by talented, sophisticated courtesans. Many poems of the major Tang poets praise famous singing and dancing ladies who are no longer always the royal palace courtesans of previous dynasties but often "freelance" talents who might move from palaces to the entourages of rich merchants or officials and back again. Tang poets such as Du Fu, Yuan Zhen (779–831), and Bai Juyi were struck by the sadness of their unstable, transient lives in contrast to the joys and opulence of which and in which they sang. It was in this later part of the Tang that the radically new form of poetry called *ci* began to evolve.

The term *ci* refers to lyrics of popular songs. The art of *ci* consisted of writing new lyrics to familiar songs, usually love songs of Central Asian origin that were part of the courtesan's repertoire and widely known at all levels of society. Since poems about professional entertainers began to appear in the high Tang, yet *ci* itself was not commonly used until a century or so later, literati officials of the highest rank seem to have been enjoying performances of the courtesans for some time before becoming artistically interested in the songs being sung. The practice of providing new words was probably widespread long before *ci* were written and included in the corpus of major poets. The "original" lyrics of these songs relating to the song's title are often forgotten. Some of the most famous *ci* written to a given tune have nothing to do with the song's title.

Although in the late Tang *ci* poems were something of a novelty, by the Northern Song dynasty (960–1126), the *ci* form dominated poetic expression. The *shi* forms of regulated verse and quatrain, which began during the Han and reached their peak in the high Tang, though still widely practiced (people still write *shi* today), were already then looked upon as stodgy, old-fashioned, and lifeless. At this point, popular forms successfully invaded the culture of writing, affirming their own style and content; they tolerated less elite distortion, and elite literary forms would never again monopolize writing. Elite writers shifted their emphasis from poetry to fiction and drama.

■ Storytellers and Novelists

▨ Classical Tales

The roots of Chinese fiction are numerous and complex; although vernacular fiction can be confidently traced to oral storytellers manipulating an originally Buddhist tradition of popular evangelism (see Chapter 12), written fictional narrative had already existed in various forms in all kinds of early texts, including poetry, philosophy, and historical and geographical records.

History provided the most powerful narrative models for fiction; ancient works like the Zhou dynasty "Zuo Commentary" on the Spring and Autumn Annals *(Zuo Zhuan)* and the Han dynasty "Records of the Historian" *(Shi Ji)* by Sima Qian were revered throughout Chinese history as models of beautiful writing as well as sources of historical and moral knowledge. Interestingly, though people doubted the existence of ghosts and other supernatural beings as early as the Han dynasty, fictional and factual narrative were not separate categories, and thus narratives of the superhuman and supernatural were viewed as a special type of history. In ancient times, whether a story was true was much less important than whom and what it was about. Such unofficial chronicles included legendary stories about historical figures as well as tales of visitations by ghosts and deities. However, the narrative is not limited to historical records; some of the most charming and fantastical early stories are retold in the works of Warring States Period philosophers, especially the Daoists (Zhuangzi, 1981; Liezi, 1990). Though travel narratives are unusual in poetry, Qu Yuan's "Encountering Sorrow" from *Songs of the South* in the Han dynasty is another extended narrative of a cosmic journey (Qu Yuan, 1985).

Another narrative genre that stressed creativity was imaginative geography. The best-known and perhaps oldest of this category is the *Classic of Mountains and Seas (Shanhai jing)*. This work preserves ancient lore about foreign lands organized into a kind of schematic map around the outskirts of the known world (China). The *Classic of Mountains and Seas* and works like it are more descriptive than narrative, but their vocabulary and imagination set the tone for later narrative treatments of fantastical events and journeys. The worldview that underlies the *Classic of Mountains and Seas* clearly reflects China's self-perception as a core of civilization surrounded by frightening, inscrutable, and barbaric peoples and also projects other fears and anxieties suggested by, for example, the frequent mention of fireproof materials and elixirs of immortality in exotic lands.

Within the written traditions, then, the origins of imaginative narrative can be identified with the ancient practice of chronicling the strange and wonderful *(zhiguai)*. Zhiguai emerged during and after the Han dynasty as generally biographical material based on popular accounts considered unsuitable for official histories. Such material included fantastical stories of historical figures, biographies of superhuman beings (especially Daoist immortals), and records of miraculous or astonishing events. In the context of popular culture, the *zhiguai* can be viewed along with the *Classic of Poetry* as being one of the earliest existing adoptions of popular or folk materials in the form of writing. But *zhiguai* were often ignored and suppressed by historians concerned with the purity of the textual legacy, and it was not until centuries later that collections like these were actively unearthed and reintroduced into the literary corpus.

An interest in the wondrous mixed with a fascination with love themes and legendary beauties led Tang dynasty litcrati to cxperiment with writing more self-consciously crafted tales in classical Chinese modeled on Han dynasty prose. This trend arose not only because of increasing interest in fictional narrative as a form of creative expression, but also as a reaction against the stilted, artificial form of "balanced prose" writing *(pianwen)* that prevailed until the late Tang in the civil service examinations discussed in Chapter 4 (Ch'en, 1961:285–317). This can be compared with the attraction to *ci* as a new form of poetry after centuries of overdevelopment of the *shi.* The classical prose movement provided a medium better suited than the ornate, symmetrical *pianwen* to naturalistic expression of emotions and narration of events. Literate gentlemen who converged on cosmopolitan Chang'an (Map 3.1), whether successful in official careers or not, brought with them from their hometowns or from the streets of the capital itself personal experiences and popular tales that helped them produce eerie, moving stories. Despite the formal classicism and political conservatism of the classical prose movement, many of the stories created or passed along by Tang writers like Yuan Zhen and Bai Xingjian (Bai Juyi's brother) became staples of popular literature and performing arts for centuries to come.

Like the *zhiguai,* these "romance tales" *(chuanqi)* included elements of the supernatural and the fantastical; more importantly, they embodied the more personal and realistic emphasis of the Tang dynasty poet-officials. The exploration of emotional and moral dilemmas—represented perhaps best by Yuan Zhen's masterpiece, "The Story of Yingying" (*Yingying zhuan;* Ma and Lau, 1978:139–145)—guaranteed that the narrative material of *chuanqi* would continue to be a major resource for both elite and popular literature in centuries to come. "The Story of Yingying" narrates a chance love affair between the ambitious student Zhang and Yingying, a talented and beautiful young woman languishing in her widowed mother's house. Zhang, however, resolves to leave her and forget about her forever when he goes to the capital for the civil service examinations. The indignant Yingying resigns herself to bitterness and eventually marries someone else but never forgives Zhang for his faithlessness, refusing to see him when he visits her after he has married. "The Story of Yingying" is a classical and emotionally raw rendition of the conflict between the demands of social convention and emotional power that ends tragically, with social convention winning—a far cry from the amusing allegorical fables of the Warring States philosophers, or the strange supernatural chronicles and far-ranging adventures that were the earliest foundations of Chinese fiction.

Yuan Zhen and other writers of *chuanqi* accomplished in fiction what writers had been doing with poetry: exploring values that turned not on rigid or abstract moral principles but on emotional sensitivity and integrity, values that held their own claim to truth but might at times have come into dramatic conflict with conventional Confucian moral duties. The artistic elaboration of an emotion-based value system is central to the Tang dynasty's contribution to Chinese literature, and it owed as much for material and themes to the thriving cultures of professional entertainment—singing courtesans, professional dancers—as to poets' and writers' own experiences and imagination.

▒ Vernacular Fiction

This new fashion in the Tang of telling strange, moving, and wondrous stories in terse, classical Chinese is only one strand of the development of Chinese narrative. Even more crucial to the later development of Chinese fiction and drama was the vehicle of oral storytelling with its roots in Buddhist popular evangelism dating back to the pre-Tang period. The contributions of Buddhism to Chinese literature were not limited to philosophical and spiritual themes but included as well the techniques and conventions of vernacular storytelling (the inclusion of a moral at the end of a tale, a mixture of poetry and prose, and an emphasis on stories about anonymous, ordinary people). For example, Buddhist source texts like the Sanskrit *Lotus Sutra* (of which Kuramajiva's popular

Depiction of a crowd gathered around a storyteller

translation appeared as early as C.E. 406; Watson, 1993:ix) already possessed all these features.

The venue of such storytelling, widespread by the Tang dynasty, was the urban or suburban marketplace. This was the focal point of the Chinese community, the hub of often multicultural commercial transactions, the meeting point of all walks of life from travelers to merchants, farmers, public officials, prostitutes, and entertainers. The entire cross section of Chinese society converged on the marketplace or square, from the county seat to the large mercantile centers and the capital. The square is crowded, and the crowd is as diverse as can be—everyone drawn by the center, the marketplace itself, where everything happens, or where at least one can hear tell of everything. This is where the stories are told, of great sages or heroes real and imaginary, remote in history or just around the corner, full of ordinary people fighting or running from the law, of great generals annihilating their enemies or entangled in political intrigue, and of ghosts, fox-spirits, gods, talking animals, sniveling cowards, and heroic prostitutes. All of this is in the hands of a single storyteller competing for his or her street audience with acrobats, magicians, theatrical troupes, blind balladeers with three-stringed guitars, and other storytellers keeping rhythm with bamboo or metal clappers or drums.

The telling of stories as such was not alien to Chinese elite culture; because of the Confucians' obsession with significance and cultural value, some of the earliest historical texts preserved are also some of China's most compelling narratives, and in late imperial times Chinese history became one of the vernacular storyteller's richest resources of material. But the official histories as well as the more exotic materials already discussed could be read only by the literate minority, which was extremely small in ancient and medieval times, and it is difficult to tell whether the same stories were being told among illiterate people at the time. What Buddhist and Buddhist-influenced storytelling had to offer Chinese narrative, then, was a form that lent itself to public performance, thus providing a bridge between literati art and a much broader, often illiterate audience. Chinese legends, mythology, and historical records provided the storytellers with new material and themes. One of the most attractive aspects of Chinese historical narrative to the storytelling, theatrical, and ultimately film and television audiences is the combination of moral character (loyalty in particular) and fighting prowess of the gallant or knight-errant. Stories of such exploits abounded in the official histories, legendary biographies, and oral tales in the marketplace. As they multiplied in the repertoire of storytellers, many such legends were grouped together in long series of tales, often loosely based on historical events.

One such repository for narrative and lore in Song and Ming dynasty storytelling was the famous story of the Tang dynasty monk Xuan Zang (596–664), whose pilgrimage to India to fetch the complete set of Mahayana Buddhist scriptures is described in Chapter 12. As in the past, the exotic foreign journey was a favorite subject of tale spinners with a taste for the bizarre and supernatural. The Xuan Zang story was gradually embellished by adding various pilgrim assistants to protect the priest from earthly and otherworldly dangers on the road. Somewhere along the line, this set of stories came into contact with the ancient Indian legends of a Monkey King of overweening ambition, and such a monkey became Xuan Zang's chief disciple.

The resulting story, *Journey to the West (Xi you ji,* 1592), then, links dozens of existing tales of the fantastical, of overcoming and outwitting animal spirits and supernatural beasts, under the premise of this sacred pilgrimage (Wu, 1977). This chain of episodes is cemented by a common set of characters centering on the monk and the monkey and other pilgrim-guardians, including a gluttonous talking pig and a dragonlike water spirit. The adventures are placed, in turn, into a cosmic context in which the monkey's mission to assist Xuan Zang is understood as penance for his past outrageous acts of mischievous hubris (he tried to overthrow heaven) narrated in the novel's opening chapters. Although the novel maintains a folksy irreverence toward traditional hierarchy, orthodoxy, and morality, the Buddha and his pantheon come out essentially invincible, and the sacred necessity of Xuan Zang's mission is never questioned.

Similar to *Journey to the West*'s snowballing of popular legends, stories of gallantry and heroism, particularly ones featuring rebellious, unorthodox figures, tended to attach themselves to the Song dynasty rebel uprising of Song Jiang (Hsia, 1971:76). Stories based on these events began to solidify during the Southern Song, gaining a wide audience for their patriotic appeal because of the Southern Song regime's status as almost a government in exile as northern China was overrun by foreign people. These legends associated martial prowess, superhuman physical strength, and a brutally straightforward loyalty with China's integrity and Han race.

These swashbuckling stories coalesced in a sixteenth-century Ming dynasty vernacular novel, *Outlaws of the Marsh (Shuihu zhuan),* which narrates the gathering of 108 colorful, Robin Hood–like heroic outlaws through a variety of adventures, in which they ultimately lead a series of successful battles against the Song imperial troops and then surrender out of patriotism and turn their energies toward assisting the Song in suppressing the evil rebel Fang La (Luo, 1981). *Outlaws,* particularly through its contribution of heroic figures like the leader Song Jiang and the colorful heroes Wu Song and Li Kui, is seminal in its contribution to the tradition of martial arts fiction *(wuxia xiaoshuo),* part of the lifeblood of Chinese popular culture to this day.

For the purposes of the *reading* audience of vernacular fiction, mere transcriptions and clever rearrangements of popular oral stories were ultimately limited in their appeal. The Qing dynasty novel *Dream of the Red Chamber (Hong lou meng,* 1791), however, is by all accounts the masterpiece of the full-length, vernacular Chinese novel (Wang, 1992). What people cannot agree on is what makes it so, and an entire scholarly tradition has been devoted to this one novel's study and interpretation. Although *Journey to the West* and *Outlaws of the Marsh* string together a vast number of almost unrelated episodes drawn from history, myth, and traditional storytelling material, *Dream* is completely original, with a series of interlocking plots revolving around the declining fortunes of the wealthy Jia, Xue, Shi, and Wang families, who have ties to the imperial court. The novel is said to be largely based on the personal experiences of its principal author, Cao Xueqin (1715?–1763). The setting is during the eighteenth century in the final glow of China's last dynasty, the Qing. A grandfather clock in the Jia family's mansion hints at China's contact with European powers, whose missionary efforts by late Qing times were a conspicuous aspect of the Chinese countryside and port cities.

Dream of the Red Chamber is remarkable in its time for its lack of physical action, the narrative's almost complete confinement to the Jia mansion and the surrounding capital suburbs, and its concentration on the relationships among a core group of young men and women, at the center of whom are Baoyu, second son of the Jia family's youngest generation; Xue Baochai, the charming, practical woman to whom he is eventually betrothed; and Daiyu, an ill-starred, frail, and gloomy beauty to whom Baoyu is more strongly attracted (though the two seem to be able only to make each other unhappy).

This triangle is nestled in countless other relationships and conflicts among these and other families, amid armies of servants, dozens of vividly realized, colorful characters, and lavish descriptions of costume, decorations, and genteel entertainments ranging from tea appreciation to poetry games and theatrical performances. The epic family saga is further placed within a cosmic frame constructed of equal parts of Buddhism and Daoism, in which Baoyu is cast not only in his earthly form of the effeminate, hypersensitive, and eccentric boy with no scholarly (social, political) ambitions who only likes to be among women, but ultimately as a superfluous stone left over from the mythical goddess Nü Wa's restoration of the damaged masonry of the heavens. This stone is cursed by the gift of consciousness with the desire to experience life in the human world, a wish granted to him by a Buddhist monk and a Daoist priest. Once his fate is sealed, a further adventure on the stone's part forms the supernatural basis of Baoyu's relationship with Daiyu: as a Divine Stone Page in the otherworldly Garden of the Goddess of Disillusionment, he is moved by kindness to water a parched fairy plant with dew, which thus incurs a "debt of tears" that Daiyu (the human incarnation of the fairy plant) must repay in the human world. Most of the other major young women characters are also spirits burdened with debts in heaven or former lives, whereas all the male characters except Baoyu himself represent the human world, the constricting influences of society, politics, money, and power.

Despite the development of the novel in late imperial China into increasingly unified and complex forms, the vitality of the oral short story was not exhausted by its absorption into novels like *Journey to the West* and *Outlaws of the Marsh*. As late as the end of the Ming and through the Qing dynasties, prominent connoisseurs of popular literature like Feng Menglong (1574–1646), Ling Mengchu (1580–1644), and Pu Songling (1640–1715) preserved in written form oral storyteller's *(huaben)* tales that were by then as many as several hundred years old. They also offered many original stories. More than any of the forms of fiction discussed so far, these stories feature characters of illiterate classes: merchants, farmers, artisans, entertainers, and prostitutes, always placed in unlikely and awkward situations and often in compelling moral predicaments (Birch, 1958; Ma and Lau, 1978). The plots of such stories rely on multiple coincidences, often also using physical objects to string events together and dramatic, even shocking scenes.

Pu Songling's somewhat later creations, written in classical Chinese rather than the vernacular, are much more homogeneous than the late Ming *huaben* stories edited by Feng and Ling. They more generally reflect the experience and imagination of the young scholar on his way to the city or capital to take part in the civil service examinations, revealing a similarity to the Tang *chuanqi*. In *huaben* tales, scholars encounter beautiful courtesans or other women who make them forget their wives, harm their reputations, or do poorly on the examinations. Pu Songling's scholars, however, are beset by all manner of supernatural beings—ghosts, demons, and fox and snake spirits—who materialize as beautiful women but also somehow get in the way of or complicate the scholar's career or family life (P'u, 1989).

This consistency of plot and narrative perspective speaks to the combination of elements in the character of the Chinese novelist that caused him to fail the civil service examinations and yet become a fertile cultural resource in his own right. It also suggests the commonality of experience among writers and readers of this sort of writing, who were almost exclusively young examination candidates themselves. These elements are equally conspicuous in the Chinese drama, which is heavily reliant on the fictional tradition for narrative material; but this brings us to another strand of the story.

■ Priests and Playwrights

Until recent years, discussions of Chinese drama in English invariably stress the "belatedness" of its appearance in comparison with other literary genres and in comparison with other cultures. However, recent research on Chinese folk ritual and drama shows that this view uncritically privileges the written literary canon and disregards folk culture. We now know that the per-

formance practices, modes of representation, and stage conventions on which
Chinese theatrical performance is based can be traced far back into shaman-
istic rituals and exorcisms of evil spirits, which continue to be practiced in
their primitive form in many parts of China to the present day.

In addition to ritual and folk practices, the performing arts also drew on
medieval palace entertainment and urban storytelling. As early as the Song
dynasty, both Kaifeng and Hangzhou had bustling theater districts nicknamed
"tiles" after their jam-packed audiences (Liu, 1966:162–163). Song "variety
plays" opened with a medley followed by a number of short pieces that may
not have been linked together by a single story or group of characters. Some
of the differences between the northern and southern theater of the Yuan and
Ming dynasties were already established by this time.

The link between oral performance and full-fledged operatic drama is
substantiated by the Jin dynasty work *Romance of the Western Chamber (Xi
xiang ji zhugong diao),* in which Yuan Zhen's above-mentioned "Story of

A Beijing acrobatic
performance

Robert Gamer

Yingying" is presented in "medley" *(zhugong diao)* format (Ch'en, 1994). That is, the story is told in the framework of a musical composition in which successive sections have different musical modes *(diao),* and each section is made up of poems that share a single mode interspersed with prose narrative passages. The reputed author, Master Dong, gave Yuan Zhen's story a happy ending.

Later in the thirteenth century, the *Western Chamber* story was adapted again by Wang Shifu to become perhaps the most famous work of Chinese drama, *Xi xiang ji (Romance of the Western Chamber),* a northern *zaju. Zaju* (also called "northern drama") inherited from previous forms like the previously mentioned "medley" the alternation of prose and verse passages, the latter of which were sung to musical accompaniment. The sung parts were limited to a single actor, providing a unity to northern drama further enhanced by its tight, four-act structure. The other major contribution of the Yuan dynasty *zaju* to operatic theater and Chinese literature in general is its unique new form of verse, called *sanqu.* Like the Song dynasty *ci, sanqu* represented a further innovation in the coordination of verse with music, allowing for a certain amount of variation and the addition of grammatical particles and colloquial expressions (Liu, 1966:186).

Although the Yuan *zaju* was associated with the capital of Dadu (modern Beijing), the southern drama that had been in existence at least since Song times was associated with the opulent and culturally sophisticated southern cities of Hangzhou and Suzhou. These Southern dramas, also called *chuanqi* like the Tang tales upon which they were often based, were extraordinarily long (running to thirty or forty scenes). They did not rise to central prominence in the history of Chinese theater until the Ming dynasty. There are hundreds of *chuanqi* plays from the Ming and Qing dynasties, but the best known are *The Lute (Pipa ji)* by Gao Ming (c. 1305–c. 1370) and especially *Peony Pavilion (Mudan ting)* by Tang Xianzu (1550–1617).

Gao Ming's *The Lute* is based on an old story of a brilliant scholar who, after achieving glory in the civil service examinations, is induced to marry the daughter of the prime minister, though he had left a wife at home and forgets about his ailing parents. After his parents pass away, the scholar is finally reminded of his neglect by his first wife, who slowly works her way to the capital by performing with her lute on the road. Tang Xianzu's *Peony Pavilion,* also known as *Return of the Soul (Huan hun ji),* is based on a vernacular story and incorporates a supernatural theme of love beyond death (Tang, 1980). It features the popular formula of a well-born young lady coming across a talented scholar, but with the twist that they only meet in their dreams. Before they can get together, the heroine Du Liniang's passion overcomes her and she dies. However, when the scholar encounters Liniang's buried portrait, the power of his love brings her soul back out of the underworld. Now united, they are confronted with the wrath of Du Liniang's incredulous father, but she persuades him the scholar is innocent, emphasizing the importance of feelings over reason. Music and stirring poetry enhance the potency of a whole series of climactic moments and confrontations. The play is a storehouse of lyrical allusions scouring the length of Chinese literary history, as well as a showcase for Tang Xianzu's gift for wordplay and symbolism.

Although later forms of theater, notably the well-known Beijing opera, are of less literary interest than these earlier masterpieces, they do give us valuable hints as to the unique stagecraft and dramaturgy of Chinese drama, of which the texts of the earlier plays give us little idea. For example, although we know that by the Yuan dynasty, dramatic roles had already been reduced into certain stock types—the "old scholar," the "clown," the "painted lady"— it is only by watching the Beijing opera that we can get an idea of how costume and makeup are manipulated to signal these roles (for example, a white spot or spots on the face to indicate a clown). We do not know for sure, but it seems safe to assume that like Beijing opera, earlier forms of theater used few props or scenic backdrops as in Western theater, relying instead on descriptive dialogue, stock gestures, and symbolic objects to suggest location and movement. Finally, the figure of the devoted opera fan, still in existence today, indicates the challenge posed by Chinese theater to the traditional literati's monopoly on literary culture. The visual spectacle of opera along with its acrobatics and musical accompaniment came together to form entertainment of great sophistication that was not yet accessible to the illiterate or only partially

Robert Gamer

A traditional Song drama performed
in Hangzhou, a former Song dynasty capital

literate. Oral storytelling, vernacular fiction, and the theater all represent the slippage over the centuries of elite culture from the hands of the literate minority. Modern technological advances were about to create the potential for even greater cultural engagement on the part of the population at large, but new forms of cultural elitism would still maintain a stubborn division between the educated and the "masses."

■ **Resisting Modern Orthodoxies**

▨ **The May Fourth Movement: Modern Cultural Orthodoxy**

The May Fourth Movement is named after a climactic student demonstration at Tiananmen Square (the Gate of Heavenly Peace in front of the Forbidden City in Beijing) on that date in 1919, passionately opposing the weak Chinese government's passive acceptance of humiliating concessions of Chinese territory to Japan in the Treaty of Versailles, which concluded World War I (the references to this treaty and movement in Chapters 4, 7, and 11 give a sense of the importance of this date). For students and writers, the demonstration represented the culmination of a ground swell of youthful antitraditionalism represented by Chen Duxiu's popular magazine *New Youth (Xin qingnian),* and the literary revolution sponsored by Hu Shi, signified by his promotion of writing forcefully and directly in the modern vernacular.

As in ancient times, cultural progress was still being measured in terms of writing. However, there was a characteristically modern, nationalistic side to the May Fourth Movement as well. After decades of humiliating military and diplomatic defeats at the hands of European countries, the United States, and Japan, both popular and elite culture in modern times were saturated by a feeling that these indignities were suffered in large part because China's political and military leaders were too effeminate, lacking in the essential qualities of the *nanzi Han* (loosely translatable as "the virile Chinese man"), the decisive, physically powerful, and charismatic leader for which Chinese history and literature provide numerous models.

May Fourth intellectuals, equipped with Western learning, knowledge of foreign languages, and an acute sense of historical crisis, were making a revolution from above by writing in a new vernacular much closer to everyday speech, using quite different techniques borrowed in part from European novelists and thinkers. They were also writing fiery essays about what the new literature was for—the destruction of old thinking and the construction of a clean, healthy, and fair new China.

The cultural agenda of the May Fourth Movement is well represented by the work of Lu Xun (1881–1936). Lu Xun's short stories represented a break from the past for the most part because they were written in the modern vernacular, a mode of expression until then alien to writing. The stories often tell of a young intellectual returning to his home in the countryside after receiving a foreign education and having been exposed to Western ideas, only to find that he can no longer fit in with the people and landscapes of his youth (Lu Xun, 1990). Unlike most writers that followed him, however, Lu Xun was a master of irony and distortion, and his vision of the world, though stridently politicized, was nightmarish and often bordered on the absurd and sinister.

But instead of signaling a triumph for popular literature, the May Fourth Movement set up a New Culture in opposition to traditional orthodox culture. Thus by the 1920s a clearly defined cultural triangle appeared: (1) traditional Chinese culture, the educational foundation of even the most radical cultural revolutionaries and the target of almost universal and incessant attack by modern writers; (2) the modern New Culture orthodoxy, based on humanism, science, and democracy—all murkily defined—and foreign (largely European) behavior, dress, and thought; and (3) mass media popular culture embodied in newspapers and magazines, radio, and film that began to emerge in the nineteenth century. This third leg of the triangle, like the first, has been neglected and disdained by historians who identify with the May Fourth Movement.

The issue is further complicated by the fact that both theorists and practitioners of the modern "progressive" or "revolutionary" art and literature, particularly in the first half of this century, consciously aligned and identified themselves with "the masses," "popular culture," or "folk culture" even as they transformed and distorted it for their own artistic and ideological ends. Apart from this explicit lip service being paid to the "popular," elites appropriating and distorting some of the same popular forms they criticize should by now seem familiar; it is very much the traditional stance of the custodians of the written word in China.

Not that the May Fourth generation and their leftist successors did not innovate a great deal. The "serious" side of modern Chinese literature, including poetry and drama, ushered in phenomena rare or nonexistent elsewhere, including a universally adopted rhetoric of "cultural hygiene" (a 1983 government-led rectification campaign attacked "cultural pollution" from abroad); the merging of individual subjectivity with national identity; and the idea of art as a dangerous weapon. This last idea not only fueled artists' and writers' sense of self-importance but also got them censored, landed them in jail, and even got them killed at a higher rate than in most other parts of the world.

The importance attributed by historians to the May Fourth Movement tends to obscure the even more profound changes in China's cultural activity brought about by the emergence of mass media in the mid–nineteenth century; the literary revolution itself was to a certain extent indebted to these changes. Newspapers, telegraph, telephone, radio, and even the railroad made it possible for a much broader swath of the population to engage in the same cultural activities. Reading news and illustrated fiction in newspapers and magazines and watching motion pictures made available in Shanghai almost as early as in New York, Paris, and London drastically changed the cultural and social life of even the most conservative. Before radical students began to dominate mass media, the commercial print media's audience consisted largely of urban sophisticates similar to the opera buffs discussed in the previous section. Printed advertisements in mass-circulation newspapers, often exploiting graphic images—even accessible to illiterates—as much as text, brought larger audiences to theatrical performances and larger markets to books and magazines. These eye-catching pictures (particularly in commercial print media, but also on billboards, shingles, and flyers) broadened the affected market substantially beyond the literate (Lee and Nathan, 1985).

In the meantime, the higher-technology mass media provided more of what a broader audience demanded: not the epoch-making, brooding short stories of writers like Lu Xun, but traditional-style vernacular novels of love, detective stories, fantastical journeys, and the exploits of superhuman martial arts heroes mixed with accounts of real journeys to Europe and the United States. Unfortunately, little of this is available in English translation, but Liu Ts'un-yan's *Chinese Middlebrow Fiction* gives an authentic taste of the miscellanies of the turn of the century and thereafter (Liu, 1984).

May Fourth thinkers associated mass media popular culture with traditional China; they were largely indifferent to or unaware of what was modern (i.e., nontraditional) about it, and so the rejection of popular fiction became one of the cornerstones of the movement. They could not see, for instance, the Western influences on Zeng Pu's *Flower in a Sinful Sea* (*Niehai hua,* 1905), on Xu Zhenya's *Jade Pearl Spirit* (*Yuli hun,* 1912), or on Zhang Henshui's *Fate of Tears and Laughter (Tixiao yinyuan,* 1930)—the latter being one of the most popular Chinese novels of the twentieth century—because they were presented in the form and language of traditional vernacular fiction. However, just like the vernacular novel and oral storytelling in previous centuries, the very popularity of what Perry Link calls the "literature of comfort" (1981:196–235) worked against the self-important authority of New Culture and thus took on a progressive value.

This is borne out by the mixed feelings modern writers and critics had about popular literature. Although they call for something radically different to blow away the cobwebs of a morally bankrupt culture, they are at the same time some of its most avid readers and promoters. Lu Xun was one of popular fiction's most strident critics, yet by assigning grudging praise to late Qing dynasty satirical works like Li Boyuan's *Brief History of Enlightenment* (*Wenming xiaoshi,* 1903) and Wu Woyao's *Strange Events Witnessed over Twenty Years* (*Ershinian mudu zhi guai xianzhuang,* 1907) in his *Brief History of Chinese Fiction* (*Zhongguo xiaoshuo shilüe,* 1959), he actually guaranteed the continued recognition of these works and others long after the cultural supremacy of the May Fourth Movement had given way to more radical visions. Zheng Zhenduo and Ah Ying (Qian Xingcun), two of modern China's most prominent leftist cultural activists, were also foremost scholars and enthusiasts of late imperial popular culture.

The New Culture movement's attitude toward popular literature was based in part on an unfortunate identification of seriousness with progressiveness: the more fun a work of literature or art, the more politically incorrect it was thought to be. Underlying this was the prejudice that the practitioners and audience of popular literature were inferior in character and intelligence to the cultural revolutionaries of the May Fourth Movement. Moreover, existing mass-media culture was incorrectly identified with an ill-defined idea of "traditional China," which was overwhelmingly viewed as an evil order to be thoroughly uprooted and eradicated.

Lao She (1899–1966), one of modern China's most unique and prolific novelists, at least implicitly defied the May Fourth generation's disdain for humor and frivolity. In works like *The Two Mas (Er ma,* 1931) and *Rickshaw Boy (Luotuo ziangzi,* 1938), Lao She creates a humorous, satirical vision of modern Chinese society that nevertheless expresses a yearning for something better. Influenced by Charles Dickens among others, Lao She had a mastery of humor unusual for a modern Chinese writer, making readers laugh without trivializing his subject matter or his characters. He exploits the fine line between comedy and tragedy so that one is constantly aware of the tragic implications of the comic situations he creates. In *The Two Mas,* he accomplishes this through the cultural and generational misunderstandings created by a Chinese father and son residing in London in the 1920s and the son falling in love with a British woman. In *Rickshaw Boy* he does so in the story of a simple, forthright laborer in Beijing who wants nothing more than to make enough money to buy his own rickshaw but is constantly thwarted by the dishonesty of those around him, the sheer scarcity of wealth, and the military instability of 1930s China.

▪ Leftist Mass Culture

Once the May Fourth Movement had passed its prime and the literary revolution gave way to revolutionary literature, leftism and communism in China inherited the movement's awkward relationship with popular culture. By the 1930s, leftist writers and critics occupied important, arguably mainstream positions in the New Culture industry. Old-style popular novels and magazines continued to sell and be written, but their audience was dwindling due to a new generation of readers with Western-style education (whose teachers had often been May Fourth activists like Lu Xun) who inherited the May Fourth hatred for old China.

Ding Ling (1904–1985) is representative of the shift from self to society that characterized the 1930s. Her *Diary of Miss Sophie* (*Shafei nüshi de riji,* 1927), one of the best-known works of modern Chinese literature, narrates through the protagonist's diary entries an ailing young Westernized woman's struggle between desire and reason as she alternately tortures, manipulates, and pursues different male friends. The work can be viewed as taking the innovations of May Fourth literature, already colored by self-obsession, sexuality, and despair, to (or beyond) their logical extremes. But only three or four years after writing this and several similar stories, Ding Ling's narrative personalities were dissolving into the masses, her febrile self-obsession transforming into enthusiastic engagement in social and historical change; she was attempting to align herself with, indeed lose herself among, workers and peasants.

This shift need not be viewed as paradoxical. The writer's attempt to become one with the people saturates the fiction, poetry, drama and reportage, and even films of the 1930s. Chinese leftists were much more keenly aware than the May Fourth generation of the power of mass media and better acquainted with its mechanics as well, and this is particularly evident in 1930s Chinese cinema. In *Street Angels* (*Malu tianshi,* 1937), for example, the familiar entertainment, fun, romance, and sensationalism of Hollywood are all exploited to advance themes of social injustice, class friction, and economic crisis, calling to mind the efforts of Charlie Chaplin. But although leftists seemed at home in the modern mass media, like their predecessors and teachers from the May Fourth movement, they were ambivalent about traditional popular and folk culture.

The urban control over mass media communications and transportation put the countryside at a greater cultural disadvantage than before. This situation has not changed substantially to the present day; the pervasiveness of television has only guaranteed the dissemination of centrally approved information and material, while local popular forms have tended to die out.

Leftists, particularly in rural base areas like Mao Zedong's Jiangxi Soviet, in a desire to unleash the revolutionary potential of the masses, went beyond the limits of literacy and explored traditional performing arts forms as potential vehicles for political propaganda. Viewing Western-style spoken dramas, the legacy of May Fourth, as boring, they turned toward traditional dramatic forms like the *yangge,* a New Year's variety show (largely song and dance) with roots in ritual performances like *nuo* exorcism and *Mulian* plays. But in their efforts to remold these forms and inject them with new moralistic content, communists failed to observe many of the features that made them work, from their coordination with the lunar calendar and characteristic bawdiness and irreverence to the formal aspects of performance and relationship between form and content. The "new *yangge,*" by displacing the old and having little appeal in itself (being an incongruous patchwork quilt of the traditional and the modern), effectively wiped out *yangge* from the areas in which it was promoted (Holm, 1991). This is characteristic of the Communist Party's kiss of death to all kinds of traditional forms clear through the Cultural Revolution (1966–1976): from storytelling to comedic dialog, from music to drum singing to dance, the Communist Party had a tendency to ruin popular, traditional art forms in the attempt to make them "modern" and useful.

■ Alternative Voices

There were at the same time modern Chinese writers not so committed to the social functions of literature as such. Shen Congwen and Xiao Hong, for example, brought to modern literature a lyrical vision of the rural countryside in which the familiar questions of national identity, ethnic outrage, and indignation at the Japanese invasions took a back seat to the vivid, subjective recreation of the rhythms and emotional structure of rural life. Both of these writers discovered and constructed a new aesthetic in the life of the Chinese countryside that had never existed in Chinese narrative literature before but that also bore no close resemblance or debt to Western literary forms.

Meanwhile, particularly during World War II, popular fiction was making a comeback and achieved unprecedented success in the novels of Eileen Chang (Zhang Ailing). In a way, Eileen Chang was the first truly modern writer in her open defiance of one of the most sacred credos of Chinese literary culture, that literature must have a positive social function. Chang's "modern *chuanqi*" take the mood of traditional romantic tales—conflicts between emotional fulfillment, social obligations, and material gain; the jealousy, manipulation, and open struggle among wives and concubines; love triangles; and so forth—bring them into the cultural soup of modern China, and expand them into a psychological dimension replete with dark and unpredictable personalities and even insanity (e.g., "The Golden Cangue"). One of Chang's most innovative contributions to modern literature is dispassionate narration of the experience of revolution and agricultural reform (an unthinkable sacrilege for a leftist writer) in such works as *Love in a Barren Land* (*Chidi zhi lian,* 1954) and *Rice-Sprout Song* (*Yangge,* 1953). Eileen Chang's importance, ignored by communist literary historians, has been vindicated not only through the influential assessments of C. T. Hsia (1971) and Edward Gunn (1980) but also through her inspiration of a whole generation of contemporary writers in all of the Chinas, from Wang Anyi in Shanghai and Lillian Lee in Hong Kong to Li Ang and Zhu Tianwen in Taiwan.

■ Contemporary Literature and Culture in the Three Chinas

Eileen Chang's predicament in 1949—whether to stay in China after the communist takeover and years of bitter civil war or go abroad and continue her career free of pressure from political persecution—was probably difficult only for personal reasons, but it was emblematic of the path of modern Chinese elite and popular cultures. Many gifted writers decided to stay; some, like Shen Congwen, sadly never wrote again, whereas others, like Lao She, adopted, willingly or not, a rhetoric and mentality vastly different from those of the works that established their reputations. Writing in the 1950s and 1960s, one was largely compelled to extol the new society, and even courageous criticisms were deeply entangled in the ideology of literature in the service of politics alone. Eileen Chang's vision would have been even less tenable than Shen Congwen's.

Modern Chinese literary history is generally marked out in terms of cataclysmic political or historical events. The importance of the May Fourth Movement to modern Chinese literature has already been noted, but there were to be many more such dates, including the anticommunist purge of 1927, the Japanese invasion of Manchuria on September 18, 1931, the outbreak of war with Japan in December 1937, the rape of Nanjing in January 1938, and the communist victory in 1949. When we get to 1949, we tend to think of things in more geographical terms, imagining completely separate cultures in contemporary mainland China, Taiwan, and Hong Kong.

This view, however, is becoming problematic. Transformation within the cultural scenes on both sides of the Taiwan Strait complicates the issue, as does the give-and-take between both Taiwan and mainland China on the one hand and Hong Kong on the other. Moreover, both mainland China and Taiwan after 1949 had their own cataclysmic political events that are comparable to those in the period before the civil war.

Taiwan's cultural scene throughout the 1950s, though perhaps less oppressive than that of mainland China, was still under tight political control. The Nationalist Party allowed and encouraged literary and artistic visions tied to the conviction that the civil war was not over and that those who fled to Taiwan and other places after 1949 would eventually return home (Lau, 1983:x–xi). But as the Nationalists' position in Taiwan solidified, a new generation of writers too young to remember the war grew up in the 1960s in a society oriented more toward economic development than military goals or political purity, a society much more saturated with mass media and popular culture, including television and a burgeoning film industry. The educational background of the newer generation of Taiwan writers (many of whom studied at the University of Washington or the International Writing Program at the University of Iowa) also led to a remarkable upsurge in the late 1950s through the early 1970s of modernist poetry and fiction in Taiwan.

The works of Ch'en Ying-chen, Huang Ch'un-ming, and Wang Chen-ho, all writers who in one way or another resisted the current of pro-American sentiment and feverish economic development, best represent this period in Taiwanese literature. These writers, whether consciously or not, preserve the modern Chinese tradition of literature as the voice of opposition to authority established by Lu Xun. They were against the status quo in Taiwan without being pro-Beijing—no small achievement under the near-totalitarian political atmosphere of Taiwan in the 1960s.

Li Yongping is often described as a conduit of "native soil literature" *(xiangtu wenxue)*, which focused on themes of home, belonging, cultural identity, and the rural Chinese experience; Shen Congwen is in some sense the spiritual ancestor of native soil literature in Taiwan. Native soil writers resisted both the sometimes affected modernism of the previous generation and the more commercialized, movie- and television-drama script phase that many writers went into in Taiwan in the late 1970s and early 1980s. They attempted to create or preserve a culture that belonged to Taiwan above all, as well as the ideal of a socially engaged literature that seemed to be fading from the modern Chinese cultural horizon in the face of feverish economic expansion. However, the lifting of martial law with the death of Chiang Kai-shek in 1975, the deregulation of journalism in 1986, and the gradual implementation of general democratic elections throughout the 1990s have led to a slackening of political intensity in Taiwanese literature, and its displacement by the popular literary marketplace as an important factor in literary success.

In mainland China, the deaths of Mao Zedong and Zhou Enlai in 1976, punctuated with particular severity by the devastating Tangshan earthquake, marked the end of an era of apparently blind faith in communism, with profound effects on the cultural scene. In the ensuing years, the rise of Deng Xiaoping and a new vision of the mission of the Communist Party and the trial and imprisonment of the "Gang of Four" for crimes committed during the anarchic Cultural Revolution set the tone for the cultural scene of the 1980s, which ushered in the rehabilitation of cultural figures who had been persecuted since the antirightist campaign of 1958 and had been in and out of prison and labor reform over the ensuing twenty years. Some of the more prominent of these, like Wang Meng, were promoted to important posts, whereas others, like Liu Binyan, were, in part through the good graces of such appointees, enthusiastically promoted in the mainstream literary press and experienced a new surge of creative work (Link, 1983). There was an outpouring of "scar" literature, humanist literature, and literature of historical reflection that reaffirmed the importance of intellectuals and artists after decades of persecution and tried to derive meaning and spiritual comfort from the therapeutic act of *suku* (recounting bitterness).

However, the literature written during this stage (in the early 1980s) did not differ artistically from the familiar conventions of socialist realism. Writers seemed to still accept the premise that literature's highest aim is the realistic depiction of social reality in progressive transformation, as Mao Zedong had himself called for in his 1942 "Talk at the Yan'an Conference on Literature and Art." This was merely a more genuine and honest way of approaching the task than had been common throughout the 1960s and 1970s, in which the bleak truths of contemporary reality were concealed under a false mask of idealism.

Around 1985, a new generation of writers emerged, writers who were too young to have gone through and to understand the turbulent and bewildering persecutions of the older writers since the antirightist campaign. These writers, like Ah Cheng, Zheng Wanlong, and Zhang Chengzhi, were teenagers during the Cultural Revolution. Many had lost a good portion of their education and held a much different view of contemporary Chinese social and cultural reality than the older generation. This view is reflected in their works, which are much less confident in the literary mission of social reform taken for granted until then in mainland China.

One of the most conspicuous trends of these writers' first departures from socialist realism is a variation of native soil literature referred to as "searching-for-roots literature" *(xungen wenxue)*. Unlike the more innocently lyrical efforts of Shen Congwen and Xiao Hong, searching for roots involves a more pronounced metaphysical mission derived in part from translations of Western philosophy and literature and in part from the rediscovery of aspects of Chinese culture that had been suppressed in the Chinese communist educational curriculum. These writers also share an interest in rewriting the rural experience without the formulas and heavy hand (with class villains and heroic workers) that were normal within the communist cultural milieu since the Yan'an days of the early 1940s. This cohort of writers inspired the resurgence of films in the mid-1980s, most notably with Zhang Yimou's debut film, *Red Sorghum,* based on the novella of the same title by Mo Yan, and Chen Kaige's adaptation of Ah Cheng's *The King of Children* in 1988.

The kind of critical retrospection represented by searching-for-roots fiction resonated with the concurrent appearance of Bo Yang's *The Ugly Chinaman* and Sun Longkee's *The Deep Structure of Chinese Culture* (Chinese works from Taiwan and the United States, respectively), adding up to a general mood of unstinting and even overwrought cultural self-criticism on the part of Chinese intellectuals. One of the lasting results of this trend was the reemergence of the intellectual as a cultural commentator, even a judge of contemporary cultural phenomena and foreign intellectual and cultural trends, for the first time after decades of Maoist disdain for intellectuals. Today, although the overall influence of intellectuals over the general public is waning, from underpaid university professors to publishing entrepreneurs to up-and-coming voices in North American and European universities, their identity as spokespersons for and interpreters and critics of Chinese culture has become firmly entrenched. Beginning with *The Deep Structure of Chinese Culture* and the *River Elegy* television series, one of the primary tasks of the latest generation of Chinese intellectuals has been to explore recent Western theoretical approaches, from feminism to liberal Marxism to cultural studies, to shed new light on Chinese culture, both traditional and modern.

Another ingredient in the cultural brew that had been fermenting through-out the late 1980s was a confidence or hope that ascendancy of the relatively liberal Deng Xiaoping regime could end totalitarianism in China. This hope kept the literature of the mid-1980s pinned under the continuing moral burden of history inherited from previous generations of modern Chinese writers. The Tiananmen Square massacre of June 1989 put an end to that hope, at least temporarily, and indirectly cast doubt on the necessity of literature's moral burden in mainland China for the first time in the century. Post-1989 writings retained many aspects that had been developing before the suppression of the democracy movement, notably a multifaceted fascination with pre-1949 China, a taste for the exotic, and a burgeoning ethnic nationalism, but now they were scarcely ever concerned with influencing society. Literature became more playful, and clear lines between "serious" literature and art and television, advertising, and entertainment film began to fade.

The shift of box office interest from the films of Chen Kaige *(Yellow Earth, The King of Children, Farewell My Concubine),* whose path-breaking reenvisioning of modern China is nevertheless committed to (at times painfully transparent or banal) historical moral themes, to those of Zhang Yimou *(Red Sorghum, Raise the Red Lantern, Ju Dou, To Live),* wrapped up in engaging stories and extravagantly beautiful images and colors and in which moral concerns become just another ingredient in his fragrant cine-matic soup, is emblematic of parallel transformations within the realm of lit-erature. Like Chen Kaige, Zhang Yimou makes a special point of adapting the fictional works of contemporary writers, and his choices reflect changes in lit-erary priorities after 1989, even when the works in question were from before that time.

It seems likely that the pop culture rediscovery of traditional and interwar China will continue for some time; there may even be a more genuine resur-gence (rather than freeze-dried preservation) of traditional performing arts. However, the temptation to fall into ruts has already proven irresistible to some filmmakers. Take, for example, the formula of building a movie around a family or village who depend for their survival on a traditional craft. The late 1980s and early 1990s were filled with films about liquor brewers, cloth dyers, rice-tofu makers, ginseng growers, sesame oil squeezers, and even fire-cracker makers, not to mention Beijing opera actors. There is also a tendency like that of the traditional theater to consolidate characters into stock roles, particularly in films with rural settings: the ancient village elder, the often mute and always male village idiot, the tautly sexual young woman and her two or three virile suitors. It is not surprising, then, that a village has been con-structed in barren northern Shaanxi province for the sole purpose of shooting these so-called Chinese westerns. Few people have caught the irony that this locale was the crucible in which the Chinese Communist Party established its political and social order in the 1930s and 1940s.

These developments in mainland Chinese film owe much to the formulas of Taiwan and especially Hong Kong entertainment film, which in turn descended from the lively Shanghai film industry of the 1920s–1940s. In keeping with the pulse of traditional Chinese popular culture, film in Hong Kong draws heavily upon traditional sources like martial arts fiction or vernacular tales of love and the supernatural. Even when the setting is contemporary, plots often center on fighting prowess, chivalric virtues and values, and outlaws and police work. Much short vernacular fiction since the Yuan dynasty consisted of detective stories, with wise magistrates like Judge Pao or Judge Dee as their heroes.

These tendencies also strongly influence television in the three Chinas, where long serial dramas reenact or completely rewrite familiar fictional or historical stories. However, contemporary domestic drama commands a much more conspicuous presence on television than in the cinema. In mainland China, such melodramas as *Yearning (Kewang)* and *Tales from the Editorial Department (Bianjibu de gushi),* though refreshingly free from the contrived moral teaching of earlier programming, often serve as barometers of sensitive social and cultural issues. Even more so was the ambitious 1986 documentary *River Elegy (He shang),* which portrays the Chinese people's futile attempts across millennia to come to terms with the cruel whims of the Yangtze River as suggestive of the people's helplessness under communist rule.

In contrast, Wang Shuo, one of the chief architects of the contemporary Chinese soap opera, reintroduces humor and irreverence with no moral strings attached. Starting out as a screenwriter of television series gave Wang insight into mechanisms of melodrama that let him create outrageously humorous situations by thwarting audience expectations and embedding inconceivable surprises. But he is best known for his characters: cynical, lackadaisical Beijingers whose moral blankness and black humor are strangely refreshing (Barmé and Jaivin, 1992:217–247).

Closer to the streets, screenplays and novels by Wang Shuo, lurid detective fiction, film magazines, martial arts novels, sex manuals, tales of the paranormal or the superhuman feats by masters of *qigong* (the art of vital force), and English-language textbooks and cassettes all clutter the most reliable indicator of mainland Chinese consumers' cultural tastes—streetside bookstalls. Whether just a tarp laid out on the sidewalk, a folding table, or a full-fledged shop with yards of shelving in a subway station or underground bazaar, bookstalls have in the post-Mao period been the backbone and richest source of information on contemporary popular literature. State-run bookstores, whose inventory is determined by the government's cultural policies, tell one very little about what Chinese people want to read, but the bookstall's very survival depends on its knowledge of the market. More recently, massive book supermarkets (often called "Book Cities") have largely displaced the state-run Xinhua operation, and their display arrangements and inventory dra-

A streetside bookstall

matically demonstrate the triumph of the market in contemporary Chinese publishing.

Even before it was legal to do so, independent book peddlers sold banned books like the anonymous Ming dynasty novel *Plum in the Golden Vase,* collections of literary works like the 1930s essays of Liang Shiqiu and Lin Yutang, or books smuggled from Taiwan and Hong Kong. Biographies of famous historical figures sell very well, whether written by Chinese authors or translated from foreign languages. Certain books by Western authors about China, like Robert van Gulik's *Sexual Life in Ancient China* and Ross Terrill's biographies of Mao Zedong and Jiang Qing, appear in usually unauthorized translations, selling many times better than the most popular books distributed through normal channels. Western literature, previously represented in Chinese almost exclusively by nineteenth-century classics and a handful of award-winning twentieth-century works, took on a more popular guise in the 1980s with the appearance of books by authors like Sidney Sheldon at about the same time that series like *Dynasty* and *Falcon Crest* appeared on television. This, of course, strongly influenced Chinese people's perception of the United States.

Teahouses are still fixtures in the cities and towns of southwestern China, set up with bamboo furniture in old pavilions or makeshift bamboo shacks with thatched roofs. In such places in the past, one would have enjoyed the entertainments of a storyteller or Chinese opera arias while chatting with friends, sipping a bowl of tea, and eating melon seeds and other snacks. Now teahouses almost invariably play videotapes of action films with the volume at the highest possible level. Another favorite entertainment is karaoke, a Japanese invention for singing along with music videos of popular recordings selected in a cocktail lounge setting. Karaoke bars, popular in Hong Kong and Taiwan for years, have now already taken mainland China by storm. Although it is tempting to deplore the violent action films blaring in teahouses and the wildfire spread of karaoke, the vitality of Chinese popular culture is unmistakable even in these new high-tech guises. We like to imagine traditional Chinese entertainments as being refined and genteel, but there is no reason to believe that traditional teahouses, theaters, and brothels were any less boisterous and chaotic than modern ones. "Boisterousness" (*renao*, literally, "hot and noisy")—may be one of the defining characteristics and values of Chinese popular culture.

High technology has also helped people pursue concerns peculiar to modern Chinese culture, such as the public discussion of serious social and political issues, national identity, and pride. The rapid spread of Internet access in China, a process that seems irreversible, is undermining the central control of information, though like television it may diminish interest in local and folk culture. While in recent years, many Internet "cafes" have become cramped, unsafe dens where preteens and teenagers skip school to indulge in online gaming and dubious Internet surfing, the Internet is of course also providing an important window to the world as well as an unprecedented means of free horizontal communication regardless of location. Most people in medium to large cities have broadband access to the Internet from their homes now, and the numbers who take advantage of this access are rapidly growing. Perusal of Chinese electronic bulletin boards indicates that the public is perhaps still less vocally concerned than in the recent past about contemporary political and social developments. But even being able to gossip about actors and pop stars or the latest biography of Bill Gates with a rapidly growing virtual community has drastically changed the political condition of contemporary China, and has drawn Chinese in mainland China into closer contact with their compatriots and other friends all over the world.

Another exciting recent development deriving from technological progress is the rise of amateur documentary filmmaking. With the now widespread availability of the digital video camera and sophisticated editing software, a new generation of filmmakers are recording the lives of visual artists and rock musicians, but significantly, also the traditional performing arts. These films are rarely produced in film studios or publicly released, but information about them is disseminated on the Internet, and cultural communities located in the larger cities screen such documentaries in addition to the more familiar activities of poetry reading, art shows, and theatrical performances. These kinds of artistic salon activities, which used to take place in private homes and officially unavailable spaces, now enjoy a greater variety of public venues in major cities like Beijing, Shanghai, Wuhan, Guangzhou, and Chengdu. Private art galleries, live music bars, bookstore-cafes/teahouses, and theater-restaurants not only are proving the cultural diversity and vitality of today's China, but are profitable businesses. These new documentaries have created a new language of images; they are a "literature" that takes the visuality and accessibility of modern Chinese culture to a new level.

■ Conclusion

The apparent triumph of popular culture over the elite in contemporary China makes an apt ending to this account of Chinese literature and popular culture. Perhaps the most significant contribution of popular culture to elite (written) literature throughout the ages is its challenge to orthodox moral values and literary forms with an alternative set of values based on sensitivity and emotional response. This is the serious message underlying its comic subversions of or perfunctory nods toward conventional morality—alternative canons that extol not moral excellence (as did the *Classic of Poetry* for the Confucians) or technical artistry, but rather grace, generosity of spirit, a great capacity for love, and emotional integrity.

These values underlie, for instance, the alternate canon of Jin Shengtan, an influential seventeenth-century editor and literary critic who honored as the "Six Works of Genius" the masterpieces of their respective genres: Qu Yuan's "Encountering Sorrow," the *Zhuangzi, Records of the Historian,* the poems of Du Fu, *Outlaws of the Marsh,* and *Romance of the Western Chamber.* The works in Jin's canon have in common—along with a marginal relation to the orthodox classics of Confucianism, which were the common denominator of everyone's literacy—values of emotional integrity, intuition, and the immediacy of experience.

Feng Menglong, a late Ming dramatist and editor of vernacular short stories and an avid transcriber of popular tunes and folk songs as well, was perhaps one of the earliest figures in China to offer vocal defense of the unique values of popular cultural forms:

> In this world, the literary minds are few, but the rustic ears are many. Therefore, the short story relies more on the popularizer than on the stylist. Just

ask the storyteller to describe a scene on the spot, and it will gladden and startle, sadden and cause you to lament; it will prompt you to draw the sword; at other times to bow deeply in reverence, to break someone's neck, or to contribute money. The timid will be made brave; the lewd chaste; the niggardly liberal; and the stupid and dull, perspiring with shame. Even though you would recite every day the *Classic of Filial Piety* and the *Analects,* you would never be moved as swiftly and profoundly as by these storytellers. Alas! Could such results be achieved by anything but popular colloquial writing? (Liu, 1966:216)

By emphasizing the popular underside of traditional Chinese culture on the one hand and the persistent traditional underside of modern Chinese culture on the other, I do not mean to claim that Chinese cultural forms are essentially unchanging, only that a large portion of cultural activity in China tends to flourish quite outside the power of cultural elites to channel, control, or appropriate it. Cultural orthodoxies are always built upon a dazzling profusion of cultural activity, commonly drawing material and techniques from it.

The idea of civil service as the only appropriate goal for the cultivation of literacy and knowledge remains prevalent in the various Chinas (mainland China, Taiwan, Hong Kong, Singapore, and the Chinese diaspora throughout the world), only partially displaced by the modern values of professionalism, science, individualism, and the autonomy of art. This is one reason the dialectics of popular and elite, entertainment and edification, common and sophisticated remain at the center of Chinese debates on culture to the present day (Zha, 1995), as they have throughout the ages. The current ascendancy of popular culture is cause for celebration only insofar as it can foster those aspects that made traditional Chinese popular culture both impossible to ignore and yet impossible for the literati to completely assimilate.

■ Bibliography

Ah Cheng. 1990. *Three Kings: Three Stories from Today's China.* Trans. Bonnie S. McDougall. London: Collins Harvill.

Barlow, Tani E., and Gary J. Bjorge (eds.). 1989. *I Myself Am a Woman: Selected Writings of Ding Ling.* Boston: Beacon Press.

Barmé, Geremie, and Linda Jaivin (eds.). 1992. *New Ghosts, Old Voices: Chinese Rebel Voices.* New York: Random House.

Barmé, Geremie, and John Minford (eds.). 1988. *Seeds of Fire: Chinese Voices of Conscience.* New York: Hill and Wang.

Berninghausen, John, and Ted Huters (eds.). 1976. *Revolutionary Literature in China: An Anthology.* White Plains, NY: M. E. Sharpe.

Berry, Chris. 1985. *Perspectives on Chinese Cinema.* Ithaca: Cornell East Asia Papers.

Birch, Cyril (ed.). 1958. *Stories from a Ming Collection: Translations of Chinese Short Stories Published in the Seventeenth Century.* New York: Grove Press.

—— (ed.). 1995. *Scenes for Mandarins: The Elite Theater of the Ming.* New York: Columbia University Press.

Bordwell, David. 2000. *Planet Hong Kong: Popular Cinema and the Art of Entertainment.* Cambridge: Harvard University Press.

Cao, Xueqin, and E. Gao. 1973–1986. *The Story of the Stone.* Trans. David Hawkes and John Minford. New York: Penguin Books.

Ch'en, Li-li. 1994. *Master Tung's Western Chamber Romance.* New York: Columbia University Press.

Ch'en, Shou-yi. 1961. *Chinese Literature: A Historical Introduction.* New York: Ronald Press.

Chang, Yvonne Sung-sheng. 1993. *Modernism and the Nativist Resistance: Contemporary Chinese Fiction from Taiwan.* Durham, NC: Duke University Press.

Confucius. 1979. *The Analects.* Trans. D. C. Lau. New York: Penguin Books.

de Bary, William Theodore, Wing-tsit Chan, and Burton Watson (eds.). 1960. *Sources of Chinese Tradition.* New York: Columbia University Press.

Denton, Kirk A. 1996. *Modern Chinese Literary Thought: Writings on Literature, 1893–1945.* Stanford: Stanford University Press.

Dolezelova-Velingerova, Milena (ed.). 1980. *The Chinese Novel at the Turn of the Century.* Toronto: University of Toronto Press.

Faurot, Jeannette L. (ed.). 1979. *Chinese Fiction from Taiwan: Critical Perspectives.* Bloomington: Indiana University Press.

Feng, Zong-Pu. 1998. *The Everlasting Rock: A Novel.* Trans. Aimee Lykes. Boulder: Lynne Rienner.

Forney, Matt. 1998. "People's Theater." *Far Eastern Economic Review* 161(3) (January 15): 48–50.

Gao, Ming. 1980. *The Lute: Kao Ming's P'i-p'a chi.* Trans. Jean Mulligan. New York: Columbia University Press.

Gernet, Jacques. 1962. *Daily Life in China on the Eve of the Mongol Invasion, 1250–1276.* Stanford: Stanford University Press.

Goldblatt, Howard (ed.). 1995. *Chairman Mao Would Not Be Amused: Fiction from Today's China.* New York: Grove Press.

Goldman, Merle (ed.). 1977. *Modern Chinese Literature in the May Fourth Era.* Cambridge: Harvard University Press.

Gunn, Edward M. 1980. *Unwelcome Muse: Chinese Literature in Shanghai and Peking, 1937–1945.* New York: Columbia University Press.

—— (ed.). 1983. *Twentieth-Century Chinese Drama.* Bloomington: Indiana University Press.

Hanan, Patrick. 1981. *The Chinese Vernacular Story.* Cambridge: Harvard University Press.

Hegel, Robert E. 1981. *The Novel in Seventeenth-Century China.* New York: Columbia University Press.

Holm, David. 1991. *Art and Ideology in Revolutionary China.* Oxford: Oxford University Press.

Hsia, C. T. 1971. *A History of Modern Chinese Fiction.* 2nd ed. New Haven: Yale University Press.

——. 1996. *The Classic Chinese Novel: A Critical Introduction.* Ithaca: Cornell University East Asia Program.

Hsu, Vivian Ling (ed.). 1981. *Born of the Same Roots: Stories of Modern Chinese Women.* Bloomington: Indiana University Press.

Hung, Chang-tai. 1994. *War and Popular Culture: Resistance in Modern China, 1937–1945.* Berkeley: University of California Press.

Huot, Marie Claire. 2000. *China's New Cultural Scene: A Handbook of Changes.* Durham, NC: Duke University Press.

Johnson, David, Andrew J. Nathan, and Evelyn S. Rawski (eds.). 1985. *Popular Culture in Late Imperial China.* Berkeley: University of California Press.

Kinkley, Jeffrey C. (ed.). 1985. *After Mao: Chinese Literature and Society, 1978–1981.* Cambridge: Harvard University Press.

Laozi. 1963. *Tao te Ching.* Trans. D. C. Lau. New York: Penguin Books.

Lau, Joseph S. M. (ed.). 1983. *The Unbroken Chain: An Anthology of Taiwan Fiction Since 1926.* Bloomington: Indiana University Press.

Lau, Joseph S. M., and Howard Goldblatt (eds.). 1995. *The Columbia Anthology of Modern Chinese Literature.* New York: Columbia University Press.

Lau, Joseph S. M., and Timothy Ross (eds.). 1976. *Chinese Stories from Taiwan, 1960–1970.* New York: Columbia University Press.

Lee, Leo Ou-fan. 1999. *Shanghai Modern: The Flowering of a New Urban Culture in China, 1930–1945.* Cambridge: Harvard University Press.

Lee, Leo Ou-fan, and Andrew Nathan. 1985. "The Beginnings of Mass Culture: Journalism and Fiction in the Late Ch'ing and Beyond." Pp. 360–395 in David Johnson, Andrew J. Nathan, and Evelyn S. Rawski (eds.), *Popular Culture in Late Imperial China.* Berkeley: University of California Press.

Leyda, Jay. 1972. *Dianying/Electric Shadows: An Account of Films and the Film Audience in China.* Cambridge: MIT Press.

Li, Yu. 1990. *The Carnal Prayer Mat [Rou putuan].* Trans. Patrick Hanan. New York: Ballantine Books.

Liezi. 1990. *The Book of Lieh-tzu: A Classic of the Tao.* Trans. A. C. Graham. New York: Columbia University Press.

Link, E. Perry, Jr. 1981. *Mandarin Ducks and Butterflies: Popular Fiction in Early Twentieth-Century Chinese Cities.* Berkeley: University of California Press.

——— (ed.). 1983. *People or Monsters? and Other Stories and Reportage from China After Mao.* Bloomington: Indiana University Press.

Link, E. Perry, Jr., Richard Madsen, and Paul G. Pickowicz (eds.). 1989. *Unofficial China: Popular Culture and Thought in the People's Republic.* Boulder: Westview Press.

Liu, Jung-en. 1972. *Six Yüan Plays.* Baltimore: Penguin Books.

Liu, Lydia He. 1995. *Translingual Practice: Literature, National Culture, and Translated Modernity.* Stanford: Stanford University Press.

Liu, Ts'un-yan (ed.). 1984. *Chinese Middlebrow Fiction from the Ch'ing and Early Republican Eras.* Hong Kong: Chinese University Press.

Liu, Wu-chi. 1966. *An Introduction to Chinese Literature.* Bloomington: Indiana University Press.

Lu Xun. 1990. *Diary of a Madman and Other Stories.* Trans. William A. Lyell. Honolulu: University of Hawaii Press.

Luo, Guanzhong. 1981. *Outlaws of the Marsh.* Trans. Sidney Shapiro. Bloomington: Indiana University Press.

———. 1994. *Three Kingdoms: A Historical Novel.* Trans. Moss Roberts. Berkeley: University of California Press.

Lynn, Richard John. 1994. *The Classic of Changes: A New Translation of the I Ching as Interpreted by Wang Bi.* New York: Columbia University Press.

Ma, Y. W., and Joseph S. M. Lau (eds.). 1978. *Traditional Chinese Stories: Themes and Variations.* New York: Columbia University Press.

Owen, Stephen. 1985. *Traditional Chinese Poetry and Poetics: Omen of the World.* Madison: University of Wisconsin Press.

Plaks, Andrew H. (ed.). 1977. *Chinese Narrative: Critical and Theoretical Essays.* Princeton: Princeton University Press.

P'u, Sungling. 1989. *Strange Stories from Make-Do Studio.* Trans. Victor H. and Denis C. Mair. Beijing: Foreign Languages Press.

Qu, Yuan. 1985. *The Songs of the South: An Anthology of Ancient Chinese Poems by Qu Yuan and Other Poets.* Trans. David Hawkes. New York: Penguin Books.

Rolston, David L. 1990. *How to Read the Chinese Novel.* Princeton: Princeton University Press.

Shen Congwen. 1982. *The Chinese Earth: Stories by Shen Ts'ung-wen.* Trans. Ching Ti and Robert Payne. New York: Columbia University Press.

Spence, Jonathan D. 1982. *The Gate of Heavenly Peace: The Chinese and Their Revolution, 1895–1980.* New York: Penguin Books.

Su, Xiaokang, and Wang Luxiang. 1991. *Deathsong of the River: A Reader's Guide to the Chinese TV Series* He Shang. Trans. Richard Bodman and Pin P. Wan. Ithaca: Cornell University Press.

Su Tong. 1993. *Raise the Red Lantern: Three Novellas.* Trans. Michael S. Duke. New York: William Morrow.

———. 1995. *Rice.* Trans. Howard Goldblatt. New York: William Morrow.

Tam, Vivienne, and Martha Elizabeth Huang. 2000. *China Chic.* New York: Regan Books.

Tang, Xianzu. 1980. *The Peony Pavilion: Mudan ting.* Trans. Cyril Birch. Bloomington: Indiana University Press.

Wang, Ch'iu Kuei. 1995. "Studies in Chinese Ritual and Ritual Theatre: A Bibliographic Report." *CHINOPERL* 18:115–128.

Wang, David Der-wei. 1992. *Fictional Realism in Twentieth-Century China: Mao Dun, Lao She, Shen Congwen.* New York: Columbia University Press.

Wang, David Der-wei, and Jeanne Tai (eds.). 1994. *Running Wild: New Chinese Writers.* New York: Columbia University Press.

Wang, Jing. 1992. *The Story of Stone: Intertextuality, Ancient Chinese Stone Lore, and the Stone Symbolism in Dream of the Red Chamber, Water Margin, and the Journey to the West.* Durham, NC: Duke University Press.

Wang Anyi. 1989. *Baotown.* Trans. Martha Avery. New York: W. W. Norton.

Watson, Burton. 1971. *Chinese Lyricism: Shih Poetry from the Second to the Twelfth Century.* New York: Columbia University Press.

——— (ed.). 1984. *The Columbia Book of Chinese Poetry: From Early Times to the Thirteenth Century.* New York: Columbia University Press.

——— (ed.). 1989. *The Tso Chuan: Selections from China's Earliest Narrative History.* Trans. Burton Watson. New York: Columbia University Press.

——— (ed.). 1993. *The Lotus Sutra.* Trans. Burton Watson. New York: Columbia University Press.

Widmer, Ellen, and David Der-wei Wang (eds.). 1993. *From May Fourth to June Fourth: Fiction and Film in Twentieth Century China.* Cambridge: Harvard University Press.

Wu, Cheng'en. 1958. *Monkey: Folk Novel of China.* Trans. Arthur Waley. New York: Grove Press.

———. 1977. *The Journey to the West.* Trans. Anthony C. Yu. Chicago: University of Chicago Press.

Wu, Dingbo, and Patrick D. Murphy (eds.). 1989. *Science Fiction from China.* New York: Praeger.

———. 1994. *Handbook of Chinese Popular Culture.* Westport, CT: Greenwood Press.

Xiao, Hong. 1979. *The Field of Life and Death and Tales of Hulan River: Two Novels by Hsiao Hung.* Trans. Howard Goldblatt. Bloomington: Indiana University Press.

Xiao-xiao-sheng. 1993. *The Plum in the Golden Vase, or Chin P'ing Mei.* Trans. David Tod Roy. Princeton: Princeton University Press.

Yang, Bo. 1992. *The Ugly Chinaman and the Crisis of Chinese Culture.* Trans. Don Cohn. London: Allen and Unwin.

Yeh, Michelle. 1991. *Modern Chinese Poetry: Theory and Practice Since 1917.* New Haven: Yale University Press.

——— (ed.). 1992. *Anthology of Modern Chinese Poetry.* New Haven: Yale University Press.

Yeh, Michelle, and N. G. D. Malmqvist (eds.). 2001. *Frontier Taiwan: An Anthology of Modern Chinese Poetry.* New York: Columbia University Press.

Yu, Pauline. 1987. *The Reading of Imagery in the Chinese Poetic Tradition.* Princeton: Princeton University Press.

Zha, Jianying. 1995. *China Pop: How Soap Operas, Tabloids, and Bestsellers Are Transforming a Culture.* New York: New Press.

Zhuangzi. 1981. *Chuang-Tzu: The Seven Inner Chapters and Other Writings from the Book Chuang-tzu.* Trans. A. C. Graham. London and Boston: Allen and Unwin.

14

Trends and Prospects

Robert E. Gamer

At Chinese New Year celebrations, parents deliver little red packets filled with coins to their children, eat noodles and dumplings, hang small wall signs, and shoot off firecrackers to beseech the gods for prosperity and long life as the future unfolds. Before we leave, we too should think about China's future; it is bound to have an enormous impact on the lives of China's populace and on the rest of the world as well. In the United States, discussion about that future tends to center around these questions:

- Will China stay unified?
- Will China's economy continue to boom?
- What will happen to Hong Kong, Taiwan, and Tibet?
- Will China become more democratic?
- Will China and its peoples blend in as responsible members of the world community?

Scholars like Edward Friedman (1994, 1995) and Baogang He (1996) foresee a divided but democratic China; they focus on factors that may transform China. Others, like Constance Lever-Tracy, David Ip, and Tracy Noel (1996), and Daniel Bell and colleagues (1995), focus on the prospects for a more united and less democratic China; they point to factors that promote continuity but may hold back change. Like all crystal balls, this one can provide differing scenarios depending on where we set our gaze. Although no one can predict China's future with any certainty, we can make some observations that at least indicate what to look for.

First of all, the authors of this volume join most other observers of China in their belief that it would be very difficult for China to withdraw from the

415

world economy. All factions of China's leaders—even those most culturally and politically conservative and its army—are deriving extensive benefits from China's economic dealings with the outside world, which began with the 1978 reforms. So are its people. And any downturn in its economic growth could result in economic and political crisis. The chapters on family, women, religion, and popular culture all point to tremendous changes in habits and expectations as a result of the economic changes. Mao Zedong's collectivization and Great Leap Forward institutions helped provide a basis for many of the cooperatives, village and township enterprises, and dependent *(guahu)* firms that are fueling China's economic advance, and these new companies can be seen as direct outgrowths and natural successors to rather than as rejections of Mao (Wei, 1998; Chan, Madsen, and Unger, 1984:213 ff.; Zhou, 1996; Croll, 1994; Yang, 1996).

Furthermore, economic reforms simultaneously give the provinces incentives to break away from and remain within a unified China. In Chapter 1, I pointed to some "creative tensions" in China's society. Each of those tensions—between Confucianism and capitalism, Confucianism and Christianity and communism, popular culture and formal traditions, regions and the capital city of Beijing, inward and outward reaching—provide China with reasons both to stay unified and to undergo social and political division.

Today, the snapping points on all those tensions are located in the vicinity of Hong Kong and Taiwan. Because Hong Kong and Taiwan are inherent parts of China's economic growth, its prosperity would be very hard to maintain without them; yet the leverage this clout gives them frightens many Beijing leaders and can lead to serious miscalculations. Likewise, calls for greater political openness by student activists and by Tibetans and minorities in the western provinces among some leaders rouse fears in Beijing that the country could break apart; that has resulted in stern measures against those activists and regions.

And finally, such moves in themselves and attempts to unify China through nationalist appeals can lead to sword-rattling by China, investor withdrawal, and retaliation by foreign governments that endanger the economic growth. Growth will also be endangered if China does not tackle the serious macroeconomic, legal, demographic, social, and environmental problems it confronts—the most serious being the growing disparity between urban and rural. Yet China is developing within itself a new generation that wants China to tackle its domestic problems, become a responsible part of the world community, and allow it to pursue both money and culture imported from the outside world; Perry Link (1992), Nicholas Kristof and Sheryl WuDunn (1994), Jianying Zha (1995), Michael Dutton (1999), and Jasper Becker (2001) all offer highly readable introductions to this new mind-set. As the old guard retires, this new generation—which is connected to the Internet (over 60 million, mostly young, Chinese are online at this point, with 81,900

Chinese websites) and increasingly conversant in English—is taking command of important institutional positions and generating a debate (discussed in Chapter 4) about how China can develop a "civil society" to tackle its problems. Furthermore, the overseas Chinese who are fueling the economies of China and the other countries of South and Southeast Asia have a strong vested interest in continued prosperity for China. Much depends upon whether these positive motives can be translated into creative solutions for China's problems.

Anyone looking at the books by the authors mentioned in the above paragraph will notice that the attitudes expressed by the people interviewed in them do not lend themselves cleanly to the black-and-white world of the "Orientalists," who write about "the Asian mind" (e.g., organization and control) as being something separate from "the Western mind" (e.g., competition and consumption), or at the other extreme, as thinking the same way we in the West do. To introduce yourself to orientalist approaches, see Said, 1979; Isaacs, 1958; Wittfogel, 1981; Tu, 1991; Hodder, 2000; Jesperson, 1999; and Munro, 2001. Samuel P. Huntington's notion that there will be a "clash of civilizations" pitting China and Islamic areas against the West derives from such Orientalism (Huntington, 1998; Gamer, 1994). Bo Yang's *The Ugly Chinaman* and the *River Elegy* television series discussed in Chapter 13 also view the two worlds in this way. Richard Madsen (1995) suggests that such attempts to explain the two worlds in simple terms create myths that are often a reflection of what we want to believe about ourselves: The Asians' old communitarian civilization with a respect for authority and concern for social order is becoming more like our new industrial civilization, and hence it will transform into a democratic society dominated by pragmatic technocrats. Madsen points out that thinking like this ignores the reality of what we are (e.g., truly pragmatic and democratic?), and that this thinking must confront reversals like the 1989 massacre at Tiananmen Square, and the attack on the World Trade Center on September 11, 2001, conducted by individuals educated in the modern technocratic tradition. Does modernization inherently move people away from traditional ways of thinking? Madsen suggests that we explore

> new moral visions . . . new American and Chinese dreams, drawing sacred power from the most resonant aspirations of their cultural traditions. These new moral visions would enable Americans, Chinese, and other peoples of the world to recognize the limitations as well as the strengths and insights of their various traditions; they would encourage them not only to tolerate but also to learn from each other and give them a realistic hope that they could see a new way forward to a just and prosperous world community. (1995:227)

The creative tensions that offer hope for China by counseling moderation at the same time make it difficult to solve problems. Hill Gates (1996) captures this dilemma succinctly. She sees part of China's strength deriving from a tension between what she calls China's petty capitalism and its tributary system. China's family-centered Confucian tradition gave families the incentive to set up small capitalist enterprises to support and enrich their members; it also gave state officials the ability to "capture" and exact tribute from those enterprises, but in a form that would keep the enterprises going and the money flowing. This spurred the economy and helped keep China unified. The arrival of Western capitalism threatened to upset this delicate balance. Its calls for open markets, contract law, and rewards for people on the basis of ability assaulted the "nepotism," relationships *(guanxi),* layers of bureaucracy, and state controls on which the old system had been based for centuries. As author after author has indicated in this volume, those Confucian values are still alive and well. Ironically, they are also a strong part of the reason why China's economy is thriving as part of the world capitalist system. In Gates's words:

> East Asia is becoming Number One not because its social formations are becoming more capitalist but because the dynamic of a tributary mode that has captured a petty-capitalist one is geared up yet further by the capture of [world] capitalism. . . . The Chinese petty capitalist mode of production does not generate all the organizations and ideology necessary to extricate the Chinese from their persisting problems. But it contains some of them and is, in any case, the cultural raw material from which their future must, inevitably, be forged. The effort to achieve social justice and a human social formation there will not succeed unless and until the Chinese take seriously their own popular traditions. (1996:276, 280)

This is where the dilemma lies: the more seriously Chinese take their traditions, the less likely they are to accept democratic reforms like a fair and impartial judicial system, protection of patents and other intellectual property rights, or the removal of government controls on business or free speech. Yet those traditions are responsible for the thrift, hard work, and entrepreneurial acumen of tightly knit families capable of setting up small businesses that have been powering China's economic resurgence. Gates is pointing directly at the problem. The Chinese must hold on to those values while seeking solutions to problems that can potentially derail economic development. And the family businesses must be willing to pass decisionmaking into the hands of professional managers who can let them grow beyond their family roots. In its long history, China's ideology has absorbed many challenges and will try to do so again. But China will seek its own solutions to such problems; they cannot be imposed from the outside world. The question is whether free markets and safe commercial contracts can be combined with the demands of *guanxi* and devotion to state and family. Gordon Redding (1990) extends this discussion to the entire Chinese diaspora.

In Chapter 3, Rhoads Murphey pointed to traditions of technology, from irrigated paddy to bamboo carrying poles, that endure even after the technological and industrial revolution has swept in from the West. Likewise, in Chapter 12, Chan Hoiman and Ambrose King pointed to the resilience of Confucian *guanxi* relationships. They say, "This streak of conservatism can be both a blessing and a curse for China's enigmatic transition into the modern world." It is a selective conservatism, stressing traditions that best suit the moment. These private networks of achieved social relationships may be weakening the open institutional channels of social organization that are also part of the Confucian tradition, resisting social change and ignoring the needs of those to whom they do not owe direct obligations (and thus undermining efforts like those Gates describes to achieve social justice and a human social formation) even as their members rush to acquire the latest designer clothes, electronic gear, fast foods, and blue jeans to wear in trendy new karaoke bars. In Chapter 13, Charles Laughlin, noting that "boisterousness" may be one of the defining characteristics and values of Chinese popular culture, pointed to the current popularity of sex manuals, pornography, martial arts, chivalric mythical heroes, outlaws, police work, and action films amid literature and videos on popular street stalls—not the sort of fare that focuses on social change or obligations. These new freedoms may actually make it harder for "modernized" coastal urbanites to understand the concerns of inland peoples (or even nearby rural people, like the young lady I wrote about in Chapter 1 who can see Beijing from a distance but has never been there) isolated from this economic growth by distance and poverty or to comprehend the spiritual aspirations of Christians, Muslims, and Tantric Buddhists, whose religions have never been syncretized into Chinese culture. Laurel Bossen indicated in Chapter 11 that the clearest advances for women have been the chance to earn and spend cash income on "frenzied consumer choices" of cosmetics, clothes, and home appliances. In Chapter 10, Zang Xiaowei pointed out that having their own incomes gives women greater freedom to choose and divorce their mates. Yet both authors indicated that women remain heavily influenced by their fathers, husbands, and loyalty to patriarchal institutions and patrilineages. All the trends surveyed by these authors—the enduring technologies, continuing *guanxi,* consumerism, recreation, and loyalty to patriarchal institutions—keep alive small capitalist enterprises and the ability of officials to exact tribute from them. The question remains whether China also can develop greater adaptation to the outside world and take the steps toward economic openness John Wong outlined in Chapter 5.

Taiwan, Singapore, South Korea, Malaysia, and other Asian countries have made great strides in democratizing and modernizing their economies. These countries, however, do not face the task of unifying large and diverse populations and territories and defending a large land base against powerful foreign competitors, and they do not contain large numbers of people still largely out of contact with the outside world. Tibet and the inland areas are not alone in wanting independence from Beijing; many in coastal provinces pursuing economic reforms have thoughts about how nice life might be if they were no longer tied down by economic and political controls emanating from Beijing. But the thousand border disputes over mining rights and control of villages serve as a warning; over the millennia, China's economy, resources, water controls, transportation, and bureaucracies have become heavily intertwined. Increasingly, modern investments cross provincial boundaries.

Part of what has brought modernity to the smaller Asian states also supports solidarity of the larger whole: the role of the overseas Chinese. As explained in Chapter 6, China is the base from which their economic power evolved. Today, many of the *guanxi* connections that hold together their power revolve around China. A turbulent and divided China would disturb not only those connections but also the stability of Asia's business climate. If problems of weak currencies, and insolvent businesses and banks (notice John Wong's warning), which have affected neighboring nations to varying degrees, were to bring a vast downturn to China's economy, the effect would be felt throughout the region. Of course, another factor that could disturb peace in Asia would be a militant China challenging Malaysia or Vietnam or the Philippines to control islands, or India over Tibetan borders, or—most frighteningly—conflict across the Taiwan Strait. Other Asian governments may wish to see China unified but not too militarily powerful, a country devoted to peace and not to war. That, too, depends upon the continuance of its economic growth. If this growth continues, in fact, China can provide a vast market and investment target for the other countries of Asia and serve as the nucleus of a powerful Asian economy (for speculation on these prospects, see Redding, 1990; Seagrave, 1995; Lever-Tracy, Ip, and Noel, 1996; Brown, 2000; and Gambe, 2000).

In the words of Ma Rong (Chapter 8), "China has never been able to survive with two nations, one rich and one poor." As Rhoads Murphey explained, when dynasties stopped addressing pressing social problems, revolt tended to ensue. As John Wong explained, the new economy is widening the gap between rich and poor, urban and rural. Considerable civil unrest is already emerging over this.

Nature may provide its own curbs to economic reform. China's people must eat, drink, breathe, and retain continued access to natural resources. Degradation resulting from economic development and the continuing rise in population endanger its ability to sustain adequate supplies of food, water, fresh air, and other staples—not to mention electricity, petroleum, timber, and other requisites of modern economic development (Schaller, 1993; Smil, 1993; Shapiro, 2001; Sanders, 2000; Edmonds, 2000). Rhoads Murphey explained that degradation of the environment has always been a problem when population grows. With the unprecedented growth of population discussed by Ma Rong, will the new measures to protect the environment discussed by Richard Edmonds in Chapter 9 be adequate to bring that degradation under control (Lieberthal, 1995:276–291)? If not, agricultural yields may decline and even world markets may not be able to supply adequate food for China's people. This possibility could result in starving children, lowered food consumption and resistance to disease (which can spread around the world during flu and pneumonia season, as was demonstrated by the 2003 SARS outbreak), and diversion of economic resources away from growth activities. This makes it imperative that China continue to work with international organizations to help seek solutions to these pressing problems at international conferences. They are unlikely to be solved without cooperation at a worldwide level.

Hence China's prospects for unity, continued economic boom, movement toward democracy, and peaceful absorption into the world community depend on the policies its leaders will be willing to craft, and on good fortune in carrying them out. A source of its strength lies in the interdependence of its regions. Rhoads Murphey pointed to the extensive cultural advances that emanated from the seagoing south while the inward-centered north imposed order; as Ma Rong said, the market economy those coastal people supply has been at its liveliest when effective rulers unify great portions of the country. The longer-term prospects for Tibet and the western provinces are more murky. Ma Rong, referring to the regions Stanley Toops introduced in Chapter 2 as China Proper and the Frontier, pointed to the "tie and tension between the interior and the coast"; although many in those regions have reasons to break away, it would be hard for them to advance economically on their own. And with the extensive Han in-migration discussed by Rhoads Murphey in Chapter 3 and myself in Chapter 6, they are no longer entirely culturally separate. Yet as indicated in Chapter 6, Tibet's religious traditions stand in contrast to those of China. Islam, the religion of many inhabitants of the vast western provinces, is even further removed from Chinese culture; it does not even share any common Buddhist themes. Like Christianity, it allows for belief in immortality, ecstasy, and salvation in heaven for individuals by an omnipotent supreme God, with punishment in hell for those who reject the appeal of his prophet on earth. In the words of Chan and King, such religions can be "tolerated as perhaps harmless pastimes for a worn-out nation" but not accepted if they "run counter to national interest." The suicide bomber seeking immortality through ecstatic detonation certainly runs counter to national interest; milder forms of such ecstasy might easily be misconstrued as running counter to it as well. Yet if China is to develop a secular syncretism between its values and those of the outside, it must develop a spiritual syncretism as well.

It is unlikely that China will adopt Western-style democracy in any kind of foreseeable future. But it is also unlikely that China can again withdraw from the world; China and overseas Chinese have become too absorbed into the world economy to allow for retreat. China has the resources, human and natural, to sustain economic growth and political unity. And behind its diversity of interests and beliefs lies a widespread reservoir of commitment to sustain that growth and unity.

China's economy, like all others, will have periods when growth slows; those are the periods when conflict could easily flare. Therein may lie the biggest problem. Perry Link (1992:195–196, 221, 273, 295) quotes a Chinese literary critic who says that Chinese intellectuals "have inherited two modes of responding to the political world: the Confucian mode of offering service to the state and the Daoist mode of withdrawing into oneself." Link observes that students may be far more interested in entering into dialogue and official channels than with actually examining ideas and solutions. A Chinese literature professor commented: "Why do all Chinese scholars abandon their work because of crisis?" Such a frame of mind impedes the process of tackling these problems; it also breeds timidity that can exacerbate problems. Instead of warning officials about the dangers of foolhardy projects, this political quiescence may tempt them into such behavior. Link himself comments about the view of wealthy people in Hong Kong who feel that Hong Kong will get special consideration only because it is a "money tree." "Do they really imagine that their wealth—fantastic by mainland standards—would cause China's rulers to keep their hands off, rather than produce exactly the opposite effect?" In contrast, Ian Buruma (2002) writes about rebels within China who resist everything to stand up for what is right in the face of this conformity. If China is to achieve a civil society that can hold on to its strengths as its role in the global economy grows, education may be the biggest challenge of all. Can it develop a responsible commitment to truth seeking and problem solving and to confronting officials with forewarnings that their policies may be at variance with both? That is something for Chinese to ponder when they deliver their coin-filled red packets and eat their noodles during New Year's; if they can tackle this challenge, they have many reasons to look to a bright future.

■ Bibliography

Angle, Stephen C. 2002. *Human Rights and Chinese Thought: A Cross-Cultural Inquiry.* Cambridge: Cambridge University Press.

Baken, Borge. 2000. *The Exemplary Society: Human Improvement, Social Control, and the Dangers of Modernity in China.* Oxford: Oxford University Press.

Barme, Geremie R. 1996. *Shades of Mao: The Posthumous Cult of the Great Leader.* Armonk, NY: M. E. Sharpe.

———. 1999. *In the Red: On Contemporary Chinese Culture.* New York: Columbia University Press.

Becker, Jasper. 2001. *The Chinese.* New York: Free Press.

Bell, Daniel, David Brown, Kanishka Jayasuriya, and David Martin Jones. 1995. *Towards Illiberal Democracy in Pacific Asia.* New York: St. Martin's Press.

Blum, Susan D., and Lionel M. Jensen (eds.). 2002. *China Off Center: Mapping the Margins of the Middle Kingdom.* Honolulu: University of Hawaii Press.

Brown, Rajeswary Ampalavanar. 2000. *Chinese Big Business and the Wealth of Asian Nations.* New York: Palgrave.

Buruma, Ian. 2002. *Bad Elements: Chinese Rebels from Los Angeles to Beijing.* New York: Vintage.

Chan, Anita, Richard Madsen, and Jonathan Unger. 1984. *Chen Village: The Recent History of a Peasant Community in Mao's China.* Berkeley: University of California Press.

Croll, Elizabeth. 1994. *From Heaven to Earth: Images and Experiences of Development in China.* London: Routledge.

Dutton, Michael (ed.). 1999. *Streetlife China.* Cambridge: Cambridge University Press.

Edmonds, Richard Louis (ed.). 2000. *Managing the Chinese Environment.* Oxford: Oxford University Press.

Friedman, Edward. 1994. *The Politics of Democratization: Generalizing East Asian Experiences.* Boulder: Westview Press.

———. 1995. *National Identity and Democratic Prospects in Socialist China.* Armonk, NY: M. E. Sharpe.

Gambe, Annabelle. 2000. *Overseas Chinese Entrepreneurship and Capitalist Development in Southeast Asia.* New York: Palgrave.

Gamer, Robert E. 1994. "Modernization and Democracy in China: Samuel P. Huntington and the 'Neo-Authoritarian' Debate." *Asian Journal of Political Science* 2(1) (June): 32–63.

Garnaut, Ross, Guo Shutian, and Ma Guonan (eds.). 1996. *The Third Revolution in the Chinese Countryside.* Cambridge: Cambridge University Press.

Gates, Hill. 1996. *China's Motor: A Thousand Years of Petty Capitalism.* Ithaca: Cornell University Press.

He, Baogang. 1996. *The Democratization of China.* London: Routledge.

Hodder, Rupert. 2000. *In China's Image: Chinese Self-Perception in Western Thought.* New York: Palgrave.

Huntington, Samuel P. 1998. *The Clash of Civilizations and the Remaking of World Order.* New York: Touchstone Books.

Isaacs, Harold R. 1958. *Scratches on Our Minds: American Views of China and India.* New York: John Day.

Jenner, W. J. F. 1994. *The Tyranny of History: The Roots of China's Crisis.* London: Penguin Books.

Jesperson, T. Christopher. 1999. *American Images of China, 1931–1949.* Stanford: Stanford University Press.

Kristof, Nicholas, and Sheryl WuDunn. 1994. *China Wakes: The Struggle for the Soul of a Rising Power.* New York: Random House.

Lever-Tracy, Constance, David Ip, and Tracy Noel. 1996. *The Chinese Diaspora and Mainland China: An Emerging Economic Synergy.* New York: St. Martin's Press.

Lieberthal, Kenneth. 1995. *Governing China: From Revolution Through Reform.* New York: W. W. Norton.

Link, E. Perry, Jr. 1992. *Evening Chats in Beijing: Probing China's Predicament.* New York: W. W. Norton.

Link, Perry, Richard P. Madsen, and Paul Pickowicz (eds.). 2001. *Popular Culture: Unofficial Culture in a Globalizing Society.* Lanham, MD: Rowman and Littlefield.

Madsen, Richard. 1984. *Morality and Power in a Chinese Village.* Berkeley: University of California Press.

———. 1995. *China and the American Dream: A Moral Inquiry.* Berkeley: University of California Press.

Munro, Donald J. 2001. *The Concept of Man in Contemporary China.* Ann Arbor: University of Michigan Press.

Redding, S. Gordon. 1990. *The Spirit of Chinese Capitalism.* Berlin: Walter de Gruyter.

Said, Edward W. 1979. *Orientalism.* New York: Pantheon Books.

Sanders, Richard. 2000. *Prospects for Sustainable Development in the Chinese Countryside: The Political Economy of Chinese Ecological Agriculture.* Burlington, VT: Ashgate.

Schaller, George. 1993. *The Last Panda.* Chicago: University of Chicago Press.

Seagrave, Sterling. 1995. *Lords of the Rim.* New York: G. P. Putnam.

Shapiro, Judith. 2001. *Mao's War Against Nature: Politics and the Environment in Revolutionary China.* Cambridge: Cambridge University Press.

Smil, Vaclav. 1993. *China's Environmental Crisis.* Armonk, NY: M. E. Sharpe.

Tu, Wei-ming. 1991. "Cultural China: The Periphery as the Center." *Daedalus* 120(2) (spring): 1–32.

Wei, Pan. 1998. *The Politics of Marketization in Rural China.* Lanham, MD: Rowman and Littlefield.

Weston, Timothy B., and Lionel M. Jensen. 2000. *China Beyond the Headlines.* Lanham, MD: Rowman and Littlefield.

Wittfogel, Karl August. 1981. *Oriental Despotism: A Comparative Study of Total Power.* New York: Random House.

Yang, Dali L. 1996. *Calamity and Reform in China: Rural Society and Institutional Change Since the Great Leap Famine.* Stanford: Stanford University Press.

Zha, Jianying. 1995. *China Pop: How Soap Operas, Tabloids, and Bestsellers Are Transforming a Culture.* New York: New Press.

Zhang, Longxi. 1998. *Mighty Opposites: From Dichotomies to Differences in the Comparative Study of China.* Stanford: Stanford University Press.

Zhou, Kate Xiao. 1996. *How the Farmers Changed China: Power of the People.* Boulder: Westview Press.

The Contributors

Laurel Bossen is associate professor of anthropology at McGill University, Montreal, Quebec.

Chan Hoiman is associate professor of sociology at the Chinese University of Hong Kong.

Richard Louis Edmonds is senior lecturer of geography, King's College, University of London, and associate member of the Center for East Asian Studies, University of Chicago. He was editor of the *China Quarterly* from 1996–2002.

Robert E. Gamer is professor of political science at the University of Missouri–Kansas City.

Ambrose Y. C. King is professor of sociology and pro–vice chancellor of the Chinese University of Hong Kong.

Charles A. Laughlin is assistant professor of Asian languages at Yale University, New Haven, Connecticut.

Ma Rong is associate director of the Institute of Sociology and Anthropology, Beijing University.

Rhoads Murphey is professor emeritus of history at the University of Michigan, Ann Arbor.

Stanley W. Toops is associate professor of geography at Miami University in Oxford, Ohio.

John Wong is professor of economics and research director of the East Asian Institute at the National University of Singapore.

Zang Xiaowei is assistant professor of sociology at the City University of Hong Kong.

Index

abortions, 300, 326; sex selective, 235, 296. *See also* child bearing; infanticide; one-child policy
acrobats, 365, 368
administration. *See* bureaucracy
Afghanistan, 210
Africa, 31, 51, 174, 206
aging, 135, 281–283, 320
agriculture: under feudalism, 32–39; since Mao, 16–130, 133, 323–327; under Mao, 73–77, 124–126, 232, 286–287, 319–322; before the Republic, 40–53, 121–124, 316; during the Republic, 316–318 . *See also* food; irrigation; land; livestock; soil; *individual crops*
AIDS, 85, 217, 240, 301
airports, 84, 132, 165. *See also* transportation
alcohol, 67, 377, 380–382, 404
Amdo, 175, 177, 187. *See also* minorities; Tibet
Amoy. *See* Xiamen
Anhui, 56
animism, 175, 342–345
Arabs, 46, 196
arms. *See* weaponry

artisans: contemporary, 93–94, 323–325; and illiteracy, 383, 391; before PRC, 38, 57, 107, 123, 142, 149, 208–210, 296, 312–313, 316–318. *See also* *baojia*; guilds; metallurgy; porcelain; silk
atomic bomb, 77–78, 206, 209–210, 234. *See also* weaponry
automobiles, 25, 94, 117–118, 132, 138, 166, 180, 266–267
Australia, 2, 156, 165, 237
autonomous regions, 92, 247–250, 330. *See also* Mongolia, Inner; Ningxia; Qinghai; Tibet; Xinjiang

balladeers, 388
banking, 98, 123, 138–139, 161–163, 174, 420. *See also* currency; International Monetary Fund; investment; World Bank
baojia, 74, 93, 123–124. *See also* *danwei*; housing
Beijing (Peking), 208, 273; economy of, 117; environment of, 258, 262, 266, 270; historic, 31, 48–49, 54–56, 92–93, 197, 228; location of, 16, 204; people in, 18, 230, 238, 404–405; university, 76, 233

427

About the Book

Understanding Contemporary China offers students a readable, well-grounded exploration of the most crucial issues affecting China today. Designed as a core text for "Introduction to China" or "Introduction to Asia" courses, it can also be used effectively in a wide variety of discipline-oriented curriculums.

Assuming no prior knowledge on the part of the reader, the book begins with an overview of China's geography and cultural history. The authors then provide thorough analyses not only of the country's politics, economy, and international relations, but also of demographic trends, environmental problems, family patterns, the role of women in development, and religion and cultural expression. Each chapter provides historical context, and each topic is covered with reference to the latest available scholarship.

All of the chapters in this second edition have been fully revised and updated to reflect the rapid pace of change in China. Numerous maps and photographs enhance the text.

Robert E. Gamer is professor of political science at the University of Missouri–Kansas City. His publications include *Governments and Politics in a Changing World* and *The Developing Nations: A Comparative Perspective.*